Pembrokesl
the Forgotten Coalfield

M. R. Connop Price

Landmark Publishing

Contents

List of Figures

Introduction

This book came into being as a Ph.D thesis prepared for the Department of History in the University of Wales, Swansea, and completed in 2002. Its intention was, and is, to provide an overview of the long history of coal mining in Pembrokeshire. The story spans seven hundred years, beginning in the thirteenth century. Although references and records of any kind are extremely sparse in the early centuries, by the eighteenth century the story becomes clearer. Indeed, this era before the steam age reached the county was quite possibly the period when the coal industry was at its busiest. Pembrokeshire had the advantage not only of numerous coal surface outcrops, but also of easy access to navigable, and often sheltered water. This was a matter of vital importance at a period when the condition of local roads was appalling.

Pembrokeshire coal was high grade anthracite - sometimes 95% pure carbon. As a consequence of geological pressures and disturbances damaging coal seams, a high proportion of the output appeared as culm, the "small" of anthracite coal. Although far less valuable than coal in commercial terms, the production of culm managed to sustain the industry until the nineteenth century, by which time many coal workings had become difficult or expensive to operate. This fact, coupled with the greater willingness by capitalists to expand and improve the anthracite industry of Carmarthenshire and West Glamorgan, caused coal mining to go into a protracted decline. Pembrokeshire was never a wealthy or technically advanced area, and belated heavy investment in collieries in the Saundersfoot and Hook districts was not sufficient to stem the relentless tide of competition from other parts of South Wales. The last phase of formal coal mining in the county ended in 1950.

The title – *Pembrokeshire - the Forgotten Coalfield* – is entirely appropriate, because Pembrokeshire's contribution to the story of Welsh coal mining has been totally overshadowed by the later achievements of the industry in the main South Wales coalfield, and in north-east Wales. Even so, the earliest attempt to describe coal mining as an activity anywhere in Wales was made in Pembrokeshire at the end of the Tudor period by George Owen of Henllys. His observations in *The Description of Pembrokeshire* are of such importance that they have been given prominent coverage in Chapter Two.

Thereafter, for many generations, the county's coal industry was left to those involved in it, or merely noticed in passing by those who were visiting West Wales. Not until 1841 was another effort made to give a broad description of the collieries, and those who worked in them. The task was performed by Robert Franks, the Inspector appointed by the government-sponsored Children's Employment Commission. As will be seen, the report, published in 1842, made sobering reading.

In the late nineteenth and early twentieth centuries several scholars showed an awareness of the Pembrokeshire coal industry, without giving it very much attention. To his credit J. U. Nef gave it a proportionate place in his massive and magnificent work, *The Rise of the British Coal Industry*. It took a Pembrokeshire man, George Edwards of Kilgetty, to make the first serious attempt to study the county's coal industry as an entity when he wrote *A Study of the Daucleddau Coalfield (Pembrokeshire)* for his M.A. thesis at Birmingham University in 1950. This admirable work, later published in a shortened form as *The Coal Industry in Pembrokeshire*, has worn well. However, Edwards did not study the coalfield in the west, on St. Bride's Bay, nor did he have very much to say about the industry prior to 1800. With the passage of time it has become apparent that the heyday of the coal industry was prior to the close of the eighteenth century, although it is entirely possible (if hardly provable) that there were peaks and troughs in the industry's performance between the thirteenth and nineteenth centuries. The present writer's book, *Industrial Saundersfoot*, published in 1982, drew on material not available to Edwards, and it endeavoured to enlarge upon the story of coal mining in the east of the county after 1750. Since then the significance of the coal industry in and before the eighteenth century has become increasingly obvious, and to put the whole story in proper perspective it is necessary to consider this period, and indeed, coal mining right across the county.

Ten years ago writing a full history of the Pembrokeshire coalfield appeared to be a large, but entirely feasible undertaking. In the event it has been a very substantial and demanding task, touching upon all manner of incidental issues not anticipated at the outset. Although extremely challenging, happily it has also been very rewarding, with insights gained into many aspects of Pembrokeshire life – and indeed human life – in centuries past. In addition to the customary sources of documentary evidence - newspapers, parliamentary papers and Royal Commissions, landowners' and coalowners' records - the thesis also draws upon fieldwork undertaken at old coal mining sites right across the county. Indeed, in the past twenty years almost every site of any significance has been viewed in the course of my many trips to Pembrokeshire. Such visits have also given rise to innumerable fascinating conversations with a wide range of people very willing to share their expertise, experience or reminiscence. Sections of this thesis rest heavily upon oral accounts of older residents of the coalfield interviewed at various dates since the 1970's. Their descriptions of mining life and working practice include numerous points which would have been lost or forgotten without their testimony. Having been privileged to know many of the last generation of men who had to endure the hardship and the grim reality of living and working in the Pembrokeshire coal industry, I cannot do other than dedicate this piece of work to the memory of all who were involved.

As the study expanded, and unforeseen avenues of enquiry emerged, I have been very fortunate to have the observations and constructive advice of a number of very knowledgeable people. First and foremost, I must thank Professor David Howell for all his guidance and encouragement as my supervisor in the Department of History at Swansea. His proposal that the main part of this thesis should have a thematic structure opened up a number of new and worthwhile perspectives on the whole subject. Particular topics within the subject have benefited greatly from specialist advice. Hermas Nicholas, who was raised in Carmarthenshire, and was formerly Deputy Chief Inspector of Mines, has been generous with his time and considerable expertise in relation to many aspects of coal mining technology and methods, labour relations and health and safety. Robin Craig, sometime Senior Lecturer at University College, London, and a well known authority on maritime history, has endeavoured to give me a basic education in his field, steering me between the Scylla of ignorance and the Charybdis of easy assumptions, towards a more thoughtful understanding of the coal shipping and trading aspects of the story. Whilst an already many-faceted study could have been enlarged substantially by devoting more time and space to coal shipping and trading, these themes really merit a separate thesis, quite distinct from the present work on the Pembrokeshire coalfield itself. In the same way this thesis does not give a detailed account of the Kilgetty iron industry, despite its close association with the coal industry. This subject was addressed in a chapter of the writer's book *Industrial Saundersfoot*, published by Gomer Press of Llandysul. Peter Claughton, a Pembrokeshire resident, and a prominent member of the National Association of Mining History Organisations, has offered much sound comment on mining history in general and Pembrokeshire mining in particular. It has been a pleasure to have his company on numerous field trips in different parts of the coalfield, and naturally I am grateful for his advice and support. Another Pembrokeshire resident, the late Terry Driscoll, formerly Senior Lecturer in Geography at Liverpool University, not only shared his professional expertise, but also his own extensive knowledge of local history, including the coal industry, on St. Bride's Bay. John de Havilland has worked long and hard, and with immense skill, and some patience to produce the required maps and plans. I must acknowledge also the long standing friendship and support of Thomas Lloyd of Cresselly, a member of CADW, the National Trust Committee for Wales and of the executive committee of the Pembrokeshire Historical Society. His encouragement has been immense, especially at certain moments when the difficulties seemed greater than the energy available to deal with them!

To mention my supervisor and half a dozen other people is not to belittle the valuable and very varied contributions of many more. The diocese of Oxford kindly approved a sabbatical which gave time to draft most of the text. This was an immense help for which I am grateful. Thanks are due, too, to the Warden and staff at St. Deiniol's Library, Hawarden, for their assistance on numerous occasions over several years. Additional acknowledgments appear in the endnotes to each chapter, although after forty years of interest in this subject it has been impossible to mention everyone. In conclusion special mention must be made to my own family (in three generations!) who have been hugely supportive throughout the years involved. In particular my wife Judy, and son David, have helped to turn reams of longhand into a presentable text, and I am deeply grateful to them. Notwithstanding so much beneficial advice and assistance I am glad to take full responsibility for the contents of this thesis.

Martin R. Connop Price, Shiplake, Oxfordshire   November 2003

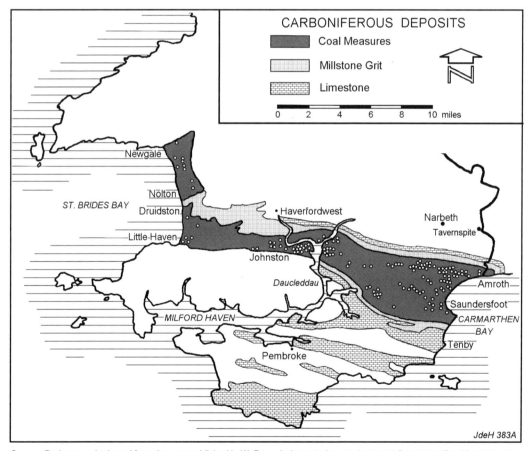

Source: Redrawn and adapted from the map published in W. Rees *Industry before the Industrial Revolution* (Cardiff, 1968), 83, University of Wales Press

Figure 1

The Geological Background

Pembrokeshire is a peninsula county famous for its rugged coastal scenery, and the upland landscape of the Prescelli hills, long believed to be the source of the "bluestones" of Stonehenge. The Atlantic coastline is deeply indented and the county measures about 30 miles from west to east, and about 35 miles from north to south. In terms of relief, North Pembrokeshire is dominated by the Prescelli hills reaching their highest point at Prescelli Top, 1760 feet above sea level. In contrast South Pembrokeshire is a plateau lying largely between 150 and 450 feet, split by the immense waterway of Milford Haven, and the numerous rivers and streams flowing into it. The principal river system is that of the Western and Eastern Cleddau draining the southern flanks of the Prescelli hills and so forming the headwaters of Milford Haven itself - in appearance very similar to the ria estuaries and inlets of South Devon and Cornwall. Pembrokeshire has the most varied and complex geology of any county in Wales or England. Many fascinating geological structures have been exposed, not only on the county's splendid sea cliffs, but also along its waterways. Not surprisingly these features have attracted the enthusiastic attention of generations of geologists.

The existence of such varied rock types and formations is a consequence of two great mountain building periods referred to as the Caledonian Orogeny (approximately 400 million years ago) and the Armorican Orogeny - sometimes described as the Variscan Orogeny (approximately 290 million years ago). In the earlier period land was raised by compression along a broadly west south-west to east north-east axis. In the later period the mountain building followed a west north-west to east south-east trend. In Pembrokeshire the evidence of these orogenies actually abut, with the older rocks from the Caledonian period being found in the north of the county, whilst younger, mostly Armorican rocks are to the south. The northern half of the county thus comprises rocks from the Precambrian, Cambrian, Ordovician and Silurian series, some being igneous, but with larger tracts of Ordovician sedementary beds now metamorphosed into slaty shales.[1]

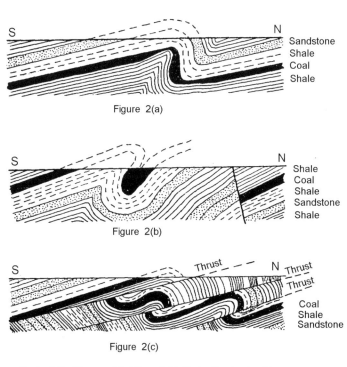

Figure 2(a)

Figure 2(b)

Figure 2(c)

Typical Faulting and Folding of Strata in Pembrokeshire

Source : A. Strahan and others *The Geology of the South Wales Coalfield Part XI : the country around Haverfordwest Memoirs of the Geological Survey, 1914.*10

The boundary with Pembrokeshire's southern geological region runs eastward from Druidston on St. Bride's Bay, by way of Haverfordwest and Narberth, to Tavernspite on the county's border with Carmarthenshire. There are two or three exceptions to this neat division, the most notable being at Newgale on St Bride's Bay. Here a small, roughly rectangular area north of the line belongs geologically to the south of it, but is detached from it by faulting and a narrow block of Ordovician slate known to geologists as the Druidston Horst.

As a result of earth movements in the Armorican period the southern area has been subjected to folding, creating a broadly west-east ridge and valley topography. Erosion of the anticlines has exposed small areas of much older rocks - for example, the Precambrian igneous rocks of the Johnston series, found in a narrow and very irregular belt between Talbenny, near Little Haven, Johnston, and the river Cleddau. The main outcrop of the Coal Measures of the Carboniferous period occupies a syncline extending across the county from St. Bride's bay to Saundersfoot bay, to numerous overfolds and thrust faults on its southern side. As a result the coalfield is considerably narrower here than elsewhere in South Wales. Although only a mile wide in the neighbourhood of Johnston, it has a width of some four miles at Saundersfoot. A particular feature of this synclinal trough is the appearance of Millstone Grit and Carboniferous Limestone both to the north and south of the coal. The limestone was a feature clearly recognised as early as the Tudor period, as is evident from the writings of George Owen. Figure 1 provides an outline of the geology of the coalfield; the structure in detail is well covered by the maps of the British Geological Survey.[2] The three sections of Figure 2 provide a diagrammatic representation of the remarkable consequences of folding and faulting as experienced in Pembrokeshire.

The evidence of George Owen

In his well known *Description of Pembrokeshire* (1603) George Owen wrote:[3]

> Our coals have been found near Talbenny and so followeth on to Johnston and there found; then at Freystrop great store, and so at Picton. It is also found by the southern vein of limestone at Jeffreston and from thence to Begelly. This first vein of coal followeth the first vein of limestone, keeping on the south side of it to the water, and so to the mouth of the Tywi [ie Carmarthen Bay]. This other vein of coal which I spake of at Jeffreston accompanieth the second vein of limestone on the north side thereof within half a mile of the limestone and passeth east to Saundersfoot and there accompanying the limestone to the sea ... In this course both of the veins of limestone and coal one thing is to be noted, that the further east the veins run, the softer groweth both the coal and the limestone, and the easier to be digged.

Whilst referring to the limestone, George Owen also mentions the small detached portion of the coalfield about Newgale and Nolton, and declares that "in Eweston, otherwise called Owenston, in Dewisland, there are coal pits where coal has been dug", and he notes that this "is a great argument that the limestone vein is not far off, for that the one is most commonly found to accompany the other".[4] Owen lived too early to recognise the bedded nature of strata, and so preferred the word "vein". Nor at this time was it realised that in the Newgale district the Coal Measures and accompanying Millstone Grit lie unconformably on Cambrian rocks. Whereas in the main outcrop only the Lower and Middle Coal Measures survive, the Newgale and Nolton district is distinctive for the exposure of the Upper Coal Measures.

George Owen's observations are of considerable importance as the earliest attempt both to describe the coal, and the steps taken to work it. His account of local mining practice will be discussed later, but here it is appropriate to note his comments on the coal itself. Owen speaks of three kinds of coal commonly found, namely "ore coal", a "string", or a "slatch". According to Owen:

the ore is the best and is a great vein spreading every way, and endureth longest. The string is a small, narrow vein sometimes two, three or four foot in bigness, and runneth downright and is always found between two rocks. A slatch they call a piece of coal by itself found in the earth, and is quickly digged about and no more to be found of that piece. The first of these three sorts is the best, then the next, and last accounted worst of all.[5]

This passage is as tantalising for what is not said as it is fascinating for what is described. What exactly did Owen mean? The term "ore coal" surely refers to a major Pembrokeshire coal seam (or "vein" in local parlance) like the Timber vein. In Tudor times the outcrop of this vein in the parish of Jeffreston, for example, must have appeared to have been "a great vein spreading every way", and ample evidence of extensive areas of working along outcrops of the Timber Vein is still to be seen. His understanding of "a string" is clearly of a smaller, less significant seam or vein. The implication of a "string" running "downright" would suggest that it was found in a near vertical position, testifying to the immense distortions which could occur in the coal measures. In fact it is known that there were veins at Reynalton, Jeffreston and Broadmoor outcropping almost to the vertical. Whereas the Timber vein was so called from the immense quantity of timber required to make safe the vein's roof, the Rock vein was so named because it usually had a reliable rock roof. The "string" referred to by Owen could also be a reference to the Rock vein as found in a few locations east of the Cleddau.

The Memoirs of the Geological Survey *relating to the Milford area include a very helpful explanation of the "string" and the "slatch" referred to by Owen. In places in Pembrokeshire, according to this account:*

The ground is traversed by overthrusts from the south, having the effect of southerly upthrows. In other cases the beds are overfolded from the south with similar results; a relatively gentle northerly rise being followed by a steep, a vertical, or an inverted middle limb, and that by a gentle rising to the north.

Figure 3(a) is an illustration of this point, whilst Figure 3(b) illustrates how on occasions coal could be squeezed out, or how the middle limb could be doubled up in a closed syncline, forming a thick vertical wall of coal, otherwise known as a "string". In the view of these writers:

The circular or elliptical pockets of coal known as "slatches" or slashes are the remains of short closed synclinal masses of coal abnormally swollen out by the squeezing down of the two sides of the syncline, and left as outliers by denudation.

This point is illustrated in Figure 3(c). [6] The quality of coal in a slatch was usually poor, and almost always comprised culm,

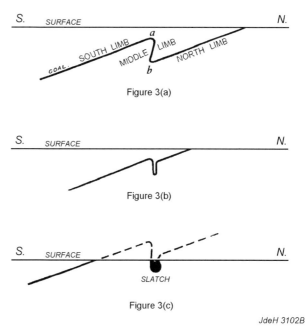

Figure 3(a)

Figure 3(b)

Figure 3(c)

JdeH 3102B

Source : T. C. Cantrill and others, *The Geology of the South Wales Coalfield Part XII : The Country around Milford* Memoirs of the Geological Survey, 1916, 115 and 116

the dust or small of anthracite. It is known that such a basin of culm was found and worked near Begelly in the 1820's.[7] Even in the twentieth century veins of coal were sometimes found to be faulted or crushed and yet unexpectedly appearing in a widened seam. Miners often referred to the dusty output of such features as "slash".

The effect of earth movements on coal measures

References already made to the folding of rock will have indicated that the main syncline occupied by the coal measures was by no means regular, reliable and unbroken across the county. The immense pressures exerted during the Armorican earth movements not only produced the syncline but also many distortions within it. As mentioned, seams could appear in any position from the horizontal to the vertical, and the higher veins were often found to be quite broken up. Lower seams were usually less damaged, but the main faults in the coalfield were usually readily discerned at depth. Accordingly faulting could seriously disrupt production by causing the loss of a vein and delay whilst miners tried to recover it in a workable state. As coal veins in Pembrokeshire were frequently very narrow, this was a serious matter. The economics of working seams as thin as 18 inches (and sometimes even less) were bound to be difficult, and any prolonged interruption in output would soon make any mining activity utterly unprofitable.

In spite of the obvious problems, some engineers of the period perceived compensations. Walter Davies quoted a work which made the assertion that faulting could be beneficial because it served to throw more strata up "near the surface of the ground as to be within our reach than could otherwise possibly be got were the strata to keep the same dip without any interruption or break".[8] In the context of the relatively primitive coal industry of the time, this view may have had some merit, but to a modern mining engineer intent on working large and unbroken seams with the latest equipment such a notion would seem ridiculous. Suffice to say that the geological problems in Pembrokeshire were much greater than in the main South Wales Coalfield, to the extent that in 1839 Sir R. Murchison was moved to say that in Pembrokeshire there were "Contortions which cannot be exceeded even in imagination, and ought to be a warning to those who speculate needlessly in culm works amid those convulsed strata".[9]

Types of coal

From early times it was recognised that South Wales had two types of coal, namely binding or "ring" coal, and stone coal. In later years these were known as bituminous and anthracite coal respectively. Pembrokeshire coal was invariably anthracite; the nearest bituminous coal was to be found in the Llanelli area of Carmarthenshire. George Owen was familiar with both kinds, although he referred to binding coal as "run" coal. He explained the term in this way: "running cole, for that when it first kindleth it melteth and runneth as waxe and groweth into one clodde" and is "noysome for smoake" and "loathesome for the smell". In relation to stone coal, however, Owen wrote: "beinge once kindled giveth a greater heate than light and delitech to burne in darke places ... this cole burneth apart and clyngeth not together".[10]

The development of the South Wales iron industry in the eighteenth century brought about the recognition of a third kind of coal, with qualities between those of binding and stone coal which was soon seen as a good coking and steam coal. Although the particular varieties of bituminous, anthracite and steam coals are usually readily identifiable, they grade almost imperceptibly into one another, and an exact definition is sometimes a matter of technical chemical analysis. Suffice to say that bituminous coals are comparatively soft, and yield a high proportion of volatile matter causing them to burn smokily. Anthracite, on the other hand, is a hard stone which in Carmarthenshire often has a metallic sheen, and in Pembrokeshire can show an oily lustre - indeed miners in the Saundersfoot area would describe the produce of some veins as "peacock" coal from its colour. Anthracite has a very low proportion of volatile matter (3% to 8%) making it virtually smokeless and an extremely high carbon content - up to 95% as found in Pembrokeshire.[11] Welsh steam coals are intermediate, both in composition and properties, and grade into semi-bituminous coals on the one hand and semi- anthracite on the other.

Compared to other parts of South Wales, Pembrokeshire was unusual for the extent to which many coal seams were contorted and crushed, and produced a very high proportion of small coal or dust known as "culm". The ratio of coal to culm found in the county was frequently 1:5, and could be as extreme as 1:20. As the coal was invariably deemed to be at least twice as valuable as the culm this was a fact of huge commercial significance. It was also a reason from time to time for both legislators and the judiciary to consider the precise legal definition of culm. Before the eighteenth century the use of the word to describe the small of stone coal, or anthracite, was well established. In time, though, the word was applied indiscriminately to "all refuse coal". This gave rise to argument, and according to Walter Davies, at length there was "a hearing at Westminster Hall, where it was decided by Lord Ellenborough, NW v Newcastle, that, in future, culm should be applied only to such refuse coal as does not bind or cake in burning - this includes two out of the three South Wales species of coal".[12] In effect the judgement said that the term could be used only in respect of the small of stone coal. According to an Act of Parliament passed in 1816 in respect of coal duties, culm was that coal capable of passing through the mesh of a riddle with holes measuring 3/8th inch across.[13] Not surprisingly, as culm was of much less commercial value, it attracted far less duty.

The Saundersfoot and Jeffreston district

The syncline in the coal measures is quite evident in this district, but the prevailing dip of the strata is to the south. This is interrupted by two major faults, both of which appear as downthrows to the north. Edwards was content to call them faults but observed that they seemed to be "rather a combination of fold and overthrust".[14] The first, named the Erroxhill fault, runs from the coast near Amroth due west to Sardis Mountain, along the south side of Kingsmoor and then down the valley of the Cresswell stream. The throw of the fault is estimated at 93 yards near Sardis Mountain, but at more than 200 yards beyond Treberth, near the junction with the much smaller Wiseman's Bridge fault. The tract north of the Erroxhill fault was found to have some of the least damaged coal veins in the coalfield, and the Lower Level vein and Kilgetty vein as worked at Amroth and Kilgetty were especially productive.

The second fault is called the Harbour fault, and this runs from Saundersfoot Harbour west north-west past Moreton and Broadmoor, and then to the south of Jeffreston. Together these faults have the effect of dividing this district into three distinct geological areas - one north of the Erroxhill fault, another between the faults, and the third to the south of the Harbour fault. However as the faults downthrow to the north, and the veins of coal rise in that direction, the veins are at a workable depth throughout the district. A number of smaller faults, usually running roughly north - south across the grain of the syncline also exist - for example, the Newton fault between Kilgetty and Begelly, the Trewern and Bramblehill faults further west, and also the Reynalton fault. It has been estimated that in the Saundersfoot area the total thickness of the coal measures does not exceed 453 yards, but it seems probable that only the lower part of the lower coal measures still exists in this district. Figure 4 provides a simplified representation of the geological faults in the Saundersfoot district , together with the location of the main coal workings. As an indication of the intensity of working in particular areas Figures 5, 6 and 7 show in greater detail mine workings at Kilgetty and Lower Level, Begelly and Moreton.

The seams which yielded the bulk of the coal were the Stammers, Rock, Timber, Lower Level and Kilgetty veins. They may be described as follows:

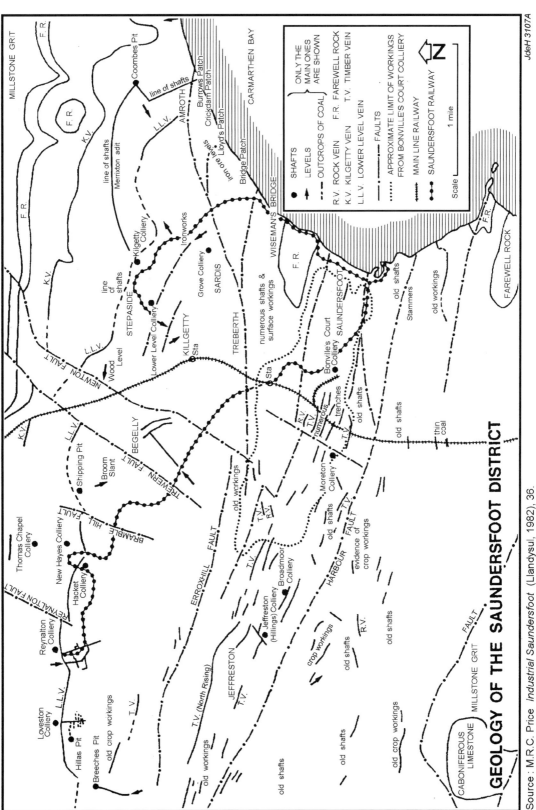

GEOLOGY OF THE SAUNDERSFOOT DISTRICT

Figure 4

Source : M.R.C. Price *Industrial Saundersfoot* (Llandysul, 1982), 36.

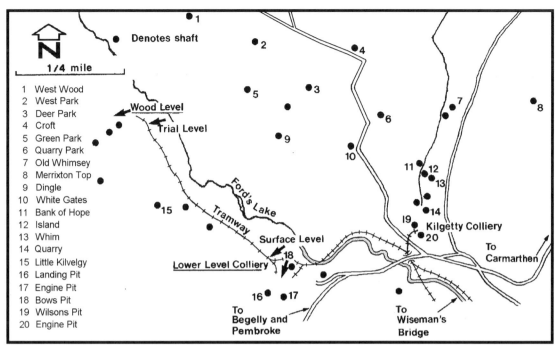

Denotes shaft

1/4 mile

1 West Wood
2 West Park
3 Deer Park
4 Croft
5 Green Park
6 Quarry Park
7 Old Whimsey
8 Merrixton Top
9 Dingle
10 White Gates
11 Bank of Hope
12 Island
13 Whim
14 Quarry
15 Little Kilvelgy
16 Landing Pit
17 Engine Pit
18 Bows Pit
19 Wilsons Pit
20 Engine Pit

Wood Level
Trial Level
Ford's Lake
Tramway
Surface Level
Lower Level Colliery
Kilgetty Colliery
To Carmarthen
To Begelly and Pembroke
To Wiseman's Bridge

LOWER LEVEL and KILGETTY

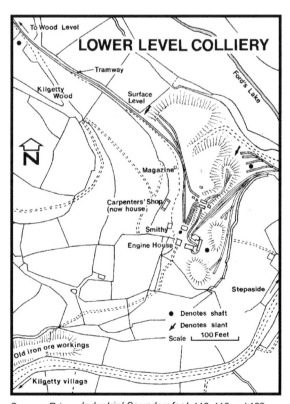

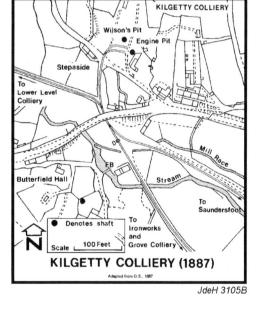

Source: Price, *Industrial Saundersfoot*, 110, 112 and 122

Figure 5

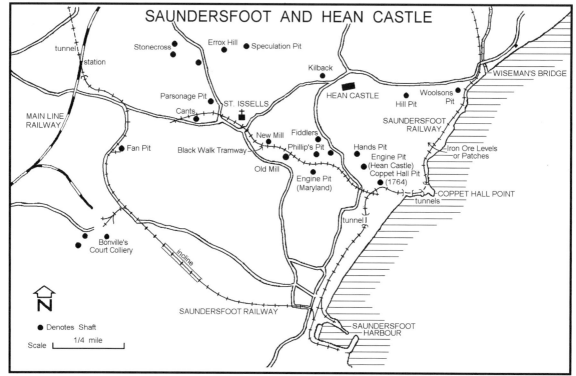

SAUNDERSFOOT AND HEAN CASTLE

Source : Adapted from Price *Industrial Saundersfoot*, 36 and 86

JdeH 3108A

Figure 6

The Stammers veins: were the highest and least important in the Saundersfoot and Jeffreston district, and appear to have been worked only to the south of the Harbour fault. Of the six veins in this group (each having the average thickness of 18 to 30 inches) four were regarded as inferior, whilst the fourth and sixth veins (sometimes called the Coal and Yard veins) were considered to be of medium quality. These dipped at an angle of 36 degrees, and by 1845 had been worked to a depth of 30 yards below sea level in the neighbourhood of Saundersfoot Harbour.[15]

The Rock vein: was worked north of the Harbour fault, and as far west as the parish of Jeffreston. It was a good quality and in thickness varied from two feet four inches at Broadmoor to four feet six inches at Moreton, where at one time an outcrop was worked as a "string". The Low vein, found in association with the Rock vein, consisted largely of culm, and varied in thickness from a mere six to twelve inches at Begelly to two feet six inches at Foxholes near Bonvilles Court.

The Timber vein had a thickness of about six feet, although when it exceeded six feet it tended to become very culmy. It was always regarded as soft, producing on average no more than one part of large coal to five parts of culm. The vein gained its name on account of this softness, because its poor roof required an exceptional amount of timber to maintain. Like the Rock vein the Timber vein was worked most extensively in the belt between the Erroxhill and the Harbour faults. It was also worked in deep trenches (sometimes described as "reens") for a considerable distance on its northern outcrop in the parish of Jeffreston. Some smaller veins of coal, including the Fiddlers and Garland, were found beneath the Timber vein, but generally these were of inferior quality.

The Lower Level vein: (sometimes called the Bonvilles Court or Summerhill vein) was found 170 to 200 yards below the Timber vein in the vicinity of Saundersfoot, but probably extended

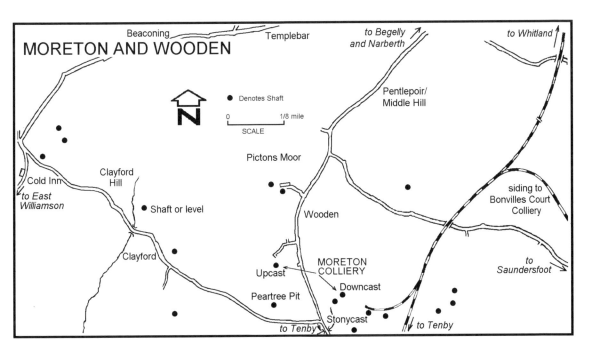

MORETON AND WOODEN

Beaconing   Templebar   to Begelly   to Whitland
                          and Narberth

Pentlepoir/
Middle Hill

● Denotes Shaft

0   1/8 mile
    SCALE

Pictons Moor

Cold Inn
Clayford
Hill
to East
Williamson

● Shaft or level

Wooden

siding to
Bonvilles Court
Colliery

Clayford

Upcast   MORETON   to
          COLLIERY   Saundersfoot

Peartree Pit   Downcast

Stonycast   to Tenby
to Tenby

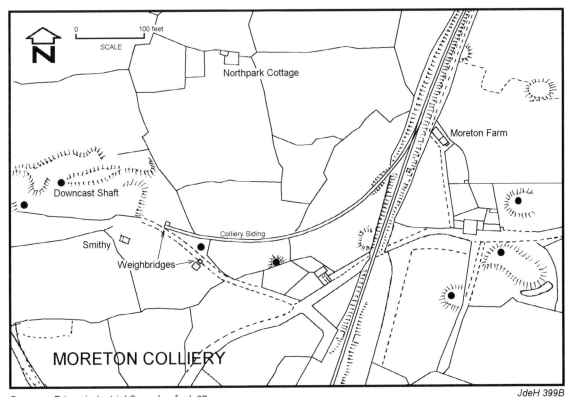

MORETON COLLIERY

0   100 feet
    SCALE

Northpark Cottage

Moreton Farm

Downcast Shaft

Smithy
Colliery Siding

Weighbridges

MORETON COLLIERY

Source : Price *Industrial Saundersfoot*, 67

JdeH 399B

Figure 7

from the Harbour fault in the south to its outcrop in the north along the line indicated on the map from Amroth to Thomas Chapel and Reynalton. In the Kilgetty area the Lower Level vein was said to be of very good quality but only about 20 to 22 inches thick. The vein sometimes produced one part coal to one part culm and although subject to patches of soft coal, the roof was firm and needed little timber.

The Kilgetty vein: (sometimes called the Scad vein) lay about 95 to 100 yards under the Lower Level vein, the interval containing a scarcely workable vein called the Catshole, and also several beds of good quality ironstone. Although the Kilgetty vein had an average thickness of just 21 inches (and was often only 18 inches thick), in 1845 Messrs. Fosters, mining surveyors, described the quality as "first rate" and "probably the best and purest anthracite in South Wales".[16] The Kilgetty vein produced up to one part coal to one part culm. In spite of their depth and thinness, the extent, quality and regularity of the Lower level and Kilgetty veins made them the most valuable in this district.

Iron ore veins: Within the coal measures several series of iron ore measures are to be found, and in the nineteenth century some of these were worked extensively in the Saundersfoot district. The most important of these were the Kilvelgy, Fiddlers and Catshole measures. In this area ironstone was usually referred to as "iron mine" or just as "mine" and ironstone veins were often described as "pins". The Kilvelgy measures lay about 40 yards below the Timber vein and 140 yards above the Lower Level vein in three workable series. The middle series of these was best, producing about nine cwt of iron mine per square yard. The upper and lower series gave about six cwt of iron mine per square yard. The Fiddlers measures lay 120 yards below the Timber vein and 60 yards above the Lower Level vein. They were very irregular, the pins sometimes being so far apart as not to be accessible within the height of an ordinary heading or level. When found in good condition they yielded about nine cwt of iron mine per square yard. The Catshole measures lay 16 yards below the Lower Level vein and had a yield comparable to the Fiddlers measures. Catshole iron mine was generally considered to be good quality .

The Landshipping District

Geologically Landshipping bears comparison with Saundersfoot, although no evidence has come to light to show that the deep Lower Level and Kilgetty veins were ever worked regularly in this district. The existence of a west - east fault (sometimes called The Old Mill fault) confined most of the mining to the valley between Landshipping Pill on the River Cleddau and Martletwy Wood, less than two miles inland. Relatively little work took place south of this fault, whilst north of it the veins worked were in descending order: the Rock vein, the Slate or Tumbling vein, the Low vein (of the Timber vein group), the Big, High or Timber vein, the Little vein and the Stinkard vein. The latter appears to have been worked in pits on the north side of Landshipping village, between the Landshipping Ferry and Rigan Pill. The Little vein was never worked systematically, but the Timber vein was found to correspond with the Timber vein of Bonvilles Court and was the principal vein of the Landshipping district. The Rock vein was also worked extensively. Figure 8 shows the main coal workings in this district, and also indicates the location of the Old Mill Fault.

The Hook and Freystrop district

This area, rather like Landshipping, is divided into narrow belts by faults running broadly west to east, some of which (from inspection in colliery workings) have been found to be overthrusts from the south dating from the Armorican Orogeny. These faults are most obvious in the neighbourhood of Hook, and are especially evident in the displacements which have been suffered by the principal seam of the district, the Timber vein. The Slide fault in East Hook is a downthrow to the north which reduces as it runs westward. The Great South fault lies further west, beyond the sites of the

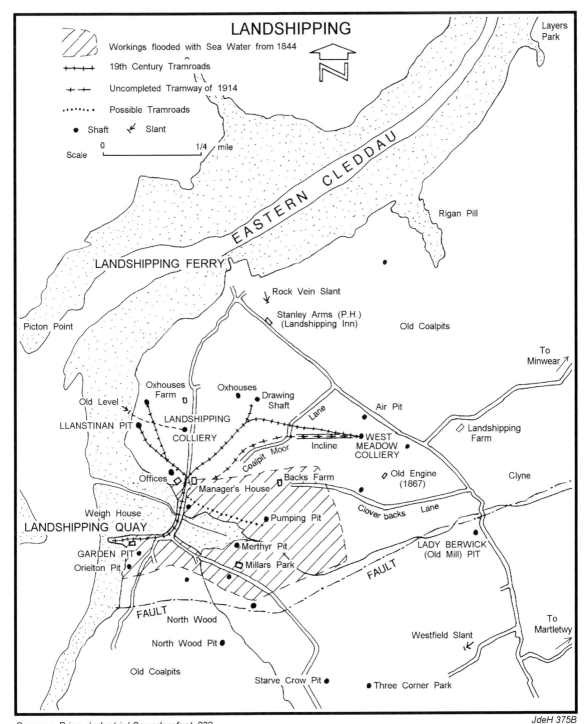

LANDSHIPPING

Workings flooded with Sea Water from 1844

19th Century Tramroads

Uncompleted Tramway of 1914

Possible Tramroads

● Shaft   Slant

Scale   0   1/4   mile

N

EASTERN CLEDDAU

Layers Park

Rigan Pill

LANDSHIPPING FERRY

Picton Point

Rock Vein Slant

Stanley Arms (P.H.) (Landshipping Inn)

Old Coalpits

To Minwear

Oxhouses Farm

Oxhouses

Drawing Shaft

Air Pit

Landshipping Farm

Old Level

Lane

LANDSHIPPING COLLIERY

LLANSTINAN PIT

Incline

WEST MEADOW COLLIERY

Coalpit Moor

Clyne

Offices

Backs Farm

Old Engine (1867)

Manager's House

Weigh House

Pumping Pit

Clover backs   Lane

LANDSHIPPING QUAY

Merthyr Pit

LADY BERWICK (Old Mill) PIT

GARDEN PIT

Millars Park

FAULT

Orielton Pit

FAULT

North Wood

To Martletwy

North Wood Pit ●

Westfield Slant

Old Coalpits

Starve Crow Pit ●

● Three Corner Park

Source : Price *Industrial Saundersfoot*, 232

JdeH 375B

Figure 8

– 19 –

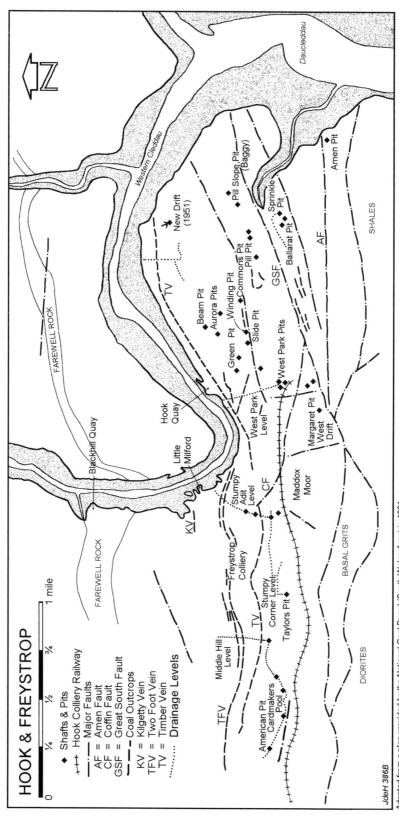

HOOK & FREYSTROP

0   ¼   ½   ¾   1 mile

◆ = Shafts & Pits
┼┼┼ = Hook Colliery Railway
——— = Major Faults
AF = Amen Fault
CF = Coffin Fault
GSF = Great South Fault
— ·· — = Coal Outcrops
KV = Kilgetty Vein
TFV = Two Foot Vein
TV = Timber Vein
······ = Drainage Levels

N

Daucleddau

Western Cleddau

FAREWELL ROCK

Blackhill Quay

Hook Quay

Little Milford

New Drift (1951)

Beam Pit
Aurora Pits
Green Pit
Winding Pit
Slide Pit
Commons Pit
Pill Pit
Pill Slope Pit (Baggy)

Sprinkle Pit
Ballarat Pit

Amen Pit

TV

GSF

AF

SHALES

West Park Pits
West Park Level

Margaret Pit
West Drift

Maddox Moor

CF

Stumpy Adit Level

KV

Freystrop Colliery

BASAL GRITS

FAREWELL ROCK

TV

Stumpy Corner Level

Taylors Pit

Middle Hill Level

TFV

American Pit
Cardmakers Pool

DIORITES

JdeH 386B

Figure 9

Adapted from a plan provided by the National Coal Board (South Wales Area) in 1981,
also G. Edwards *A Study of the Daucleddau Coalfield (Pembrokeshire)*, 1950

former West Park and Margaret Pits. The Coffin fault, a north-south fault, a little to the west of Hook Quay, appears to have inhibited mining operations between the Freystrop and Hook districts. Figure 9 depicts these faults, as well as the outcrop of the Timber vein, and the more important pits. The Rock vein was also exploited in many of these workings. As a consequence of faulting, it is appropriate to refer briefly and separately to the geological features of Freystrop.

Between Little Milford and Freystrop Cross some lower veins were worked, the lowest being the Kilgetty vein. It was found at a depth of 50 yards in the Portobello shaft. It is believed that the same shaft cut through the narrower Plot vein at 14 yards. Another thin vein, the Ten inch, was worked along the outcrop on each side of the main road 300 yards north of Freystrop Cross, and evidence of this activity may still be seen on the south side of Little Milford Wood. The highest of this group of veins was the Two foot, which was worked extensively both west and east of Freystrop cross, and again the surviving crop workings may still be seen in or near Little Milford Wood. The principal vein in both Freystrop and Hook is the Timber vein. The main crop of the vein appears west of Little Cranham, and it runs along the ridge past Freystrop Cross to the escarpment overlooking Hook Quay and the Western Cleddau. The thickness of the vein varies substantially, probably as a result of overthrusting on the soft strata beneath the Timber vein and at times the vein disappears from the outcrop altogether. Early in the twentieth century it was reported that these features were "rendered conspicuous by the long trenches of enormous width and depth ending abruptly at both ends; between them are gaps of 100 to 300 yards where there is no trace of working and it is believed that the vein has been pinched out altogether".[17] Although there are still numerous signs of workings along the Timber vein outcrop, they are no longer as spectacular as they were in the nineteenth century. The workings at Freystrop were drained largely by a long level running down to the Western Cleddau known as the Stumpy Adit Level. In 2001 the outflow from this level was still to be seen at Stumpy Corner, 200 yards south east of Little Milford. West of Freystrop Cross the ground was drained by a separate level running from the vicinity of Middle Hill Chapel towards Little Milford. The last workings in this neighbourhood were those of the American Pit, south west of Little Cranham, and Cardmakers Pool Colliery nearby. The Timber vein was lost between the village of Johnston and a point about 500 yards west of the American Pit.

The Nolton and Newgale coalfield

This small detached coalfield is separated from the western extremity of the main Pembrokeshire coalfield by the Druidston Horst, a raised strip of Ordovician slate bounded by a fault on each side. This area of Coal Measures extends into the parishes of Nolton, Roch, and Brawdy, where to the north of Newgale Marsh and Eweston they are bounded by a fault and much older Cambrian Rocks.

In geological terms the whole area is said to have a sigmoidal structure, with strata curving in the shape of a reversed "S", most notably just south of the Maidenhall fault which runs north-west to south-east across this coalfield. North of this fault the dip is to the south, whilst south of the Maidenhall fault the dip is mostly westerly towards the sea. In the extreme north of the area, the Eweston coals are believed to be a folded continuation of the Newgale coals in which the principal veins are the Three Quarters, the Five Foot, and the Stink veins. These and the Yard vein were worked extensively in the nineteenth century from Southwood colliery, the main colliery of the Newgale district. The ground south of the Southwood workings, abutting onto the Maidenhall fault, is extremely disturbed, and only shallow and small scale mining activity was undertaken in this location.

The Nolton district lies south of the Maidenhall fault, and is bounded on the east by the Folkeston (or Folkestone) fault, which in turn separates this district from the Hilton and Simpson district. The Nolton coals occur in conjunction with Sandstone, but both the Newgale and the Hilton and Simpson coals are associated with shales. The geological evidence suggests that the Nolton coals actually overlay the coals of both the other districts, and indeed Nolton has the

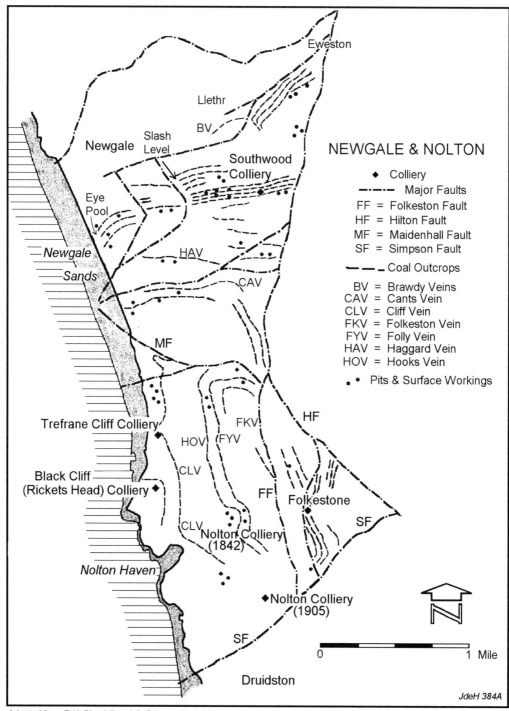

NEWGALE & NOLTON

- ◆ Colliery
- —·—·— Major Faults

FF = Folkeston Fault
HF = Hilton Fault
MF = Maidenhall Fault
SF = Simpson Fault

— — Coal Outcrops

BV = Brawdy Veins
CAV = Cants Vein
CLV = Cliff Vein
FKV = Folkeston Vein
FYV = Folly Vein
HAV = Haggard Vein
HOV = Hooks Vein

•• Pits & Surface Workings

Eweston

Llethr

BV

Newgale

Slash
Level

Southwood
Colliery

Eye
Pool

Newgale

Sands

HAV

CAV

MF

Trefrane Cliff Colliery

FKV

HF

HOV

FYV

CLV

Black Cliff
(Rickets Head) Colliery ◆

FF

Folkestone

SF

CLV

Nolton Colliery
(1842)

Nolton Haven

◆ Nolton Colliery
(1905)

SF

0   1 Mile

N

Druidston

JdeH 384A

Adapted from R.H. Blundell and G. Price
Report on the Pembrokeshire Coalfields, 1955

Figure 10

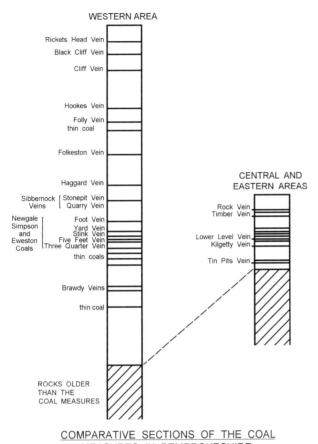

WESTERN AREA

Rickets Head Vein
Black Cliff Vein
Cliff Vein

Hookes Vein
Folly Vein
thin coal

Folkeston Vein

Haggard Vein

Sibbernock ⌠ Stonepit Vein
Veins ⌡ Quarry Vein

Newgale ⌠ Foot Vein
Simpson │ Yard Vein
and │ Stink Vein
Eweston │ Five Feet Vein
Coals ⌡ Three Quarter Vein
thin coals

Brawdy Veins

thin coal

CENTRAL AND
EASTERN AREAS

Rock Vein
Timber Vein

Lower Level Vein
Kilgetty Vein

Tin Pits Vein

ROCKS OLDER
THAN THE
COAL MEASURES

COMPARATIVE SECTIONS OF THE COAL
MEASURES IN PEMBROKESHIRE

Source : A. Strahan and others *The Geology of the South Wales Coalfield Part XI
the country around Haverfordwest* Memoirs of the Geological Survey, 1914, 11.

Figure 11

only outcrop of the Upper Coal measures in Pembrokeshire.[18] The principal vein or seam on the seaward side of the Nolton area is the Cliff vein, but further inland the Folly vein is the widest with an average thickness of four feet. These and the other veins in the district parallel the Folkeston fault by running roughly north to south; the fault itself is thought to be a downthrow to the west of 1000 feet or more. The smaller, triangular Hilton and Simpson area is contained within converging faults within which the Newgale series of coals run in a north-south direction. Figure 10 provides a simplified picture of the complex distribution of coal seams and faults in this district. Figure 11 offers a comparison between the Coal Measures in the Western (or St. Bride's Bay) area, and those in the central or eastern areas of the county, where only the Lower Coal Measures could be exploited.

Little Haven and Broad Haven

In this district the Coal Measures largely consist of shales, with some relatively thin coal seams. However, as a result of much older Precambrian and Palaeozoic rocks having been overthrust over the coal bearing strata, surface coal outcrops were seldom found, and it is possible that the Coal Measures are concealed at depth for over a mile south of the old workings on the Crane vein, the principal vein of the Little Haven district. It has been suggested that this situation may prevail eastwards at least as far as Bolton Hill, near Johnston. Very little evidence remains of mining activity in this district, although the large pond inland from Broad Haven beach was formed in the nineteenth century by colliers digging for culm, and is sometimes referred to as "the Slash pond". Figure 12 illustrates the position of the very few small pits in this district, and also the Southern Thrust fault, forming the southern edge of the coalfield on St. Bride's Bay.

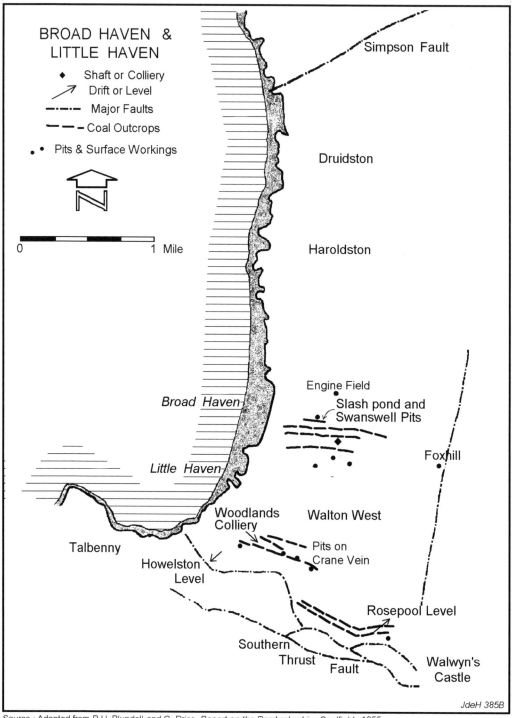

BROAD HAVEN &
LITTLE HAVEN

♦ Shaft or Colliery
↗ Drift or Level
—·—·— Major Faults
— — — Coal Outcrops
• Pits & Surface Workings

0 _____ 1 Mile

Simpson Fault

Druidston

Haroldston

Broad Haven

Little Haven

Talbenny

Engine Field
Slash pond and
Swanswell Pits

Foxhill

Woodlands
Colliery

Walton West

Pits on
Crane Vein

Howelston
Level

Rosepool Level

Southern
Thrust Fault

Walwyn's
Castle

JdeH 385B

Source : Adapted from R.H. Blundell and G. Price *Report on the Pembrokeshire Coalfields*, 1955

Figure 12

[1] A. Strahan and others, *The Memoirs of the Geological Survey: The Geology of the South Wales Coalfield*, Part XI (London: HMSO, 1914), and T. C. Cantrill and others, *The Memoirs of the Geological Survey: The Geology of the South Wales Coalfield*, Part XII, (London: HMSO, 1916). Notwithstanding these dates these continue to be an invaluable source in respect of the complex geology of Pembrokeshire.

[2] See British Geological Survey 1:50,000 map sheets 209 (St. Davids); 226/7 (Milford Haven); and 228 (Haverfordwest).

[3] Dillwyn Miles (ed.), *The Description of Pembrokeshire: George Owen of Henllys* (Llandysul: Gomer Press, 1994), 91. Although it is clear that by Owen's time there was a general understanding of the geology of the coalfield, there seems to have been districts where the detailed geology was not understood. In 1717, for example, a lease was granted to work coal and culm in Portfield, near Haverfordwest, a locality apparently at least a mile north of the coalfield (N.L.W. Haverfordwest Deeds, MS. 1281).

[4] Miles (ed.), *The Description of Pembrokeshire*, 70.

[5] Ibid., 93.

[6] Cantrill and others, *The Geology of the South Wales Coalfield*, Part XII, 115-16.

[7] Strahan and others, *The Geology of the South Wales Coalfield*, Part XI, 160.

[8] Walter Davies, *General View of the Agriculture and Domestic Economy of South Wales* (London, 1815), vol 2, 332-33.

[9] Sir R. Murchison, *Silurian System* (London, 1839), This observation was quoted by T. W. Harcourt Roberts in his paper on the Nolton and Newgale Coalfield in September 1948. A copy is deposited at the Pembrokeshire Record Office.

[10] Miles (ed.), *The Description of Pembrokeshire*, 90.

[11] H. Stopes, *Malt and Malting* (London, 1885), 41, quoting R. Meade *The Coal and Iron Industries of the United Kingdom* (London, 1882).

[12] Walter Davies, *General View of the Agriculture and Domestic Economy of South Wales*, vol 2, 335.

[13] 56 Geo III, cap 127. This definition was repeated in 1819 in 59 Geo III,cap 52. However this was not constant, in every age. *The South Wales Coal Annual* , 1903, for example, mentions "rubbly culm", being "the nutty small passing through longitudinal bars $1^{1}/_{4}$ inches apart". By then anthracite dust was called "duff".

[14] G. Edwards, *A Study of the Daucleddau Coalfield (Pembrokeshire)* (Unpublished M.A. thesis, University of Birmingham, 1950).

[15] Messrs. Fosters' report to Sir Richard Phillipps, 1845 – National Library of Wales, Picton Castle MS 4099.

[16] N.L.W., Picton Castle MS. 4099, as above. A detailed account of coal working in the Saundersfoot area is to be found in the present writer's *Industrial Saundersfoot* (Llandysul, Gomer Press, 1982).

[17] Strahan and others, *The Geology of the South Wales Coalfield*, Part XI, 159.

[18] One vein in Nolton, low down in the Upper Coal Measures, was called Smiths, as it was semi-coking, suitable for smithing work.

The Chronological Development of the Coal Industry

It is believed that the Romans found coal during their occupation of Wales, but there is no evidence that it was ever exploited in any significant or systematic way. The earliest coal miners in South Wales were probably monks, and there are references indicating that monks at both Neath Abbey and Margam Abbey were using coal in the thirteenth century. Indeed, the first reliable record of the use of coal is at Neath in the year 1248. Although there were a number of monastic settlements in Pembrokeshire, most notably at St. Davids, there is no evidence that monks ever dug coal in Pembrokeshire.[1]

No one can say exactly when coal was first mined in the county. T.W. Harcourt Roberts, for many years managing director at Hook Colliery, recorded an agreeable story which he attributed to about the year 1200. According to this tale a storm blew a Spanish ship off course, and instead of making landfall in Cornwall to collect a cargo of tin, it found shelter in the safety of Milford Haven. The crew sailed further up the waterway until they reached Hook. There, it is said, they saw the local inhabitants burning "stone coal", or anthracite, and they realised that this would be a better fuel for tin smelting than charcoal. Quite soon they had acquired a cargo of coal and gone back to Spain. The charming conclusion to this story is that, months later the Spaniards are reputed to have returned and bartered Spanish daffodil bulbs in exchange for coal. The daffodil bulbs doubtless offered little attraction as food, but it is said that until recent times wild daffodils have grown in profusion around Hook and Llangwm.[2]

Maybe this legend contains a memory of the first ever export of coal. If its authenticity is extremely suspect, it is probably correct to the extent that it suggests that the Pembrokeshire coal industry and coal trade began in the thirteenth century. William Rees implies that a coalmine at Roch, near St. Brides, may have been working in the thirteenth century, but gives no details.[3] A better indication of the earliest commercial use of Pembrokeshire coal occurs in Medieval Latin records relating to the construction of the castle at Aberystwyth in 1282. Mention is made of the purchase of limestone from Tenby, and also five hundred cart loads of coal from David the coal-dealer for £7. 10s. 0d., and one hundred cart loads of coal from Ada de Munfort, £1. 10s. 0d. After totalling 2s. 0d for haulage the coal cost £9. 2s. 0d, although significantly it was noted that of the six hundred 'caratatis', "three hundred remain at Christwell in the care of David the coal-dealer under the security of John de Lodeshope, and three hundred are at Tenby". In this one remarkable document there is evidence not merely of coal mining in Pembrokeshire, but of a significant industry with established traders and shipping places. The mason ordering the coal and limestone for Aberystwyth plainly had no hesitation in turning to Pembrokeshire for these materials, which does imply that the county is very likely to have been the source of coal and lime for other major building projects in the thirteenth century.[4] The reference to Christwell is also interesting, in that it points to Cresswell having an association with coal shipping from the thirteenth to the nineteenth century – a span quite possibly unique in Wales.

This evidence of a coastal trade in coal and culm is strengthened by the fact that in 1301 "sea coal" was being used at the King's silvermines at Byrland in Devon, and it is very probable that this originated in West Wales.[5] The construction of the first stone pier at Tenby in 1328 cannot have been entirely coincidental; it points to a growth in coastal traffic. According to a survey of the Bishop of St. David's properties made in 1326, the Bishop's tenants at Lamphey were expected to provide the service of carrying coal when required for lime burning in their locality.[6] Four years later in 1330, there is evidence of coal pits near Begelly, and at Freystrop and Roch, as well as a drift mine in the Coedrath Forest.[7] There is a separate reference to coal pits at Roch in the year 1392.[8]

The Saundersfoot area, known in the fourteenth and fifteenth centuries as Goytrath, or Coedrath, developed early. At this period Goytrath was included in the estate of the Earl of Pembroke, and his accounts provide numerous references to coal mining in the years between 1324 and 1331;[9] as, for example, "1324 - A mine of sea coal .... paying a yearly rent of 16s. 4d." In 1331, however, an entry refers to: "Mine of Sea coal, nil, because no one worked it during the time of this account." At much the same period another entry notes both the price of coal, and its intended use: "150 Bushels of coal, bought for making lime 6s. 3d. – i.e. $\frac{1}{2}$d. per bushel."

The year 1348 saw the onset in Wales of the Black Death, a virulent and persistent scourge which is thought to have reduced the total population of the whole country by 40 per cent over 40 years. Whilst it is not possible to quantify the impact of this grim disease upon Pembrokeshire, it must have seriously disrupted community and commercial life, and delayed progress in the coal industry.

In these early centuries references to the local coal trade emerge like rare glimpses of sunlight through an autumn fog. The Francis Green papers provide a reference to coalpits at Roch in 1382.[10] The first mention of the coal in conjunction with the church comes in 1385, when a small cargo of 40 bushels was unloaded at Porthclais, the tiny harbour serving St. David's Cathedral.[11] The entry was duly made in the cathedral records:

Item. For coal bought, 40 bushels at 2d per bushel – 6s. 8d.
For carriage of the same from Porthcleys to the churchyard – 7d.

By 1399 coal mining in the Swansea area was well established, and well organised within the limitations of the time. The distinguished mining historian J. U. Nef refers to the accounts of the Kilvey colliery in the years to 1400, showing that it employed over thirty people.[12] Even so, the emerging industry in West Wales was completely overshadowed by the dramatic events of a very turbulent age, not least the revolt of Owain Glyndwr very early in the fifteenth century. Indeed, a French Army supporting Owain Glyndwr wintered in Pembrokeshire in 1405-6.

The earliest reference to coal in the fifteenth century is provided by Richard Fenton in his book *An Historical Tour through Pembrokeshire, 1811*.[13] Describing Henry V's grant of the Lordship of Haverfordwest, he says:

In a deed I have seen, Rowland Lenthall is named Lord of Haverfordwest (1439) which is held 'in capite' and he seals it with the seal of his Chancellory. In another deed, he grants coal mines in Roch 'carbones lapidees' and is styled 'Lord of Haverford and the manors of Roch and Pill.'

Almost fifty years later, in 1486, it is thought that coal mines near Tenby, and some other mines, probably formed part of a grant made as a reward for the service by Jasper Tudor, Earl of Pembroke, to Thomas Morice of Tenby at a yearly rent of 40s.[14] The coal mine near Roch, for which a sum of 66s. 8d. was being paid in 1453, seems to have been destroyed in the Wars of the Roses about 20 years later. In 1500 Richard Robyn and Jenkyn More took over the lease and the pit was back in production.

Once again the story is obscured for many years, suggesting that mining in Pembrokeshire continued only on a modest scale. At the start of the sixteenth century it is thought that mining may have suffered some decline, and after an apparently unsuccessful period in the possession of Henry Rowe, the coal pits of Coedrath were let to William Williams in 1529.[15] According to the terms of the lease William ap David Williams was granted:

All those coal mines whatsoever lying within our view of Coedrathe, Co. Pembroke, which are now in decay and which used to be arrented at 53s. 4d. yearly, with leave to dig, erect and reconstruct at the said mine at his pleasure, paying yearly rent of 46s. 8d. to the Kings Exchequer at Pembroke.

The new tenant was not especially successful, because by 1545 the rent was reduced to 40s. per annum. Other tenants followed at even lower rents, until in 1568 John Catherne proposed to surrender his lease unless allowed free use of the forest to replace the decaying timbering of the mine.

In the late 1530's, after the unification of Wales and England in 1536, Henry VIII asked his chaplain and librarian John Leland to tour his kingdom inspecting libraries in colleges, cathedrals and abbeys to produce an account of the antiquities of England and the Principality. When he visited south Pembrokeshire he made passing reference to the coal industry, and wrote:

> From Tenbigh I went to the cole pittes on a hill top two miles of, not far from the Severne shore. And a good mile beyond them I rode through a wood not veri greate, but yet the fairest than I remember that I saw in Penbrokeshire.

A little earlier Leland wrote:

> But the ground in the divers partes of Penbrokeshire berith se coles, wherewith communely the people make fier and with firres as thei do also about Cairmardine [Carmarthen], though ther be better plenty wood. Bi one of thes coles pittes being a four miles from Llanfith [Lamphey] I cam.[16]

Leland makes it clear that coal had become a domestic fuel used by ordinary people. In the sixteenth century this use seems to have become as important as lime burning. Indeed, court records of 1551 indicate that when Owen Nash of Jeffreston dug for stone coal he was motivated by domestic requirements rather more than other commercial considerations.[17] Even so, in Tudor times Jeffreston was well established as a notable centre of the industry. In October 1577, a special commission of inquiry was held in the district to take evidence about weights and measures in use.[18] Seven witnesses were called to confirm that "at the cole pittes of Jeffreston" cole was measured by the hundred, and that "the hundred of sea cole and colne dothe contayne 1x barrels and not above". Only three of these witnesses actually lived in the parish of Jeffreston. Two lived in Yerbeston parish, one at Loveston and one at Knightston, near Tenby – a hint of the expansion of the industry.

"Mines of coal" in Loveston parish were referred to in a deed dated 1562, and "mines of coles called Masterland and Grenehill in Bigelly parish" (but very close to Jeffreston) were included in a sale in 1573.[19] The considerable extent of mining in the Begelly area is indicated by the alarm expressed in 1581 about the safety of the Narberth to Tenby road, as it passed through an expanse of open and unprotected coal pits.[20] Further west, the coal mine at Roch was leased by three different parties between 1565 and 1583.[21]

Clearer evidence of the growth of the coal trade in the Elizabethan period is provided by the invaluable work of E.A. Lewis on the Welsh Port Books.[22] These began to record shipments in 1559-60, as required by an Act of 1558. Originally the whole of West Wales from Barmouth to Worms Head was deemed to be one port, namely Milford. Later Tenby was recognised separately as a shipping place within the port of Milford. Although Lewis found very little information about trade between Wales and Ireland before the time of the first Port Book, he was satisfied that "Milford, Haverford and Tenby shipping took an active part in the carrying trade which thrived between Ireland and Bristol in the later Middle Ages". Certainly fishing, and trade with Ireland were the most notable maritime occupations in Pembrokeshire by 1566, and in Lewis' view the outward traffic in coal and culm constituted "the most important branch of commercial intercourse between Wales and Ireland in Elizabethan times". Although coal was usually shipped in the summer months, the Port Books reveal that between Michaelmas 1565 and Michaelmas 1566, 59 tons of culm and four tons of coal were sent overseas from Milford.

The table below provides additional figures for overseas shipments, derived from the work of J. U. Nef, using figures supplied to him by E. A. Lewis.[23] As will be seen, the record is incomplete. Although there is no information available on foreign exports from Milford in the years 1585-87, there is mention of the shipment coastwise in 1585-86 of 18 weys and 500 barrels of coal. At this period shipments were made to destinations as varied as Plymouth, Dartmouth and London, as well as Aberystwyth and Pwllheli. On 10 June 1587, 10 weys of coal, together with six pieces of frise (cloth) were exported from Tenby to France on board the LE JONAS DE TENBYE. On 25 September 1588, the PHENIX of Tenby sailed to Rochelle in France with nine pieces of frise and five weys of coal. At this time the French ports were linked more often in the coal trade with Swansea and Neath than Pembrokeshire.

The use of different measures is an awkward feature of these early Port Books records. This difficult subject is discussed in Appendix A. For the purposes of the following table of overseas shipments, J. U. Nef's interpretation is observed: he regarded the hundred as equivalent to 8 tons, the chaldron as about 2 tons, the wey at Milford and Tenby as $^4/_5$ of a ton, and the barrel as about $^2/_{15}$ of a ton. The destinations to which these shipments were dispatched are shown in diagrammatic form in Figure 13.

| Period | Milford Shipments | | Tenby Shipments | |
	Coal	Culm	Coal	Culm
1566-1567	5 weys	30 chaldrons	-	-
1593-1594	$14^2/_3$ hundreds	$29^3/_4$ hundreds	$1^3/_5$ hundreds	-
1598-1599	$29^2/_3$ hundreds	$40^3/_4$ hundreds	19 weys	-
1600-1601	$19^7/_{30}$ hundreds	$63^1/_2$ hundreds	8 weys	$^1/_2$ hundred
1601-1602	$32^1/_3$ hundreds	$43^1/_2$ hundreds	33 weys	4 hundreds
1602-1603	$31^1/_2$ hundreds	60 hundreds	30 weys, 40 barrels	$1^1/_2$ hundreds

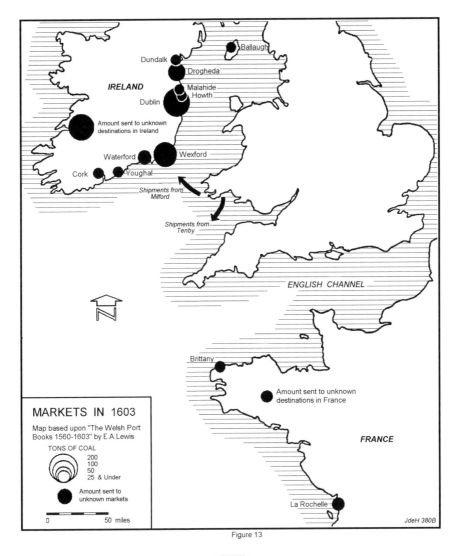

Figure 13

Appendix B includes tables covering coal shipments between Milford and Ireland between 1559 and 1603, together with a table derived from the Port Books for a later period, covering coal and culm shipments from Milford and Tenby between 1660 and 1710.

The Port Books provide a useful but clearly patchy record of the coal trade in Tudor times. Quite apart from any clerical errors and omissions there may have been, it is impossible to say how far the records of trade are also affected by the problems of smuggling and piracy. As a result, even very knowledgeable writers have found it difficult to assess the value of the figures available. For example, one writer has suggested that in 1593 coal exports from the whole of South Wales amounted to only 464 chaldrons, or well under 1,000 tons. J. U. Nef doubted such a low figure, even allowing for the possibility that some shipments may have escaped the attention of customs officials.[24] Furthermore he made the point that individual cargoes were increasing in size, and by the end of the sixteenth century would usually be 12 or 14 tons. What is clear is that notwithstanding occasional dips in the volume of trade, in the later part of the sixteenth century the shipping of coal and culm was increasing rapidly. George Owen, the celebrated Pembrokeshire historian of the Elizabethan period, placed coal in only eighth position amongst the country's exports, but at the time the coal trade and the coal industry were of ever increasing importance.

The evidence of George Owen

Owen's account of the coal industry is an outstanding record for its time, and it repays careful reading.[25] Whilst it is clear that by the end of the sixteenth century much had been learned about the structure of the coalfield, knowledge was far from complete. No doubt miners had acquired their insights by trial and error and intuition, but the details given by Owen are such as to show that they also had a considerable amount of practical experience. Although conditions were often difficult, Elizabethan miners were quite capable of following a vein of coal:

> The coal is first found out by a small appearance thereof which they call the edge, which being found they search which way the vein leaneth and on the contrary side they begin to sink, for the coal is found to lie slope in the ground and seldom downright. The coal being found, the workmen follow the vein every way until it end or be letted by water or rock. The vein for the most part will not be passing five or six foot deep so that the coal is carried stooping, for they commonly leave a foot of coal in the bottom undigged to serve for a strong foundation, except they find the rock under foot they call the 'Doonstone', which if they find, then they dig clean all the coal, and further than that stone they look for no coal. And overhead they are driven to timber their work to keep the earth from falling, which is chargeable, but in some grounds they have a rock above and then they save much labour and cost in sparing of timber.[26]

Although Owen does not refer to any coal seams by name, this description of mining operations indicates that the miners of his day were familiar with both the Rock Vein and the Timber Vein.

Plainly, as the industry had grown there had been significant developments in working methods:

> The digging of this coal is of ancient time used in Pembrokeshire, but not in such exact and skilful sort as now is, for in former time they used no engines for lifting up of the coals out of the pit, but made their entrance slope so as the people carried the coals upon their backs along stairs which they called 'landways', whereas now they sink their pits down right foursquare about six or seven foot square, and with a windlass turned by four men they draw up the coals a barrelful at once by rope. This they call 'a downright door'.[27]

The engines referred to in this passage are simply windlasses – equipment that became known in Pembrokeshire as the 'druke and beam'. It is clear that in the earliest days in Pembrokeshire the mines were either drifts or opencast, for ease of access. Owen's testimony continues:

In these works the water springs are trouble some, which they avoid by sinking a great pit right under the door to which all the water will run, and from thence draw it up with a windlass by barrels or else by making a 'level', as they call it, which is by a way digged underground somewhat lower than the work to bring a passage for the water. This is very chargeable and may cost sometimes £20 and oftentimes more. They now most commonly sink down twelve, sixteen, or twenty fathoms before they come to the coal, whereas in old time four fathoms was counted a great labour. When they find it they work sundry holes, one for every digger, some two, some three or four as the numbers of diggers are, each man working by candlelight and sitting while he worketh. Then have they bearers, which are boys that bear the coals in fit baskets on their backs, going always stooping by reason of the lowness of the pit. Each bearer carryeth this basket six fathoms where upon a bench of stone he layeth it, and meeteth him another boy with an empty basket which he giveth him and taketh that which is full of coals, and carryeth it as far, where another meeteth him, and so till they come under the door where it is lifted up.

The organisation of a typical mine at this period is also described in some detail:

In one pit there will be sixteen persons, whereof there will be three pickaxes digging, seven bearers, one filler, four winders, two riddlers, who riddle the coal when it is a-land, first to draw the small coal from the big by one kind of riddle, then the second riddling with a smaller riddle with which they draw small coals for the smith from the culm, which is indeed but very dust, which serveth lime burning. These persons will land about eighty or hundred barrels of coal in a day. Their tools about this work is pickaxes with a round poll, wedges, and sledges to batter the rocks that cross their work.[28]

Elsewhere in this account Owen records that "The lords of the land hath either rent, or the third barrel after all charges of the work deducted." He continues by making the observation that:

All times of the year is indifferent for working, but the hot weather is worst by reason of sudden damps that happen which oftentimes causeth the workmen to swoon and will not suffer the candles to burn, but the flames, waxing blue of colour, will of themselves out.[29] They work from six o'clock to six o'clock and rest an hour at noon and eat their allowance, as they term it, which is $1/2$d in bread to every man and 4d. in drink among a dozen. This is of custom on the charge of the pit, although they work on their own charge. All their work is by candlelight throughout the year.

The fascinating point here is that whilst the men would work at their own expense, presumably finding their own tools and equipment, it was the custom for the 'allowance' of food and drink for workers to be treated as part of the running costs of the undertaking, and thus an additional expense for the colliery lessees or proprietor.

Having drawn attention to the unpleasant atmosphere of the mine and the hazards of gas, Owen again refers to a source of 1561, the memoranda on The Queen's Remembrancer's Roll, and goes on to declare that:

The dangers of digging these coals is the falling of the earth and the killing of the poor people; or sudden stopping of the way forth, and so die by famine; or else the sudden irruption of standing waters in old works. The work men of this black labour observe all abolished holy days cannot be weaned from that folly.[30]

It would seem that the miners held both to tradition and some superstition in maintaining the holy days abandoned by the Protestant reformers. Overall Owen was candid rather than complimentary about Pembrokeshire labourers and their unfortunate lot, and observed that they are:

held in such continual labour in tilling of the land, burning of lime, digging of coals, and other slaveries and extreme toils, as while they live they never come in shape, favour or comeliness to be accounted among the number of personable men.[31]

Owen's careful description of the characteristics and virtues of Pembrokeshire coal also warrants lengthy citation:

> This kind of coal is not noisome for the smoke, nor nothing so loathsome for the smell as the ring coal [bituminous coal] is, whose smoke annoyeth all things near it, as fine linen, and men's hands that warm themselves by it, but this stone coal yieldeth in a manner no smoke after it is kindled and is so pure that fine cambric or lawn is usually dried by it without any stain or blemish, and is a most proved good drier of malt, therein passing wood, fern or straw. This coal for the rare quality thereof, was carried out of this country to the city of London to the late Lord Treasurer Burghley by a gentleman of experience to show how far the same excelled that of Newcastle wherewith the city of London is served, and I think if the passing were not so tedious there would be great use made of it ...[32]

In Elizabeth's reign the consumption of timber for building, ship building, pitwood and charcoal increased significantly. Although useful figures are lacking, it is clear that the demand for coal increased also, causing many people to have great concern for its future availability. With hindsight it is obvious that these anxieties were exaggerated, but they probably influenced a decision taken in 1599 to impose a customs levy amounting to 5s. per Newcastle chaldron, or 4d. per barrel, on all coal exported overseas. Initially "overseas" was defined as including Ireland, Scotland, the Isle of Man and the Channel Isles. The Irish and others complained, and between 1601 and 1603 coal shipped to all these destinations was exempt from duty. Initially George Owen had something to say about it, and observed that this was:

> after the rate of 4d. for every barrel, whereas the price of the barrel is but 6d., so that the custom is near as much as the price of the coal; and the like custom was demanded for the culm, which was sold but for 1d. the barrel for which the Irishmen who are served from this country and the seamen greatly complained, alleging their trade impaired, and that it would turn to the decay of shipping; but the country people well liked of it, as that which might be the means to stay the transporting, which hath greatly enhanced the price, and is feared that in time will wholly wear out the coal, and so leave the country destitute of fuel; but upon complaint of Her Majesty's subjects of Ireland, this imposition is remitted for the Irishmen.[33]

The importance of coal, and particularly the cheaper culm, for ordinary people has sometimes been overlooked by students of George Owen. However he states clearly: "This coal may be numbered as one of the chief commodities of this country and is so necessary as without it the country would be in great distress." Earlier in *The Description of Pembrokeshire* he writes:

> The lower parts, as the hundreds of Narbeth and Roose, make some gain by selling of sea coal by sea to Ireland and France, but generally the country people dislike with the selling of this commodity lest in time it grow so scarce that the country shall want it, being the greatest fuel, as it hath enhanced the price thereof.

Owen's suggestion that the "sea-coalles" were only eighth amongst the county's exports may have misled some of his readers as to the industry's true significance.[34] Carefully considered, Owen's evidence suggests that the country trade in coal, and especially culm, was substantial, although probably not as important as shipments for export. In any event, by now coal was without doubt, Pembrokeshire's "greatest fuel".

The Seventeenth Century

Initially, it has been suggested, coal was exported to Ireland as a convenient return cargo while the balance of trade favoured Ireland. During the sixteenth century, however, the use of this fuel became a habit which persisted, and so the export of coal to Ireland steadily increased. According to A. K. Longfield this trade was conducted largely by Irish-owned ships. He noted that the Milford Port Books for the period February to September 1587 showed that, of twenty-four vessels engaged in the trade, all but three were owned in Ireland. Over half of the shipments from Milford were destined for Wexford in small ships belonging to that port.[35] To some extent this situation may reflect the fact that prior to 1570 there was a serious shortage of experienced mariners and suitable trading vessels in West Wales.[36] The rapid growth in trade in the Elizabethan era appears to have changed this position entirely by the end of the century.[37]

In the first half of the seventeenth century this pattern was maintained, with a further expansion in overseas shipments from Milford. The following table, based on the Port Book evidence noted by Nef, indicates both the fragmenting nature of the records, and the continued use of different volume measures. Whilst it does not suggest a notable upsurge in trade following the lifting of the tax on Irish shipments, it does point to a considerable increase in the exports of culm by the 1630's, by which time some export duties had been revised and increased.[38]

Period	Milford Shipments		Tenby Shipments	
	Coal	Culm	Coal	Culm
1604-05	$28^2/_3$ hundreds	$36^1/_4$ hundreds	26 weys	-
1605-06	36 hundreds	$39^1/_8$ hundreds	-	-
1607-08	-	-	275 barrels	140 barrels
1633-34	$46^1/_3$ hundreds	$110^1/_2$ hundreds	2 hundreds	-
1636-37	$65^1/_2$ hundreds	$228^1/_3$ hundreds	-	-

After 1638 the Port Books for Milford invariably refer to overseas shipments by the chaldron measure; the term was not used for coastwise shipments before 1665-66. From time to time in the seventeenth century coal duties were varied, but given the somewhat limited figures available an assessment of their impact upon trade would be a difficult and possibly inconclusive exercise. Although the shipment figures plainly point to an expansion in the coal industry, duties of any kind must have been a disadvantage to coal producers and coal shippers alike. Given Pembrokeshire's long and remote coastline they must have experienced both the temptation and the opportunity to avoid paying duty. Accordingly the accuracy and the completeness of the available records is open to question. Nevertheless, for what they may be worth, the Port Book figures for the years 1660-1710 are given in Figure 14.

The fluctuations in coal shipments before 1650 may be some measure of the problems encountered by those in the coal trade when it was looked upon as a source of income for the Crown. The uncertainty and turmoil of the Civil Wars cannot have been easy for anyone involved in the trade, and the position in the 1650's is obscure owing to a gap in the Port Books during most of the period of the Protectorate.

Shipping in the Bristol Channel and the Irish Sea was sometimes hampered by the activity of pirates and privateers. The latter were usually only a problem at times of conflict with France or the Netherlands,[39] but piracy occurred in Pembrokeshire waters as early as the 1570's, and on at least one occasion the notorious Welsh pirate John Callice defied the authorities by coming ashore at Milford and lodging at Haverfordwest.[40] A century later the problem remained, together with some fraud and deceit in trading practice. By 1682 the Treasury was keenly aware of the prevalence of fraud in shipping coal, lead and tin from England to Ireland, and a customs officer named Silvanus Stirrup was appointed to detect abuses. This was no easy task, and whilst Stirrup may have had only limited success, he played a useful part in the compilation of an extensive survey of Irish trade in the early 1680's.[41]

By the seventeenth century Pembrokeshire anthracite had found a range of uses, most notably lime burning and malting. George Owen said simply that coal "is a most proved good drier of malt", although in the absence of other evidence, it would seem that at the time this usage was local rather than widespread. In addition, stone coal was used for some smithy work, although Owen acknowledged that it was not as good for this purpose as bituminous coal.[42] As anthracite has a

Figure 14

YEAR	MILFORD				TENBY			
	Coastwise		Overseas		Coastwise		Overseas	
	Culm	Coal	Culm	Coal	Culm	Coal	Culm	Coal
1660 (½ year)	3 tons	46 hun.	-	-	-	-	-	-
954 hun.								
1661-62	-	-	381½ cha.	536 cha.	-	-	-	-
1663-64	-	-	683½ cha.	469 cha.	-	-	-	-
1665-65	2,396 cha.	151 cha.	591 cha.	444½ cha.	-	-	-	-
1666-67	-	-	-	-	515 hun.	200 bar.	-	-
1668-69	-	-	1,221 cha.	566½ cha.	-	-	20 cha.	-
1669-70	-	-	95 cha.	1,566½ cha.	-	-	55 cha.	-
1670-71	6,434 cha.	1,254 cha.	-	-	-	-	-	-
1671-72	-	-	1,063½ cha.	392 cha.	-	-	-	-
1672-73	4,282 cha.	221 cha.	-	-	1,942 cha.	104 cha.	-	-
1680-81	5,513 cha.	1,234 cha.	1,834½ cha.	1,175 cha.	-	-	-	-
1682-83	-	-	-	-	4,005 cha.	644 cha.	12 cha.	26 cha.
1687-88	11,232 cha.	913 cha.	856 cha.	1,015 cha.	2,500 cha.	1,108 cha.	-	-
1709-10	5,094 cha.	178½ cha.	995 cha.	97 cha.	-	-	-	-

Abbreviations: bar. = barrels, cha. = chaldrons, hun. = hundreds

Sources:The Welsh Port Book - Ed. E.A.Lewis (1927), and The Rise of the British Coal Industry - J.U.Nef (1932)

relatively low sulphur content it might have been adequate for the manufacture of cast iron, but it is unlikely to have been satisfactory for making wrought iron. This may be one reason for the importation of small quantities of other grades of coal from the seventeenth century onwards.

Earlier, in the Elizabethan period, the usual fuel for smithy work was charcoal, but by the start of the seventeenth century charcoal, and the woodland to provide it, was in short supply. This problem was just as acute in Pembrokeshire as anywhere else. Owen not only lamented the scarcity of woodland in the county, but also mentions that efforts had been made to convert peat into charcoal for smithying. Although his references to charcoal are few, it appears to have been produced in some quantity because on occasions it was exported. (In 1593, for example, Sir Francis Godolphin shipped 100 packs of charcoal to St. Ives in Cornwall).[43] However, at least one corner of the county seems to have had a satisfactory supply of timber, namely Blackpool, on the Eastern Cleddau. A forge had been established at this spot at the beginning of the sixteenth century, and it had passed into the ownership of the Barlow family by purchase in 1546.[44] In 1635 the Barlows let the forge to George Mynne of Surrey, and in addition to this evidence for a timber supply it is known that at the same period timber was sold for use in nearby coal pits.[45]

Other uses were found for Pembrokeshire anthracite in the seventeenth century. In 1615 Robert Mansell acquired a patent for the exclusive manufacture of glass. Doubtless aware of the special properties of Pembrokeshire coal, Mansell tried to work glass in a furnace which he had erected near Milford Haven. The cost of transporting the product to London evidently exceeded all the advantages obtained by location close to the source of fuel, and Mansell moved the glassworks to Newcastle on Tyne, where the coal was reported to be better suited for the purpose.[46] On the other hand, Northumberland coal did not compete well against Pembrokeshire coal when it came to salt drying, and shipments of anthracite were dispatched to London and ports in East Anglia for this use. Later in the century it is believed that the particular qualities of Pembrokeshire culm were valued for use in hothouses, and J. U. Nef suggested that this might explain why this culm found a market all over the western world, but usually only in small quantities.[47] Within Pembrokeshire itself, and specifically within Haverfordwest, there were at least two references to the purchase of coal for use at "the pest house" in 1652, a year when the plague was a serious hazard in the county.[48]

Some broad impressions of the development of the coal industry, and coal mining communities, may be obtained by comparing figures for the population of coalfield parishes in 1563 and 1670. These figures cannot be regarded in any way as reliable as modern census figures, but they may be a guide. In 1563 the Bishop of St. Davids was asked to provide the Privy Council with information about the ecclesiastical livings in his diocese, and to state the number of households in each parish. A comparison with 1670 is possible because in that year a list was prepared of hearth tax payers in each parish.[49] Figure 15 provides a map of parishes on or very close to the Pembrokeshire coalfield.

Between 1563 and 1670 it is evident that most Pembrokeshire parishes saw a significant population growth, and many on or near the coalfield doubled or almost doubled in numbers – for example Begelly, Jeffreston, Lawrenny, Martletwy, Minwear, Reynalton, Slebech, Boulston, Burton, Freystrop, Nolton and Walton West. In a few such parishes the population was almost static, or actually decreased, between 1563 and 1670 – for instance Johnston,

PEMBROKESHIRE - THE FORGOTTEN COALFIELD

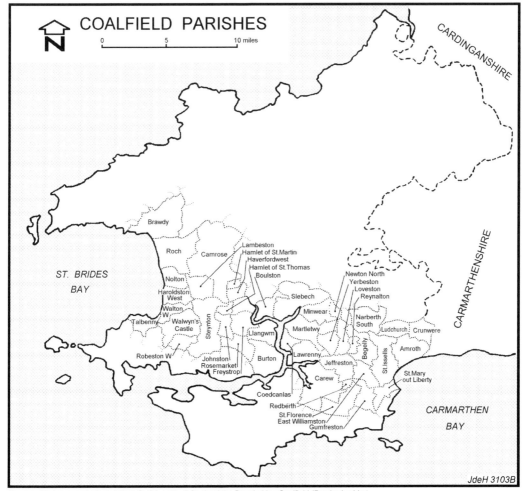

Source : Redrawn and adapted from G. Edwards *A Study of the Daucleddau Coalfield (Pembrokeshire)*

Figure 15

Loveston, St. Issells and Tenby. Whilst it might be said that the gap of 107 years between the two dates is sufficiently far apart to conceal a number of other, briefer population trends, if there is one general movement it is towards a growth in population along the shores of the Cleddau, with a slight decrease in population on the east coast around Tenby and St. Issells. Weighing the evidence, Brian Howells has concluded that:

> The development of mining and the opening up and colonisation of woodland were responsible for the fact that the rate of rural population increase during the years 1563-1670 was greater in Narberth than in any other hundred [of Pembrokeshire] except Cemais.[50]

As regards towns, the case of Tenby is particularly interesting. After some prosperity in the Middle Ages, the town was incorporated as a free borough in 1581. In the seventeenth century, though, the town went into decline. In the words of Margaret Davies:

> Plagues, Civil War, loss of trade and fishing to ships from other ports and a farming hinterland which was less productive than that behind Pembroke all seem to have contributed to this decline.[51]

In 1623 the Mayor and corporation said simply "the ... traffic of foreign merchants is not so much frequented in this place as in times past".[52] If Tenby continued to ship coal as the Port Books testify, decline was to persist throughout the seventeenth century. Indeed towards the end of the century it was reported that "the port and town of Tenby is very near to utter ruine and desolation ... the peere for preserving shipping is in danger to fall to decay",[53] The reasons for this decline may be several, but the evidence of the population figures, and also the Port Books, would suggest that the growth of the coal industry in the seventeenth century was largely along the banks of the River Cleddau. It seems reasonable to suppose that there was some population movement away from Tenby and St. Issells to find employment in mining.

Evidence of particular coal workings in the seventeenth century are regrettably rare. In 1612 Arthur Owen, third son of John Owen of Orielton, became owner of "lands and coal mines at Coedcanlas and Freystrop".[54] In 1648 the estate of Griffith White included the coal mines in Begelly parish, and also coal mines in the parish of Loveston.[55] In 1664 James Philipps of Tregibby, near Cardigan, granted a lease of Folcaston [near Nolton] "with creeks, quays, quarries, coal and culm", to Anthony Stokes of Roch parish, gentleman, for lives.[56] The Picton Castle papers include an agreement in respect of Sir John Philipps' coal works and quay at Freystrop in 1699.[57]

Figure 14 demonstrates the dramatic increase in coal shipments in the second half of the seventeenth century, especially with regard to coastal traffic. Even more significant are the figures for actual shipments made in different years, as observed by Barbara George - 41 in 1617, 243 in 1638, 322 in 1662, 470 in 1680, and no less than 502 in 1698.[58] An important aspect of this increase was the trade to Ireland. Whilst L. M. Cullen noted that Irish shipments from Whitehaven grew rapidly after 1660, so that by 1677 half the coal used in Dublin came from that port,[59] he was probably incorrect in saying that culm exports from Milford and Tenby were dependent on the Dublin market.[60] Rather was there a long tradition of shipping coal and culm to lesser ports on the south and east coasts of Ireland, many of which were much closer to Pembrokeshire. The general advance in trade was not entirely uninterrupted. After peaking in the 1680's there was a recession in the 1690's, the causes of which have been explained by John Hatcher. "Wars with Holland and France harmed overseas trade, and sharply increased duties on coastal shipments damaged the market throughout the coastal regions of Britain."[61] By the end of the century trade began to make progress, and the key to it all was the sea. In Pembrokeshire development was most marked by the sheltered waters of the River Cleddau and Milford Haven. In the eighteenth century the sources available to the researcher increase considerably, and it becomes possible to identify periods of activity at particular pits, and to discuss the development of infrastructure and operating practices.

[1] E. W. Evans, *The Miners of South Wales* (Cardiff: University of Wales Press, 1961), 1; J. Harry, *The Pembrokeshire Coalfield* (Dyfed County Council, 1990), 10 and 11.

[2] T. W. Harcourt Roberts, *Historical Survey of the Pembrokeshire Coalfield*, 1947, quoted by J. Harry, *The Pembrokeshire Coalfield*, 11.

[3] W. Rees, *Industry before the Industrial Revolution* (Cardiff, University of Wales Press, 1968), 11 and footnote 39.

[4] Public Record Office, Kew, *History of the Kings Works, Vol. 1 C47/2/2/7* and C47/2/4/2d; R. F. Walker, "William de Valence and the Army in West Wales, 1282/83", *Welsh History Review*, 18 (1997), 419. I am grateful to Dr. Walker for drawing my attention to this reference. I am also grateful to C. J. Spurgeon, formerly employed at Aberystwyth Castle on behalf of the Royal Commission for Ancient Monuments in Wales, for his private communication dated 1 October 2001,stating that the lime kiln at the castle "was clearly operating from the outset of work in 1277". He also noted a claim made by I. D. Sanders, *Ceredigion*, 1959, 319-336, that coal, lead and chalk shipments were made to Aberystwyth in 1277-80. Numerous castles and church buildings in West Wales date from the Norman period, and whilst no direct evidence is available in other cases about the use of coal and culm, I am indebted to the late Terry Driscoll of Roch, Pembs, for the advice that the clinker of culm has been found in the mortar of Roch Castle.

[5] Robert L. Galloway, *Annals of Coal Mining and the Coal Trade* (1st ed. reprinted, Newton Abbot: David & Charles, 1971), 29; Evidence in the accounts of Thomas de Sweneseye (*Archaeological Journal* No. 108, (1870), 318, then Master of the King's Mines in Devon and Cornwall.

[6] *The Black Book of St. David's* (Cardiff: University of Wales Press, 1902), 89.

[7] W. Rees, *Industry before the Industrial Revolution*, 35.

[8] Pembrokeshire County Library, Haverfordwest, Francis Green MSS., Vol. 25, 428. I am indebted to the late Terry Driscoll of Roch for drawing my attention to this reference.

[9] Henry Owen (ed.), *A Calendar of Public Records relating to Pembrokeshire*, vol. 3, The Earldom of Pembroke and its members (London: Honourable Society of Cymmrodorion, 1918), 84, 130, 140.

[10] Francis Green, "Pembrokeshire in Bye-gone Days", *West Wales Historical Records* Vol. ix (1920-1930), 83-86.

[11] "Liber Communis", a record of the accounts of St. David's Cathedral for 1385, by Hugh Felton quoted by P. B. S. Davies, *Pembrokeshire Limekilns* (St. Davids: Merrivale Press, 1997).

[12] J. U. Nef, *The Rise of the British Coal Industry* (1st Edn. London, 1932), Volume 1, 14.

[13] R. Fenton, *An Historical Tour through Pembrokeshire, 1811*, (London: Longman et. al., 1811), 211.

[14] Rees, *Industry before the Industrial Revolution*, 82.

[15] H. Owen (ed.), *A Calendar of Public Records relating to Pembrokeshire*, Vol. 3, 66, 193.

[16] John Leland, *The Itinerary in Wales – John Leland, in or about 1536-1539*: extracted from his Mss., arranged and edited by Lucy Toulmin- Smith (London: George Bell and Sons, 1906), 115 and 117.

[17] National Library of Wales, 25/8/14b.

[18] Public Record Office, E178/3493: Court of Exchequer – Special Commission of Inquiry, 1577.

[19] F. Jones, "White of Henllan", *The Pembrokeshire Historian*, 5 (1974), 64.

[20] N.L.W. Great Sessions records, Wales 4, Pembroke 775/6.

[21] W. Rees, *Industry before the Industrial Revolution*, 82, footnote 39.

[22] E. A. Lewis (ed.), *The Welsh Port Books (1550-1603)*. (London: Honourable Society of Cymmrodorion, 1927) xxiv.

[23] Nef, *The Rise of the British Coal Industry*, Vol.2, Appendix D, 380.

[24] Ibid. Vol. 2, Appendix B, 362-363; H. A. Lloyd, *The Gentry of South West Wales, 1540-1640* (Cardiff: University of Wales Press, 1968), 89, declared "The unwisdom of estimating the quantity and nature of maritime commerce in this locality on the evidence of the extant port books alone, is obvious. Much trade must have gone unrecorded, for customs officials, when diligent, cannot have had an easy task."

[25] Those interested in studying George Owen's work in greater detail would do well to study Brian Howells (ed.), *Elizabethan Pembrokeshire: the evidence of George Owen*, Pembrokeshire Record Series, 2 (Pembrokeshire Record Society, 1973), and also Dillwyn Miles (ed.), *The Description of Pembrokeshire: George Owen of Henllys* (Llandysul: Gomer Press 1994).

[26] D. Miles (ed.), *The Description of Pembrokeshire*, 92.

[27] Ibid., 91.

[28] Ibid., 93.

[29] Ibid., 93. This appears to be a reference to choke-damp (carbonic acid gas) which would extinguish a naked flame, and could also suffocate an unwary coal miner.

[30] Ibid., 94.

[31] Ibid., 46.

[32] Ibid., 90.

[33] Ibid., 94 As a consequence of maritime links with Ireland many Irish people emigrated to Pembrokeshire. This clearly caused George Owen concern as he wrote (D. Miles, ed., 43) "As for the Irishmen, they are so powdered among the inhabitants of Roose and Castlemartin that in every village you shall find the third, fourth or fifth householder an Irishman, and now of late they swarm more than in times past by reason of these late wars in Ireland."

[34] Ibid., 61; E. A. Lewis (ed.), *The Welsh Port Books 1550-1603,* xxiii, declares on the evidence of the Port Books that "the outward traffic in coal and culm constituted the most important branch of commercial intercourse between Wales and Ireland in Elizabethan times". On the basis of this assertion the student may wonder whether Owen himself underestimated the size and significance of this trade.

[35] A. K. Longfield, *Anglo-Irish Trade in the Sixteenth Century* (London: Routledge, 1929), 171-172. Cardiff was also prominent in the Irish trade, and Chester shipped coal for Dublin.

[36] G. Dyfnallt Owen, *Elizabethan Wales* (Cardiff: University of Wales Press, 1962), 124.

[37] Ibid., 128. He also quotes George Owen in support.

[38] Nef, *The Rise of the British Coal Industry,* Vol. 2, Appendix D, 380.

[39] W. Rees, *Industry before the Industrial Revolution,* 114, provides several illustrations of such incidents.

[40] G. Dyfnallt Owen, *Elizabethan Wales,* 144, 131. At the same period it seems the integrity of customs officials was very much open to doubt. George Clerk, a searcher, was accused of accepting bribes – even from the Mayor of Tenby.

[41] L. M. Cullen, *Anglo-Irish Trade, 1660-1800* (New York: 1968), 144.

[42] Miles (ed.), *The Description of Pembrokeshire,* 90.

[43] H. A. Lloyd, *The Gentry of South West Wales 1540-1640* (Cardiff: University of Wales Press, 1968), 86.

[44] Sir F. Dashwood, *The story of Blackpool Mill* (Narberth: 1975), 3.

[45] National Library of Wales, Slebech MS 441.

[46] W. Rees, *Industry before the Industrial Revolution,* 66.

[47] Nef, *The Rise of the British Coal Industry, Vol. 1*, p. 117. He notes that cargoes from Milford were destined for Flanders, Holland, Norway, France, Spain, Portugal and the West Indies, as well as Scotland and ports on the East Coast of England. Shipments seldom exceeded 100 tons to any destination in a year, but in 1681 an exceptional 448 tons were shipped from Milford Haven to Rotterdam.

[48] B. G. Charles (ed.), *A Calendar of the Records of the Borough of Haverfordwest, 1539-1660* (Cardiff: University of Wales Press, 1967), 115, 135.

[49] Brian Howells, "Land and People, 1536-1642" in Brian Howells (ed.), *Early Modern Pembrokeshire, Vol. 3, Pembrokeshire County History* (Haverfordwest, 1987), 2, 3.

[50] Ibid., 18.

[51] Margaret Davies, *The Story of Tenby* (Tenby: 1979), 20.

[52] B. Howells, "Land and People, 1536-1642", 18.

[53] W. Harrison, *Some aspects of Tenby's History* (Tenby: 1979), 2.

[54] F. Jones, "Owen of Orielton", *The Pembrokeshire Historian*, No 5 (Haverfordwest: 1974), 11.

[55] F. Jones, "White of Henllan". Griffith White's grandfather, also Griffith White, had an interest in coal mines at Loveston as early as 1562. In 1573 he acquired the mines at Masterland and at Greenhill in Begelly parish.

[56] F. Jones, *Historic Pembrokeshire Houses and their Families,* extended edition (Newport, Pembs: 2001), 81.

[57] N.L.W., Picton Castle MS 579.

[58] Barbara George, "Pembrokeshire Sea Trading before 1800," *Field Studies*, Vol.2, No 1 (1964), 15.

[59] Cullen, *Anglo-Irish Trade 1660-1800,* 82.

[60] Ibid., 81.

[61] John Hatcher, *The History of the British Coal Industry*, Vol.1 (Oxford: Clarendon Press, 1993), 140.

Landlords and Leases

Until the early nineteenth century the operation and development of the Pembrokeshire coalfield was controlled by the only local inhabitants with significant money or property - namely the landed gentry and a relatively modest number of prosperous yeomen. For them there was no great distinction to be made between using their land for agriculture or for mining. The latter was seen simply as an alternative source of income - and sometimes much more remunerative than farming. The one drawback with mining was the likelihood that such activity would ruin the land for any future agricultural use. As early as 1571 it was observed that land in the parish of Begelly was so full of pits as to be both dangerous and unworkable.[1] At this period though, there was no stigma attached to an involvement in mining, and some saw it as a positive virtue. In 1744, for example, John Campbell of Stackpole expressed the hope that "the mines" would rescue his family finances.[2] Although the Cawdor family (the Campbells) held property in the parishes of Loveston and Jeffreston, they do not figure prominently in the story of Pembrokeshire coal mining however. Their lucrative mines were outside the county.

Other landowners were blessed with property in Pembrokeshire containing considerable coal deposits. The Philipps family of Picton castle owned coal pits in the parishes of Begelly, St. Issells, Amroth and Freystrop as well as on their own immediate estate about Picton Castle itself.[3] The Owens of Orielton owned a sizeable colliery at Landshipping, and also had interest in pits at Jeffreston, Reynalton and Hook.[4] The Allens of Cresselly and the Barlows of Lawrenny possessed pits near Cresswell Quay,[5] as did the Hamiltons and Grevilles, who also had land at Begelly.[6] The Powells of Greenhill owned pits in the parishes of Begelly, Jeffreston and Llangwm,[7] whilst the Wogans of Wiston had pits in their land at Hean Castle near Saundersfoot.[8] The various owners of Slebech had small pits near Landshipping, and in the parish of Martletwy.[9] The Pryses of Gogerddan (Cardiganshire) owned pits at Moreton near Saundersfoot, and appear to have had other lesser interests in the parish of Jeffreston.[10]

A recital of these names of the landed gentry amounts to a statement of their domination of the Pembrokeshire coal industry in the middle of the eighteenth century. In this period prior to the Industrial Revolution, and prior to the development of the capital market, the industry could only function through their interest, and their willingness to involve others. As coal proprietors they had the option of being directly involved in the exploitation of their mineral resources, but usually they preferred indirect involvement, either by delegating management to an agent, or by letting coal mines to contractors, or even subcontractors, whose activities would be monitored by an agent. As a result the major landowners retained some say in strategic thinking about the future development of their coal and culm, but so long as the terms of leases and agreements were observed they had very little scope for tactical, or day to day decision making. Even so, G. E. Mingay made several significant but generalised points as regards the involvement of landlords:

> Although in the eighteenth century it became common practice to lease out mines and works to private entrepreneurs, the landlords or their stewards often filled an important role in directing, financing and generally encouraging projects, and their royalties included payments for wayleaves or transport rights, streams used for power, land taken up by workmen's cottages, and for the timber supplied by the estate. Landlords resorted to the courts to obtain full rights to minerals under commons and waste land, and small freeholders or customary tenants whose

rights hindered exploitation were bought out. The development of mining was thus a factor in the decline of peasant ownership.[11]

It has to be said that Pembrokeshire does not offer obvious examples in every instance, but Mingay reflects fairly both the climate and the trends of those times.

The advantages in leasing out coal mines were considerable, even though in the eighteenth century there was a scarcity of lessees with sufficient funds for the task, and the banking system was too weak to offer much support. Usually the coal owner, in Mingay's words, "provided the land and perhaps some buildings and transport facilities; the pits or works, equipment, tools, wagons, and horses were the responsibility of the lessees".[12]

In the late eighteenth century at least three landowners preferred to have a more direct involvement. J. B. Allen of Cresselly and Sir Hugh Owen of Orielton and Landshipping chose to work some of their pits, and to lease out others. Lord Milford was not only involved in working his own collieries, but on occasions he leased pits from other landlords – for example, the Moreton colliery near Saundersfoot from 1764 to 1779,[13] and a colliery at Amroth in 1802.[14] His interest was so considerable that at times he resembled Sir John Lowther in West Cumberland in the seventeenth century, in his readiness to try to buy adjoining properties with promising reserves of coal.[15] In 1789, for example, he contemplated the possibility of selling over 2,400 acres to give himself a chance of purchasing an important mineral estate at Begelly.[16] In 1798 he managed to acquire Killanow farm in Amroth parish,[17] and within a few years it was producing coal or culm.[18]

In these activities, Lord Milford was not typical. Most landowners preferred to lease their pits, and as a result, routine managerial functions were in the hands of lessees, or those appointed by them. It was their responsibility to monitor output and sales, and to ensure good accounting. It was their task to supervise the work force and to maintain the coal mine and its equipment. As good education was a privilege accorded to few in eighteenth-century Pembrokeshire, finding men fit for these responsibilities was not a simple matter. The precise measurement of coal was always difficult, and it was relatively easy for a collier to perpetrate some deception over the amount of coal or culm he or she had hewn or moved. In practice it seems that men with considerable experience, but limited literacy, undertook these tasks for lessees, often using tallies to keep note of quantities dug or raised.[19]

For lessors it was essential to have capable men to assist in monitoring activity and protecting the landlord's best interests. The Picton Castle papers include a memorandum book of 1705 in which a colliery agent or steward noted all he had learned from a mine at Freystrop, where the lessor was Lady Pakington and the lessee a Mr. Longman. It appears that in August 1705, Mr Longman was doing well, and his progress to a depth of 23 fathoms (or about 140 feet) provided guidance in the setting of terms for other mineral leases.[20]

In the case of absentee landlords, like the Pakingtons, who lived in Worcestershire, or like Harcourt Powell, who had houses in both Berkshire and Suffolk, the appointment of an estate steward or agent was especially necessary. These were always men of practical ability, and some education. Charles Hassall, who worked for a while in the late eighteenth century for Sir Richard Philipps, could be considered to be minor gentry in his own right, as well as a leading authority on good agricultural practice at that period.[21] Richard Knethell of Hook certainly aspired to gentry status; a qualified attorney, and sometime steward of the Great Nash estate, it is believed he was also clerk to the Wogans of Wiston. At various times he was lessee of coal pits not only in the Hook and Freystrop area, but also in the Begelly and East Willamston district.[22]

Arguably the most able of these men was Thomas George of Hook. In 1787 he was appointed as sole agent at Hook for both Sir Hugh Owen and John Harcourt Powell, and there is no doubt that they relied heavily upon his advice. In 1791 he assisted in the building of a ballast quay at Hook and in the following year he is believed to have been prominent in a meeting of colliery agents endeavouring to settle the price of coal.[23] Colonel Colby as trustee of the Orielton estate, consulted Thomas George in 1800 regarding the development of a mine at Amroth,[24] and in 1804 he travelled to Llanelly to inspect a Trevithick steam engine, and went on to

Swansea in the hope of finding a type of steam engine suitable for use at one of the Pembrokeshire pits.[25] As his expertise and competence became widely recognised, so his salary increased, and early in the nineteenth century he was able to obtain a lease to Sir Hugh Barlow's small colliery at Nash.[26] By 1811 he managed to take a lease of three lives at Great Nash farm and Thomas George effectively joined the ranks of those who might be considered yeoman farmers.[27]

Not all colliery agents were so successful. At the end of the eighteenth century John Cossens was agent for the Orielton estate in Amroth. In 1800 Colonel Colby leased the White Bone colliery to Lord Milford, and Cossens was asked to supervise activity at the pit.[28] By 1804 output was falling, and trade was in decline. A year later Cossens, who sometimes reported to Thomas George, observed that "the goods have been very poor which have prevented the trade".[29] In brief only culm was being produced, and Lord Milford was losing interest in the pit. As these unfortunate circumstances continued Cossens himself appears to have been out of favour – possibly for letting too many people enjoy too much credit for too long. Attached to a list of colliery debts is a statement dated 24 October 1807, signed by Colby, to the effect that Cossens "is no longer Agent to my colliery near Amroth church".[30]

In 1850 it seems that there was a distinct possibility that Captain Thomas Stephenson, then Harbourmaster at Saundersfoot, might be asked to act as mineral agent to Sir Richard Philipps (Lord Milford). A neighbouring landowner and colliery proprietor, J. M. Child of Begelly, was alarmed, and he wrote to Lord Milford to dissuade him. In Child's view Stephenson was:

> an honest, honourable, sober and well intentioned man who would zealously discharge any duty entrusted to him to the utmost of his ability. At the same time I cannot hide from you my decided opinion that as Mineral Agent he is totally incompetent as he must be deficient in all the qualifications requisite for such an appointment, such as Viewing, dialling, sinking, boring, ventilating, mapping, the application of machinery and some notion of mechanics which are indispensable in the prosperity and well doing of a colliery.[31]

Following such comprehensive criticism, J. M. Child felt obliged to be constructive, and instead spoke warmly of the qualities of H. P. Goode of Haverfordwest. Suffice to say that Mr. Goode was appointed!

If the better colliery agents provided instances of men who managed to advance their status by their involvement in the coal industry, there were others who regarded the industry as an interesting and challenging way to diversify their commercial interests. Thomas Kymer of Robeston Hall was a prosperous London merchant in the middle of the eighteenth century, and whilst he tried to develop a stake in Pembrokeshire coal and culm it appears that as an outsider, and a Whig, he was not entirely popular with the Tory landed gentry.[32] In the 1760's, at a time when a number of collieries in Pembrokeshire had failed, he turned his attention to the Gwendraeth valley in Carmarthenshire.[33] Here he became involved in both coal and timber production before embarking in 1769 upon the construction of Kymer's canal running inland from Kidwelly.

Kymer's contemporary, Abel Hicks, had the advantage of being a Pembrokeshire man. Until 1769 he managed a 200-acre-farm on St. Bride's Bay, and also ran a coasting business which shipped coal and culm from Pembrokeshire around the coast of Wales and over to Ireland. Given such interest it was logical for him to go into partnership with two other men for the purpose of coalmining, and in so doing he gained a greater prominence in the community.[34]

In 1813, Thomas Bowen was a principal figure in the Union Bank of Haverfordwest;[35] some years later a Thomas Bowen of Johnston Hall was the main lessee of the Falkeston colliery at Nolton.[36] Similarly in 1825, David Saer was the prominent figure in the Pembrokeshire Bank of Haverfordwest;[37] at the same period a man of the same name was a lessee of a pit at Summerhill, Amroth.[38] A few years later T. S. Biddulph, who is believed to have been a member of the Biddulph and Cocks banking house in Swansea, acquired an interest in a colliery at Amroth.[39] These would seem to be additional instances of men who, having enjoyed success in another business, chose to commit some of their wealth to the Pembrokeshire coal industry.

Notwithstanding these examples it is not always easy to discern whether some men became prosperous and more prominent because of their involvement in the coal industry, or whether they took up such interests because they had enjoyed some financial success elsewhere. In 1950 George Edwards drew attention to the case of the Cresswell colliery in 1787.[40] Here, he asserted, "there were large numbers of workmen adventurers who either singly or in groups and with little capital, undertook what were usually small concerns". At this date the Cresswell colliery:

> Consisted of nine workings, each controlled by different men who paid a royalty to the land owners Sir Hugh Owen, John Harcourt Powell, and Hugh Barlow. Five of these workings produce less than 500 tons during that year and only one topped the 2,000 tons mark.

Edwards evidently relied upon Nef in calculating these tonnages, but his belief that the pits were run entirely by workmen with little capital is open to discussion. The name of Alex Smith appears in relation to four of the nine coal works at Cresswell, and the name of William Smith in relation to three, including the most productive, simply named "Level". Both men may have been involved also in the operation of the pit known as "Smiths Hill", described briefly as "worked by partners". Although these names are the most obvious, William Belth is referred to in respect of two of the workings, one of which was actually named "Belth". As those working coal had to have the means to buy timber, iron, candles, rope, powder, tools and other essentials, it must be doubtful if these men were mere workmen with little capital. Rather were they businessmen seeking to make a profit in the hazardous enterprise of coal mining, although it is not clear whether they had made progress by pursuing such investments, or whether, like Knethell and Hicks, Saer and Biddulph, they had made money in some other business and then had chosen to diversify into mining. Five examples of colliery accounts relating to Cresswell between 1770 and 1827 appear in Appendix M, including a simplified account for 1787.

In the eighteenth century landlords and lessees alike were very well aware of the commercial potential of coal, culm and other minerals. However their increased appreciation of the value of their land could bring them into conflict with neighbours or partners. Boundary disputes were quite common, and were not confined to the immediate vicinity of coal mines. One of the most bitter and complex disputes arose at Cresswell Quay. The main quay at Cresswell was owned by John Allen of Cresselly, and near it he had built coal yards, or "coal folds", to store coal, culm and limestone. Another coal shipper, George Barlow, maintained that these coal, culm and stone banks trespassed onto his land. In 1744 there was a court case about ownership, which appears to have gone in Allen's favour. On 3 April 1745 however, two of Barlow's men began to throw Allen's limestone off the site. They were asked to stop and took no notice, even when asked by Allen in person. Barlow's agent, Thomas Davies, arrived with others and urged his men to continue. Allen, in his turn, objected to the route being used by Barlow's men in bringing coal to the quays. Davies insisted that the way was Barlow's freehold and he was following orders in using it. By now the temperature was rising rapidly. Allen, his wife and his labourers tried to stand in the road to block the coal carts. Mrs Allen actually threw stones at the cattle drawing one of the carts, and one of the labourers hit a horse with a stick. The skirmish ended in acrimony when Allen was caught by the corner of a coal cart and was dragged along, injuring his right leg. Far from being penitent, Barlow's men returned the next day to continue moving Allen's limestone. Not surprisingly the dispute ended up in court.[41]

A somewhat similar argument arose fifty years later at Saundersfoot, where the legal title to the same coalyard was disputed by Sir Richard Philipps and Edward Loveden, who had come into possession of the interests of the Pryses of Gogerddan. In 1793 Loveden built a wall around the coalyard claiming it as his own. A workman named Henry Parsell deposited coal and culm in the yard, and was then sued for trespass by Sir Richard Philipps. It emerged that when Philipps' men had endeavoured to pull down Loveden's wall some months earlier, Loveden had asked Parsell to bring an action against them. Unfortunately the outcome of this dispute is not clear, although the hostility between Philipps and Loveden is quite apparent.[42]

In 1788 there was a court case demonstrating the possibility of landowners solving a dispute amicably and sensibly. At this time Harcourt Powell owned two thirds of the land and minerals in a property named West Hook. The other third was owned by Sir Hugh Owen. A boundary dispute arose with a neighbouring landowner, Richard Wright, which related not only to the position of veins of coal and culm under the boundary, but also to the use of a shaft nearby which had been sunk at the expense of Powell and Owen, but which was also used by Wright for the benefit of his pits. In the event the parties agreed to refer the issue to the arbitration of Hugh Savage of Haverfordwest, and to abide by his decision to be given by 1 May 1789. [43]

A different kind of difficulty arose at Bonvilles Court colliery, Saundersfoot, sixty years later. The owner of most of the minerals was Captain J. M. Child of Begelly House. In letting the coal seams beneath his land to the recently formed Bonvilles Court Coal Company he had prohibited any underground working within forty yards of the house and outbuildings known as Bonvilles Court. Suspecting that this provision had been breached he asked J. W. Rees, Charles Griffiths and Jeremiah Phillips to carry out an inspection below ground. Initially they were refused access, but on 21 May 1849 they descended the landing pit and explored the workings. They discovered that the requirements of the lease had been broken, that three or four accessible coal seams had been left uncut, and that furthermore the heading they were following extended well beyond the boundary of the mineral lease actually passing directly under one of the buildings. Whilst this could easily have given rise to a dispute, it seems to have been treated more as a deficient way of working requiring correction. [44]

Disputes over methods of working were not unusual. In 1740 for instance, Walter Pryse brought a legal action against Francis Meyricke, who was lessee of a small colliery on his land at Vadson, in the parish of Begelly. The argument turned on the right of Meyricke (or his sub-tenant named Roch) to sink new air pits in the land they had leased. In the event it was decided that the lessees had such rights, but the case demonstrated the anxiety felt by landlords to avoid unnecessary damage to their land. [45] Earlier, in 1721, Sir John Philipps had been concerned over the right (or otherwise) of the Rector of Begelly to allow a lessee, John Powell, to work coal on the Begelly glebe land, and then convey it across Picton estate land. It was argued that in this case any such right would be for the benefit of the Rector himself and not someone else. A conclusion was not reached before the Rector vacated the living, somewhat confusing the outcome. [46]

The landed gentry naturally socialised together, and although they might have different political or property interests, in many cases there was a spirit of cooperation between them. In 1787 Richard Wright, a landowner at Hook, agreed to lease his West Park Level to John Harcourt Powell and Colonel Colby for 99 years. As the rent was only a peppercorn, it must be supposed that this was a co-operative move by Wright towards his lessees to enable them all to have the benefit of this drainage level. [47] In 1792 for example, J. B. Allen wrote to Colonel Colby, uncle of Sir Hugh Owen, then a minor, about a project:

> to drive a level from Cresswell Quay into a colliery called Grove for the sum of £250, when I had not the least idea that any person would have engaged in it for £1000. It is a scheme of great advantage to your nephew and myself. It will not only work two or three small veins already known which could not be worked by other means, but it will also tend to discover whatever veins may be in those lands.

Accordingly Allen suggested that Colby should ask his agent, Thomas George, to carry out an inspection. [48]

With a promptness impressive in any age, Thomas George duly made his report the next day. He noted that: "The level they bring in is about 300 fathoms distant and would be about two years driving", but also that it "is likely to dry the whole of this field being about five fathoms deeper than that already in that land". He also remarked that there was talk of extending this new level further east under another field where the existing level was only twelve fathoms from the surface. However there was a question to be resolved regarding the extent of Sir Hugh Owen's ownership and royalty. [49]

It is likely that J. B. Allen and Colonel Colby were able to cooperate in this case, because although there may have been some tension between the Allens and Owens in earlier years, there is no indication of anything other than goodwill between these two men in their dealings at Cresswell Quay. As early as 1755 there were five quays, or sections of quay in use at Cresswell.[50] Two were owned and operated by the Allen family, and one a little further west, on the south side of the Cresswell river, was controlled by John Wogan. Between the two Allen quays was a wharf operated jointly by Sir William Owen, Thomas Powell and Hugh Barlow. This shared use no doubt reflected the fact that in the parish of Reynalton the Powells and the Owens shared their mineral royalties in the ratio two thirds to one third, and in the parish of Jeffreston in the ratio one third to one sixth, the remaining half going originally to the Barlows and in the nineteenth century to the Lort Philipps family.[51] Opposite, on the north bank of the river in the parish of Lawrenny, was a quay and coal folds owned by George Barlow. It would seem (although it is not certain) that this quay, reached by a ford across the river, may have been the consequence of the dispute between John Allen and George Barlow in the 1740's. A plan of Cresswell Quay in 1755, and a plan of 1905 for comparison may be found in Figure 16.

It will be clear from these agreements and disputes that the precise terms of mining leases were of considerable importance. In the earliest years of the industry it is likely that landowners engaged labourers to work coal on their behalf. Indeed, there is a long tradition in Pembrokeshire that agricultural workers might be employed in coal mining when farm work was slack - another manifestation of the landowners' view that mining was simply another way of earning an income from the land. It is not known when landowners began to grant formal leases of their coal seams to those men willing to carry the assorted risks involved in mining. There are few documents surviving relating to the coal industry before 1700, and the nature of the earliest agreements must be rather speculative. Given the fact that the majority of the population was then illiterate, it must be wondered to what extent agreements were based on long-established Pembrokeshire practice or were even oral. Evidence that there were established (but not defined) Pembrokeshire customs is alluded to in a few existing documents - including a lease dated as late as 1838.[52] There is no doubt that illiterate men were sometimes parties to formal leases. In 1789, for example, a court case revealed that the lessee of the Redwalls Colliery had had the terms of his lease read out to him before he applied his mark to the deed. Such a procedure may have satisfied the legal requirements of the time, but the observance of the terms depended entirely on the lessee's memory and sincerity.[53]

Simply to suggest the possibility of some early oral agreements is to raise many questions. Coal mining was always an expensive and risky activity, and those involved in it needed confidence in the certainty and reliability of all their dealings. Anyone working coal would require a term long enough to justify his investment in the people and the equipment needed to raise the commodity, and also clauses to protect him against unexpected increases in payments during that term. If the agreement related to an existing coal mine, the funds required by the lessee could vary from the moderate, in the case of a fully equipped going concern, to the immense, in the case of an old pit needing extensive repair. If the agreement was for the opening up of a new pit or pits, the lessee would not only require considerable capital to embark on the venture, but also a landlord patient enough to wait for the mine to be developed before expecting significant returns. Given the limited technology available, and the difficulties of Pembrokeshire geology, this process could take years. Shafts had to be sunk, drainage levels driven, and winding gear set up - but in reality coal lessees (in every period) could very rarely afford elaborate preparation, and would try to win and sell coal as soon as possible.

In the light of long experience there evolved two forms of payment for mining leases. One was the dead rent (or ground rent), a basic fixed rent, usually quite moderate, and payable in all circumstances, whether coal was being dug or not. This encouraged a lessee to work coal to begin to cover his costs, and it discouraged any thought of not working the mine to a strict output and, perhaps, inflate prices in the district.

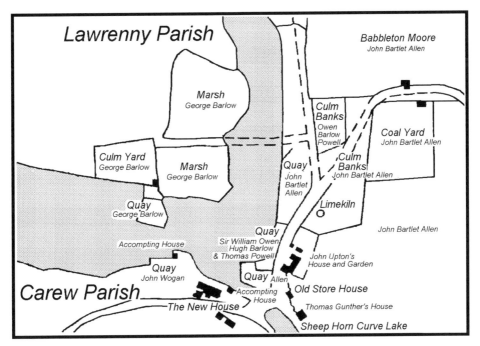

Cresswell Quay 1755

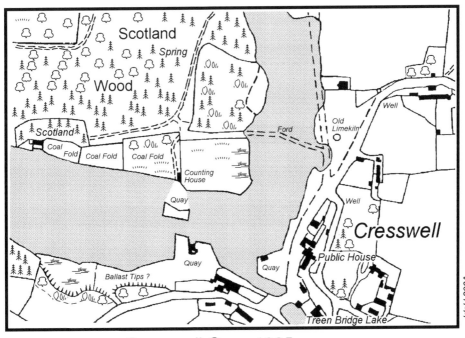

Cresswell Quay 1905

Source : M.R.C. Price "Coal, Culm and Creswell Quay,"
The Journal of the Pembrokeshire Historical Society No.6, 1994/5

Figure 16

The other form of payment was the royalty, or "Lord's part", a charge set in proportion to the quantities of coal and culm raised and sold. In the nineteenth century many leases comprised both a fixed rent and a proportional element, but in the preceding century the emphasis was placed firmly upon the royalty. In 1737, for example, in the lease of Jeffreston Mountain colliery, an "entire third part" of all the coal and culm landed "had to be payed to the lessor" who also had an option on purchasing the rest.[54] In 1760 however the same colliery was leased for a quarter of the returns, less transport and shipping in respect of coals sold off the landlord's quay at Cresswell.[55] In 1781 the small Woodlands colliery at Little Haven was leased subject to a royalty of one third;[56] when let again in 1806 the royalty was one fifth.[57]

Substantial royalty payments were a feature of Pembrokeshire leases well into the nineteenth century. In the lease of Kilgetty colliery in 1811 the Lord's part was a quarter of all profits,[58] and a similar royalty was required at the nearby Lower Level colliery in 1822.[59] Some years earlier, a number of Picton Castle estate leases had been granted on the basis of one third being payable as the Lord's part – for instance in the case of the Begelly collieries in 1806[60] and the pits at Poor Shipping, near Kilgetty, in 1801.[61] A. H. John refers to such agreements as "primitive mineral leases, in which the product of the mine was divided up between the landlord and the working capitalist", and he compares them unfavourably with leases employed at the same period in the Swansea and Carmarthenshire districts, which depended upon tonnage royalties.[62] Even at the time the royalties were much criticised. In 1807 the well-known coal viewer Edward Martin asserted that:

> the royalties in Pembrokeshire are very high. Some proprietors or owners of coal land have one third, some one quarter and others one sixth of what the coal or culm sells for to shipping, after deducting the expense of conveyance or carriage; but the exact proportion of royalty or Land-money should be fixed and depend on the thickness and position of the veins of coal, the quality of the coal and contiguity of the colliery to shipping.[63]

There may have been more to the matter of royalties than mere greed on the part of landlords. In the eighteenth century there was a considerable variation in weights and measures across South Wales, and in the coal trade in Pembrokeshire volume measures prevailed. As measures varied, so some variation in payments was to be expected. Pembrokeshire appears to have retained volume measures up to the end of the 1830's – almost certainly longer than any other coal mining district in South Wales. In the circumstances it is hardly surprising that the county persisted with this form of royalty, and only gradually went over to tonnage royalties.

Even after coal became measured by weight rather than volume, the traditional practice continued for a time. An un-named mineral surveyor visited Pembrokeshire in March 1840, to gather information about colliery lettings. His prime concern appears to have been a lease on the Southwood colliery at Newgale, but the minutes of his enquiries make interesting reading.[64] He consulted (amongst others) the notable land surveyor, H. P. Goode. He declared that the royalty paid to the landowner:

> varies from one third to one fifth of the sales. This variation appears to arise not only from the difference in the expense of raising the coal in different situations, but also from the facilities of working (such as levels etc) sometimes afforded by the owner of the land.

The report went on to note the use of weight measurements when it mentioned H. P. Goode's advice that:

> One shilling per ton for culm, and two shillings and sixpence for coal is taken for the Lord's share in some collieries. A fixed or sleeping rent is generally reserved in the coaling leases, both to secure a certain income to the proprietors of the land, and to make it the interest of the lessees to work the coal to a considerable extent.

The general trend in nineteenth-century Pembrokeshire was for the proportion requested in royalty to diminish. Royalties further east in Wales were undoubtedly much lower. According to the 1830 coal commission they averaged about one tenth in South Wales.[65] By the 1850's Pembrokeshire leases were generally being granted on a tonnage basis. In 1851, for example, Thomas Stokes of Hean Castle, Saundersfoot, leased Woolsons colliery at Wiseman's Bridge to David Parsell for a payment of one shilling per ton of twenty cwt. of coal sold.[66] This cannot have been an entirely successful arrangement, because in the following year Stokes executed another lease of the property to Parsell for payments of just sixpence per ton of 21cwt![67] By the later part of the century leases for even the smallest pits provided for tonnage royalty payments. When William Hilling was granted a lease to work coal at East Willamston in 1889 the ground rent was £10 per annum (not payable in the first year) and the royalty was 7d per ton on all coal raised.[68]

Royalties and rents were not the only source of coal income for a landowner. Although colliery leases often included provisions for the use of all the land needed for mining operations, on occasions surface land for spoil tips, reservoirs, water courses and additional shafts could be let separately. In addition many landowners received wayleave income from the carriage of coal and culm over cart roads from the pit to the relevant shipping place. At or near the quay, charges might be levied for stocking coal and culm in coal folds, as well as for loading it across the quay. In brief so many charges could be imposed in the process of winning and shipping coal that the price was invariably inflated before the commodity ever left the county. It is also likely, but not clearly demonstrable, that coal-owners like the Owens of Orielton at Landshipping were at an advantage in that they had control of the whole process, and were able to avoid some of the charges levied by middle men elsewhere.

Two concessions were commonly made by landlords to lessees in the nineteenth century. One was to permit coal or culm used within a colliery – for example in the mine's own steam engines – to be free of royalty.[69] Second and similarly, the coal allowed to individual colliers was usually free of royalty. According to the Royal Commission on Mining Royalties, 1890, free coal for colliery use might amount to 5 per cent or even 10 per cent of the total quantity worked.[70]

Some of the earliest documents extant touch on the business of carting coal from the pits of Pembrokeshire. Frequently landowners holding property off the coalfield would impose a duty on a tenant to assist in the carriage of coal and culm to his residence or other premises. A lease of 1618 provides a good illustration of leases of this kind. In 1618 William Scourfield, the owner of New Moat in north Pembrokeshire, agreed to let the property for an annual rent of 13s. 4d., two capons, one bushel of oats (Haverfordwest measure), the labour of one man for a day at harvest, the labour of one man for a day to stack furze, the labour of two man-days to shear sheep, and the carriage of one barrel of coal from the coal pits to the landlord's property at Sealyham.[71] The duration of the lease, by the custom of property law, was for the duration of the lives of three named persons. It was a measure of the changelessness of Pembrokeshire life that when New Moat was let again, 165 years later, by Hugh Scourfield to Price Gibby, not only was the lease for a term of three lives, but the consideration was £24 per annum, plus two fat hens, and the provision of carts to convey two loads of coal and culm over a distance of ten miles.[72]

Such leases were common, and examples may be found in several muniment collections. Curiously, in the circumstances, the carriage of coal and culm between a colliery and a shipping quay could be a requirement of a coal mining lease, but it was by no means a standard provision. Usually carriage and sundry other items would be treated as expenses to be deducted before the payment of royalty to the landlord, as in accounts for 1785-86 relating to Hook colliery.[73]

In 1790 the accounts in respect of Cresswell Quay make note of payments "for carriage, quayage, and boatage", and in the same document, in relation to Landshipping, there is mention of payment for "cleaning the docks, repairing quays, trippers etc". There is also a reference to "stemming money", described as "an allowance given to captains who load as customary" (coal and culm).[74] An account book of 1809 at Picton Castle not only includes payments to labourers and colliers at Kilgetty, but also a payment to John Callen "for a watercourse and a private road through Merrixton".[75]

The duration of mining leases was another difficult issue, especially when the lessee faced the labour of opening up and developing a new colliery. The landlord usually hoped for an early return, but mining investment was invariably long term and lessees needed time to see their investment pay. In the late eighteenth century or early nineteenth century it might take anything from two to four years to develop a coal mine, and even an established mine might require re-equipping and so be unproductive for a time. In the circumstances the old practice of granting leases for a term of three lives was unsatisfactory, because there could be no certainty as to how long the lives would last. During the complex and long running dispute over the use of coal quays at Cresswell, John Allen urged Harcourt Powell to lease his quay because the death of Sir William Owen would end a term of three lives and confront Powell with much more expensive alternatives.[76]

Even so, the term of three lives remained in regular use in Pembrokeshire leases well into the nineteenth century. It was employed also for purposes ancillary to mining – for example, in 1779 on the grants of rights of way for a colliery access road in the parish of Amroth,[77] or, in 1793, on the grant of a reservoir and water course to supply the pits at Hillsend and Coom Mills, Amroth.[78] The surrender of the lease for three lives of coalfield property at Cranham near Freystrop in 1811 mentioned not only the annual rental of £63 and six hens, but also the duty of providing a cart for a day to move hay or culm for the lessor.[79]

Several instances have been seen of a lease for three lives being employed at a later date, the most surprising coming as late as 1853 in a substantial lease of coal and culm in the parishes of Begelly, Amroth, and St. Issells by the Picton Castle estate to the Pembrokeshire Iron and Coal Co. for an annual rental of £500.[80] By then, however, it was almost invariably the case that leases were granted for a specific term of years, very seldom less than 21, often 31,[81] and sometimes as much as 40 years,[82] 51 years,[83] or 60 years.[84] Until the second half of the nineteenth century there could be legal objection to the grant of long leases. On many settled estates, leases of a duration longer than 21 years were prohibited, but several Acts of Parliament after 1856 allowed life tenants to have wider discretion.[85] Whatever the length of the term it was usual for the lessees to have a right to surrender the lease if the coal was exhausted, or became unworkable. Sometimes it was agreed such a provision could take effect after three years, or, perhaps after seven years, but on other occasions 24 months' notice or even 12 months' notice of termination might be accepted. A lease would often include a clause allowing the lessee to underlet, subject to the landlord's consent.

A lease of Begelly colliery for 21 years from January 1838, provides an illustration of a typical nineteenth-century Pembrokeshire mining lease. The landlord, Captain J. M. Child of Begelly House, received a rent or royalty of 1s. per ton of culm, and he expected his lessee Lewis Pocock to raise at least 10,000 tons per annum. According to the conditions the lessee had to be willing to make dams to prevent flooding underground, and he had to keep the works in good repair. He was required to fill in unnecessary pits, and to keep and be able to produce books and maps of the workings. He was prohibited from committing waste – that is to say inappropriate despoliation of the surface land. The lessee also had to allow Captain Child to purchase on the determination of the lease any part of the plant on the premises used in conjunction with coal mining, the power to determine on two years' notice being granted. The lessee was not compelled to work any particular portion of the coal seams, provided he worked some in order to achieve the stipulated output. Unfortunately the very reason this lease is noteworthy is that the lessee could neither raise nor sell enough coal or culm to meet the conditions, and in 1848 these circumstances gave rise to a tortuous dispute.[86] Long experience taught landlords and lessees alike to try to use the lease to protect their interests in both the short and the long term. The requirement to be able to produce books and maps of the workings was not common a generation earlier, although there might have been explicit provisions allowing the landlord or his agent to inspect the workings, and to ask to see books of accounts. Such a lease, dated 1801, is to be found in the Jones muniments. The term is exceptionally short - just 14 years - but the option to determine could not be invoked for seven years, after giving six months' notice in writing. It is also notable for a provision declaring that failure to work coal for more than three months in any one year (harvest time excepted) or any other default, would allow the landlord to repossess the property.[87] After all these matters had been given careful consideration, and notwithstanding the optimism of many such lessees, these ventures could very easily end in frustration and failure. In July, 1835, James Williams and John Hume became partners in working the New House colliery, near Slebech, as tenants of Sir Richard Philipps.[88] Within a year they were in deep financial trouble. It seems that Williams owed money to Hume, and Hume owed money to two Haverfordwest men, John Walters, a banker, and Joseph Marychurch, described as an ironmonger but also trading as Marychurch, Owen and Llewhelin, timber merchants. The outcome was that in June 1836, all Hume's stock in trade was assigned in trust for his creditors.[89]

In the first half of the nineteenth century, apart from a very few landowners working coal on their own behalf – Lord Milford, for example, or the Owens at Landshipping - coal mining in Pembrokeshire appears to have been a patchwork of businessmen lessees mixed with small contractors, most struggling to make ends meet in working relatively shallow and ill-equipped pits. Sometimes they did not have mineral rights in sufficient ground to justify the sinking of a new pit. In 1848 there was a problem faced by Henry Leach, a landowner at Loveston. He sought the advice of a mining engineer or surveyor named William Hulm, who recommended his making an arrangement with a neighbour named Protheroe for access to more ground. Alternatively he suggested letting most of his coal veins to Messrs. Pocock, a company or partnership who were working pits nearby.[90] Such limited mining operations did not match the needs of the time. The Industrial Revolution had made available the technology to permit deeper and far more productive coal mining. The Owens, through Colonel Colby as trustee, were the first to make any appropriate investment, but in this remote and relatively impoverished county it was difficult to generate fresh finance for new equipment and methods. Banking in Pembrokeshire was almost non existent before the 1780's, and the lack of currency and insufficient sources of credit led to numerous trades people issuing trade tokens, notably in Haverfordwest.[91] The fact that it was Colonel Colby who moved first to adopt the new technology was hardly a coincidence; he not only commanded all aspects of activity at Landshipping, but he could also anticipate benefits accruing specifically to the advantage of the Orielton estate.

For the successful application of the new technology and methods the sums required were much greater than any previously considered normal in mining, or indeed any other industry.[92] Technological advance was the vital means of overcoming what Michael Flinn has described as "the general and remorseless tendency within an extractive industry towards diminishing returns and rising marginal costs".[93] The lack of capital compelled men to form partnerships, initially unlimited liability companies, and then later, joint stock companies. A few years after Colonel Colby, Lord Milford followed his lead by acquiring steam engines in 1809 and 1811 for use at the Kilgetty colliery. Further steam engines for use in Pembrokeshire were obtained in the 1820's. This relatively slow response is indicative both of the limitations of the capital market, and the sheer expense of buying and running such engines. Not only were Pembrokeshire coal proprietors often reluctant to invest, but as mentioned in the next chapter, for fuel the engines required the importation of suitable coals which were also subject to certain duties. Overall, there can be little doubt that the restrictive legal and institutional framework of the capital market inhibited investment in Pembrokeshire. A. H. John gained the impression that in South Wales there was:

> a considerable section of people who, had the laws of bankruptcy been different, would have been willing to finance industrial development on the Welsh coalfield during the nineteenth century. The real difficulty lay in requirements of early nineteenth century law whereby an investor placed the whole of his property at the risk of a concern over which he possessed, at best, only partial control. Until the introduction of limited liability the shareholder's entire property was available to meet the debts of a concern of which he was a partner, or even the smallest shareholder.[94]

The investor's sense of vulnerability in these circumstances was not trivial. Not only were the risks and the responsibilities for an enterprise spread by the formation of a partnership or unlimited company, but the effect of taking out loans was to give a say to the lender. Furthermore, if the proprietors agreed contracts for delivering coal and culm they had the effect of giving merchants an influence over production. No longer were operation and output at the complete discretion of the landlord, his agent, or his lessees. In the new order both the financing and the practise of coal mining became more akin to other trades

For some members of the landed gentry these changes may have been hard to accept, but whatever their attitude, it may well be argued that the failure of the coal industry to modernise was really a failure of the capital market to make adequate banking and credit facilities available in West Wales. Although numerous local banks appeared, most were undercapitalised and some were very short lived. Several closed in the banking crisis of late 1825[95] and early 1826 which for a time virtually paralysed trade on the coalfield west of Swansea. In A.H. John's words: "In the face of this severe restriction of credit facilities by banks on the coalfield, the larger companies fell back upon their connections in other parts of England."[96] In addition in 1826 legislation was passed to enable the Bank of England to open a branch in Swansea offering more reliable facilities.[97] A new confidence seems to have been established, because by 1828 Sir Richard Philipps was actively seeking to develop Picton estate land in the Saundersfoot district. The key to this development was the passing of an Act of Parliament in 1829 for the construction of the Saundersfoot Railway and Harbour Co.[98]

The passing of this Act effectively marked the end of the old era and the start of the new. Although not the first partnership to describe itself as a company (the Tenby and Begelly Coal Co, for example, was formed in 1825[99]) it was probably the first to introduce local industry to all the formalities of company law and shareholding. Others soon followed (for instance the Kilgetty Colliery Co.[100]) and within twenty years the Pembrokeshire Iron and Coal Co. had been formed to finance and oversee the development of coal and iron works on the Picton estate near Saundersfoot.[101] When registered in 1857 it became one of the earliest joint stock limited liability companies in the county. The dominant figure in the undertaking was Charles Ranken Vickerman, a London solicitor, whose father had been legal adviser to both Sir Richard Philipps and Lord Milford.[102]

In view of the long association between the Picton Castle estate and their London lawyers, it might be supposed that the relationship with the Pembrokeshire Iron and Coal Co. would be entirely positive. In reality as an industrialist C. R. Vickerman's aims and ideas did not always correspond with those of Sir Richard Philipps. In 1850 J. M. Child of Begelly was moved to tell Sir Richard that he believed "that a collision must ultimately take place sooner or later between yourself and your tenants, the Pembrokeshire Coal and Iron Company" over different interpretations of terms in the company's lease.[103] J. M. Child did not think highly of the company's management, and indeed the directors had numerous arguments among themselves. By the time of its registration in 1857, only three of the eleven directors of 1853 were still in office, but by then their attitudes and outlook were much happier. The several leases concluded between the Picton estate and the P.I. & C.Co in respect of land at Kilgetty and Thomas Chapel were amongst the earliest Pembrokeshire leases to refer consistently to imperial weights.[104]

Initially C. R. Vickerman enjoyed his involvement in local industry, because very soon he committed his immense personal fortune to the Pembrokeshire Iron and Coal Co. and the development of the Kilgetty ironworks. Although the establishment of the ironworks proved to be difficult as well as expensive, Vickerman was not a man to be deterred easily. Whilst there was no more than a year when both furnaces were in use together and several periods of complete inactivity, for over twenty five years C. R. Vickerman worked hard to make something of his investment. In the meantime, in 1863, he not only had the satisfaction of controlling the Bonvilles Court and Kilgetty collieries and the Saundersfoot Railway and Harbour Co., but he also purchased the Hean Castle estate, and became resident in Saundersfoot for several months each year.[105]

By the 1870's C. R. Vickerman was the single most important figure in the Pembrokeshire coal industry, and although there were some other men of note elsewhere on the coalfield, the survival of many Vickerman family papers makes the study of Charles Ranken Vickerman especially interesting. In 1872, for example, he appears to have been so conscious of the burden of running his collieries and ironworks that he decided to sell his industrial concerns to a company formed for the purpose of maintaining them and providing new capital. When the Bonvilles Court Coal and Iron Company was duly formed in May 1873, Vickerman retained a shareholding in the business.[106] An enthusiastic prospectus, typical of the period, was issued to invite subscriptions, and this is reproduced in Appendix C. Several improvements were made by the new company, but very soon it was overtaken by an economic depression. Labour disputes hastened the end of ironmaking at Kilgetty in June 1874, and as conditions deteriorated further the new company was compelled to go into liquidation in 1876. When the property and plant of the B.C.C. & I.Co. was auctioned in May 1878, C. R. Vickerman was the only bidder. As a creditor owed more than £100,000, he was allowed to buy it all back for little more than £10,000.[107] Accordingly he regained possession of the works with the additional benefit of the capital investment made since 1872 – a sum believed to be about £50,000.

As a wealthy man in an impoverished part of Wales it is hardly surprising that C. R. Vickerman was not especially popular. His presence symbolised the fact that in Pembrokeshire, as in many parts of South Wales, industrial development now depended primarily upon English money rather than the Welsh landed gentry. The fact that he was willing to risk his capital, and that his expenditure made a substantial contribution to the local economy, was not fully appreciated. In a difficult financial climate C. R. Vickerman himself felt the strain, and indeed tried to sell his properties again, but without success.[108] Correspondence survives from 1880 when, as landlord of the Moreton Colliery, Vickerman had reason to write to the colliery company's advisers, Messrs. James & Edwards, over arrears of rent. The colliery company evidently hoped for some subsidy or allowance in sinking a new pit. When he declined, they complained. C. R. Vickerman felt the time had come to mention the realities as he saw them:

> How is it then, that I suffered, at your earnest request, the rent to fall into arrears for two years…? Or how came I to sell you an engine at less than I should have accepted from any other parties – and given you six months for payment? One would suppose from your letter that your rent had never been more than six weeks in arrear. The simple fact is I have to pay my rents within that period, and to enable me to do so I must get in the rents owing to me. The landlords you refer to "who afford substantial assistance towards sinking operations" *are not to be met with in this part of the world* [author's italics]. I and my friends have expended nearer £100,000 on 'sinking operations' and have never had – nor expected – one shilling assistance from any landlord.[109]

As a lawyer by background, Vickerman was always vigorous in his own defence, but his directness, and his ability to argue his case, did not always endear him to others. At times there were tensions with the local community, and these became apparent in hearings conducted by the Royal Commission on Land in Wales in 1894. Two local men criticised C. R. Vickerman for giving notice to tenants when he acquired the Moreton and Trevayne estates in 1872. In response he argued that notices had been issued by the vendor prior to the sale, and in any case the whole issue was greatly complicated by under-letting.[110] According to H. M. Vaughan, this Commission was set up for largely political reasons.[111] Certainly C. R. Vickerman did not think he was given a fair hearing, and his relationship with the Saundersfoot district remained somewhat uneasy until his death in January 1897, at the age of 79.[112] By then his fortune was mostly spent, and in 1899 his son, C. H. R. Vickerman, sold the Hean Castle estate to Sir William Thomas Lewis, a prosperous coal owner in Glamorgan, later elevated to the peerage as the first Baron Merthyr of Senghenydd. The Vickerman family moved to St. Issells House adjoining the harbour at Saundersfoot.

[1] N.L.W., Great. Sessions, Wales 4, Pembroke 775.6.

[2] N.L.W., MS1352B, fo. 231; Carmarthenshire Record Office, Derwydd MS 179.

[3] N.L.W., Picton Castle papers.

[4] N.L.W., Owen and Colby MSS 1137, 2306.

[5] R. Fenton. *A Historical Tour through Pembrokeshire*, 247, 274.

[6] N.L.W., Hamilton-Greville MSS 6-8, 11.

[7] Pembrokeshire Record Office, Particulars of the estate of Harcourt Powell, 1778, H/DX/238/1 and D/EE/ 7/338.

[8] N.L.W., Haverfordwest (Williams and Williams), MS 13073.

[9] N.L.W., Slebech MSS 5530, 7466.

[10] N.L.W., Gogerddan Papers (uncatalogued), box 29.

[11] G. E. Mingay, *English Landed Society in the Eighteenth Century* (London: Routledge, 1963), 192. W. R. Morgan, *The Story of Begelly* (Llandysul: Gomer Press, 1980), mentions a Commission of Inquiry at Begelly in January 1856, into Lord Milford's rights to Kingsmoor Common. It appears that for many years he had allowed nearby residents to dig culm on Kingsmoor Common for 1d. per year, but that the extent of his ownership was disputed by a neighbouring landowner, as well as some local people. See also N.L.W., Lucas MS 2799.

[12] Mingay, *English Landed Society in the Eighteenth Century*, 193.

[13] N.L.W., Gogerddan Papers (uncatalogued), box 29: Dispute between Edward Loveden and Lord Milford concerning Moreton colliery.

[14] N.L.W., Owen and Colby MS 1879, 2283.

[15] J. V. Beckett, *Coal and Tobacco: the Lowthers and the economic development of West Cumberland, 1600- 1760* (Cambridge: Cambridge University Press, 1981), 44-45.

[16] N.L.W., Picton Castle MS 1691.

[17] N.L.W., Picton Castle MSS 1427-1428, 269.

[18] N.L.W., Picton Castle MS 4093.

[19] When the Merrixton drainage adit serving the pits at Kilgetty was reopened in the 1930's, the colliers engaged in the clearance operations entered the old underground workings of Coombes colliery, Amroth.

They were surprised to fine two or three "nests" near the entrance to former headings. Each nest contained several clay balls – a reminder of a method of counting trams filled with coal in the days before the ordinary collier was numerate.

[20] N.L.W., Picton Castle MS 585.

[21] N.L.W., Great Sessions, Wales 4. 824.1: Pembrokeshire Great Sessions, Spring, 1789.

[22] N.L.W., Eaton, Evans and Williams MSS 6961, 6965 (Hook); N.L.W., Eaton, Evans and Williams MS 918: rent roll.

[23] N.L.W., Owen and Colby MS 2276.

[24] N.L.W., Owen and Colby MS2334.

[25] N.L.W., Owen and Colby MS 2154.

[26] Pembrokeshire Record Office, D/LLW/298. The accounts for 1806-7 indicate that the output of the colliery was almost entirely culm, most of which was sold locally.

[27] W. G. Thomas, *Llangwm through the Ages, Part I, 1244-1800* (Haverfordwest: 1989), 57.

[28] N.L.W., Owen and Colby MSS 2334-2336.

[29] N.L.W., Owen and Colby MSS 2283, 2342.

[30] N.L.W., Owen and Colby MSS 1880.

[31] Pembrokeshire Record Office, D/RTP/Sir RBPP/6/ 81. Dialling is believed to mean surveying.

[32] Carmarthen Record Office, Dynevor MSS. This view was expressed to the writer by the late Raymond E. Bowen, as a result of his research in the Dynevor muniments.

[33] Carmarthen Record Office, Dynevor MSS 1-2: letter dated February 1764. According to the late Raymond E. Bowen the Dynevor muniments include a note written by Richard Evans, Kymer's agent, referring to a sales office at Tenby. Unfortunately its purpose is not explained, but it may be surmised that either Kymer was dealing in Pembrokeshire coal when his own collieries could not satisfy demand, or that Kymer was trying to take orders away from Pembrokeshire coal owners.

[34] F. Green, 'Dewisland Coasters in 1751', *West Wales Historical Records*, Vol. VIII (1919-20).

[35] F. Green, 'Early Banks in West Wales', *West Wales Historical Records*, Vol. VI (1916),129.

[36] Pembrokeshire Record Office, D/HIG/36.

[37] *The Cambrian* of Swansea 31 December 1825, reported the failure of Messrs Phillips and Co. of Haverfordwest, and Messrs. Saer and Co. of Narberth and Haverfordwest. The next issue contained a fulsome apology in respect of "Saer, Thomas and Co," acknowledging that in fact all demands had been met. However damage had been done, and the bank did fail in 1826. See also Green 'Early Banks in West Wales'.

[38] N.L.W., Eaton, Evans and Williams MS 1573 and 2175.

[39] R. O. Roberts, 'Bank of England Branch Discounting 1826-1859' in W. E. Minchinton (ed.), *Industrial South Wales 1750-1914* (London: Frank Cass & Co. Ltd., 1969), 173. One bank could guarantee another – for example Cocks, Biddulph and Biddulph of Charing Cross provided guarantees for their friends Biddulph Brothers and Co., Carmarthen, in 1830.

[40] Edwards, *A study of the Daucleddau Coalfield (Pembrokeshire)*, 41.
Also N.L.W., Owen and Colby, MS 1138

[41] N.L.W., Great Sessions, Wales 4. 814.3: Pembrokeshire Great Sessions, gaol files, Spring 1746. N.L.W. Trenewydd MMS 320 indecates that the dispute at Creswell Quay continued until 1755.

[42] N.L.W., Great Sessions, Wales 4. 825.5: Pembrokeshire Great Sessions, gaol files, Spring 1794.

[43] N.L.W., Great Sessions, Wales 4. 823.6: Pembrokeshire Great Sessions, gaol files, Autumn 1788.

[44] N.L.W., Haverfordwest (Williams and Williams), MS 13089.

[45] N.L.W., Francis Green MSS.

[46] N.L.W., Picton Castle MSS 1434 and 4074.

[47] N.L.W., Lucas MS 3805.

[48] N.L.W., Owen and Colby MS 2094. A three-cornered dispute regarding a drainage level at Middle Hill arose in 1764, the interested parties being J.Child, Mrs Barlow and R. Knethell of Hook, NLW.. Eaton Evans and Williams, MSS 6961-6963.

[49] N.L.W., Owen and Colby MS 2219.

[50] Cresselly estate map of 1755 in possession of T. Lloyd, Esq, Cresselly.

[51] These figures are based on analysis of colliery accounts in the Owen and Colby MSS, for example MS 1137.

[52] N.L.W., Haverfordwest (Williams and Williams) MS 20068.

[53] N.L.W., Great Sessions, Wales 4. 824.1: Pembrokeshire Great Sessions, gaol files, Spring 1789.

[54] N.L.W., Corston MS 40.

[55] N.L.W., Corston MS 82.

[56] N.L.W., Jones MS 42.

[57] N.L.W., Jones MS 82.

[58] N.L.W., Picton Castle MS 4092.

[59] N.L.W., Picton Castle MS 4079.

[60] N.L.W., Picton Castle MS 4115.

[61] N.L.W., Picton Castle MS 4114.

[62] A. H. John *The Industrial Development of South Wales 1750-1850* (Cardiff: 1950), Appendix C, 183.

[63] N.L.W., Gogerddan Papers (uncatalogue]ı, box 29: Letter from Edward Martin to E.Jones, November 1807.

[64] Addendum to Walters' diaries and notebook regarding the coal industry at Nolton and Newgale. Privately owned, but a copy is in the author's possession.

[65] House of Lords Select Committee of inquiry into the Coal Trade, 1830. Parliamentary Papers Reports from Committees, Vol 8, 1830.

[66] N.L.W., Haverfordwest (Williams and Williams), MS 13094.

[67] N.L.W., Haverfordwest (Williams and Williams), MS 13099.

[68] Pembrokeshire Record Office, D/LLC/484.

[69] Pembrokeshire Record Office, D/RTM/HP4/292. Joseph Cadman, mining engineer, commenting on a proposed lease at Hook in 1886, observed that it was unusual to charge a royalty on coal consumed by pumping and winding engines.

[70] Royal Commission on Mining Royalties, 1890, referred to in J. H. Morris and L. J. Williams *The South Wales Coal Industry. 1841-1875* (Cardiff: University of Wales Press, 1958), 118.

[71] N.L.W., Lucas MS 3749.

[72] N.L.W., Lucas MS 3910.

[73] N.L.W., Owen and Colby MS 1138.

[74] N.L.W., Owen and Colby MS 2308.

[75] Accounts of William Evans to Lord Milford: Account Book May-November 1809, held at Picton Castle. I am grateful to Thomas Lloyd of Cresselly for drawing attention to this reference.

[76] Pembrokeshire Record Office, D/POW/H/163.

[77] N.L.W., Picton Castle MS 4079.

[78] N.L.W., Picton Castle MSS 4084, 4085.

[79] N.L.W., Lucas MSS 3868, 3869.

[80] N.L.W., Picton Castle MSS 4101,4102.

[81] N.L.W., Picton Castle MS 4114.

[82] N.L.W., Picton Castle, MS 4097.

[83] N.L.W., John Francis collection, Lewis of Henllan MS 5.

[84] N.L.W, Haverfordwest (Williams and Williams) MSS 13094 and 13099; also at N.L.W., Picton Castle MS 4104, 4105, 4109.

[85] J. T. Ward, "Landowners and Mining" in J. T. Ward and R. G. Wilson (eds.) *Land and Industry* (Newton Abbot: David & Charles, 1971), 66.

[86] N.L.W., Haverfordwest (Williams & Williams), MSS20067, 20068.

[87] N.L.W., Jones MS 82.

[88] N.L.W., Haverfordwest (Williams and Williams), MS 19660.

[89] N.L.W. Haverfordwest (Williams and Williams), MS 19009.

[90] Pembrokeshire Record Office, D/LLC/546. Document DB/13/117 provides another example of such a collaborative arrangement. In this instance Revd. J. H. A. Phillips and two others sought to create a viable mineral property at Freystrop in 1868.

[91] Noel and Alan Cox, *Tokens, Checks, Metallic Tickets, Passes and Tallies of Wales, 1800-1993* (Cardiff: 1994), 71, illustrates two copper tallies issued at Landshipping colliery.

[92] D. J. Davies, *The Economic History of South Wales prior to 1800* (Cardiff: University of Wales Press, 1933), 142.

[93] Michael W.Flinn, *The History of the British Coal Industry*, (Oxford: Clarendon Press, 1984), Vol. 2, 311.

[94] A. H. John, *The Industrial Development of South Wales*, 53.

[95] Green, "Early Banks in West Wales", 150 and 161.

[96] A. H. John, *The Industrial Development of South Wales*, 51.

[97] R. O. Roberts, 'Banks and the Economic Development of South Wales', in C. Baber and L. J. Williams (eds.) *Modern South Wales: Essays in Economic History* (Cardiff: University of Wales Press, 1986), 65.

[98] 10 George IV, Cap 108, 1829.

[99] Pembrokeshire Record Office, HDX/951- the original ledger of the Tenby and Begelly Coal Co. survives, and covers the period from 1825 to 1833.

[100] The original Kilgetty Colliery Co. was essentially a partnership formed in 1834. It came to an end in 1843, and so is not to be confused with the Kilgetty Anthracite Colliery Co.of 1935-1941.

[101] The Pembrokeshire Iron and Coal Co. was formed originally on 20 July 1847, but was reconstructed by Deed of Settlement dated 16 May1853. It was provisionally registered under the Companies Act on 14 May 1857,and incorporated as a company under the Joint Stock Companies Act 1856, 1857 on 5 June 1861.

[102] Obituary to C. R. Vickerman printed in an unidentified newspaper on 27 January 1897.

[103] Pembrokeshire Record Office, D/RTP/Sir RBPP/6/81.

[104] Pembrokeshire Record Office, D/RTP/Sir RBPP/6/79 provides an example of such a lease. It relates to the letting of the Thomas Chapel colliery from 25 May 1852.

[105] Hean Castle was auctioned at the Gate House Hotel, Tenby on 9 September 1863 (advertisement in *Haverfordwest and Milford Haven Telegraph*, 15 July 1863).

[106] These events are described in greater detail in Price, *Industrial Saundersfoot*, 28, 29. Records and returns relating to the Bonvilles Court Coal and Iron Co. Ltd are at the Public record office under reference BT31/1835/7163. A very short lived company of similar name formed in 1876 is filed under BT31/2230/ 10560.

[107] Vickerman papers (privately owned). Memorandum showing position of the works and ownership, 9 January 1882.

[108] Vickerman papers, W. S. Gresley's Report, 9 November 1878.

[109] Vickerman papers, Letter from C. R. Vickerman to Messrs James & Edwards, 110, Cannon Street, London, 22 August 1880.

[110] Parliamentary Papers, 1894, xxxvii, *Royal Commission on Land in Wales*: evidence of C. R. Vickerman on 20 April 1894.

[111] H. M. Vaughan, *The Squires of South Wales*

[112] For further detail see Price, *Industrial Saundersfoot*, 31.

Mining Technology and Methods

Any attempt to describe working methods in the Pembrokeshire coalfield in the space of a single chapter is bound to be incomplete. Given that the industry was in existence for seven centuries, and was active at dozens of different locations across the county as late as 1800, it is not feasible to consider every aspect of the story. Rather does this chapter endeavour to point to the main concerns for all those who devoted their energies to finding and working anthracite, and to give some illustrations of the ways in which they dealt with the problems they encountered.

Whilst it is not possible to improve on George Owen's excellent account of coal mining in the Tudor period, brief mention must be made of two approaches to mining in the medieval period. The first was outcropping - in Pembrokeshire sometimes called "smutting". As coal seams in the county were notoriously distorted, and outcrops could appear in any position from the horizontal to the vertical, so outcropping consisted of working the exposed seam manually to the extent practicable in any given location. Some sites might require timbering to support the sides and roof; others might be restricted by lack of ventilation or drainage. Eventually all the coal obtainable against these limitations would be won, and the outcrop abandoned.

The second method of mining might be considered a development of the first. Once the early colliers became aware of the likely position of a coal seam below ground, their logical course of action was to sink a pit to reach it. Nowadays such workings are sometimes described as "bell" pits, meaning that in underground section they could assume the shape of a bell as the miners worked out from the pit bottom in all directions as far as possible. Given the disturbed geology of South Pembrokeshire, and the friability of many of the coals and shales, it is debatable whether the county possessed many true bell pits. Instead it is probable that most small pits had to be sunk with considerable care, and given substantial support at every stage of their development. Examination of mining maps and plans reveals numerous instances of such pits being sunk along the alignment of a coal outcrop, or just to the dip of it to allow coal to be worked to the rise from the pit bottom. However it is quite likely that many of the pits were sunk as small air pits to provide ventilation rather than as more substantial shafts for working and winding coal. Given the amount of support needed for all workings below ground in the Timber vein, for example, it is probable that colliers soon preferred to tunnel in pursuit of the coal seam rather than use their supplies of costly timber simply to maintain a series of working shafts.

The expansion of the coal industry in and after the Tudor period naturally encouraged landowners and colliers alike to seek for new seams or deposits of coal, by boring and by pit sinking. These methods will now be given particular attention, as will the main methods of gaining access to coal by the development of shafts and slants. Further sections will describe the use and development of other technical features.

Pit sinking

Over the generations Pembrokeshire miners acquired considerable local knowledge of both the potential, and the position of coal veins in their own district, and on occasions debate might be enriched by local folklore! When the time came to consider opening a new pit the miners would begin by using a pointed bar, about twelve feet long. The sharpened, or chiselled end was driven into the ground to a depth of perhaps eleven feet, before being extracted. If the bar had passed through any coal or culm, a slightly hooked indentation behind the end of the bar would be sufficient to bring up evidence of the find. If several borings in the same vicinity produced the same positive result, colliers might feel confident that it would be worth the time and effort to sink a pit.[1]

Plainly such a method could only provide an indication of the condition of the shallowest veins of coal. By the late eighteenth century a more elaborate technique employing a set of boring rods was widely adopted. The rods were suspended from a large timber tripod by block, pulley and rope. Each rod might be anything from four to nine feet long, and each could be screwed end-on into the next. The drill head, or boring bit, might be as much as five inches in diameter, and this was attached to the lowest rod. At the uppermost end a four-armed bracehead was fitted, and two men might be detailed to rotate the bracehead to enable the rods to screw further into the ground. A newly cut tree trunk might be used to provide additional vertical pressure, having enough spring to help another two men to lower and raise the rods as required. Eventually a scoop, or a hollowed tube, might be lowered into the hole to obtain a sample of the soil or rock encountered.[2] Such methods were probably employed at Hook colliery in 1785 when work was in hand on the sinking of a new pit. The colliery accounts reveal that the cost of pit sinking varied from 2s. 6d. per fathom, paid to J. David & Co., and 5s. per fathom, paid to Owen Griffith & Co.[3]

If boring to find coal was time consuming and tedious, boring to open up a new pit was hazardous as well as arduous. In 1842 R. H. Franks described a procedure known in Pembrokeshire as "pouncing":

> Pouncing is another name for boring, taking the means for the end. It is, however, difficult to describe the nature of this labour. It was performed by three women and two men placed opposite to one another, and pressing the ends of two logs acting as levers, which operate on a circular bore. It was certainly not proper work for females, although it appeared to me less irksome than other kinds of labour which women submit to in these parts.

Anne Thomas, aged 17, a pouncer at Kilgetty colliery, told Franks:

> I have only been six months at these works. My work has usually been winding up the coal from below the ground. Pouncing is much harder work than the windlass; it hurts the back. We only pounce when sinking a new shaft, and rest frequently. Indeed we could not continue long at such hard work.[4]

To the modern mind the fact that seventeen-year-old girls were employed in such a way is both astonishing and shocking. By the nineteenth century no one could have been in any doubt that pit sinking was dangerous, and yet skilled work. Possibly Franks' report served to give the importance of the task greater recognition, because only seven years later there is evidence of a shortage of capable pit sinkers. George Taylor, writing to Sir John Pakington from Freystrop, said:

> I hope to ... commence sinking the other Tumbling Vein pit .... next week, but shall be compelled to send for more sinkers and engineers for there is none out of employ in this neighbourhood that will seek such work in either the Engine or the new Tumbling Vein pits in sinking under the pumps.[5]

Pit sinkers had to deal with the extreme problems of solid rock and running water. Frequently coal is found only at depth, and rock strata may well be encountered first. Although there is no evidence of explosives being employed in Pembrokeshire before the nineteenth century, gunpowder is believed to have been used at Neath by 1710,[6] and may well have been tried in Pembrokeshire during the eighteenth century. Before any form of blasting power became available, the old miners often used to light a fire on or against a difficult area of rock they wished to break, and when it was hot it would be doused with cold water. The sudden change in temperature usually caused the rock to crack. A more elaborate technique involved boring holes into the rock strata, before covering the surface with "hot", unslaked lime. Water was then added, and a timber plug placed across this section of the shaft. Before long the rock would expand and crack, perhaps to a depth of two or three feet. The process might then be repeated. Although this method, like most others, was very laborious, it was apparently quite effective.[7]

The problem of running water in pit sinking would arise with alarming suddenness if the sinkers met a natural spring. Indeed, the only answer in such a case might be to abandon the site and move on to another. More often the difficulty was confined to water seeping into shafts, and in Pembrokeshire this was as common in working collieries as in newly formed shafts. Lining a shaft with stone or brick could be very beneficial, but it was time consuming and expensive. The practice of "tubbing", or lining a shaft with wood, is usually said to have begun in North East England in the eighteenth century.[8] Given Pembrokeshire's long experience with the Timber Vein, though, it may well be wondered if "tubbing" did not start in the county at a much earlier date.

Shafts and slants

As outcropping of coal gradually exhausted surface seams it became necessary for colliers to dig deeper. If coal was found on a cliff, bank or hillside a slant (sometimes called a drift) down into coal would probably be appropriate, the lie of the coal seam and considerations of access, haulage, and drainage determining the angle of slope or slant. In Pembrokeshire such slants were normally used to gain access to relatively shallow workings; deeper workings were entered by shaft. In 1998 an open slant could be seen in Rhode Wood, between Saundersfoot and Monkstone Point, and another was in woodland near the village of Loveston. Almost certainly both were exposed by the failure of the traditional method of "tallating" abandoned slants and shafts. The practice of tallating involved throwing old trees, branches and rubbish of all descriptions into the slant or shaft, before putting a timber cap topped with soil over the entrance. This procedure might make the pit safe for many years, but eventually the timber would rot and the capping collapse.[9]

Slants or drifts offered the collier the advantages of easy accessibility and an almost immediate opportunity to win coal and earn revenue from the work done. Unfortunately there were also some disadvantages. Often the maintenance of roadways angled into the seams could be expensive – depending, of course, on the condition of the seam. Furthermore the very nature of the slant meant that coal produced had to be hauled to the rise, whilst water from the outcrop would tend to run into the mine. Over time there was an increasing preference for winning coal by sinking shafts. The advantages of this method were perceived to be easier maintenance, and better arrangements for raising the coal to the surface. For example, a shaft could be sunk in a position to enable coal to be worked to the rise, thereby permitting gravity haulage to carry the coal cheaply and simply to the pit bottom for winding.

In George Owen's day the deepest shafts were said to be 20 fathoms or more (i.e. 40 yards and over). This suggests that by 1600 colliers were already working close to the limits of adit drainage. Admittedly in the vicinity of Hook and Freystrop, on the ridge above the Western Cleddau, adit drainage is believed to have been effective at up to 80 yards in the eighteenth century.[10] In 1780, though, the West Park shaft at Kilgetty was put down 84 yards to the Kilgetty vein, and by 1787 a shaft at nearby White Gates had reached the same vein at the same depth. Very early in the nineteenth century a depth of 94 yards was achieved at the Thomas Hill pit, Amroth, and soon after it is believed that the Engine Pit at Begelly was sunk 106 yards to the Timber vein. The Union pit at Begelly, which was developed in the 1820's, reached the Timber vein at 120 yards.[11]

Over twenty years elapsed before any deeper shafts were sunk in Pembrokeshire. In 1846 the Tower pit of the Bonvilles Court colliery reached the Lower Level vein at 168 yards, and further north near Thomas Chapel the New Hayes shaft was put down to the Kilgetty vein at 155 yards in 1854. By then plans were afoot for a huge shaft at Grove, near Kilgetty, to provide coal for the furnaces of the Kilgetty Ironworks. In the Grove shaft the Lower Level Vein was found at 132 yards and the Kilgetty vein at 210 yards, although initially the latter was not proved, and sinking is thought to have continued for an additional 70 yards. Measuring 18 feet by 15 feet the Grove shaft was built as a bratticed, or divided shaft, and from the outset appears to have been fitted with two cages capable of taking two trams each, the earliest colliery shaft so equipped in the county. Even in 1873 the Grove colliery was described as "one of the largest and finest in the Principality",[12] but by then (or very soon after) cages were also installed in shafts at Bonvilles Court and at Lower Level. Later they were provided at Hook and Kilgetty and it seems very probable that they were also used at Moreton colliery. In the late 1860's the upcast shaft at Moreton was deepened and reached the Lower Level Vein at 316 yards. Accordingly this became the deepest colliery shaft in the county, although it was used for less than twenty years.[13]

From the 1860's onwards very few new shafts were constructed in the Pembrokeshire coalfield. The American pit at Freystrop was sunk at the time of the American Civil War, and in the 1870's a shaft and slant were provided to serve the Meads colliery at Jeffreston. Otherwise there was little activity until the late 1880's when a small colliery was opened at Yerbeston with access being gained by both a slant and a shallow shaft. In the 1890's the Lady Berwick shaft at Landshipping proved to be an unfortunate failure when it was put down on a geological fault.[14]

The Edwardian era witnessed three significant sinkings in the Hook and Freystrop district. First, two shafts at the American pit were enlarged and fitted with cages for a new Freystrop Colliery company, but ultimately with little success.[15] Next "Boggy" or Pill pit, near Hook Pill, was provided with both shaft and slant access, but again the development was not a long-term success.[16] The Margaret pit at Hook, developed between 1907 and 1910, fared rather better, but was replaced in the 1930's by the West Drift. The small mines operating at Reynalton and Loveston after World War I were both drift mines, whilst Broom and Kilgetty collieries of the 1930's were new developments based on older workings. Accordingly the Margaret pit has a modest claim to fame as the last entirely new shaft to be sunk in Pembrokeshire.[17]

Drainage

The earliest known use of drainage adits in the British Isles was in the fourteenth century when shallow levels were excavated to assist the working of silver lead mines at Bere Ferrers in Devon. In 1327 an adit a hundred yards in length was recommended at Bere Ferrers;[18] by the end of the century it is believed that there were some up to half-a-mile long. However the labour costs involved in driving and maintaining adits were high, and their use seems to have lapsed in favour of simple mechanised pumps as early as 1480.

Knowledge of the construction of adits doubtless reached other mining areas in the course of commerce and trade, and by the Tudor period were widely used. In the sixteenth century coal miners in the inland Nottingham coalfield were employing quite refined drainage techniques including not only lengthy drainage adits but also horse-drawn rag and chain pumps, and possibly even a suction lift pump. Whilst there is no evidence of drainage adits in Pembrokeshire as early as the sixteenth century, the technical knowledge to develop them would have been readily available. It may be debated whether the landowners in such an impoverished part of Wales had the resources to spend on the driving of adits, but by then it must have been very clear that only such an investment would enable coal to be mined in Pembrokeshire at greater depth. The rapid expansion of the coal industry in the sixteenth century implies additional investment and new methods; the most likely explanation is that in the Tudor period numerous drainage adits were driven inland from the river Cleddau or from tributaries like the Cresswell River, enabling new pits to be sunk and new areas to be worked.

The earliest reference to adit construction in Pembrokeshire so far seen is in a letter dated 25 August 1760, written by Alexander Smith when apparently acting as agent to the landlord, Harcourt Powell. A pit at Langdon, near Jeffreston, had flooded, and could not be cleared without a drainage adit, or level being extended into its workings. The lessee saw the problem as an opportunity to obtain a new lease. Alexander Smith reported:

I have been talking with John Williams who is Partner and have the management of the work. He seems inclinable to drive a Levell and set a gin if necessary to clear the water if you please to give them a time of twenty one years for working the vein at Langdon. The sooner you please to determine this the better as it will take some time to drive the Levell and to get the water out to land goods for next year.[19]

West of the Cleddau, J. Harcourt Powell owned land at Hook, where the Green pit was sunk in the 1780's. It appears that part of the escarpment between the new pit and the Western Cleddau was owned by Richard Wright, because in 1787 Wright granted a 99-year-lease to Harcourt Powell allowing him to use the West Park Level which ran through his land.[20] Similarly in 1792 Thomas George wrote to Colonel Colby, trustee of the Orielton estate, regarding a proposed new level to be driven in a field at Cresselly, near Cresswell Quay.[21]

Driving these adits required skill and determination. As the intention was always to provide drainage at the greatest depth in the mine that the lie of the land would allow, the mouths of adits were usually sited at or very near existing streams or waterways. At a tidal location like Landshipping it was obvious that the mouth of an adit needed to be above the high water mark. In the event of an exceptionally high tide provision was made to seal the mouth of the adit with an iron plate, or a large wooden board. When an adit disgorged into a fresh water stream such precautions might be ignored. Such was the case at Thomas Chapel, and on at least two occasions the colliery workings were flooded after torrential rain – the second instance causing the deaths of two men.[22]

Drainage adits required considerable maintenance if they were to be kept free from obstructions, and be able to serve their purpose. If a colliery fell into disuse the adits would soon become blocked, and the works inundated. In 1900 the important Stumpy Adit Level between Freystrop and Hook was cleared when the reopening of Maddox Moor pit was proposed. In the 1930's, when a decision was taken to reopen Kilgetty colliery, the first requirement was the cleaning out of the three-mile-long adit between Merrixton and the coast at Amroth. Two men were asked to begin the task at Amroth, and in grim conditions they laboriously worked up from the sea towards the first pit served by the adit, the long-closed Coombes colliery. In due course they retreated to the beach to eat their sandwiches, and as they sat the adit suddenly spewed out a torrent of boulders and mud, loosened by their activities earlier. The flow continued for several hours, and although experienced colliers, the men were shaken by their escape.[23] Figure 17 illustrates this lengthy adit and the numerous pits served by it.

As indicated by Alexander Smith's letter of 1760, the horse gin could be used to raise water from coal pits. An outline description of a horse gin or whim is given later in this chapter in the section headed "winding". Although evidence of particular examples of horse gins applied for drainage purposes is slight, the method was probably used widely. At some collieries water wheels, then often described as "water engines", were employed for pumping. When Dr. Charles Collins visited the Saundersfoot area in 1806 he remarked that: "In working the coal nothing but water engines are used, and few machines of any kind, and no steam engines."[24]

This may have been an accurate statement as regards the Saundersfoot district at this date, but not so in relation to the whole of Pembrokeshire. A waterwheel was used at Coombes colliery, Amroth, in the early nineteenth century and a lease of 1793 permitting Lord Milford to use springs, ponds and streams at Craig-y-borion above Amroth to supply water to his collieries was doubtless related to it.[25] Other waterwheels are believed to have been operational at Kilgetty, one being specifically mentioned in a lease of 1817.[26] However the largest and last waterwheel at Kilgetty was built as late as 1839.[27] Designed by Thomas Dyson, then engineer to the Bedford Level in eastern England, this wheel was of the overshot type, which gained additional power from the weight of the water cascading on to it from above. A leat over a mile long was constructed along the side of the valley running north west from the colliery, and a wooden launder supported on tall timber uprights conveyed the water to the top of the 40-foot-wheel. Although the wheel is thought to have been disused by 1900, in its active days it was one of the sights of the district.

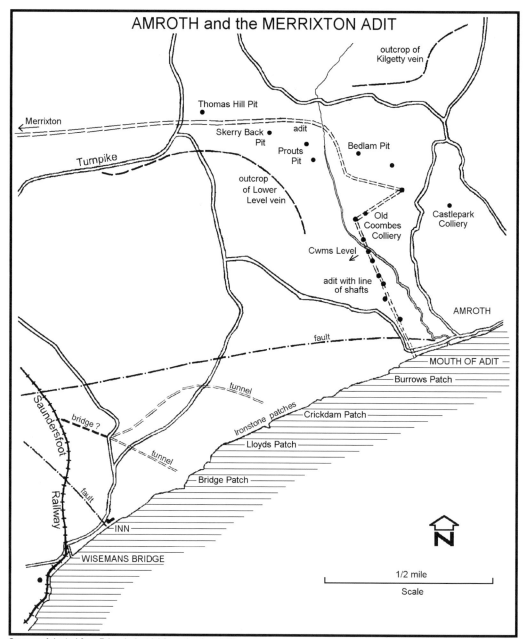

AMROTH and the MERRIXTON ADIT

outcrop of
Kilgetty vein

Thomas Hill Pit

← Merrixton

adit

Skerry Back •
Pit

Bedlam Pit

Prouts
Pit •

Turnpike

outcrop
of Lower
Level vein

Old
Coombes
Colliery

Castlepark
Colliery

Cwms Level

adit with line
of shafts

AMROTH

MOUTH OF ADIT

fault

Burrows Patch

tunnel

Crickdam Patch

Saundersfoot

Ironstone patches

bridge ?

Lloyds Patch

tunnel

Bridge Patch

Railway

fault

INN

WISEMANS BRIDGE

N

1/2 mile

Scale

Source : Adapted from Price, *Industrial Saundersfoot*, 126

JdeH 3106C

Figure 17

As already seen, the problem of providing adequate ventilation in mine workings was well known in the time of George Owen. In that era the only solution was to go to the trouble and expense of sinking air pits down to the workings to improve the natural circulation of air, but the benefits of such effort might be moderated if the site was sheltered, or the air still.

In the first half of the eighteenth century the idea arose of setting up a furnace near the bottom of a shaft to draw air towards itself and to encourage the circulation of air in mine workings. This notion originated in North East England, and in the same area by the 1750's attempts were being made to guide the ventilation current through underground workings by timber and brick stoppings, and by trap doors. As experience accumulated these methods became more effective, and were soon widely used. Whilst it is not known when they were introduced into Pembrokeshire it is very probable that they arrived with the sinking of numerous deeper shafts in the 1780's and 1790's.

The primary purpose of all ventilation is and was to disperse noxious and inflammable gases, and to provide miners with a suitable working environment. Deeper mine workings meant greater hazards to health and safety, and certainly greater risk of gas explosion. Although the dangers in the shallower pits were less, none could be considered entirely safe. Firedamp – methane – was identified as a problem at the Moreton colliery in 1778.[28] Although the workings were not then deeper than 80 yards, it seems that the measures taken to deal with it were entirely unsatisfactory. Over thirty years later a letter to Edward Loveden, the then owner of Moreton Colliery, stated that:

> The backwardness of it [the colliery] was more owing to the want of air, than want of meeting goods. The workers could not go down 4 or 5 fathoms with the candle, though they made use of every means that is customary, by sinking air pits.[29]

In the nineteenth century collieries at both Begelly and Broadmoor were troubled by firedamp, and Wilson and Smith's Colliery at Broadmoor acquired a name for being a fiery pit. Once again, though, the real difficulty was probably wholly deficient ventilation. Other collieries nearby, for example Kilgetty, appear to have been little troubled by gas, and in Pembrokeshire generally firedamp does not seem to have been a major problem.[30]

There is also some evidence that a number of pits in the county encountered that mixture of gases known as "blackdamp". The main ingredient of blackdamp is carbon monoxide, produced by the oxidation of coal. However anthracite and other high rank coals oxidise very slowly, so this should not have been a serious problem in Pembrokeshire. Here again the assumption must be that those mines troubled by blackdamp had woefully inadequate ventilation.[31]

Following legislation in 1850, the first government inspector of mines with responsibility for South Wales was appointed in 1851. H.F. Mackworth's report in 1852 was highly critical of Pembrokeshire pits. He wrote: "There is hardly an instance of the employment of artificial ventilating power throughout the year and in collieries wherein I measured the quantities of air it was this summer less than half that required for the health and vigour of the miners."[32] Rather curiously, Robert Franks, who visited Landshipping colliery on behalf of the Children's Employment Commission of 1842, reported that ventilation there was by means of "a blowing machine, and by lighting a fire at the mouth of the pit". Unfortunately the blowing machine is not described, but this is the earliest reference to any kind of mechanical contrivance being used for the purpose in Pembrokeshire.[33]

In 1852 Mackworth was called as a witness before the Select Committee on Coal Mines, chiefly in relation to his report on a gas explosion at Middle Duffryn colliery in the Aberdare valley. In his evidence he made mention of other aids to ventilation and safety. "A good ventilation", he declared, "makes the chance of the accumulation of gas remote; the adoption of the Davy lamp in the same colliery reduces the chance of accident by the multiple of the other." He went on to recommend the recent invention of the steam jet as a supplement to furnace ventilation, especially in difficult conditions and emergencies. However he acknowledged that the application of steam jet ventilation depended upon the provision of a steam boiler at approximately 50lbs per square inch, the steam jet operating by expanding and pushing the air. He was also questioned about the new ventilation machines devised by Struvé and Brunton, and considered that in some cases a Struvé ventilator would ventilate a mine, although at a higher capital cost than a steam jet.[34]

A series of appalling explosions in British coal mines generated great concern about underground ventilation, and the work of Struvé and Brunton was soon followed by others. The ventilator conceived by Lemielle was first used in England in 1860, and in the following year John Nixon was granted a patent for his design. Two years later Schiele patented his ventilating fan. In 1863 the first ventilating fan designed and built by Waddle of Llanelly was installed at Bonvilles Court colliery, Saundersfoot – a unique instance of Pembrokeshire being at the forefront of mining technology.[35] Thereafter the shaft in question was always known as the Fan pit.

The early mines' inspectors themselves contributed greatly to the interest taken in matters of ventilation. Although their recommendations carried no powers of enforcement, their observations were noted – sometimes more by the press than by the proprietors of collieries. Following the death of two men in an accident in Thomas Chapel in 1854 the *Pembrokeshire Herald* was moved to observe that the Inspector of Mines had never visited the county following a fatality. Had the writer studied Mackworth's evidence to the Select Committee the reason would have been obvious. The inspector was then expected to visit over 400 collieries in an area of at least 1,300 square miles, Mackworth calculating that it would take him four years to visit every one of them. In due course the number of inspectors was increased, and the area to be covered by each inspector was reduced, and some assistance was provided to help them.[36]

By 1860 the Inspector of Mines in South and West Wales was Thomas Evans, and in his report for that year he referred to a gas explosion at Moreton Colliery on 20 October 1860, which caused three deaths. He found the management to be at fault, and was scathing in his criticism:

> The manager, John Thomas, is ignorant of the ordinary and common rules of ventilation; and at the Coroner's enquiry I pointed out his responsibility, and many direct violations of the rules by the manager, overman and fireman. The colliery is laid out without the slightest regard to safety, and although the coroner's jury did not think anyone to blame, the magistrates thought otherwise, and when I afterwards summoned the owner before the magistrates they imposed a penalty. If mines are to be under the direction of such men, and the lives of persons employed depend upon their management, I fear my list of deaths will certainly not decrease.[37]

By 1861, Thomas Evans expressed his concern about the use of bratticed or divided shafts, the downcast side being used for winding, and the upcast for ventilation. He reported that:

> In Pembrokeshire there is now a colliery at work; it is about 180 yards deep, divided by a thin wooden brattice (about 1½ inches thick) with a furnace at the shaft bottom. I have known the ventilation most defective, almost at an explosive point near the furnace; the responsibility of working such a colliery has been pointed out to the manager, and now they are under notice of arbitration.[38]

Evans did not name the colliery, but the depth quoted approximates to that of the shaft at Bonvilles Court. In the circumstances maybe it is not surprising that the first Waddle fan was installed there in 1863! However, following the Hartley colliery disaster in County Durham in the same year, single bratticed shafts were seen as a serious danger. In 1872 such shafts were outlawed by legislation requiring every mine to have at least two separate means of access.

By 1871 Thomas Wales was the inspector of mines for the area, and on 22 November of that year two men were killed by a gas explosion at Hook, and eleven others hurt. Wales inspected the workings the next day and calculated that air was passing at the rate of 5,000 to 6,000 cubic feet per minute. He did not think this a large quantity nor was it properly applied. He found that the air reaching the coal face was very small indeed, and protested that: "Men ought never to be allowed to work, not even with a safety lamp where gas is lodged. From what I have seen in some collieries in this county and in Carmarthenshire there is a tendency to introduce the safety lamp as a substitute for proper ventilation."[39]

In truth effective means of mechanical ventilation came very late for most mines in Pembrokeshire. Although the technology existed in the second half of the nineteenth century, by then most pits were either too small to benefit, or facing such a financial struggle to survive that their management was disinclined to make the investment. It appears that a Waddle ventilating fan was installed at the West Park pit at Hook in the 1880's, and a small fan of unknown make at Freystrop in about 1902. As late as 1891 furnace ventilation was employed at the Trefrane Cliff and Lower Level collieries.[40] Although no relevant mine records are available it is thought that one of Pembrokeshire's last collieries, Kilgetty, was equipped with a small electrically driven fan in the 1930's. Broom colliery had no fan, but rather an air compressor on the surface pushing air through pipes into the workings, with the old Broom shaft acting as the upcast, and the former Shipping colliery drift as an alternative access. The short lived colliery at Loveston is also believed to have been ventilated by an air compressor. Certain dead end stalls in the Timber vein at Hook were ventilated only by compressed air fed through a one-inch diameter pipe. Not surprisingly the air was badly polluted and very unhealthy.[41]

Lighting

In the twenty-first century everyone is so accustomed to efficient artificial lighting in streets and homes and transport systems that the poverty of lighting in coal mines prior to the twentieth century almost defies belief. Colliers everywhere had to rely upon tallow candles well into the Victorian period and sometimes even later. In Pembrokeshire a miner's candle was commonly 3 to 4 inches in length, and could be relied upon to give a little light for an hour or two. Every miner needed a good supply of candles for every shift, so the daily consumption of tallow candles was considerable. In addition to providing some meagre illumination in the stall or heading or place of work it was usual for larger candles to be placed at intervals along mainways to assist the work of hauliers and trammers. Siting such candles required some care; they could not be placed in any spot where gas was likely to gather, nor could they be exposed to too strong a flow of air intended to ventilate the mine. It is said that rudimentary clay shields might be fixed close to the flame if it was in danger of being blown out. In any event it was necessary for the candles to be replaced at least once in every shift.[42]

About the year 1730 Carlisle Spedding invented a flint mill comprising a small steel disc which, by means of a cogwheel and pinion, revolved rapidly in contact with a piece of flint. The ensuing sparks produced a glimmer of light which did not ignite firedamp, and yet was sufficient to work by. Whilst no specific reference has been found to confirm the use of this flint mill in Pembrokeshire, its usage is quite likely, because Spedding's device was widely adopted in the eighteenth century.[43]

In 1811 the first experimental safety lamp was introduced by Dr Clanny of Sunderland. Within a few years both George Stephenson and Humphrey Davy had designed safety lamps, the essential feature of which was the provision of a metal gauze between the flame and the atmosphere in the colliery. The gauze effectively inhibited the flame from igniting any accumulated gas, although when the flame was lowered it would give the collier warning of the presence of gas by turning blue. Its value as a means of lighting was somewhat limited, although certainly brighter than the candle and more long lasting. As the years went by safety lamps were improved, but it is very doubtful if they were employed in Pembrokeshire at all before the 1840's. The earliest known references to safety lamps both occur in 1864. In July of that year the *Mining Journal* reported the imprisonment of two Bonvilles Court miners who broke rules by opening their safety lamps underground. A month later three miners at the Nash and Sprinkle colliery were more fortunate, simply incurring fines for having their lamps open, notwithstanding the fact they caused a small fire.[44] It must be debatable whether the management really understood the value and importance of the safety lamp at this period. Following an explosion at Hook on 22 November 1871, which caused two fatalities, The Inspector of Mines, Thomas Wales, criticised the ventilation and insisted, as we have cited earlier, that men should never have to work, not even if they were in possession of a safety lamp, where gas was present.

In truth the safety lamp was not in general use for many years. As late as 1913 the report of the Inspector of Mines made mention of workmen being burned in local collieries when firedamp was ignited by the use of naked lights.[45] Furthermore it is also known that men worked in the Rock Vein at Hook with naked lights until the 1930's.[46] The hazards and the difficulties were so considerable that it now seems miraculous that Pembrokeshire men managed to produce so much coal and culm over so many centuries. Small wonder, too, that so many of them were religious.

Timbering and roof support

According to William Linnard in his pioneering book *Welsh Woods and Forests,* Welsh woodlands comprised mixed hardwoods, containing a preponderance of oak, and this was reflected in the types of wood chosen for use as pit wood below ground. Hardwood, he asserted, was needed in two forms. First, poles were required to make props, posts, collars and arms for roof support. Second, shorter corded material was wanted to make what was known in the industry as "cogs" or "cogwood", meaning the timber used to create a criss cross type of framework stacked up to the roof either ancillary to the main pit props, or to give roof support where there were vacant spaces not filled by waste. Linnard concluded that both types of timber were obtainable from woodland thinning or from coppice felling.[47]

In making these points Linnard appears to have been addressing the circumstances of the eighteenth century and early nineteenth century. Over time it was realised that hardwood was of limited usefulness in relation to mine support. Frequently such timber is not straight, difficult to work, too heavy and also too expensive. However, cut into manageable blocks – in later years customarily 24inch x 6inch x 6inch – hardwoods had a place in the construction of chocks in underground locations requiring permanent load-bearing support or at the edge of areas supported by waste. Overall, though, the best pit timber was obtained from Scandinavia. Being long-grained, straight and free from knots, it was superior in compression and so ideal for props or posts. Red barked timber from France had a somewhat twisted grain, but proved to cope best under tension. Accordingly this was often employed for the making of timber "collars", or cross beams.[48]

So much good timber was cut in World War I that in the years afterwards most home grown timber was of desperately poor quality. Even so, some was used in Pembrokeshire mines to the detriment of timbering standards. In the main anthracite region of South Wales it was used only for cogwood, although by World War II it was of a better quality and more widely employed. By then the policies of the Forestry Commission were having a beneficial effect, producing increasing amounts of pit timber grown in the Scandinavian manner.

In Pembrokeshire, mining conditions created an additional requirement for pit wood. The Timber Vein was worked heavily east and west of the Cleddau and, as has been mentioned, it required substantial timber support. Indeed in places it required almost continuous propping with total roof cover. This was achieved by weaving branches of hazel and willow into the roof supports known as "drivers" supplementing these with any other broken branches or woody material available which might contain falls from the roof of the seam.[49] Acquiring such material became a cottage industry for women in Freystrop and Hook, and to this day some elderly residents can recall the efforts of their forebears in this respect. The best known of all the women engaged in the task was known as "Martha the Dungell", but she and her friends received very modest payment for their hard work.[50]

In the earliest days of the coal industry much of South Pembrokeshire was heavily wooded, with the extensive Coedrath Forest covering the Saundersfoot district and the larger Narberth Forest adjoining the Eastern Cleddau. The growth of the coal industry through the Tudor period made severe inroads into local timber stocks, and by the seventeenth century the commodity was becoming harder to obtain and much more expensive. Narberth Forest was Crown property, but in the reign of James I the steward is alleged to have ignored the King's regulations for the protection of trees. It appears that for many years private deals were done and profits made at the expense of the Crown, a 'dishonest' practice encountered in all aspects of Crown manorial rights in these years. In 1632, long after James's death, it was ascertained that of 8,000 trees once marked with the king's initials, only 10 per cent were still standing.[51]

In the circumstances the management of woodland for later colliery use became increasingly important. In 1713, for example, seven acres of woodland were acquired to supply timber for

SOUTH WALES TIMBERING METHODS

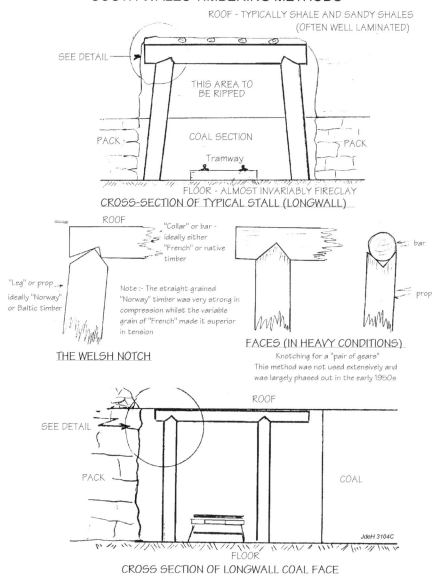

Source : Hermas E. Nicholas, former H.M. Deputy Chief Inspector of Mines

Figure 18

TIMBERING AT BROOM COLLIERY 1935-1939

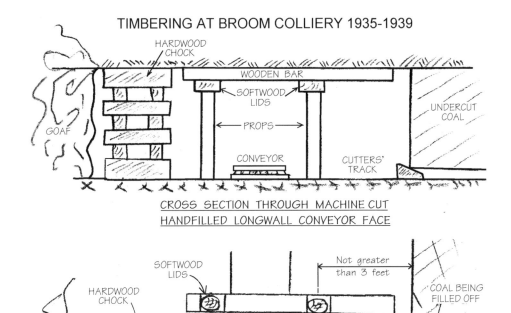

CROSS SECTION THROUGH MACHINE CUT
HANDFILLED LONGWALL CONVEYOR FACE

PLAN OF SUPPORTING SYSTEM
FOR MECHANISED FACE LINE

This is a typical (all wood) support system
With the substitution of handcutting, no conveyor and softwood dirt filled cogs for
the chocks it would be the system of support suitable for stalls and topholes

Source : Hermas E. Nicholas, former H.M. Deputy Chief Inspector of Mines

Figure 19

use at what was then called Cardmakers Pool colliery at Freystrop. The colliers of the time reportedly described the wood as "the best they ever saw for that use".[52] Timber was also in heavy demand for building, ship-building and for charcoal manufacture. By way of example, in 1635, the Barlows of Slebech let a forge at Blackpool on the Eastern Cleddau to George Mynne, who in 1636 became a partner in a small ironworks built at Whitland six miles to the east. The partners had the right to cut timber for charcoal within a twelve-mile radius of Whitland, but by 1638 there were complaints about the rapid deterioration of the district.[53] Not surprisingly, by the beginning of the nineteenth century, it appears that coal as well as charcoal was being used at Blackpool.[54] Even before then, in the late eighteenth century, it is clear that local supplies of timber were quite inadequate for the Pembrokeshire coal industry. The records of one small port on Cardigan Bay – Aberdovey – reveal that between 1791 and

1794 no less than 27,000 oak poles were exported, mainly as pitwood to Milford Haven.[55]

Mines across South Wales were subject to "squeeze" – the tendency of workings to close up under superincumbent pressure – a circumstance more pronounced in this area than elsewhere, as the whole strata in South Wales appears to be subject to geological compression. Even when mine workings were well maintained the effects could be dramatic. In the Timber Vein at Hook, for example, props nine feet high could be reduced to four feet in a fortnight by both pressure from above and the lifting of the floor. At one period in the 1920's the Timber Vein was so damaged that one shift of men worked for six weeks at virtually the same spot shoring up and maintaining access to enable the other shift to work coal and culm.[56] The "squeeze" effect was both costly and dangerous. In 1871 the Mines Inspector T. E. Wales objected to the local practice of allowing coal hewers to carry out timbering in their own stalls. As they were paid for cutting coal rather than setting timber, there was a tendency for men to be both brisk and careless in their way of working. Wales advocated the employment of men for the specific task of timbering, who would be paid for the proper performance of their work. This was not regarded with enthusiasm by either employers or employees, and as there were vested interests on both sides, change was difficult. In 1887 the then Mines Inspector J. T. Robson criticised the practice again, and attributed the higher accident rate from roof falls in South Wales to its continuing use. Eventually special rules regarding timbering underground were introduced in South Wales, and became effective in the western part of the coalfield from 1 October 1895. [57]

The extreme instance of "squeeze" at Hook just mentioned could not be cured by a better rulebook, but after the colliery was taken over by Watts, Watts and Co. in 1934 the whole approach to such problems was transformed. The new owners wanted a well ordered and well laid out colliery, and they were prepared to invest heavily to achieve it. Thereafter timber arrived at Hook by the shipload from Scandinavia, nuts and bolts by the ton, and steel arches often known as "rings" by the wagonload from the steelworks of GKN.[58] The first all-steel pit prop was invented in 1861, but little progress was made in this area of technology before 1896. Another 40 years or so elapsed before steel props became commonplace, and in 1947 there was a most significant development when the Dowty company introduced their hydraulic prop. These were never used in Pembrokeshire, and similarly it is doubtful if steel props (rather than "rings") were ever employed in the county. Until the developments of the mid 1930's the county's mines relied upon pitwood and traditional Welsh timbering techniques, as illustrated here in Figure 18. The reopening and redevelopment of Broom colliery between 1932 and 1935 included the provision of a longwall conveyor face, for which a rather different timbering method was required. This is shown in Figure 19.[59]

Systems of Winding

According to George Owen, in the late sixteenth century pits were entered by a slope or slant, and workers carried coal out on their backs. Where shafts were used, coal and colliers alike were wound up and down, usually by four men turning a windlass – a device long known in Pembrokeshire as the "druke and beam". Coal was carried in a basket, bucket or barrel, whilst colliers either used the same, or sat astride a horizontal bar of iron or wood known as "the clatch iron". As pits became deeper the work became harder, and by the nineteenth century it was common for windlasses to be set up not only on the surface but at different levels below ground, so that a basket, barrel or tub of coal might have to be wound by three or four different windlasses before coming to the surface. The whole process had its hazards because in the earliest days ropes were of uncertain quality and strength, and because the only brake on the actual winding was the physical strength of the person or persons at the windlass handle. In due course catches were fitted to prevent the windlass winding back, and ropes became more reliable, but it remained heavy work quite capable of causing injury to the winder. Ironically, in the seventeenth century, it seems to have become the custom to entrust the task to women, who usually coped well with it.

The seventeenth century also saw the introduction of the cog and rung horse gin. In this device a horizontal drum was positioned over the top of the shaft perhaps six feet square, and it was turned by horse by means of an arm secured to an adjacent vertical shaft on which a large cog wheel was fixed which meshed with a pinion at the end of the drum shaft. The rope around the drum was double ended so that the weight of the empty tub or barrel descending would assist the raising of the loaded tub or barrel on the other end. Unfortunately there are very few specific references to these gins in operation, although it is very probable that they could be seen in all the main coal mining parishes. An inspection by the writer of the site of a long-closed pit at Brince in Jeffreston parish in 1992 revealed a circular area close to the pit suggestive of such an arrangement. It must be admitted, though, that after a lapse of 150 years, other explanations are possible.

The whim gin (or "whimsey") was a development of the basic horse gin. Here a large diameter drum mounted on a vertical axis or shaft was turned by horses or oxen hitched to a long wooden arm or lever secured to the axle. The ropes from the drum went over two pulleys on the top of a head frame located over the shaft, and thus went down into the shaft. As pits became deeper more horses or oxen were required to work these devices to produce an increased output, but of course this also increased costs. The name "Whim pit" for an eighteenth-century shaft at Kilgetty points to the use there of this type of gin.

The eighteenth century witnessed further technical developments. The water wheel, which had been used in the seventeenth century for mine drainage (by lifting water in a series of buckets), was adapted for winding. This was achieved by replacing a single wheel with a double wheel, the buckets in which were set in opposite directions. Accordingly the double wheel could be driven either way by diverting the water to different sets of buckets. The reversible water wheel proved to be an important advance over the horse gin, both in economy of operation and in speed of hoisting. However, it is doubtful if it was ever used in Pembrokeshire. Whilst it has been suggested that the large water wheel erected at Kilgetty in 1839 was of this design, the only available picture of the wheel does not support this contention. This impressive water wheel was possibly the last one ever built for use in the British coal industry.[60]

The principle of the balanced hoist mentioned earlier was adopted also for the water balance system of winding. This method was particularly appropriate at a site with a plentiful supply of water, or at a mine that was provided with natural drainage by adits. Again no certain location in Pembrokeshire is known for the use of the water balance, but there were numerous suitable sites at Hook and Freystrop, and at Amroth, Kilgetty, Thomas Chapel, and in the parishes of Jeffreston and Loveston. It operated on the basis that a descending tank of water was heavier than an ascending tub of coal, so enabling the former to bring the latter to the surface, where it could be held by a brake. Once emptied of water at the pit bottom the tank would be brought up again by the heavier tub (or tub and cage) descending. Such an arrangement worked especially well if there were clean, clear drainage adits at the pit bottom to take away the discharged water. Otherwise the water released had to be pumped up to the drainage adit level.

The earliest steam engines used in mines were the Newcomen atmospheric pumping engines first introduced in 1712. In some coal districts these were a great aid to mine drainage, although none was erected in Pembrokeshire. Seventy years were to pass before the engineer James Watt devised an engine wherein power could be applied to both sides of the piston alternately, so providing a continuous cycle of operation and the steady pull appropriate for winding operations. The earliest steam engine in Pembrokeshire was erected by Colonel Colby in the period when he was managing the estates of Owens of Orielton. In 1800 he spent £1,900 in acquiring the engine for the Landshipping colliery.[61] Other local landowners were long reluctant to invest heavily in the technology of the Industrial Revolution and in a coalfield beset by water and frequent geological difficulties. After a few years other coal proprietors started to follow Colby's example, and in 1810, for example, payments were being made on behalf of Lord Milford for mortar "for the steam engine house at Kingsmoor".[62] By the 1840's several collieries had more than one steam engine. If a report in the *Cambrian* newspaper in March 1840 is to be believed the Kilgetty colliery then had one engine in use for both pumping and winding.[63] The failure to invest more in this way was to make the decline of the Pembrokeshire coalfield more certain, even if not more rapid.

The introduction of steam winding at the larger pits enabled iron tubs to be used in shafts, although these could inflict some damage on the walls of shafts, pump rods and other equipment if they bumped the sides. By 1836 a successful system of winding with cages and shaft guides had been introduced in North-East England. Broadly speaking this system was reckoned to double the quantity of coal that could be lifted in any given time. Grove colliery at Kilgetty was the first in Pembrokeshire to have this equipment when it was completed in 1856. Even then the improvement was only slowly taken up in the county. One difficulty was the need to stop production in order to widen and modify shafts. Another was the fact that transport facilities at several collieries were inadequate for the conveyance of an increased output. Plainly without transport facilities to match there was little point in making the investment necessary to double output!

When steam engines were under repair, or shafts required maintenance, it would be necessary to resort to the system of capstan winding – that is to say having the rope wrapped round a capstan at the top of the shaft and in control of a group of men responsible for lowering or raising it. This method had obvious dangers. In August 1866 the Pembrokeshire press reported on the inquest into the death of William Parcell at Bonvilles Court colliery. With another man he was being lowered on a wooden stage from the capstan on the surface when the rope jerked and Parcell fell to his death. On this occasion six men were at the capstan to control the winding rope but they could not prevent one section of rope slipping off another onto the capstan causing the disastrous jerk.[64]

The final phase in the development of winding came with the introduction of electricity, although in Pembrokeshire only those pits at work after 1920 made use of this source of power.[65] Even then, arguably only Hook, Broom and Kilgetty collieries in the 1930's used it efficaciously. In 1927 a power house with electricity generators was built at Hook Colliery: it was located near the new West Drift, with an electricity substation nearby. In addition to steam and electric winders, there were also electric air compressors and associated switchgear.[66]

Working methods

At the beginning of the nineteenth century the pillar and stall system of mining was the customary technique for working coal in South and West Wales. In this method mainways were driven into the coal, and then cross-headings cut to follow the coal to the rise to simplify both drainage and haulage. The distance between cross-headings could vary from colliery to colliery but the 70 yards usual at Hook was quite common. Cross-headings were not necessarily cut at right angles to the mainways; if the coal was inclined steeply they would be set at an angle to reduce the gradient in the heading. The actual angle of the heading would be determined by the need for ponies to be able to bring down loaded trams on fully spragged wheels. Whatever the angle of the cross heading, the working stalls were usually set parallel to the main levels, as shown in Figure 20. The width of the stalls and the width of the pillars left to support the roof would vary according to the thickness of the seam and the cleat of the coal.[67]

Pillar and stall working continued in use into the twentieth century, and most of the observations made here about working are derived from information and advice received from former colliers.[68] At Kilgetty and Wood Level the custom was to work a stall with an average width of 12 feet (5 feet below centre and 7 feet to the rise), leaving pillars in place with a width of about 6 feet. If the official intention was to create stalls which were twice the width of the pillars, the reminiscences of some colliers suggest that the stalls were sometimes widened to about 14 feet, and the pillars reduced to no more than 4 feet wide. Plainly this was advantageous in increasing the proportion of coal won but it did involve colliers and overmen

PILLAR and STALL and LONGWALL WORKING compared

(BASIC) PILLAR & STALL METHOD - HAND GOT

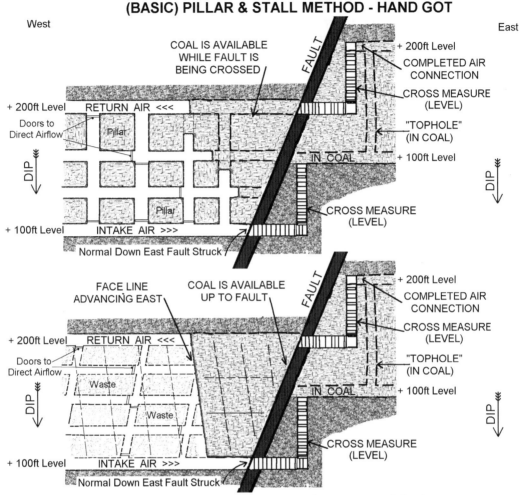

West

East

COAL IS AVAILABLE
WHILE FAULT IS
BEING CROSSED

FAULT

+ 200ft Level

COMPLETED AIR
CONNECTION

CROSS MEASURE
(LEVEL)

+ 200ft Level

RETURN AIR <<<

Doors to
Direct Airflow

Pillar

"TOPHOLE"
(IN COAL)

IN COAL

+ 100ft Level

DIP

DIP

Pillar

CROSS MEASURE
(LEVEL)

+ 100ft Level

INTAKE AIR >>>

Normal Down East Fault Struck

(BASIC) LONGWALL METHOD - HAND GOT

FACE LINE
ADVANCING EAST

COAL IS AVAILABLE
UP TO FAULT

FAULT

+ 200ft Level

COMPLETED AIR
CONNECTION

CROSS MEASURE
(LEVEL)

+ 200ft Level

RETURN AIR <<<

Doors to
Direct Airflow

"TOPHOLE"
(IN COAL)

Waste

IN COAL

+ 100ft Level

DIP

DIP

Waste

CROSS MEASURE
(LEVEL)

+ 100ft Level

INTAKE AIR >>>

Normal Down East Fault Struck

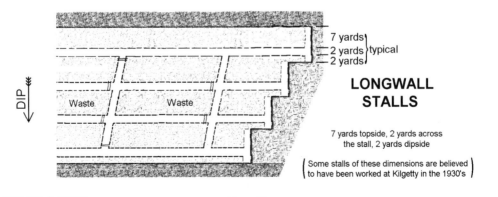

7 yards ⎫
2 yards ⎬ typical
2 yards ⎭

LONGWALL
STALLS

DIP

Waste   Waste

7 yards topside, 2 yards across
the stall, 2 yards dipside

⎰ Some stalls of these dimensions are believed ⎱
⎱ to have been worked at Kilgetty in the 1930's ⎰

Source : H. E. Nicholas

Figure 20

in making a fine judgement as to whether the practice was actually safe. In contrast, at Hook, both stalls and pillars appear to have been wider, the stalls being laid out with centres 30 or 33 feet apart and the pillars being about 10 feet wide. Superincumbent pressure on narrow pillars tended to break up the coal within the pillar, and was likely to cause the floor around it to lift. Wider pillars usually provided better security for stalls and headings and when an area was worked out they might be "robbed" of additional coal before the stalls were finally abandoned and packed up ("gobbed up") with waste. This practice not only gave renewed support to the roof but helped to minimise the risk of gas gathering in the old workings.

One of the notable features of Pembrokeshire mining was the narrowness and irregularity of coal seams. Although Bonvilles Court was a good colliery by the standards of the county, the Timber Vein was often barely 3 feet high, and the Kilgetty vein a mere 18 to 24 inches high. At Broom colliery one seam had a thickness of no more than 16 to 18 inches, although it could rise to 3 feet before opening out further and deteriorating in quality to become the kind of friable culm sometimes called "slash". At Hook colliery the coal seams were the best in Pembrokeshire, with the Rock Vein measuring 3 feet 6 inches to 5 feet and the Timber Vein typically 6 feet to 7 feet and occasionally as much as 15 feet. Not surprisingly Hook colliers considered their mine to be better than Bonvilles Court, even though its plant and equipment were not superior until Hook benefited from the capital investment made in the mid 1930's by Messrs. Watts, Watts and Co.

Whilst there was considerable variety in styles of pillar and stall working, they all involved a good deal of waste. Not only was a substantial amount of coal lost by the need to leave pillars, but the thinness of so many seams meant that miners had to spend much time and expense ripping away rock to create a space large enough in which to work. Driving new headings and opening up new stalls was a skilled job, involving much ripping of the roof and timbering to make them usable. In Pembrokeshire ripping out the roof was known as "on the con", that is to say "on the company", and not making money with the men receiving a day wage only, and not the additional sums payable on a coal cutting contract. Any coal extracted in the course of this work was usually small, and said to be "not enough for salt", or not enough for profit.

The usual practice was for three men to be allocated to each stall – a leading collier, an assistant collier (or "butty"), and a boy to help with moving the coal to the dram in the heading. Preparing a stall for work could take as much as two hours. Coal cutting commenced by the leading collier removing a thickness of coal from the bottom of the seam with a small pick or mandrel. In the wider seams at Hook he might undercut the coal by a foot or more, but in Bonvilles Court he might take as little as six inches. Timber was used to support the undercut coal until the leading collier was ready to let it fall either under its own weight, or assisted by wedges or lever bars. The top edge in the Kilgetty vein is said to have been marked by a thin layer of what the men called "grizzle", thought to be a form of fireclay, grey-white in colour. In this particular case, when the vein was narrow, they found it easier to go in over the coal and remove it all.

Plainly this work was unpleasant. Quite apart from the dust of coal cutting, in the thin seams of Pembrokeshire a collier might be crouching (or even lying) in his stall for hours, struggling to wield his mandrel. Indeed, one type of mandrel had a short handle and a single pointed end designed to make it easier and safer to use in such a confined space. Similarly, a notably small flat shovel was employed to clear the coal away from the face and into the dram, tub or skip. At Bonvilles Court the colliers soon found that pads of hardened skin developed on their hips and elbows and shoulders. At Broom colliery and at Hook prior to the 1930's the conditions were often wet, and everywhere the ventilation within the stall was poor.

The defects and difficulties involved in pillar and stall working provided an incentive to find better techniques. In time this led to the introduction of the longwall method, a broad term covering numerous local variations. In many instances in Pembrokeshire "longwall stall" would be the preferred system of extraction. A major attraction was the way in which this technique helped miners to maximise extraction rates at a relatively low capital cost in areas

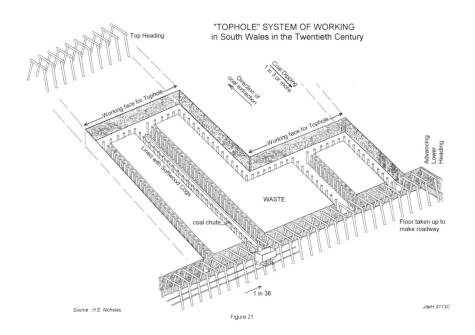

"TOPHOLE" SYSTEM OF WORKING
in South Wales in the Twentieth Century

Top Heading

Coal Dipping
1 in 3 or more

Direction of
coal extraction

Working face for Tophole

Working face for Tophole

Lined with Softwood Cogs

Advancing
Lower
Heading

WASTE

coal chute

Floor taken up to
make roadway

1 in 36

Source : H.E. Nicholas

JdeH 3113C

Figure 21

with limited and irregular coal reserves. It also offered the possible benefits of improved ventilation, relatively low technological demands, and compactness giving ease of supervision.

Generally speaking in the longwall stall system the main roadways would be set at a gradient of about 1 in 36 to the rise to facilitate horse and hand haulage down from the coalface. Levels would then be driven off the main rise and dip roadways at intervals of about 80 to 100 yards. The angled headings from the levels would be set to enable stalls to be opened up working "x" yards to the rise and "y" yards to the dip, roughly parallel to the levels. At intervals dictated by local conditions the headings, usually roadways sloping to the rise, would be advanced from the lower level to intersect and cut off the stalls. However, the miners would continue to advance the stalls towards the next intended heading, where the process would be repeated.[69] The reader is referred again to Figure 20 and will observe how this system tended to create a "stepped" coalface.

Cutting headings and stalls on the appropriate alignment was an important and responsible task, on which depended the successful and profitable working of the entire coalface.[70] Accordingly those men who were skilful enough to do it would be given extra pay. Within each longwall stall at Bonvilles Court colliery the men were asked to work three yards dipside and eleven yards landside, that is to say, to the rise. As the work proceeded, and the stalls were worked into one another, it was customary to support the roof with substantial cogs of pit timber. As the area of working moved on, the practice was to fill the spaces left vacant by the excavation of coal by packing them, or "gobbing back", with stone from earlier roof ripping operations, or with spoil brought down by blasting to open new headings. Stepped longwall stalls worked at Broom and Kilgetty collieries in the 1930's were somewhat similar, but significantly larger than those at Bonvilles Court, being anything up to one hundred in plan. At all these collieries occasional use was made of "topholes", headings driven up into coal when required by distortions in the strata. This is illustrated in Figure 21. The larger collieries like Hook and Bonvilles Court also had cross measures drifts, or slopes driven at an angle from one seam into another. The 'K' pit into the Kilgetty vein at Bonvilles Court was a cross-measures drift as well as the main access to the Kilgetty coal.

Until the first half of the nineteenth century almost all underground workings in Pembrokeshire appear to have been created on the pillar and stall principle, even though a lack of capital and geological difficulties frequently prevented the orderly development of mines. However, H. F. Mackworth in his report for 1852 makes the surprising generalisation in relation to

Pembrokeshire that "as is usually the case with thin seams, the working faces are carried on by longwall, and the whole of the coal is brought out of mine".[71] The writer believes that this statement indicates that the Bonvilles Court form of longwall stall mining was already established in the very few Pembrokeshire pits the newly appointed inspector had visited. As Mackworth admitted to the Select Committee on Coal Mines in 1852 and has been remarked earlier, this area covered 1,300 square miles included over 400 collieries. By his own estimate it would take him 3 to 4 years to visit each one.[72] At this date he must have seen very little of the Pembrokeshire pits, and cannot have fully appreciated the diversity of practice in the county.

Longwall working in South Wales probably originated in the 1820's. Morris and Williams note that in 1837, R. J. Nevill of Llanelly offered to lend Sir John Morris of Swansea two or three colliers "who are used to longwork" in order to instruct his men in the technique.[73] The very thinness of seams in West Wales doubtless encouraged the adoption of such methods, simply to improve the economics of the industry. However longwall also had the advantage of easing arrangements for ventilation, even when "stepped" working faces were in use. This benefit does not appear to have been acknowledged very quickly in South Wales. As late as 1859 the then mines inspector, Lionel Brough, declared that in Glamorgan and Monmouthshire where seams were thicker the longwall technique was but in its infancy.[74] Twenty years of considerable change followed and his successor, Thomas Wales, was able to say in 1881 that longwall prevailed in most workings in his area.[75] What he did not say was what form the longwall working took. Once it became clear that it was possible to remove most, if not all, the coal by the longwall approach, it was logical to try to eliminate any kind of stall by creating a long working face which itself could be used for the passage of air circulating through the mine. At a stroke, conditions for miners could be improved and colliery working could be made much more efficient. This said, Pembrokeshire did not take full advantage of the longwall method. Examination of the limited number of mining plans available suggests that Bonvilles Court did not progress beyond its own version of longwall stall operation in the Lower Level Vein. The older workings at Bonvilles Court, like those at nearby Moreton, contained long and sinuous mainways and untidy sections of pillar and stall mining, all pointing to the management giving priority to making a return on coal rather than the careful development of the colliery underground.

The Trefrane Cliff colliery was redeveloped in the 1890's, but even at this period the workings were laid out systematically for pillar and stall operation, presumably because undersea working was contemplated, for which activity longwall would have been hazardous. The underground layout at the Commons pit at Hook was also a tidy form of pillar and stall, as was the layout at the later Pill pit ("Boggy pit") less than a mile away. In contrast, though, the historic workings at West Hook were distinctly untidy. Here there is some evidence of attempts to work two mining districts in a systematic way but also evidence of such ideas being frustrated by faulting and other geological problems. The mining plans show that pillars were removed in certain districts as soon as they became exhausted, and they also indicate that after the colliery was taken over by Watts, Watts and Co. in 1934 a serious attempt was made to develop a new and deeper district to the north. The hope was that this area, at least, might be laid out for effective longwall operations, but regrettably the conditions encountered seemed to have inhibited development work at an early stage. As a result the only longwall section at Hook (modest at that) appears to have been in the west of the workings in the vicinity of an abandoned shaft known as Waddy's pit.[76]

The small and short lived colliery at Reynalton was a redevelopment of much earlier workings which were almost certainly pillar and stall. However it is thought that one aspect of mining at Reynalton may have been the removal of pillars in districts formerly worked. The similarly small colliery at Loveston is believed to have been worked on the pillar and stall basis, and so the only collieries in Pembrokeshire which saw any development were those at Broom and Kilgetty. The latter is thought to have adopted a version of longwall stall working, whilst the former was laid out for working by an open face system, giving two longwall faces of about

100 yards each which were notable as being the only Pembrokeshire coal faces on which mechanical coalcutters were installed, with conveyor belts employed to move the coal away. Although well laid out, this arrangement was not ideal in the wet conditions and uncertain geology of Broom. As indicated in figure 19, cogs of timber were used to support old workings far more than waste, and this was hardly sufficient in a mine where the roof was sometimes unstable. Working below ground in Broom could be alarming if the roof "took a set", and settled more heavily on the pit timber.[77] The fact that this sometimes happened points to the difficulty experienced in trying to control the roof when supported by timber. Although always unpleasant for the miner, such accidents were only really frightening for the inexperienced. In the end geological and water problems vitiated the best intentions of the mine owners, and Broom like Kilgetty, closed early in 1939.

Loveston colliery closed earlier, as a result of the traumatic disaster of 26 May 1936, when colliers broke into old uncharted workings, causing their own mine to be inundated with the loss of seven lives. Although the deaths were the subject of an inquest, there was never a formal public enquiry into the accident, but simply a report from the Mines Inspectorate stressing the hazards of mining near old workings. As it is doubtful whether Loveston had ever been visited by an inspector it is thought that the disaster caused considerable concern and heart searching within the Inspectorate. At all events by 1937 the Pembrokeshire Precautions against Inrushes Committee had been formed within the Swansea area, and it took a long hard look at all mining activity then in operation or in contemplation. It is believed that the Committee's demand for sensible precautions was a major factor in the sudden cessation of mining at Broom and Kilgetty in 1939. There was certainly a genuine hazard at Broom, in the form of the flooded New Hayes shaft nearby. In the absence of accurate plans no one could say how far to the west it was safe to work from Broom, and if the pumps were stopped it became possible to see the water level rising within a matter of minutes. Even so, the Committee remained in being until the early 1950's, but once work had stopped on coal exploration at East Hook in 1951 (ironically very close to the waters of the Western Cleddau) there was no more for it to do. It is believed that their papers relating to the Loveston disaster, and their subsequent deliberations, were destroyed in a cull of old documents in the late 1960's.

Underground haulage

The later chapter dealing with Health and Safety will make mention of the conditions experienced by the young people who acted as hauliers underground in 1841, the year of R. H. Franks' visit to Pembrokeshire on behalf of the Children's Employment Commission. In the years after that Commission's report improvements were made in underground haulage. Mainways were enlarged, tramways relaid, and steel trams introduced. By the 1870's horses or ponies were employed in some pits, having an iron bar attachment to the tram known as a "shaft and gun", assisting braking, and so preventing the tram colliding with the pony on a downward slope. These animals were normally stabled below ground, where they were supervised by an experienced ostler. He would ensure that they were fed and watered and well treated. The stables were built in brick, and limewashed to discourage any bugs or insects which might spread infection to the horses or ponies. If an animal suffered any injury or sickness a vet would be called to treat it. On one occasion a pony was purchased for work at Bonvilles Court colliery without anyone observing that it was in foal. In due course the vet was called to check its condition, and the foal was eventually born underground – an occurrence C. R. Vickerman believed might well have been unique. [78] By 1900 there was stabling for ten horses at Bonvilles Court, although at that date they were being used by just three horses, one pony and one donkey.[79] At the same period the stables for ten horses at Grove colliery were not in use, but stables and pit ponies were being employed at Hook colliery. In about 1935 an unexpected flood in the workings of the Margaret pit at Hook caused nine ponies to be drowned in their stalls.

By then machinery was being employed for underground haulage in some of the larger

Pembrokeshire collieries. David Parsell's compressed air locomotive for underground work was not a great success; it is believed to have been tried out on the underground tramway at Moreton colliery.[80] Stationary haulage engines working with cables or wire ropes seem to have been much more useful. The largest was probably the 14-inch haulage engine installed below ground in the engine slant for the K pit, at Bonvilles Court, in the 1880's. It was equipped with 1200 yards of steel wire rope, with sheave wheels and guides, and worked until the colliery closed in 1930.[81] Appendix D provides a detailed account of the plant and equipment employed by the Bonvilles Court Coal Company in 1900. Appendix E provides particulars of equipment for sale at Hook colliery in the same year. In this case, though, the list is not comprehensive, but simply a statement of plant and equipment included in the sale.

Coal Preparation

For centuries the only important distinction made by the coal industry for the customer was the distinction between coal and culm. The idea that these commodities might require further grading or preparation for the consumer (apart from the removal of rubbish) did not enter the thinking of anyone in Pembrokeshire before the nineteenth century. According to Angela John primary riddling or sieving of coal underground was a task undertaken by women. There was then a secondary riddling process at the surface, which at the time of the Children's Employment Commission was carried out using hand riddles, or a large stationary riddle. Later in the century, females were restricted to surface work, and at Lower Level colliery, Kilgetty, their tasks included moving trams and tipping their contents down to the screens, and also sorting stone and spoil from coal at the screens. Typically there might be ten women so employed "picking as quick as lightning".[82] By 1900, however, Bonvilles Court colliery was equipped with "revolving and shake screens at the pits mouth for separating the coal from the nuts, peas and small culm", whilst Kilgetty colliery had screens for separating coal and culm, and "one revolving screen elevator and travelling belt for the manufacture of nut coal".[83]

When work was under way to reconstruct and modernise Freystrop Colliery in 1903, the *Pembrokeshire Herald* reported that the coal raised would be screened into five sizes or qualities - duff, fine culm, peas, nuts and large. The first two categories were deemed self explanantory, although there was mention of a proposal to use small coal to make smokeless fuel "briquettes" at Freystrop. The report continued:

> The peas are used largely for boiler and steam producing purposes, and for burning in American stoves and ranges. There is a large demand for it. The nuts are chiefly used for horticultural purposes and for Dawson gas engines, whilst the special purpose of the large coal is for malting. Large quantities are sent away regularly to the Midlands and to Ireland for this purpose.[84]

Although anthracite coal was a high value product, in the twentieth century customer expectations continued to rise, and by the 1930's the market was extremely demanding. Thorough screening became an essential requirement. French buyers, in particular, were quick to object if they found any stone in the coal. Recognising the need for improvements the Hook Colliery Company installed new screens and a washery near the Margaret pithead in 1932. Although by then the Bonvilles Court Colliery was closed, the screens and a washing facility were retained in working order, and enhanced, in anticipation of the reopening of Broom Colliery. Coal washing also took place at the Kilgetty Colliery, where a Blacket barrel was installed when the mine was renovated in 1936. The barrel was a simple but quite effective means of separating stone from coal, because when rotated at slow speed the stone would lodge in the barrel's internal spiral, and be pushed out at the top, whilst the coal (having a lower specific gravity) was cleaned and washed through. Although no details have survived of the equipment then available at Bonvilles Court, it is likely to have included another Blacket barrel.[85]

[1] Information given to the writer in 1984 by a former collier, Owen Gwyther (1912-1986), a resident of Broadmoor.

[2] Flinn, *The History of the British Coal Industry*, Vol.2, 71.

[3] N.L.W., Owen & Colby MS 1138.

[4] *Children's Employment Commission Report, 1842*, Part 2, 576, Evidence of Anne Thomas to R. H. Franks.

[5] N.L.W., Lucas MS 736: Letter from George Taylor to Sir John Pakington Bt. MP. dated 18 July 1849.

[6] Flinn, *The History of the British Coal Industry*, Vol.2, 75.

[7] Information given to the writer in 1987 by David Jenkins of Hook, whose family worked in the coal industry at Hook for many generations.

[8] Flinn, *The History of the British Coal Industry*, Vol. 2, 76. According to the *Haverfordwest and Milford Haven Telegraph* of 25 December 1912, the Wigan Colliery Co. intended boring for coal to a depth of 4,000 feet at Johnston. This ambitious idea was soon forgotten!

[9] The practice of tallating was described to the writer in 1989 by a former collier, Ivor Howell of Kilgetty. A tallated shaft at Woolson's pit, Wiseman's Bridge, collapsed unexpectedly in 1987. For many years the site had been used as a caravan park. In the 1990's it was largely overgrown.

[10] T. W. Harcourt Roberts, *Historical Survey of the Pembrokeshire Coalfield*.

[11] Strahan and others, *The Geology of the South Wales Coalfield*, Part IX, 174, 175.

[12] Vickerman papers (privately owned), Messrs Lewis & Biddlers' report, 1 February 1873.

[13] C. R. Vickerman acquired the Moreton estate in 1872, so became one of several landlords to the Moreton colliery. After closure in 1887 the lease was given to him, and the deep shaft of over 150 fathoms seems to have been retained intact until 1901. In 1900 it was said to be equipped with a nearly new double winding engine. Memorandum on Bonvilles Court Coal Co., 26 November 1900.

[14] Pembrokeshire Record Office, DX/143: Report on Landshipping Estate by J. Foster Brown.

[15] *Pembrokeshire Herald*, 23 October 1903.

[16] The development of Hook Pill pit, otherwise known as "Boggy", is mentioned in the *Pembrokeshire Herald*, 20 August 1903. Unfortunately the local nickname for the pit proved to be entirely justified as it was stopped by water problems within a few years.

[17] When the Margaret Pit was opened it had another shaft 200 yards away to the north-east as an upcast, or air shaft. This second shaft is thought to have been an existing shaft enlarged and repaired. After the opening of the West Drift at Hook, the Margaret was closed and in due course filled in.

[18] P.F. Claughton, *Combe Martin: The History and Archaeology of SilverLead Mining* (Unpublished paper, 1996).

[19] Pembrokeshire Record Office, D/POW/H/61.

[20] N.L.W., Lucas MS 3805.

[21] N.L.W., Owen & Colby MS 2219.

[22] *Pembrokeshire Herald*, 31 July 1854.

[23] Account given to the writer in 1978 by the late W. Phillips of Wisemans Bridge, one of the colliers who had undertaken the task. The Merrixton adit is thought to have been the longest in Pembrokeshire.

[24] Diary of Dr. Charles Collins, 1806 carried in the *Narberth Weekly News*, May 1934; also referred to by T. R. Perkins "The Saundersfoot Railway", in *The Locomotive*, 15 September 1934.

[25] N.L.W., Picton Castle MS 4084/5.

[26] N.L.W., Picton Castle MS 4096. An account book for May to November 1809, held at Picton Castle refers to payments made to John Callen "for one half of the water engines at Merrixton Bottom". I am indebted to Thomas Lloyd of Cresselly for this reference.

[27] Pembrokeshire Record Office, S.R. & H. Co. Minutes, 3 June 1839.

[28] N.L.W., Gogerddan uncatalogued papers: J. Woolstenhulme's report on the Moreton colliery, 30 September 1778.

[29] N.L.W. Gogerddan uncatalogued papers, box 29: Letter from Owen Thomas to Edward Lovedon regarding the condition of his Moreton Colliery, 8 February 1809.

[30] *Children's Employment Commission Report*, 1842, Part 2, Evidence of Lewis Wilson, 572: Evidence of Samuel Singleton, 575.

31 I am grateful to Hermas Nicholas, retired deputy Chief Inspector of Mines, for this helpful observation.

32 P.R.O., POWE 7/1.

33 *Children's Employment Commission Report*, 1842. Part 2, 572. Lewis Wilson of Broadmoor colliery said that at his colliery a fan was occasionally employed. By implication it was of little worth.

34 H. F. Mackworth, Evidence to Select Committee on Coal Mines, 1852, paras. 444-483.

35 South Wales Institute of Engineers, *Transactions*, Vol. V, p203. The Waddle fan survived the abandonment of Bonvilles Court colliery and remained in position until 1991. In that year the Fan pithead was reduced in height for safety reasons, and unaware of the history involved, the workmen allowed the fan to drop into the flooded shaft.

36 *Pembrokeshire Herald*, 31 July 1854, and H.F. Mackworth's evidence as in footnote 34 above, para. 509.

37 P.R.O., POWE 7/4. According to J. H. Morris and L. J. Williams, *The South Wales Coal Industry, 1841-1875*, 54, the influence of the Mines Inspectors "revealed its results most clearly in the improving efficiency of ventilation where, even before the inspectors had the power to compel compliance, managers had every incentive to act on good advice when it was proffered".

38 P.R.O., POWE 7/4.

39 P.R.O., POWE 7/7.

40 P.R.O., POWE 7/27.

41 Information given to the writer in 1984 by the late Owen Gwyther of Broadmoor, a collier who had worked at Broom, Loveston and Hook.

42 Information given to the writer in 1985 by the late Osborne Evans of Kilgetty who had been employed at Bonvilles Court colliery.

43 Beckett, *Coal and Tobacco*, 171, 172. Carlisle Spedding was Sir John Lowther's colliery steward at Whitehaven.

44 *Mining Journal*, July and August 1864.

45 P.R.O., POWE 7/49.

46 Letter to the writer from Owen Gwyther of Broadmoor, dated 23 November 1983. In the same letter he described the Timber Vein single stall working and only ventilated with compressed air.

47 W. Linnard, *Welsh Woods and Forests* (Cardiff: National Museum of Wales, 1982), 95.

48 I am indebted to Hermas Nicholas, former Deputy Chief Inspector of Mines, for this advice. There is a local tradition, which cannot be proved, that this type of timber "collar" was invented in Pembrokeshire.

49 R. Keen, *Coalface* (Cardiff: National Museum of Wales, 1982), 12, includes the reminiscence of W. E. Bowen of Hook as regards coal cutting and timbering.

50 I am grateful to Miss Betty Phillips of Hook for this reminiscence. According to a disbursement account for Cardmakers' Pool colliery, Freystrop, now held at Picton Castle, in May and June 1788, payments were made for "burdens of boughs" at 1d. each. I am indebted to Thomas Lloyd of Cresselly for this reference.

51 G. Dyfnnallt Owen, *Wales in the Reign of James I* (Woodbridge, Suffolk: Boydell Press, 1988), 178.

52 Linnard, *Welsh Woods and Forests*, 96.

53 N.L.W., Slebech, 441; M. C. S. Evans, 'The Pioneers of the Carmarthenshire Iron Industry', *Carmarthenshire Historian*, IV (1967).

54 N.L.W., Slebech MSS 3403, 3409.

55 Linnard, *Welsh Woods and Forests*, 96.

56 I am indebted to David Jenkins of Hook for this information. His father was a collier at Hook at the relevant time.

57 T. Boyns, "Work and Death in the South Wales Coalfield 1874-1914", *Welsh History Review*, Volume 12, No 4, 514.

58 P.R.O., COA/38/817. This file reveals that at the time of closure of the West Drift at Hook, the main intake had concrete arching for 70 yards and 9 foot steel arches for 440 yards. There were also substantial lengths of steel arching in both the intake and return roads serving the workings in the Tumbling Vein. The first use of steel props in the anthracite coal industry is believed to have been at Pantyffynnon colliery, Carmarthenshire.

59 I am grateful to Hermas Nicholas for his advice on the method of timbering adopted at this period for the longwall conveyor, as illustrated in Figure 19.

60 A drawing, believed to be of this waterwheel, by the Tenby artist Charles Norris, is owned by Cardiff Free Library.

61 N.L.W., Gogerddan uncatalogued papers: Letter of H. Jeffreys, dated 29 March 1807.

62 Accounts of William Evans to Lord Milford, Michaelmas 1810, Lady Day, 1811, held at Picton Castle. I am grateful to Thomas Lloyd of Cresselly for this reference.

[63] *The Cambrian*, 4 April 1840. For a least a century the steady but relentless thud of those steam pumping engines was a familiar, if tedious sound for coalfield residents.

[64] *Haverfordwest and Milford Haven Telegraph*, 6 August 1866.

[65] P.R.O., POWE 7/50 records that in 1914, there was no electricity in any of the Pembrokeshire mines.

[66] P.R.O., COA/38/817.

[67] I am grateful to Hermas Nicholas for clarifying my understanding of these matters.

[68] I am indebted especially to Ivor Howell of Kilgetty who died in July 2002, aged 90, and also to the late Osborne Evans of Kilgetty, the late Howard Prout of Sardis, near Wiseman's Bridge, and the late Owen Gwyther.

[69] I am indebted to Hermas Nicholas for his expert guidance on the matter of longwall working.

[70] I am indebted to three former colliers, now deceased, namely Ivor Howell of Kilgetty, William James of Kilgetty and Howard Prout of Wiseman's Bridge for this information.

[71] P.R.O., POWE 7/1.

[72] P.R.O., HO 87/53.

[73] J. H. Morris and L. J. Williams, *The South Wales Coal Industry, 1841-1875*, 60.

[74] P.R.O., POWE 7/4.

[75] P.R.O., POWE 7/17.

[76] I am indebted to Hermas Nicholas for his guidance on the interpretation of the surviving underground plans for these collieries.

[77] The information relating to Loveston and Broom collieries was given to the writer by the late Owen Gwyther of Broadmoor.

[78] J. Harry, *Living and Working in the Pembrokeshire Coalfield* (Dyfed County Council Education Dept., 1990), 35, it was unusual for mares to be employed underground.

[79] Price, *Industrial Saundersfoot*, Appendix 2, 218.

[80] Patent No.1596/1873.

[81] Price, *Industrial Saundersfoot*, 219.

[82] Angela V. John, *By the Sweat of Their Brow: Women Workers in Victorian Coal Mines* (London: Croom Helm, 1980), 80, 85. A footnote to the text attributes the comment relating to Lower Level to the oral testimony of Martha Jane Richards who was interviewed in 1970.

[83] Price, *Industrial Saundersfoot*, 217, 219.

[84] *Pembrokeshire Herald*, 23 October 1903.

[85] I am grateful to Hermas Nicholas for this information. His father, a well known mining engineer, was one of several advisers to the Kilgetty Anthracite Colliery Co. at the time of its renovation.

C. R. Vickerman   Mrs D. Evans

Labour and
Labour Relations

5

Following George Owen's fascinating account of the organisation and activity of Elizabethan coal miners in Pembrokeshire, very little is recorded relating to colliery labour in the ensuing one hundred and fifty years. Even the admirable Owen does not tell us of the precise relationship between landlord and labourers; it is not clear if the groups of sixteen or seventeen people engaged in the coal pits of this period were employed as workmen to a contractor, or whether instead they had some form of partnership stake in the enterprise. A. H. John was quite confident that in Pembrokeshire contractors were employed to win coal.[1] He pointed out that:

> the contractors undertook to raise a stipulated amount each day, week or month, at a fixed price, and to deliver the coal to the wharfs. Although this contract was not so common on the anthracite coals as in the hinterland of Newport it is evident that it existed on all parts of the coalfield ... In Pembrokeshire, for example, the Redwall colliery was let by task in 1788, when "ale was provided for the bidders,"[2] and almost sixty years later the Kilgetty collieries were sub let to four men who hired colliers to cut coal at $6^{1}/_{2}$d. per square yard.[3]

The use of contractors was by no means universal. There is evidence that in 1737 a partnership of six yeomen took a lease of the colliery at Jeffreston Mountain Park, between Jeffreston and Cresswell Quay.[4] Fifty years later the numerous pits comprising the Cresswell colliery were let to various partnerships of businessmen, amongst whom there may have been one or two whose involvement was merely financial.[5] Such an arrangement had two main advantages. First it enabled men of skill, but no great prosperity, to contemplate the possibility of raising capital for development. Secondly, it spread the risk, and made it more likely that together the partners could cover their commitments in times of financial hardship. As noted in a previous chapter, however, a few large coal proprietors preferred to work their coal on their own account, apparently dispensing with both contractors and partners. In 1807 the very capable Thomas George was asked to report to the landowner, Edward Loveden, on the prospects for a new pit at Moreton, near Saundersfoot. In his report he offered an illustration of the financial implications:

> If every single company was made up of two men, two women and two boys, their yearly pay, at least would be £70. Timber, candles, iron rope, powder etc. would be little less than £50, say £30, added to £70 makes £100. Six such companies would expend yearly £600, consequently they must sell goods worth £900 at the Pits Mouth...[6]

Such a statement says much about the state of mining at Moreton. Here, early in the nineteenth century, when most coalfields had already adopted steam power and other innovations of the Industrial Revolution, the leading coal surveyor in West Wales is suggesting that a landowner might employ a few small companies, hardly larger than families, to work his pits, probably on a contract basis. This could almost be described as cottage industry coal mining, and yet it was by no means the last instance to occur in the county. Even so, as the Moreton case demonstrates, such an arrangement could never be financially profitable to the labourers, let alone give them much chance to protest about their lot. Indeed, Brian Lewis rightly pointed out how such small sub-contracting companies impeded the formation of trade unions. He wrote of these workers:

> Many were not wage labourers in the strict sense, but sub-contractors or partners in "butty" gangs. This meant that until the middle of the century, when mines grew into major industrial

units, the struggle of employee and employed was not in clear perspective. Rugged individualism survived long after other workers had sought strength in collective action.[7]

By this period the coal industry gave employment to a substantial number of people, although it is not possible to assess the precise size of the work force. If essential and ancilliary occupations are included - like blacksmiths, carters and lightermen - the total might be about one thousand. Small pits could be found right across the coalfield, but, by definition, they were undertakings with only a few workers. Other collieries had sizeable payrolls. In 1777, Moreton colliery employed thirty-eight people, eight of whom were women. They received just 4d. per day, while the men were paid 8d. or 9d. per day. The same year the Begelly colliery had a labour force of seventy-seven, including thirteen women and a number of boys. They were being paid 3d. or 4d. per day, just half the amount being paid to the men.[8] Later, in 1840, a hundred were employed at the Begelly colliery. The accounts for Hook colliery for the year 1785-86 indicate that eighty-one people were engaged in mining operations, twenty-seven being female.[9] Here the women may have considered themselves fortunate to have been paid 6d. per day; men were paid 8d. or 9d. per day, all payments being made fortnightly. A number of other workmen were employed to sink shafts, drive levels and repair equipment.[10] Output figures suggest that at this period the Landshipping colliery was one of the largest, if not the largest in Pembrokeshire, although the exact number employed is not known. We shall see that in 1841 this colliery provided work for 163 people.[11] Similarly the extensive complex of pits at Cresswell and and Jeffreston (quite apart from those in neighbouring parishes) undoubtedly gave work to a great many.

The rates of pay down to the 1780's cited above were very low. To some extent an improvement came in the next twenty years, so that by 1806 the usual pay for a man was one shilling each day, while women earned between 6d. and 8d. for winding coal at windlasses, or by working on coal banks, or by loading carts.[12] Rates were still very low, however, and John Curr, a notable Yorkshire mining engineer who visited Pembrokeshire at this time expressed astonishment at the low earnings. In his home area men might be paid anything from 2s. 6d. to 4s. each day.[13]

In Pembrokeshire, where so many lived in abject poverty, there was understandable concern over food prices. When prices reached very high levels rioting broke out in Pembrokeshire as elsewhere, colliers and other industrial workers playing a prominent part. The 1790's saw several years of poor harvests and acute food shortages. It seems that some large farmers were tempted to exploit these circumstances by withdrawing grain, thereby exacerbating the scarcity and increasing the price. Even worse, some corn dealers continued to export grain in spite of the shortage. On 18 August 1795, the angry miners of Hook gathered together to march to Haverfordwest. On their arrival fighting broke out in Quay Street, causing such alarm that the Riot Act was read, and the men were obliged to withdraw.[14] Even so, as the weeks went by many thoughtful middle and upper-class people expressed their sympathy for the lower orders, and attributed their plight to the actions of profiteering farmers. By 1796, John Campbell of Stackpole, later Lord Cawdor, was deemed to be another villain of the piece for his preference for high prices, but there was no quick conclusion to the problem.[15]

Although the shortages eased for a while, in 1800 there was serious scarcity again, and further discontent. James Thomas, the agent for the Orielton estate at Haverfordwest, wrote to Colonel Colby, then trustee of the estate during the minority of Sir Hugh Owen, reporting on a meeting held to raise subscriptions for the relief of the poor. He advised Colonel Colby that he had pledged £50 on behalf of Sir Hugh, and added: "I hope you will not object to it, as a consequence thereof the Landshipping colliers will be relieved from an absolute state of starvation which is the general state of the lower class of people in this country."[16] There was self interest as well as humanity in their decision, because Thomas had noted that several inhabitants of Haverfordwest had "received anonymous letters declaring that unless some immediate means were adopted for the relief of the poor, that they were determined to relieve themselves". Recent cases of criminal damage at Merlin's Bridge were taken to be a sign of such intent. Three days later Colby received a letter from a correspondent in Pembroke making the interesting point that the poor of that district were not in distress because their subscription had been set up in good time. Nevertheless this writer applauded the subscription at Haverfordwest because he realised "the other part of the county has been suffering want in the extreme".[17]

The relationship between farming and coal mining in Pembrokeshire was always close, notwithstanding the damage done to agricultural land by mining.[18] Landlords' agents usually took a keen interest in both topics. Hugh Wilson, the agent to J. Harcourt Powell at Cresswell Quay, wrote to his employer in February 1815, to express concern over the difficulty he encountered in collecting rents and the sums owed for culm.[19] His reports often had as much to say about the state of agriculture as about the state of the coal industry.[20] In the nineteenth century some miners were fortunate to have the benefit of a small plot of land on which they might keep a cow or a pig; many augmented their meagre wages by helping out farmers at busy periods.

Humanitarian interest in conditions faced by the working classes grew during the early decades of the nineteenth century, and a number of measures were passed by parliament to ease their lot. The Factory Act of 1833 was intended to improve conditions in manufacturing, and with this legislation enacted, Lord Ashley (later the Earl of Shaftesbury) showed his concern about conditions in the coal mines, not least as regards the employment of children. In October 1840, the Children's Employment Commission was established with the coal industry as its first priority. The inspectors appointed to investigate began work with commendable speed, their brief being enlarged to enable them to notice the position of young persons in the industry (i.e. those aged between 13 and 18). They decided for themselves to consider also the circumstances relating to the employment of females.[21]

As already noted, Robert H. Franks was the inspector appointed to visit pits in South and West Wales including Pembrokeshire. He visited eight collieries in the county, and listed all those employed. What emerges clearly is the very small size of these separate and diverse undertakings. Several (Kilgetty, Begelly, Hean Castle and Landshipping) employed a significant proportion of youngsters; Begelly and Nolton gave work to relatively few females.

PERSONS EMPLOYED

NAME of MINE	OCCUPIERS	MALES			FEMALES		
		Adults	under 18	under 13	Adult	under 18	under 13
Kilgetty	Messrs Heptonstall & Co.	44	27	13	36	6	4
Begelly	Messrs Pocock & Child	50	21	12	10	7	-
Broad Moor	Messrs Wilson & Co	38	11	6	44	3	-
Hen Castle	Messrs Stokes & Co.	58	18	13	20	9	1
Thomas Chaple	Messrs Morgan Hughes & Co.	-	-	-	-	-	-
Landshipping	Colonel Owen	95	23	14	18	12	1
Hook	Messrs Harcourt & Co.	-	-	-	-	-	-
Nolton	Messrs Bowen, Whitton & Co.	24	14	3	4	-	-
		309	114	61	132	37	6

This list provides the only reference in the report to coal mining in Hook. It is known that new developments were in hand at Hook at this period and it seems probable that at the time of Franks' visit no mining was taking place. In the case of Thomas Chapel colliery it is likely that mining operations had been halted by accident or breakdown.[22]

Robert Franks soon discovered that in Pembrokeshire colliers' lives were often short and extremely hard. David Morgan, the manager of Broadmoor colliery, declared that most men were unable to work by the age of 55 or even 50. Thomas George Noote of Begelly described the assorted injuries and diseases suffered by the men, and maintained that these reduced average life expectancy to about forty years.

The ratio of women to men in the coalfield as represented in the table was higher than elsewhere in South Wales. Indeed, on the basis of the national figures contained in the Children's Employment Commission report, Angela John has claimed that the proportion of adult women then employed was higher than in any other area of Britain, although Scotland had a greater number of young girls.[23] The typical use of female labour was described by Richard Brough, manager of the Begelly colliery, as "working at windlasses below, wheeling and screening coals above". Ann David, aged 13, who worked at Begelly, hauled skips or tubs with her sister, moving about sixty loads in a shift. They put in eleven or twelve hours work each day, and were paid on piece rates. Hannah Bowen, aged 16, was a windlass woman, working an eight-or-nine-hour shift. She is recorded as saying that she could draw up four hundred loads weighing one and half hundredweight to four hundredweights each, although the period of times in which she achieved this is not stated. Other women were engaged in riddling, or sieving, another process which required considerable strength.[24]

If conditions for the adults and teenagers were grim, those for the youngsters were worse. The six Pembrokeshire collieries listed as having employees all had under thirteens on the pay roll, although no information was given about the boys at Nolton. In the case of Landshipping colliery, it was stated that children started work at the age of about eight and their main task was to look after the air doors. This was deemed to be light work, and so was frequently allocated to young children. At Broadmoor the mine owner Lewis Wilson said that children could begin work from the age of seven. Occasionally a child of six might be at work in a colliery. James Bowen, the surgeon, disliked such arrangements. He asserted that the practice of taking children into the mines at such an early age was bound to shorten their lives, and he proposed a lower age limit of twelve. Lewis Wilson, never one to favour great reform, argued instead that "a limitation of age would be a barrier to their being brought up to working habits".

Although colliery foremen and managers claimed that children worked no more than eight to ten hours per day, Franks discovered that many seldom worked less than twelve hours, and some fourteen or even fifteen hours each day. In all this time they had no regular meal breaks; children just had to eat their bread and cheese, and whatever else they had, as circumstances might permit. Many of the adults interviewed by Franks confirmed these facts, and acknowledged that they might work shorter hours than the children. A thirteen-year-old haulier at Kilgetty, William Absalom, pointed out to Franks that the "men go away when they please, as they do work by the job, but we must work whether we like it or not".[25] Sometimes this happened because children and young people were not allowed to finish until they had moved a certain quota of coal each day. The agent for the Kilgetty colliery, Richard Hare, observed that the mainways at Kilgetty were no more than three feet, or three foot six inches high, so that only young people could work in them. Whilst this did not say much for the colliery or its standards of maintenance, Hare plainly thought it a satisfactory explanation for children spending long hours in the dark, dank recesses of a claustrophobic mine. Indeed, he admitted that children were often underground longer than the usual eight to ten hours because a lot of time was lost in cutting away the heads and ends of rock in the workings to create more room. Lionel Brough, a mining engineer from Neath, told Franks that one of the coal veins required so much timber support that they couldn't keep mainways in a fit state for horses. As a result they were "so low and narrow that boys only can tram the coal from the hewers to the bottom of the pit".

R. H. Franks interviewed several children from the collieries in the Saundersfoot district and most had a significant point to make about their working conditions. For example, James Davies, aged eight, said:

I have been below one year and I earn 10d. a week which my father takes. I work with my brother, who is eleven, pushing trams. I have never been hurt, and I work longer than my father. I have been to Sunday school, but never to day school.

Benjamin Thomas, an eight-year-old boy at Broadmoor colliery, described the work as very hard, and added:

My father is dead and my mother winds below with my sister; they earn three shillings each week. My three brothers work below; they earn three shillings and sixpence. They all work at skip hauling ... the boys do not wear shoes in this pit.

R. H. Franks heard these comments and noted that Benjamin Thomas was a "very pitiful looking fellow".

Plainly colliers of all ages had ample reason to complain about their conditions, and without the prompting of Robert Franks it must be very doubtful if they would ever have been heard at all. The 1842 report shocked and disturbed many in Victorian society, but it did not have an immediate impact in Pembrokeshire. The law was changed, to be sure, prohibiting the employment below ground of boys under the age of ten, and of females of any age. Unfortunately, though, the Mines Act, 1842, lacked bite, because it made no provision for penalties, or for further inspections. Such was the lack of employment opportunities in Pembrokeshire, that impoverished families were quite ready to ignore the law, and even if mine managers and agents had a mind to try to enforce the law the fact that the actual mining was sometimes undertaken by sub-contractors made it harder to adopt effective controls and to apportion responsibility. Asserting that mineral agents might only visit a colliery once a month, Angela John has suggested that the law was being evaded in West and South Wales well into the 1850's.[26]

Many of the colliers Franks spoke to reported that they were paid in money, rather than in goods and services. The latter was an idea dating back at least to feudal times, and was sometimes seen as an effective way for an employer to exert control over his workforce. Payment in goods and services through a company store was known as the "truck" system, and although often used in the main South Wales coalfield, it does not appear to have been a serious issue in Pembrokeshire. Where large landowners directly employed the whole work force it was not difficult for them to exploit their position.[27]

Whilst the 1842 report emphasised working conditions, the colliers and their families were even more concerned about their wretchedly low wages. It might be supposed that the militancy of the Rebecca movement in West Wales would have stirred a much more forceful and demanding attitude amongst the miners, and certainly by 1857 there was a possibility of unrest. In that year the Pembrokeshire Iron and Coal Company's directors felt that:

In order to avoid the ruinous effects of Combinations and Strikes among the Miners and Colliers it was absolutely requisite to be always in possession of much larger stocks of materials than had at one time been considered necessary.[28]

Two years later, in May 1859, a period of depression compelled this company and the Bonvilles Court Coal Co. to dismiss a sizeable number of men, and to lower the wages of the rest. Already poorly paid, the men could not contemplate their families facing destitution. On 16 June 1859, they held a meeting at Kingsmoor Common, Begelly, and decided upon a disciplined march to Merrixton Bottom (Stepaside), Saundersfoot and Bonvilles Court. This demonstrated their difficulties, and enabled them to express their views to any other colliers they might meet. According to the *Pembrokeshire Herald,* those still at work were "gently reproved ... for clandestinely breaking the covenant they had all agreed to".[29] A week later another meeting was held on Kingsmoor Common, but J. M. Child, a coal owner who lived close by at Begelly House, was "too well acquainted with his men to expect a riot, and there was none".[30]

Twenty years after the Children's Employment Commission the collieries were careful not to employ children aged under 12, but the youngest were still started on the job of tending the air doors. Billy Howells began in this way, but soon moved on to tramming. Years later he recalled this work:

> From "tending the door" I went to be what is known in the coal pits as "small boy". It simply means this. In every stall two men would work together cutting the coal and from there two boys would tram the coal in little trams bringing out and emptying them into the big trams that were drawn by horses to the bottom of the pit from where they were brought to the top in carriages or cages. These two boys would consist of a "big boy" and a "little boy". The ages of the big boys would range from 15 to 20, and that of the little boys from 12 – 15. There would be several stalls joining one another and from each stall was a road leading out into a "heading". This was steep, and therefore the trams would be spragged – that is, sticks made for the purpose would be put in the spokes of as many of the wheels as it was necessary to stop them from going round... as a rule the whole four of the wheels would need spragging. At the bottom of these headings there was the "trip" where all the little trams were tripped, or emptied into the big ones.

Noting that the big boy would have to ensure all the work was done, Billy Howells expressed the opinion that "of all the positions held by a boy in a coal pit, that of small boy is by far the worst". At some length he described the punishments meted out by some big boys, and declared that the small boy would certainly know "more kicks than halfpences". Mercifully there were others who showed some care.[31]

In the 1860's there was an increasing trend for workmen and their families to emigrate in the hope of improving their lot. By 1865 the exodus from South Wales was assuming serious proportions, and causing growing concern. In 1866 *The Llanelly and County Guardian* offered an opinion, and although written from the perspective of the more industrialised part of Carmarthenshire, the comment would have been widely applicable.

> Last year a vast number of colliers and ironworkers with their wives and families emigrated from the mining districts of South Wales to America – in fact it was with difficulty many of the works could be kept fully and regularly going. At the beginning of the present Spring a similar movement pervaded the district ... and fears began to be entertained that the operation of the iron works and the collieries, more especially the latter, would again be seriously interfered with. Several letters however have lately been received from those who went out last year giving a most deplorable picture of the state of things in the United States, and warning those at home to stay where they were well off. This has had the effect of materially checking the emigration movement, and most of those making preparation to make their departure have changed their minds ... being at last convinced that a moderate rate of wages and regular employment are to be preferred to the uncertain result of emigration to the States.[32]

Given the content of this article, it may be wondered if it was entirely truthful; Welsh employers were clearly anxious not to lose any more of their workforce. Although the gradual decline of the coal industry in Pembrokeshire may have exacerbated the problem, there can be no doubt that emigration was a serious issue. According to the Census returns the number of colliers in the county dropped from 926 in 1851 to 853 in 1861 and to 646 in 1871. Even then the movement was not halted; records of the Primitive Methodist Pembroke Dock district showed that 25 of their members emigrated to America and elsewhere in the summer of 1871 as a consequence of "the Kingsmoor coalmasters ceasing to work their pits".[33] By 1881 the number of colliers in the county had fallen to just 477.[34] The issue of emigration will be considered further in chapter 10.

Occasional disputes and demonstrations appear to have been the pattern until the 1870's. In 1872 the newly formed Amalgamated Association of Miners, under the presidency of Thomas Halliday, won considerable benefits for members during a strike in Glamorgan. On 24 April 1873, 130 colliers gathered at the Miners' Arms, Begelly, and adopted unanimously the following resolution: "That having seen the good results arising from the Miners Union during the late strike in South Wales, the meeting feels it desirable that they should form a branch in connection with the same without delay."[35] This decision brought a new and wider kind of trade unionism to the Pembrokeshire coalfield, demonstrating that the men were aware of events on a larger stage. The formation of the union branch was timely, because conditions for the coal industry were deteriorating and wage rates were at risk. Indeed a year later the *Tenby Observer* tellingly noted that: "it is obvious that Pembrokeshire is pretty much a law unto itself as regards wages".[36] During May 1874, the Bonvilles Court Coal and Iron Company gave notice of a 10 per cent wage reduction. Not surprisingly there were meetings of the men on Kingsmoor Common, and at one such gathering it was decided to ask the company to allow the men to work for a fortnight at former pay rates. William Foley, on behalf of the management, agreed (in the words of the *Tenby Observer*) "with a kindness and forbearance that has distinguished all his dealings with the men".[37]

Thomas Halliday visited Saundersfoot a few days later and obtained a trivial concession, albeit this was insufficient to impress the men. On 16 June 1874 they went on strike, although after talks they agreed to return on 29 June to work for two weeks at a five per cent reduction in wages. During July the men tried to win acceptance of a "closed shop" policy from the employers, in return for an ongoing cut of five per cent.[38] In reality they were in no position to bargain, and when William Foley refused, they had to admit defeat and return to work anyway. This setback was less serious than the fact that during the dispute the furnaces at Kilgetty Ironworks had been blown out. Although done as an economy measure, it proved to be permanent, and so removed a significant source of employment and income from the district.

Unfortunately trading conditions did not improve, and in January 1875, most South-Wales coal owners sought to impose a 10 per cent wages cut, which soon led to a miners' strike. In Pembrokeshire it seems the employers did not press for the cut before March, and then when the men stopped work the *Haverfordwest & Milford Haven Telegraph* observed that they "seemed determined to follow the example of their brothers over the hills" in going on strike.[39] This may not have been fair comment, because a colliers' meeting held at Kingsmoor Common to consider the issue produced a majority of only seven in favour of strike action. Whilst local trade unionists were aware of events elsewhere in South Wales, the available reports indicate that they had many misgivings, not least because it was recognised that the men were unlikely to receive any relief.

In the main South Wales coalfield a settlement was reached at the end of May, whereby the men accepted a 12$\frac{1}{2}$ per cent cut in wages on the understanding that thereafter wages would be determined by a sliding scale linked to the selling price of coal, and monitored by a joint committee of employers and men. It took about a fortnight for the end of the strike to be acknowledged in Pembrokeshire, but on 16 June 1875 a newspaper report appeared relating to the Saundersfoot district:

> Following upon the resumption of work in the Glamorganshire coalfields, we are pleased…to notice the termination of the equally disastrous struggle between betwixt capital and labour which has so long existed at the Bonvilles Court and Grove Pit collieries. As a sure sign of work being about to commence the horses have today "Monday" been sent down into the pits: numbers of men have also once more commenced taking their tools in, but it will be some days before a general start can be made, as the pits are necessarily out of order, but not to any serious extent, and workmen are already attending to the requisite repairs. A general feeling of thankfulness is apparent throughout the district that the sufferings of scores of families will now terminate.[40]

Local press reports all indicate that effective union leadership was provided from outside Pembrokeshire, suggesting that union activity within it was still in its infancy. Accordingly it is not clear whether unionists were able to function to the extent possible elsewhere in South Wales. Up to 1860, for example, colliers had been obliged to accept the employer's verdict as to the weight of coal worked. Legislation was then passed permitting the men to elect check weighmen to verify the figures. Later Acts of Parliament strengthened this position, and also allowed the men to appoint their own union officials. In the words of Brian Lewis:

> It is true a checkweighman appointed by the men was not easily victimised. Fair and accurate weighing resulted, but with it came professionalism. The union leader became a full time official who was set apart from his followers because his job was different. The men who were appointed to this post usually had characteristics in common. They were sober, respected and businesslike, but because their livelihood depended on the pit remaining open, they were also under pressure to conform. In 1860 the law said that the checkweighman had to be appointed from among a colliery's employees, and, although management could not dismiss an official (so appointed) it was not compelled to reappoint him after a strike or lock-out.[41]

Checkweighmen, in brief, tended to counsel caution, and as union officials became increasingly immersed in matters of negotiation and procedure. In Pembrokeshire in the 1870's there were clearly local union officials, but as the press very rarely mentioned any by name it must be doubtful whether they exerted much influence upon their usually unsympathetic employers.

There can be little doubt that these protracted disputes created considerable difficulties for the employers as well as the employees, and it is not entirely clear whether the former in Pembrokeshire accepted the sliding scale principle as it applied in other parts of South Wales. In the summer of 1876 the reconstituted Bonvilles Court Coal Co. was in serious financial difficulties, and by September the management was pursuing the old and unwelcome ploy of imposing a wage cut- this time of 15 per cent. The men went on strike in October, until Thomas Halliday appeared on the scene to urge a return to work pending negotiations. Unfortunately his proposal to resolve the matter by arbitration was refused by the main proprietor, C. R. Vickerman, and, accordingly, the local press, which hitherto had shown most sympathy for the employers, now expressed more concern for the strikers and their families. Noting that rents and the cost of food had not been reduced, the *Haverfordwest and Milford Haven Telegraph* asserted that the wage cuts "have gone as far as they ought".[42] Before the end of the year the Bonvilles Court Company had effectively collapsed, and a new company – The Bonvilles Court Coal & Iron Co. (1876) Ltd. – had been formed to take over from it.[43] Unfortunately this concern was under-capitalised, and no more able to make the business profitable than its predecessor. In November 1877, it went into liquidation, although the liquidator managed to maintain some coal mining activity, presumably to benefit creditors and retain the value of the assets.[44]

The Bonvilles Court Coal & Iron Co. was not alone in its difficulties at this period. The Saundersfoot & Tenby Colliery Co., formed in 1875 to maintain mining at Moreton, Broadmoor and Jeffreston, went into liquidation in November 1878.[45] The Jeffreston Anthracite Coal Co. formed in 1876, appears to have been at a standstill by the same date,[46] and in the winter of 1878-79 the coal trade in the Saundersfoot district was in a deeply depressed state. In January 1879, most miners were put on short-time working, and by March mining families were suffering severely. C. R. Vickerman was well aware of their plight, and a newspaper report in March claimed that "notwithstanding the severity of the past winter, he had kept all his labourers fully employed". Whether the claim was entirely accurate may be debatable, but he did go on to propose that those workmen in need of relief be employed "in repairing and improving several very useful roads not chargeable to the parish". The idea met with widespread approval, and a small committee was formed to gather subscriptions to enable the plan to be put into effect. Fortunately the colliers were able to resume full time working at the end of April.[47] By now, though, the ranks of those seeking employment in the industry was thinning further. As noticed earlier, by 1881 the number of colliers in Pembrokeshire was half that of 1851.

The lot of the ordinary colliers was not comfortable. Plainly they faced much uncertainty over their employment in both the long and the short term and if many had not possessed a

patch of land, they and their families might well have starved. The benefit of these smallholdings was referred to by Messrs. Bidder and Lewis in a report for the Bonvilles Court company
in 1873, who pointed out that these enabled the men to keep their cow and pig:

> The influence is still felt, by the fact that ... Wages ... In this district are always and invariably
> quite 33 per cent or 50 per cent below the standard of other mining districts in South Wales.
> Sometimes they will leave and "go to the hills", as the phrase is, attracted by higher wages. But
> they mostly return from Merthyr, Aberdare, etc declaring that they are really no better off for
> the higher wages, but rather the reverse. The cost of lodging, and the increased cost of food more
> than counterbalancing the higher pay, added to the discomfort and inconvenience of separation
> from kith and kin.[48]

The painful realities of life as a collier in the 1880's are evident in the memoirs of James
Thain of Stepaside, reproduced in Appendix F. They provide a sharp contrast to the somewhat
impersonal reports produced by officials, or paid-for by coal owners. After some years Thain
emigrated to North America, but fortunately in old age he set down these recollections of his
experience as a young man working in the Kilgetty and Saundersfoot district some of which
now seem surprisingly rosy.

The appalling problems of the 1870's and 1880's were probably felt just as keenly west of
the Cleddau, but information about the smaller pits in this district at this time is slight.
Economic depression was by no means the only problem at Hook. By 1883 James Wilson,
proprietor of the colliery since the 1840's, had lost his grip. A letter from an anonymous
employee to the solicitors acting for the landlord, Mr. Harcourt Powell, paints an amazing
picture of the situation then prevailing at Hook:

> It appears that Mr. Wilson and especially Mrs Wilson, who is the colliery manager, now have
> made up in their own minds to stop Hook Colliery. Mr Wilson it appears is gone simple minded,
> and his wife is manager. They have noticed lots of people and lowered others, and only giving
> men with familys (sic) 1s.0d. or 2s.0d.per day...

The wage cuts aside, the position of Mrs. Wilson, as acting manager, was totally illegal. Not
only were women now barred from underground work, but the 1872 Coal Mines Act required
the appointment at each mine of a specified, qualified manager exercising personal daily
supervision. According to the evidently disaffected employee, the colliery foreman was a fool,
and Wilson had not gone underground in weeks. With more anger over the threat to the
colliery than to the obvious illegalities being perpetrated, the writer asked that Mr. Powell be
made aware of the problems, including the point that:

> Now they are ... Saying that the culm is under water and none to be got at but that is false. There
> is a pit he have stopped could land culm for two years without little expense and there is
> thousands and thousands of tons of culm that the colliers know of, and the best of prospects and
> thousands locked up by his mismanagement ... He will lock up a place of culm on purpose to
> spite the men and keep wages down. Some is thinking of shooting them if the Lord don't remove
> him shortly ...[49]

Given this extraordinary incompetence and lack of trust, there had to be change. It came in
January 1884, when the mine was sold to Messrs. Roberts and Canton who already had
interests in mining at Nolton and Newgale.[50] They were also in a position to make further
investment, and a new Hook Colliery Company was formed for the purpose. Whether this
proved profitable is open to question; the 1880's were a time of depressed prices and increasing
competition from other areas producing anthracite coal - most notably the Gwendraeth Valley
and Mynydd Mawr districts of Carmarthenshire. The small pits at Nolton and Little Haven
closed in or by the 1870's with only the Southwood colliery at Newgale lasting into the
1880's.[51] By then the Cardmakers' Pool colliery at Freystrop was also at a standstill. In the
Saundersfoot district the Moreton colliery closed in 1887, and after a brief revival the last pit

at Begelly was abandoned in the early 1890's.[52] Something of the effect of this period of depression may be seen in Figure 22, indicating the collieries and employees at work in 1891.

The sliding scale arrangement introduced in South Wales in 1875 was intended to protect workers from any arbitrary action taken by employers. In spite of some amendments to the sliding scale, it seems it tended to stifle effective union activity. If the full sliding scale ever operated in Pembrokeshire, it cannot be said to have been beneficial. In 1881 the average wage for a workman at Bonvilles Court was 1s.6d per day, whereas in 1873 it had been 2s. to 2s.6d. In 1873 miners at Bonvilles Court could earn as much as 3s.6d per day, but after the disastrous 1870's they did not recover such rates before the turn of the century.[53] A pay sheet from the Grove and Lower Level collieries at Kilgetty, dated March 1897, shows that engineers and boilersmiths were among the highest paid, the former receiving 2s.7d per day. A woman trammer at the same pits received a mere 1s. per day![54]

Given such a low wage rate, it is remarkable that even in the early 1880's one colliery company at least had half a dozen pensioners! The Hook colliery, so sadly mismanaged before 1884, granted pensions of 2s. per week to three retired labourers, and the widow of of the master of the colliery sloop. Two other widows received larger sums. One, Margaret Bowen, was granted no less than 5s. per week. Her husband, a foreman, had been killed in the New Aurora pit. Another, Mary Owens, had lost her husband in a gas explosion in the Commons pit. Her allowance was 2s. per week.[55]

Hook colliery was the setting for a new kind of industrial dispute in 1891. In 1890 miners at Hook had formed a branch of the National Labour Federation; gradually other miners were persuaded to join and then to create a fully unionised workforce. By 7 September 1891, the only man refusing to pay a union subscription was a certain Richard Davies. Tiring of this, the other men carried a resolution demanding his dismissal on pain of strike action. Somewhat to the surprise of the management who regarded the whole idea as "ridiculous", a strike ensued.[56] One or two members of the union showed a willingness to work, and they also incurred the hostility of the men, but again the management was unwilling to dismiss the men and hand power and prestige to the union. Such was the need for employment that the situation could not continue for long, and it appears that it was resolved when Davies and the others elected to leave the district. Even so, the union evidently remained in place at Hook, albeit without the approval of management. When the South Wales Miners' Federation was formed in 1898, the smallest branch represented on the Federation Council was that set up at Saundersfoot.[57] There was no branch at Hook, presumably because the men were already associated with the National Labour Federation. The desire of the Saundersfoot men to join a union may have been increased by their experience of a dispute in January 1894. In that month C. R. Vickerman gave colliers at the Kilgetty colliery two weeks' notice in a response to a demand for a 10 per cent-advance on their wages.[58] The Bonvilles Court men then made the same demand, but in reality they were in no position to succeed, because viewed from the employers' position these collieries were barely profitable anyway. Clearly, Saundersfoot was a lively place in the 1890's in so far as workers' militancy was concerned, agricultural labourers of the same district having agitated in Michaelmas 1891 for a 2s. a week wage rise, encouraged by visiting delegates from the newly formed Labourers' Federation in South East England.[59]

The formation of the South Wales Miners' Federation followed a long dispute over the revision of the 1875 sliding scale agreement determining mine-workers' wages. The main hope of the men was to win a guaranteed minimum wage, but ultimately they had to settle for a revised form of the sliding scale. In the case of anthracite collieries it was agreed that the percentage paid in wages would be 5 per cent less than that paid at other South Wales collieries, but on the other hand, the miners' one day monthly holiday – "Mabon's Day" – was retained in anthracite producing areas for several years.[60] Although Mabon's Day ended across most of South Wales in 1898, Mabon himself became president of the South Wales Miners' Federation which was founded because the dispute had exposed the miners' lack of effective organisation and funding.[61] Although a district union, by 1899 it had 104,000 members.

PEMBROKESHIRE - THE FORGOTTEN COALFIELD

Mode of Working, Lighting, and Number of Deaths from Accidents, and Number of Persons Injured for the year 1891

No.	Name of Mine	Name or Number of Pit, Slant, or Level	Name of Seam	Mode of Working — Long-wall (L.W.) Pillar & Stall (P.S.)	Mode of Lighting — Safety Lamps (S.L.) Naked Lights (N.L.)	Diameter or Dimensions and Depth of Downcast and Upcast Shafts: Downcast: Diameter or Dimensions in feet	Downcast: Depth in feet	Upcast: Diameter or Dimensions in feet	Upcast: Depth in feet	Particulars of Ventilation: Mode of Ventilation with Description	No. of Currents	Airways: Length of Splits (Yards)	Airways: Sectional Area (Square feet)	Average Total Quantity of Fresh Air per minute (Cubic feet)	Persons Employed: Underground (A.)	Above-Ground (B.)	Above-Ground (C.)	Gross Total (A.) (B.) (C.)	No. of Deaths from Accidents	No. of Persons Injured	No. of Days in which Coal or Iron-stone has been Drawn	REMARKS
											PEMBROKESHIRE											
374	Begelly	Meadow pit	Low vein	P.S.	N.L.	6	96	6	42		—	—	—	—	9	2	—	11	—	—	287	
375	Bonvilles Court	Bonvilles Court pit Upcast	Lower level vein Kilgetty vein	P.S. & L.W.	N.L. & S.L.	12¾ x 10 — —	522 — —	— 9 11	 360 204	Waddle fan. 15' dia	3	4,500 514 200	30 30 30	33,000	128	36	5	169	1	—	284	
376	Kilgetty	Lower level pit Upcast	Kilgetty vein	P.S. & L.W.	N.L.	9	500	12 x 5	630	Furnace 8' x 6'	2	2,000 1,862	30 30	6,300	104	53	6	163	—	—	289	
377	Hook	West Park pit Upcast	Timber vein	P.S.	S.L.	8½ x 7½	324	6 x 5½	264	Waddle fan	1	836	30	8,545	86	29	24	130	—	1	283	Working double shifts
378	Landshipping																					
379	Trefane Cliff	Slant	Four feet	P.S.	N.L.	—	—	—	—	Furnace	1	—	14	2,100	25	10	—	35	—	—	305	
380	Yerbeston	Slant		—	—	—	—	—	—	—	—	—	—	3,000	6	10	—	16	—	—	—	Re-opening

Source : Report of H.M. Inspector of Mines, 1891, P.R.O. POWE 7/27

JdeH 3114A

Figure 22

At the beginning of the twentieth century there were numerous district unions serving men employed in the British coal industry but by 1908 these local unions had become affiliated to the Miners' Federation of Great Britain. Founded in 1889, this body took over negotiations with both Government and the employers in respect of wages, hours of work, recruitment policy and the like. In South Wales the level of wages was generally lower than in most other coalfields, and so the chief concern of unionists was always to try to improve wage rates. In 1912 government proposals on a minimum wage were rejected by coal-owners in South Wales and Scotland, and between 26 February and 1 March over a million men came out on strike. This historic dispute was described by R. Page Arnot as being "of a magnitude that had never occurred in any single industry in any country of the world".[62] Naturally Pembrokeshire miners constituted only a tiny part of this vast movement, but according to one press report 350 Saundersfoot men "were among the first to leave work in the country".[63] Another newspaper noted that whilst the men wished to remain peaceful "as a precaution three extra constables had been drafted to Saundersfoot and one to Stepaside. The local people were indignant about the drafting of extra police into the district."[64]

At this period coal was such a vital commodity in economic life that the government of the day could not afford to relax and do nothing. On 29 March 1912, the Coal Mines (Minimum Wage) Act was passed ostensibly guaranteeing every collier a wage of 6s.6d per day. The reality was otherwise, primarily because some provision was made for regional variations. Only Bonvilles Court and Hook collieries were operative in Pembrokeshire, although development work had started on reopening Reynalton colliery. The proprietors of these mines were not members of the influential Monmouthshire and South Wales Coal Owners' Association, but in the face of this legislation appealed for their assistance and support. J. S. Roberts of the Hook Colliery Company set out his position for the benefit of the Joint District Board established under the Act. Of 139 men employed, none then earned more than 3s.4d per day, plus a fuel allowance worth $1\frac{1}{2}$d., and Roberts pointed out that "these rates are much lower than the rates paid in other parts of the coalfield, and it will therefore be necessary, as previously stated, that we shall apply for exemption from any award of the general minimum that the independent chairman may fix".[65]

Several surviving documents help to explain Roberts' stance. In one he refers to the colliery's isolated position, and the lack of any rail connection, mentioning also some of the severe geological problems faced at Hook. In another he says: "the seam worked at present produces culm only, so fine that there is scarcely sufficient grit in it for steaming the boilers". In the same paper he mentions that the company supplies the men with all their tools and free fuel for domestic use, and he assesses the rental for a house with a plot of land, $\frac{1}{2}$ to 1 acre, at £3 per annum. In a further note he observes (and reiterating the point we have seen made earlier) that "all our men keep livestock of some kind- poultry, pigs, a cow, and some of them two or three cows. And I find that Hook men working in Carmarthenshire and Glamorganshire collieries are always willing to return when they have an opportunity of getting employment here."[66] Similar arguments were presented by C. H. R. Vickerman, the proprietor of Bonvilles Court colliery, and both he and Roberts asserted with some justification that if the Glamorgan standard was applied in Pembrokeshire their collieries would probably close.[67] In the event Pembrokeshire was exempted from the standard established for other parts of South Wales, and Pembrokeshire miners continued to go to work for a sum nearly 50 per cent. below the official national minimum wage! That said, the minimum wages agreed for those working underground in Pembrokeshire was a significant improvement, even if the *Haverfordwest & Milford Haven Telegraph* misrepresented the miners' feelings when it declared that the award "had been received with great satisfaction".[68] In truth it was just another chapter in the long history of low wages, but given the precarious position of the Pembrokeshire collieries there was no more that the miners could do.

In World War 1 control of the coal industry was assumed by the government in the national interest. At the end of that exhausting conflict it was proposed by the Sankey Commission in

1919 that the coal mines should be taken into public ownership, and the men given higher wages. In 1921 however, the government returned the collieries to the coal owners, even though most of them lacked the means to improve wages or to invest in new technology. Many coal proprietors faced declining markets, both at home and abroad, and the general response was to impose sudden and severe wage cuts. It is debatable whether the marketing problems of anthracite coal producers were as serious as those in other sectors of the industry, but wage cuts were enforced in the same way. The consequence was a strike lasting from 1 April to 1 July 1921, which ended in another defeat for the miners. No doubt it was fortunate for them and their families that the dispute coincided with a warm spring and summer, but in Pembrokeshire many of the men sought to supplement their resources by working over old tips in search of discarded coal, or by digging between tides into coal seams exposed on beaches- as at Wiseman's Bridge, for example. Their hardship was severe, and their views on the coal owners' stance can be imagined. Even so, a collier had to be careful how he expressed himself; in 1921 a Begelly man employed at Bonvilles Court was overheard "speaking his mind", and was soon sacked![69]

Although there was a brief boom in the British coal industry in 1922 and 1923, trading conditions deteriorated thereafter. By 1925 the coal owners felt moved to seek another reduction in wages, and an increase in working hours. To stave off another dispute the government provided a temporary subsidy and set up a Royal Commission to review the industry, headed by Sir Herbert Samuel. The recommendations of the Royal Commission proved to be very sympathetic to the owners. Not only did it reject nationalisation and the continuance of subsidies, but they advocated a cut in wages and the possibility of extending the hours of work. The proposals incensed the Mineworkers' Federation, and were seen as a potential threat by the rest of the trade union movement. On 1 May 1926, the day after the coal subsidies ended, the strike began. On 4 May, many other unions came out in support of the miners, giving rise to the General Strike. A disagreement between the General Council of the Trades Union Congress and the Miners' Federation as to who was ultimately responsible for negotiating an end to the dispute caused the General Council to call off the action by other unions. The miners maintained their stoppage for six months, although in Pembrokeshire it received more solid support at Bonvilles Court than at Hook.[70]

Such a major dispute had implications for almost every part of the community. In addition to the obvious concerns about the welfare of the miners and their families, memories of the closure of Reynalton colliery in the wake of the strike of 1921 were enough to cause concern over the deteriorating state of the county's two surviving deep mines. Furthermore, as the miners were not being paid, there was an inevitable drop in the takings of local traders and retailers. The miners themselves were naturally desperate for some alternative income, especially if they had a family to support. Some managed to get seasonal work as agricultural labourers, but such employment tended to be brief. Many men went onto the beaches like those at Saundersfoot and Wiseman's Bridge to dig where thin coal seams had been exposed in the cliffs or above the sand. Even so, digging on the cliffs could be dangerous because of the risk of rock falls, and digging on the beach could be frustrating because it was only possible to get down six or seven feet between the tides. Others went to old spoil tips, and worked over them again trying to find any discarded fragments of culm to use or sell. A few might form a small team to sink a shallow pit in search of coal, as for example at Begelly in 1926, where three men dug coal in a small pit at Parsonage Lane. Another Begelly man used a "druke and beam" to raise culm from a small pit behind his house, and he sold the produce locally.[71] Other ventures were more successful. A trial pit dug by three men at Hook eventually became a shaft 100 feet deep. Locally this little pit was known as "Think, Spit and Consideration", each word in the name reflecting a notable characteristic or quality of one of the trio involved in working it.[72]

During the strike the miners' families suffered extreme hardship. At the beginning of June the Board of Guardians of the Narberth Union received applications for assistance, the first test case being that of Uriah Thomas of Amroth. He applied for relief for himself, his wife and four children, and assured the Board that he was getting no strike pay whatever. After much debate a majority favoured dealing with the case as if an application from a widow and four children.[73] Soon the St. Issell's and Begelly Relief Fund was established to provide for needy children at Stepaside, Begelly, Pentlepoir and Saundersfoot. Soup kitchens were set up, and by 9 July it was reported that 10,500 free meals had been provided at a cost slightly under 1³/₄d. per meal. Whilst the organising committee were thankful for the "fine response" to their appeal, funds were insufficient to extend the scope of their work.[74]

Earlier, on 18 June 1926, the *Pembrokeshire County Guardian* concentrated upon the needs of the many impoverished families west of the Cleddau by reporting that:

> Committees have been formed both at Hook and Freystrop to deal with the distress in those areas arising out of the coalmining dispute, and the efforts of these devoted workers must command the respect of all.... Farmers and others are contributing liberally in kind, and money contributions have been received. Under the auspices of the Pembrokeshire Education Committee soup kitchens have been set up for the children attending elementary schools at Hook and Freystrop, where between 30 and 40 children are given a midday meal of soup, with meat and potatoes, and tea after school...We are informed that the mayor of Haverfordwest has decided to open a fund on behalf of distressed families in the Hook colliery district.

Early in July it was learned that the miners' union agent was planning to visit Hook to persuade working miners to stop work until a national settlement was achieved. The police heard of this occasion, and, thinking that some sort of public order offence might be committed, sent what was described as "a car load of constables, including the deputy chief". The men at Hook considered themselves responsible citizens, and felt that this was not only an instance of over-policing, but in the words of one collier "an unwarrantable attack on the peaceful villagers, and thereby more likely to stir up strife than maintain peace". In the event there was no trouble. This was a reflection of the calm state of affairs of the Pembrokeshire coalfield as a whole; in contrast to the mining communities in south-east Wales and other areas of Britain, the Pembrokeshire colliers were moderate in their political stance and on the whole there was a remarkably low level of militancy and violence.[75]

Certainly in the Saundersfoot district there was little public discontent, and the difficult issues raised by the dispute seem to have been approached in a rather formal way. In particular, the problems of poverty were handled initially under the direction of the Narberth Board of Guardians rather than by ad hoc committees and appeals. According to the *Pembrokeshire County Guardian,* 2 July 1926, "the Relieving Officer acting on behalf of the Board agreed to a formidable list of applications for relief from the mining district, and he suggested that relief be given by way of loan. This was agreed to."

Notwithstanding the use of loans, before the end of July one or two voices were heard challenging the Board's policy. By giving relief "to men who refused to work", it was argued, "they were only encouraging vagrancy and encouraging people not to work". The chairman, Revd. J. O. Evans, then declared that "it was their duty to give relief to anyone who is in need".[76] The issue was deferred for a while, but it was raised again in late August when a motion proposing that relief be stopped was dismissed. It was reported that funds for the soup kitchens in the Saundersfoot district had already given out, so that if the relief offered by the Board was reduced the children would go hungry. The issue became increasingly contentious as the strike dragged on, and it seems that local committees grew in importance. It was noted that in the week ending 2 October the number of children's meals provided by the local committee for Begelly, Saundersfoot, Pentlepoir and Stepaside totalled 1,193.[77]

Eventually, in the middle of October, the strike was broken. *The Pembrokeshire County Guardian* for 22 October 1926, referring to developments at Bonvilles Court colliery, noted that:

> Following upon the fresh terms offered by Mr. Vickerman ... a mass meeting of colliers was held at Kilgetty on Tuesday evening. The local agent was present and the proceedings were very animated. A majority of 25 was recorded in favour of standing by the Federation, but there were

large numbers of neutrals...Since the meeting those who voted to resume have taken action and are signing on. Up to 6pm on Wednesday, eighty men had signed ... And it has been arranged that the pit ponies are to be taken down this morning.

As the so-called "new" conditions were similar to those in force at the start of the strike, subject to further review at the end of the year, it cannot be said that the miners won anything. As Pembrokeshire colliers were so poorly paid anyway, it can be claimed that for them, even more than the miners in other districts, the outcome of the strike of 1926 was a bitter experience. Indeed, for some it was a life-changing event, because they lost their jobs in the industry. At Hook colliery, for example, "forty to forty-five men were idle in consequence of other men filling their places."[78]

The miners were not the only losers in 1926, because the colliery companies were also damaged by this long dispute. In the case of Bonvilles Court it can be argued that whilst the effects were not fatal immediately, they contributed to the eventual downfall of an already ailing concern. In spite of some new investment at Bonvilles Court in 1927, the management could not find a way to turn a fundamentally marginal mining operation into even a modestly profitable business. Matters were made worse in the summer of 1929 when one of the several thin seams being mined became virtually unworkable. Output fell and the employers went back to the old tactic of proposing a 10 per-cent reduction in the men's wages.[79] This was rejected by a meeting of miners held at Kilgetty late in July, who also dismissed any suggestion of slackness on their part. It was pointed out that many of the underground stalls were so small as to make physical movement virtually impossible; in certain places, according to one press report, "men were unable to reverse an axe, this movement having to be carried out with the assistance of a "butty [colleague]".

On 8 August 1929, the *Pembrokeshire Telegraph* reported as follows:

> Last Saturday 110 miners employed at "K" pit, Bonvilles Court, ceased work in compliance with notices served by the management...Hopes are entertained that action will be taken in placing the local economic conditions before the responsible government department with a view to developing the anthracite industry of the neighbourhood. A number of steamers were in the Saundersfoot harbour last week, and large cargoes were shipped. The prospective closing down of Bonvilles Court colliery was no doubt responsible for this unusual activity.

Two weeks later the same paper noted that 250 were at work at the colliery, with 60 or 70 still idle as a result of "the failure to arrive at a settlement of the wages dispute". However the newspaper expressed the view that the trouble might only be temporary, and indeed a week later the paper was able to record that a settlement had been reached.[80]

Unfortunately this settlement could not remedy the basic facts about Bonvilles Court - that it had become an old and high-cost mine working thin and fractured seams. A mineral surveyor's report made it clear that there was no prospect of making useful extensions to the workings, and so by March, 1930 it was realised that the colliery would have to close. The last shift was worked on 17 April 1930, and although forty men were retained for some weeks to undertake dismantling operations, by June all 320 men were out of work. *The Pembrokeshire Telegraph* reflected the mood of the moment: "the district is overspread with painful anxieties, and among all sections of thoughtful people a belief in the necessity of immediate intervention gathers weight".[81] No intervention came. This closure was the single most severe closure in the decline of the Pembrokeshire coal industry, and some indication of that decline is given by Figures 23 to 32, which depict the location of different mines in operation between 1841 and 1951. Appendix G lists in tabular form the numbers of men employed at the different collieries in operation between 1891 and 1950.

Many years later Owen Gwyther of Broadmoor, who had worked at Bonvilles Court, described the situation faced by the miners and their families in 1930:

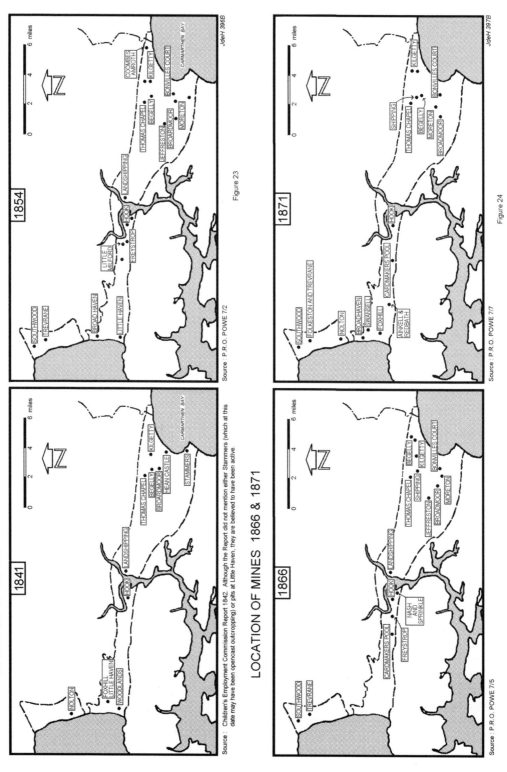

LOCATION OF MINES 1841 & 1854

1841

1854

CARMARTHEN BAY

Source : Children's Employment Commission Report 1842. Although the Report did not mention either Stammers (which at this date may have been opencast outcropping) or pits at Little Haven, they are believed to have been active.

Source : P.R.O. POWE 7/2   Figure 23

LOCATION OF MINES 1866 & 1871

1866

1871

Source : P.R.O. POWE 7/5

Source : P.R.O. POWE 7/7   Figure 24

- 94 -

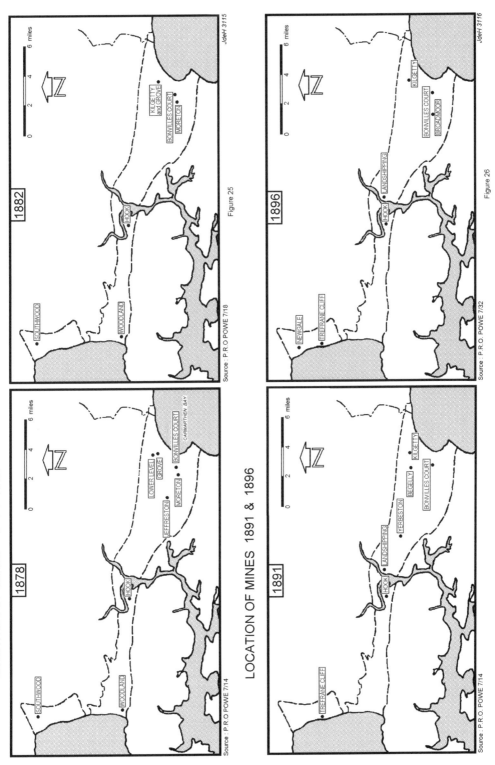

LOCATION OF MINES 1878 & 1882

LOCATION OF MINES 1891 & 1896

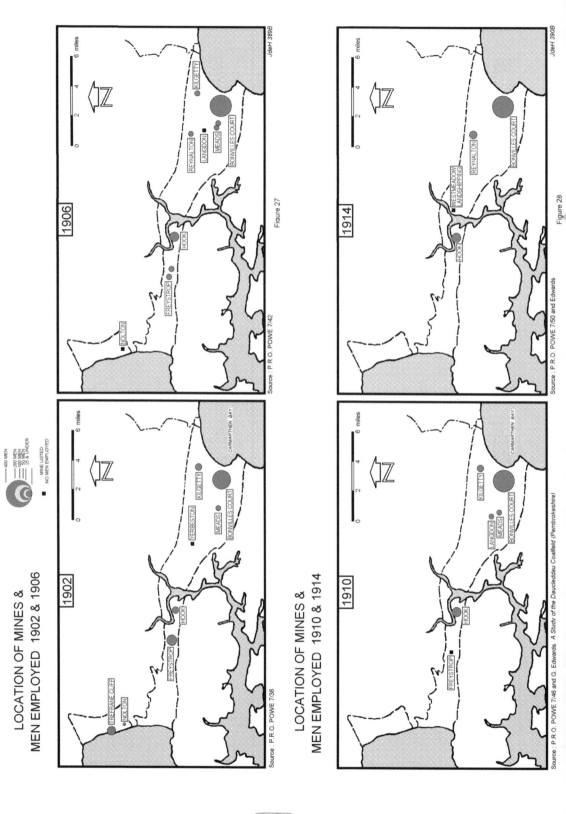

LOCATION OF MINES &
MEN EMPLOYED 1902 & 1906

Source : P.R.O. POWE 7/38

Figure 27

LOCATION OF MINES &
MEN EMPLOYED 1910 & 1914

Source : P.R.O. POWE 7/46 and G. Edwards A Study of the Daucleddau Coalfield (Pembrokeshire)

Figure 28

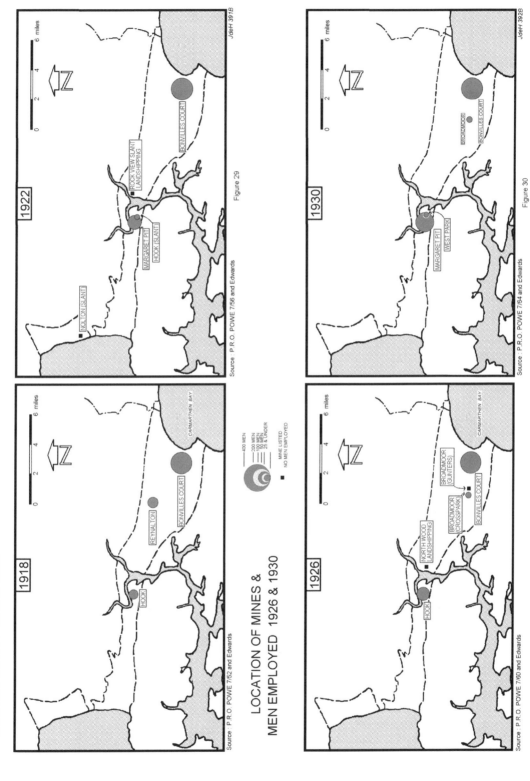

LOCATION OF MINES &
MEN EMPLOYED 1918 & 1922

1918

CARMARTHEN BAY

HOOK

REYNALTON

BONVILLES COURT

0 2 4 6 miles

N

Source : P.R.O. POWE 7/52 and Edwards

1922

KILGETTY (SLANT)

ROCK VIEW (SLANT)
LANDSHIPPING

MARGARET PIT
HOOK (SLANT)

BONVILLES COURT

0 2 4 6 miles

N

Source : P.R.O. POWE 7/56 and Edwards

Figure 29

JdeH 391B

LOCATION OF MINES &
MEN EMPLOYED 1926 & 1930

1926

NORTH WOOD
LANDSHIPPING

HOOK

BROADMOOR
(GUNTERS)

BROADMOOR
(CROSSPARK)

BONVILLES COURT

CARMARTHEN BAY

0 2 4 6 miles

N

400 MEN
200 MEN
100 MEN
25 & UNDER

MINE LISTED
NO MEN EMPLOYED

Source : P.R.O. POWE 7/60 and Edwards

1930

MARGARET PIT
WEST PARK

BROADMOOR

BONVILLES COURT

0 2 4 6 miles

N

Source : P.R.O. POWE 7/64 and Edwards

Figure 30

JdeH 392B

LOCATION OF MINES &
MEN EMPLOYED 1934 & 1938

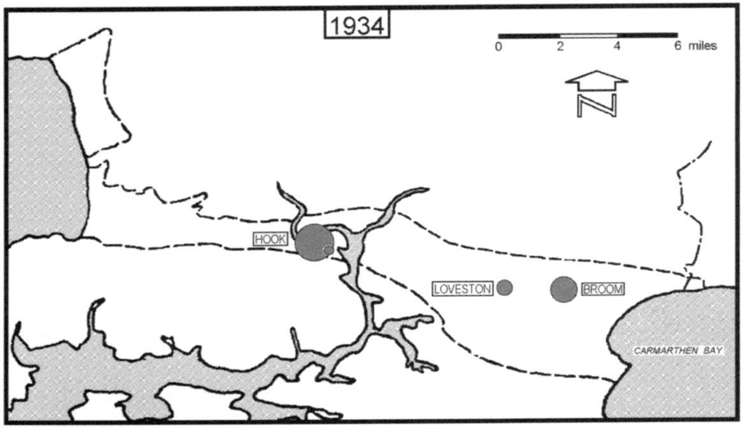

1934

LOVESTON
BROOM
HOOK

6 miles
N

CARMARTHEN BAY

Source : P.R.O. POWE 7/68 and Edwards

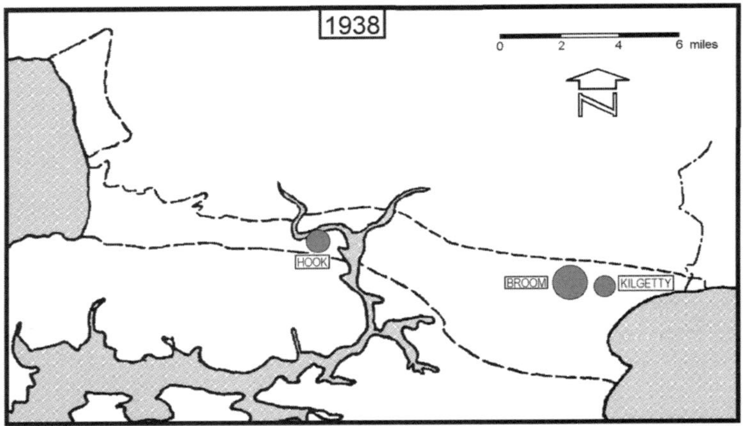

1938

HOOK
BROOM
KILGETTY

6 miles
N

Source : P.R.O. POWE 7/72 and Edwards

Figure 31

JdeH 393B

LOCATION OF MINES &
MEN EMPLOYED 1946 & 1950

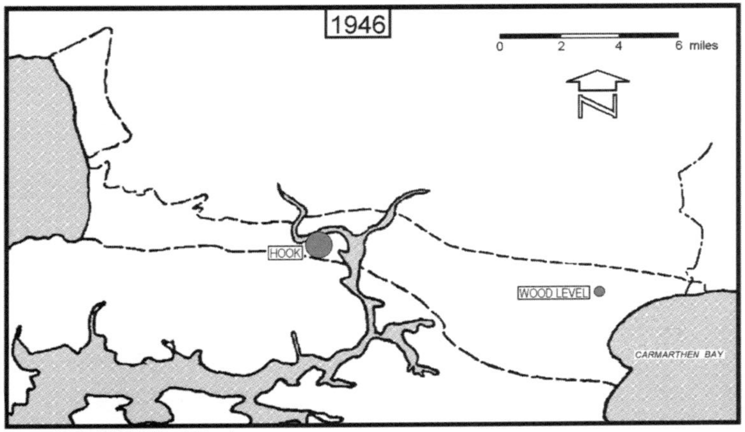

1946

HOOK
WOOD LEVEL

6 miles
N

CARMARTHEN BAY

Source : P.R.O. POWE 7/73 and Edwards

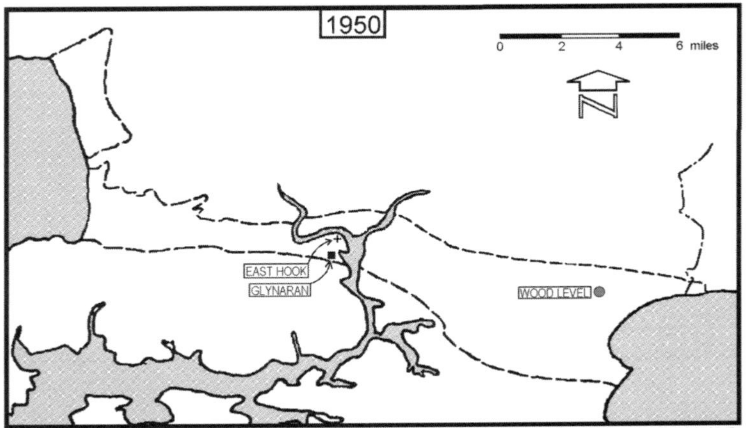

1950

EAST HOOK
GLYNARAN
WOOD LEVEL

6 miles
N

Source : P.R.O. POWE 7/76 and Edwards

Figure 32

JdeH 394B

Conditions of life at that time were very low and indeed if it had not been for the abundance of rabbits and the large gardens many people would have starved. Unemployment benefit was very low and to a lot of people, non-existent. If you were single and living with parents you very often had nothing. People were told to sell their belongings, pianos, gramophones, furniture etc. - anything that was considered to be the smallest luxury. It was at this time that a batch of men were selected to go to work in Hook Colliery. Wages at that time were labourers 25s. per week, whilst coal face workers were graded 1st and 2nd and were paid 35s. and 37s.6d. The men were expected to pay their own board and lodging and to keep their homes and families going in this area (ie Saundersfoot and Kilgetty). This was of course impossible and most men refused with the result that nearly all, including myself, were refused further benefit for six weeks.[82]

In fact Owen Gwyther and a sizeable number of other men from the Saundersfoot district did eventually work at Hook, even though the Hook Colliery Company had its own difficulties in the wake of the disputes of the 1920's. The sale of the mine to Watts, Watts & Co. of London brought a welcome infusion of fresh capital, and output increased as Hook won some of the business previously satisfied by Bonvilles Court. Although there was a brief slump in production in 1936, Hook coped comparatively well through the 1930's. The same could not be said of the small mine at Loveston which was opened in 1932; having produced a very modest 3,500 tons in 1934, it was effectively closed by a disaster in May 1936, which killed seven men.

Closer to Saundersfoot, there was also an effort to revive the coal industry. The collieries at Broom, near Thomas Chapel, and at Kilgetty were re-opened in 1934 and 1937 respectively. Output at Broom using electricity and modern machinery reached 30,000 tons in 1936 and about 28,000 tons in 1938, whilst in the same year Kilgetty managed to raise about 17,000 tons.[83] This was not enough to make the pits really profitable, and these enterprises were always at the mercy of the difficult geology of the Pembrokeshire coalfield. By the end of 1938 the problems at Broom had become considerable, and the colliery closed in January 1939. Serious faulting at Kilgetty might have been overcome if additional capital had been available for the purpose, but the company was not in a position to provide it. Appeals for government assistance were not heeded, and notice of closure was given. Arthur Horner, president of the South Wales Federation of Miners, remarked bitterly that it was:

> a scandal that in a case like this, where the company is anxious to work, and where there are prospects of remunerative results…that there should be no government assistance forthcoming.

However he went on to make a telling observation:

> From certain points of view the existence of coal production in Pembrokeshire … is an anachronism and a danger to the wage standards of the men in other parts of the Welsh coalfield … In view of the fact that there is no other prospect of alternative employment, it will be a great shame if these workmen and their families are rendered permanently destitute.[84]

It may be surmised that Arthur Horner was not entirely sorry to see the Pembrokeshire pits close down.

Kilgetty colliery duly closed in February, 1939, throwing 262 men out of work. Of the 224 men who joined the unemployment register at Tenby, eventually over half were to find some employment in wartime construction work.[85] In addition a number of new military and defence establishments were created in Pembrokeshire, and some men were recruited into the armed forces.

[1] A. H. John, *The Industrial Development of South Wales*, 77,78.

[2] N.L.W., Jones MS 81.

[3] *Children's Employment Commission Report, 1842*, Part 2, 575, 576.

[4] N.L.W., Corston MS 40.

[5] N.L.W., Owen and Colby MS 1137. Alexander Smith's name is recorded as a partner in relation to five out of nine workings in 1787, and he was clearly heavily committed to the coal industry as a business. Certain other names occur only once, and have not been seen in any other references, and so may have been interested only as investors, or "sleeping partners".

[6] N.L.W., Gogerddan Papers (uncatalogued), Box 29: Letter from Thomas George to Edward Loveden, 11 March 1807.

[7] Brian Lewis, *Coal Mining in the Eighteenth and Nineteenth Centuries* (London: 1971), 69.

[8] N.L.W., Picton Castle, MS 4076 provides information not only about the Moreton and Begelly collieries, but also Ridgeway, at Saundersfoot, where seven were employed.

[9] N.L.W., Owen and Colby, MS 1138.

[10] N.L.W., Owen and Colby, MSS 2306-2310.

[11] *Children's Employment Commission Report*, 1842, Part 2, 471.

[12] "The Diary of Charles Collins, 1806", *Narberth Weekly News*, May 1934.

[13] N.L.W., Gogerddan Papers (uncatalogued), Box 29, Report of John Curr, 1806.

[14] D. J. V. Jones, *Before Rebecca* (London: Allen Lane, 1973), Chapter one; W. G.Thomas, *Llangwm through the Ages, Part I*, 64.

[15] Francis Jones, "Agrarian Disorders at Pembroke", *Treasury of Historic Pembrokeshire* (Newport, Pembs: 1998), 138. There had been disorder over food prices and shortages on earlier occasions, most notably when there were corn riots in Pembrokeshire in 1740. See also D. W. Howell, *The Rural Poor in Eighteenth-Century Wales* (Cardiff: University of Wales Press, 2000).

[16] James Thomas to Colonel Colby, 5 June 1800, published in B. E. Howells (ed.), *Pembrokeshire Life 1572-1843* (Pembrokeshire Record Series, I, Haverfordwest), 84.

[17] P. Adams to J.Colby, 8 June 1800, published in *Pembrokeshire Life 1572-1843*, 85. Resentment and some vandalism occurred prior to the disturbances in 1795. In 1794 there was a court case in which John Daley, a collier of Coedcanlas, was charged with firing a gunshot through a window at the home of David Wilkins of Martletwy, yeoman, and clerk to the Landshipping colliery. (N.L.W. Great Sessions 4.825.5: Pembrokeshire Gaol file, Spring 1794). Such disturbances were not unique to Pembrokeshire. For similar reasons they occurred on other coalfields in 1795 and 1800 – for example, north-east Wales.

[18] D.Williams "The Acreage Returns of 1801 for Wales", *Bulletin of the Board for Celtic Studies*, Vol. XIV parts i-ii (1950 and 1951). The crop returns for both St.Issells and Begelly parishes noted a shortage of corn because of the need to use land "for grazing the teams of cattle that convey coal and culm to the shore".

[19] Hugh Wilson to J.Harcourt Powell, 22 February 1815, B. E. Howells (ed.), *Pembrokeshire Life 1572-1843*, 88.

[20] Cornwall County Record Office, Truro. Harveys of Hayle Mss DDH 1/2/54 H. Wilson to Harveys 2 April 1830 quotes the price of oats in South Pembrokeshire. Similarly in his letter of 24 November 1830, to Harveys, DDH 1/2/247.

[21] *Children's Employment Commission Report, 1842*. The background to the setting up of the Commission is discussed in Michael Pollard: *The Hardest Work under Heaven: The Life and Death of the British Coal Miner* (London: Hutchinson, 1984), 73, 74.

[22] *Children's Employment Commission Report, 1842*, Part 2,471. Whilst the owners of Thomas Chapel are recorded correctly here as Morgan Hughes and Co., the report later speaks of Thomas Chapel as being in the ownership of Messrs Stokes and Co. There appears to have been a confusion between Thomas Chapel and Hean castle colliery, the latter being Messrs Stokes' property. Witnesses allegedly speaking as colliers at Thomas Chapel almost certainly were colliers at Hean Castle.

[23] Angela V. John, *By the Sweat of their Brow* (London: Croom Helm, 1990), 38.

[24] *Children's Employment Commission Report, 1842*. The section relating to the evidence gathered by R. H. Franks at the various collieries in Pembrokeshire is to be found on pages 572-580.

[25] William Absalom is reported as working for Ben Howard, the contractor. Ann David, mentioned two paragraphs earlier, worked for John Nash, a contractor. Clearly coal mining contractors, or sub-contractors, were still a feature of the industry.

[26] Angela V. John, *By the Sweat of their Brow*, 56. In Pembrokeshire this legislation may have been evaded for much longer, with the connivance of colliery officials. In 1998 Ivor Howell of Kilgetty recalled how as a young man he had spoken with the then elderly Hetty Thomas, who had been employed at Kilgetty in the late nineteenth century. Evidently she claimed to have worked underground if required, but whenever a Mines Inspector was due to visit she was allowed to be absent for a day or two on full - albeit modest - pay.

[27] R. P. Roberts, *The History of Coal Mining in Gower from 1700 to 1832* (Unpublished M.A. Thesis, University of Wales, 1953).

[28] Vickerman Papers: Pembrokeshire Iron and Coal Company minutes, 16 September 1857. I am indebted to Mrs. D. Evans for allowing me to study these minutes. As regards the Rebecca movement, see D. J. V. Jones, *Rebecca's Children* (Oxford: Clarendon Press, 1989).

[29] *Pembrokeshire Herald*, 24 June 1859.

[30] *Pembrokeshire Herald*, 1 July 1859.

[31] Billy Howells' unpublished reminiscences, c 1891, 'A Debtor to Grace,' 34, 35. I am indebted to Roscoe Howells of Amroth for giving me the opportunity to study these reminiscences.

[32] *Llanelly & County Guardian*, 10 May 1866.

[33] Pembrokeshire Record Office, Haverfordwest: Minute books of the Primitive Methodist Pembroke Dock Station. Emigration was by no means a new development in Pembrokeshire. During the food shortages of the 1790's and early 1800's some had opted to take their chances in North America, but the motivation was sometimes religious dissent rather than hunger. See H.M. Davies, "Very Different Springs of Uneasiness": Emigration from Wales to the United States of America during the 1790s', *The Welsh History Review*, Vol. 15, 3, (1991), 368.

[34] Margaret C. Gilpin, "Population Changes round the Shores of Milford Haven from 1800 to the Present Day", *Field Studies* Vol.1, 2, (1960), asserts that between 1841 and 1891 the mining parishes of Freystrop, Coedcanlas, Martletwy and Carew were overpopulated "and a very large proportion of their inhabitants moved to industrial districts of South Wales, or emigrated". Terry Driscoll of Roch, who has studied census returns for the parishes of Nolton and Roch, believes that the population decline in those parishes between 1871 and 1891 owed far more to a collapse in agriculture than the closure of the small pits in those parishes. Also see P. N. Jones, *Mines, Migrants and residence in the South Wales Steamcoal Valleys: the Ogmore and Garw Valleys in 1881* (Hull: Hull University Press, 1987), 25, 26, 50. By detailed analysis of census returns the author points to significant inward migration from South Pembrokeshire, with a particular concentration in the Upper Ogmore Valley. He mentions the coalfield in Saundersfoot but sees a link between the work of David Davies in building the Pembroke & Tenby Railway, and his subsequent involvement in colliery development in the Ogmore Valley.

[35] *Tenby Observer*, 24 April 1873.

[36] *Tenby Observer*, 30 April 1874.

[37] *Tenby Observer*, 11 June 1874.

[38] *Tenby Observer*, 25 June 1874.

[39] *Haverfordwest and Milford Haven Telegraph*, 24 March 1875.

[40] *Haverfordwest and Milford Haven Telegraph*, 16 June 1875. The A.A.M. suffered a severe setback in the disputes of 1875, and although it did not expire immediately, within a few years the remnants of the A.A.M were absorbed by the more moderate National Miners Union, which had most of its support in the North of England and Scotland.

[41] Brian Lewis, *Coal Mining in the Eighteenth and Nineteenth centuries*, 73,74.

[42] *Haverfordwest and Milford Haven Telegraph*, 18 October 1876.

[43] The company returns of the Bonvilles Court Coal & Iron Co formed in 1873 are held at the Public Record Office, Kew, reference BT31/835/7163. The returns relating to the Bonvilles Court Coal and Iron Co. Ltd (1876) are to be found under reference BT31/2230/10560.

[44] P.R.O., J15/1337: Chancery Division, 29 November 1877, and J15/1385, Chancery Division, 7 February 1878.

[45] Company returns at Public Record Office, Kew, BT 31/217/1023.

[46] Company returns at Public Record Office, Kew, BT31/ 2255/10769.

[47] *Pembrokeshire Herald*. 2 May 1879.

[48] Vickerman papers (privately owned), Messrs Lewis & Bidder's Report, 1 February 1873. Given the rural character of Pembrokeshire, comparisons with more industrialised coalfields are difficult. In the Forest of Dean, however, some miners also had the benefit of a smallholding or cottage and garden. They also had more independence than the wage labourer colliers in Glamorgan. See, for example, Royden Harrison (ed.), *The Independent Collier*, (Brighton: Harvester Press, 1978).

[49] Pembrokeshire Record office, D/RTM/13/46.

[50] *Haverfordwest and Milford Haven Telegraph*, 23 January 1884.

[51.]The Trefrane Cliff colliery (sometimes called Black Cliff) was at work at Nolton in the 1890's.

[52] Price, *Industrial Saundersfoot*, 72, 109.

[53] Vickerman papers (privately owned) *Messrs Lewis & Bidder's Report*, 1 February 1873. The report notes that "after recent rises" the wages for colliers were 3s.6d. per day, masons 3s.0d. to 3s.6d, carpenters 3s.0d. to 3s.4d., labourers 2s.0d. to 2s.6d.

[54] Angela. V. John, *By the Sweat of their Brow*, 197,198, provides further comment on the wages of women.

[55] Pembrokeshire Records Office D/RTM/HPO/209.

[56] *Pembroke Dock and Pembroke Gazette*, 24 September 1891.

[57] R. Page Arnot: *South Wales Miners (a History of the South Wales Miners Federation, 1898- 1914)*, (London: G.Allen and Unwin, 1967), General Appendix 1, 379.

[58] *Pembrokeshire Herald*, 2 February 1894.

[59] D. W. Howell, *Land and People in Nineteenth Century Wales* (London: 1978), 109.

[60] *The South Wales Coal Annual, 1903*, 163.

[61] E. W. Evans, *Mabon (William Abraham 1842-1922)*, (Cardiff: University of Wales Press, 1959), 66.

[62] Arnot, *South Wales Miners*, 290.

[63] *Haverfordwest and Milford Haven Telegraph*, 6 March 1912.

[64] *Pembrokeshire County Guardian*, 8 March 1912. The importing of extra police was deeply resented, and seen as "a serious and unjustifiable imputation on their [the colliers'] character".

[65] *Haverfordwest and Milford Haven Telegraph*, 8 May 1912. Although no pits were active at Nolton at this moment, there had been mining in the district in the Edwardian period. A document relating to Nolton and dated 12 December 1911, declared that "Labour is plentiful and cheap, and there is no trade union in the district!": Pembrokeshire Record Office D/MDC/5/5/10,11. I am indebted to Terry Driscoll for drawing my attention to this reference.

[66] Pembrokeshire Record Office, D/HR/10.

[67] This view was endorsed by a local Liberal M.P., Walter Roch: *Haverfordwest and Milford Haven Telegraph*, 29 May 1912.

[68] *Haverfordwest and Milford Haven Telegraph*, 19 July 1912.

[69] W. R. Morgan, *A Pembrokeshire Countryman looks back* (Tenby: Five Arches Press, 1988), 113.

[70] The late Owen Gwyther, who moved to Hook colliery in 1930, remarked in a letter to the writer dated 23 November 1983: "Trade unionism came to Hook later than to Bonvilles Court" and "although the Union was established when I went there it was a long way from being 100%; it was also frowned on by the management." For a wider background to the dispute in South Wales see Chris Williams, *Democratic Rhondda: Politics and Society 1885-1951* (Cardiff: University of Wales Press, 1996), 119-150.

[71] W. R. Morgan, *The Story of Begelly*, 48. The 1926 strike had consequences for many families not dependent on the coal industry. Although the last of the small pits on St. Bride's Bay had been abandoned by 1921, in 1926 the need for coal caused several local men to dig on tips in the Nolton and Little Haven districts.

[72] Account given to the writer by David Jenkins of Hook in 1987.

[73] *The Pembroke and County Guardian*, 4 June 1926.

[74] *The Pembroke and County Guardian*, 9 July 1926.

[75] *Pembrokeshire County Guardian*, 9 July 1926. There was some resentment over the police presence in the Saundersfoot district, but the resident police sergeant in the village, Sgt. Nicholas, was greatly respected. For the militancy surrounding the miners in South East Wales, see Hywel Francis and David Smith, *The Fed: A History of the South Wales Miners in the Twentieth Century* (London: Lawrence and Wishart, 1980), Ch.2.

[76] *Pembrokeshire County Guardian*, 30 July 1926.

[77] *Pembrokeshire County Guardian*, 15 October 1926.

[78] Hywel Francis and David Smith, *The Fed*, Appendix III, 505.

[79] *Pembrokeshire Telegraph*, 25 July 1929.

[80] *Pembrokeshire Telegraph*, 22 August 1929, and 29 August 1929.

[81] *Pembrokeshire Telegraph*, 1 May 1930.

[82] The late Owen Gwyther in a letter written to the writer, 1 December 1983.

[83] *The Telegraph Almanack*, 1937, not only noted the appalling accident at Loveston on 26 May 1936, but also a one-day strike at Broom Colliery, on 14 September 1936.

[84] *The West Wales Guardian*, 6 January 1939.

[85] Edwards, *A study of the Daucleddau Coalfield (Pembrokeshire)*, 93.

Health and Safety in the Pembrokeshire Coalfield

For generations health and safety in mining were secondary to the winning of coal, and although experience and better mining methods were of some benefit to a miner's well being, the risks were always considerable. In the Elizabethan era George Owen referred to the difficulty of working in hot weather "by reason of sudden damps which often times causeth the workmen to swoon, and will not suffer the candles to burn". In addition to gas, he described the dangers of coal mining as being "the falling of the earth and killing of the poor people; or stopping of the way forth, and so die by famine; or else the sudden irruption of standing waters in old works". Clearly Owen had no doubt that coal mining was a hazardous undertaking.

Little or nothing was done to moderate these risks for several centuries. The hazards Owen described remained all too real in the eighteenth century. Two accidents which occurred in 1742 were of a kind which would have been entirely familiar to Owen. On 16 April 1742, John Hugh was winding culm out of a pit at Freystrop, and in endeavouring to clear the movement of his windlass he fell down the shaft, and was killed.[1] A few weeks later, on 5 June, William Thomas was at work in a coalpit at Amroth when "the earth fell on him", and he died immediately.[2]

In February 1761, an inquisition (post mortem) was held in St. Issell's parish into the death of a collier named Thomas Evan, "being about to go to work in a certain coal pit called Gallant in St.Issell's parish, and being fastened to a rope to go down into the said pit, the rope accidentally broke and Evan fell to the bottom of the pit and instantly died". Not surprisingly the verdict was "accidental death".[3] A similar conclusion was reached at an inquest held at Amroth two months later. In this instance a collier named John Harry had been at work in the Castle Back pit, "and being about to raise or draw water out of the said coalpit, a damp or dead air suddenly gathered in the said coal pit which suffocated the said John Harry, who died instantly".[4] As a final example, on 24 December 1761, Lewis David was at work at Semletts Close Engine Pit, in the parish of Jeffreston, endeavouring to draw water out of the pit, and died by falling down the shaft.[5]

It was not necessary to work in the coal industry to encounter its dangers: the available records do not say if Richard Hendy worked as a collier, but he was making his way home in the dusk of 22 February 1762, passing by the side of some flooded coal pits at Freystrop, and he fell in and drowned.[6] Misfortune suffered by Richard Rees was of a kind only a collier could experience. On 19 March 1762, he was standing on scaffolding in the Five Acre Field pit at Jeffreston when a board broke and he was killed.[7] The only redeeming aspect to this unhappy catalogue is that instances of multiple deaths are relatively rare. Whilst a search of the records of almost any parish on the coalfield may reveal an occasional mining fatality, a note of some more serious accident seldom occurs. In the parish records of Freystrop, however, it seems that three men were killed in one incident in 1803.

In June 1839, the existence of new forms of transport, and new dangers, was highlighted by a coroner's inquest, again in the parish of Freystrop. In this case the inquest was into the death of Letitia Cozens, who was "run over by a wagon on a tramroad in the said parish".[8] Two other inquests held in July 1839 were of a much more familiar kind. Ezekiel Mathias was at work in a pit in Johnston parish when water broke in from other workings and he was drowned.[9] Michael Thomas had the misfortune to fall into the Underhill Pit at Jeffreston, and was killed.[10]

The Cambrian newspapers of Swansea took an interest in mining mishaps in all parts of South Wales, and on 4 April 1840, described an accident at the Quarry pit, Kilgetty colliery. By an unofficial arrangement James John was left in charge of the winding engine as well as the pumps, his official responsibility. During a short absence from the site he entrusted all the machinery to one David Davies, who previously had been dismissed for bad conduct. As workmen were waiting to go down the shaft, Davies took matters into his own hands, and safely lowered a tram containing five of them. According to the report:

> the second tram with five children had not been lowered more than five fathoms when the engine ran away and the poor victims were precipitated to the bottom of the pit. On taking them up William Morris, aged 14 was in the last agonies of death; John John, aged 15 was so severely injured that he only survived until the following morning; John Phelp had both arms broken; John Phillips was severely bruised but not dangerously hurt, and W. Ennorth miraculously escaped without the slightest injury.

At the inquest the jury could not agree whether the cause of death was negligence or simply accidental.[11]

If this event demonstrated the importance of having reliable and responsible men in charge of essential colliery functions, an incident in the following year demonstrated the unpredictability of some hazards in mining. On 10 June 1841, 22 men and 2 girls were at work in a pit at Cardmakers' Pool colliery at Freystrop. Water broke in from old workings, and very quickly reached a depth of about 16 feet. In the words of *The Cambrian* report:

> through this 20 of the men were drawn up by a chain leaving the remaining two men and two girls in the pit. Providentially they were able to gain a spot out of reach of the water, although in a state bordering on despair...after a night spent in total darkness, they were eventually rescued unharmed at 11 a.m. the next morning.[12]

In the 1840's two important events occurred which helped to sharpen awareness of health and safety issues. The first was the official inquiry of the Children's Employment Commission, which produced its report in 1842. The second was the disaster at Landshipping, easily the most serious accident in the story of the coal industry in Pembrokeshire. These will now be examined in turn:

The Children's Employment Commission

We have seen that the Commission appointed Robert H. Franks to gather evidence on their behalf in South and West Wales. He visited 62 collieries in Glamorgan and Monmouthshire, and another eight in Pembrokeshire. In the mines in the former counties it was estimated that 30 percent of the work force of 5,222 comprised young people under the age of 18. Furthermore 562 of these youngsters (including 27 girls) were aged under 13. Matters were even worse in Pembrokeshire. Here the proportion of women in the mines was even higher, because Franks believed there was no other work available for them. The pittance earned by the husband was insufficient for a family to live on, and so they needed the extra earned by the wife - and also the children - simply to survive.

In Pembrokeshire some women and girls were employed sorting coal from culm, or tipping spoil onto spoil banks. Many others, we have seen, were employed on the "druke and beam", or windlass. Although the largest collieries might have a steam engine to provide power for winding trams, tubs or buckets into and out of shafts, windlasses were often used below ground to draw coal out from the deeper workings. Small collieries, without suitable steam power, usually had windlasses set up on the surface. Operating a "druke and beam" was always hard work, but quite young women might be assigned to the task, and be obliged by their poverty to continue with it even when ill or pregnant.

At this period in Pembrokeshire it was widely recognised that when a pit was in full production, a collier could take his child into the mine to help. The extra pair of hands entitled him to claim an extra allowance, even if the child was too small to do any useful work.

Accordingly one colliery manager was noted as saying: "Young boys are taken down as soon as they can stand on their legs".[13] Several adult witnesses, including Lionel Brough, argued that it was necessary to employ young children for haulage of skips underground. The custom clearly had financial benefits for poor families, but as Lionel Brough observed, it also served to acclimatise the children to the grim environment of the coal industry in which most of them would spend their working lives.[14]

In the evidence given to Franks it is clear that in some collieries the wages of children were paid to their fathers, although there is also mention of work in some collieries being undertaken by contractors. In this event, it is probable that the contractor was responsible for meeting the wages of the child or a parent on his behalf. Either way the colliery proprietor would not be directly responsible for the pay, or even the employment of the child. Although it is doubtful if Franks visited every colliery in the county, to judge from his report, it seems clear that the number of young children who were actually on colliery payrolls was not very large - 61 males and only six females under the age of 13 in Pembrokeshire.[15] Franks did however speak to numerous children in the mines, including boys aged seven and eight, so it may be supposed that in this respect the official figure is possibly an underestimate.

Very young children were employed as "trappers" - that is to say they had to open and close air ventilation doors when miners or trams were passing through. If they were lucky they might have the dim light of a candle; often they might just have to sit in the dark with only the rats for company. Even so, it was a vital task because the doors were essential to the ventilation system of the mine, and the dispersal of dangerous gases. The older children, aged perhaps ten or more, would usually be employed in tramming- hauling trams, skips or corves from the coalface to the foot of the shaft or drift. The loads they had to move using a girdle and chain could be quite considerable - at Begelly colliery, for example, it was said that each skip contained $1^1/_2$ cwt. of coal, and each tram $5^1/_4$ cwt.[16] At Nolton colliery the corves contained 6cwt. of coal, although these would not be hauled by anyone under the age of 13.[17]

Colliery owners freely acknowledged that young children were employed in their pits. Lewis Wilson of Broadmoor stated that they usually started at the age of seven.[18] Richard Hare, the agent for the Kilgetty Colliery, pointed out – we have noted earlier - that although the task of tramming coal underground was hard, it could only be done by children because even the main roadways were only 3ft.6inches high. At this colliery the youngsters were expected to draw trams or skips containing no more than $1^1/_2$ cwt. Physical strength was clearly important, and Hare went on to acknowledge that as children under ten were of little value below ground a limit to their age would be an advantage.[19] This view was echoed by Thomas Stokes, the proprietor of the Thomas Chapel colliery, who somewhat sanctimoniously blamed the parents for trying to get their offspring to work as soon as possible because they needed the money.[20] Captain Child of the Begelly colliery was surely more honest in acknowledging that the women in the mines "worked harder than the slaves in the West Indies".[21] The comparison was reasonable, in more than one sense, because in the absence of other work, and lacking the means to move elsewhere, the poor people of the district had scarcely more choice than slaves.

Such heavy and arduous labour in a severely confined working environment was inimical to health, not only for women and children, but also for the men. However the men faced certain other risks because so many of them worked at the coal-face, or in other areas especially exposed to dust and noxious gases. The amount of gas encountered in some of the mines was considerable. At Broadmoor colliery, for example, fire damp (methane) was experienced, and although the owner admitted to Franks that one man had recently been killed in an explosion, he claimed that the gas was dispersed by careful ventilation.[22] At nearby Begelly the colliery manager acknowledged that there was a considerable amount of gas in the pit, but declared that he was "not aware of any recent accident".[23] The trustee of Sir John Owen's Landshipping colliery agreed that his mine was not free of gas, and although as we have seen he referred to the use of a blowing machine and a fire to help the circulation of air, he admitted there was no special provision for ventilation.[24] At Kilgetty colliery the agent expressed the view that the mine was well ventilated, but an underground steward for his part acknowledged that there was much carbon dioxide in the workings. He declared with candour that the conditions caused the men a great deal of ill health as they grew older, and indeed caused more problems "than at any other mine in the county".[25]

James Bowen, a surgeon from Narberth, gave some telling evidence to R. H. Franks. He asserted that the population of Begelly and East Willamston was about 1,163. Although farming was important, it was mainly a mining population, and he was well aware of their health and habits. He drew attention to the diseases of the lungs and air pipes suffered by many of the colliers, and expressed the opinion that much of the bronchitis was caused by their work with anthracite coal. He also said that the average life span of a collier was around 40 years, and that few reached the age of 45. In the entire population he thought there were only six miners who had reached the age of sixty – a fact confirmed by another witness, the Revd. Richard Buckby, the Rector of Begelly.[26] Another surgeon, Thomas George Noote of Begelly, not only echoed these sentiments, but declared firmly: "The practice of taking children into the mines does materially tend to injure the health, in consequence of the inhalation of impure air producing a constriction of the muscular fibres of the bronchiae, thereby causing asthma."[27]

In making his report to the Children's Employment Commission in December 1841, R. H. Franks began by stressing the unwholesome character of work in the collieries, and asserting that it was "productive of diseases which have a tendency either to shorten life or reduce the number of years of useful labour". He went on to point out that "the health and strength of children and young persons are deteriorated at early ages", and he called for a restriction of the age at which children should be allowed to work in the mines, and a ban on young girls undertaking such labour. Unfortunately the priority Franks gave to issues of health does not appear to have been followed by others associated with the Commission. Graphic drawings in the final report, showing women and children at work in the mines, shocked a hitherto unsuspecting public. Thereafter the main pressure was for social reform, primarily to end the use of child labour. Many of the miners disagreed, anticipating that such change would mean even more severe poverty. However, in 1842 an Act of Parliament was passed forbidding the employment underground of women and children under the age of ten. As the legislation did not offer any solution to the problem of poverty, and as only one inspector was appointed to oversee the Act in Wales, it will be seen that it was not enforced effectively in Pembrokeshire for many years.

The Landshipping disaster, 14 February 1844

This accident occurred when the tidal waters of the River Cleddau broke through into mine workings under the river, drowning forty of the fifty-eight colliers underground at the time. The report carried by *The Carmarthen Journal* two days later was so vivid that much of it is quoted here:

> About half-past three or four o'clock, in the afternoon of Wednesday, when there were 58 persons at work down below; the parties at the mouth of the pit became aware of some accident having occurred by a powerful current of air making up the pit, so strong, to use the language of one of the bystanders, as to bear up a band when held unrelentingly over it; and the same instant the water at a little distance from the shore, became much agitated, eddies being visible to a considerable extent. Shortly afterwards, several persons rushed out into the shaft of the pit shrieking wildly for assistance. The man at the whim immediately put three horses to the gallop, and succeeded in rescuing 4 men and 14 boys when the water rushing with tremendous force up towards the mouth of the pit, which filled at the rate of 7 fathoms in a minute, rendered all further exertions unavailing.

From the mouth of one of the survivors we received the following account:

He and another man were alarmed by a rushing wind, stronger than any storm he had ever witnessed, which completely carried them off their legs, and at the same time extinguished their lights. He called to his companion to stand still, as he thought it was occasioned by the explosion of fire damp in same part of the works; but having discovered his mistake, he at once saw their only chance was to fly to the mouth of the pit; in his way thither, his companion appears to have lost his footing, as he heard him exclaim 'O Lord, have mercy on my soul.' He himself was overtaken by the water, which almost prevented his progress, dashing him several times against the sides of the pit; when he got into the light, he rushed past another man who was about to get into the bucket, and was hauled up in safety, the water following him so closely, that the next and last man was only saved by climbing up the side of the pit, until the buckets which descended to the other was raised, reached him. The water appears to have broken in at a comparatively small distance from the shore, and 33 persons being at work a good way farther in, their retreat was instantly cut off, the water pouring down in a body between them and the entrance of the pit; the remaining seven were at work, nearer out, must have been overtaken in their endeavours to escape.

A very violent explosion took place yesterday morning in the middle of the river, occasioned by the pressure of the water on the air confined in the recesses of the pit, large pieces of timber being thrown up to the height of from thirty to forty feet.[28]

The scene of the disaster was the Garden Pit, where the pithead was no more than thirty yards south of Landshipping Quay. One of the notable elements in this account is the reference to the use of a horse whim for winding the large buckets used in the pit. The very fact that a whim was being used, rather than steam power, suggests that the Garden Pit was an old shaft, probably reopened for further use. This appears to be supported by an article published in *The Times* five days after the event, which declared that the shaft "had not for about three years previously been worked, for the reason, it is said, that it was not considered safe to carry on operations there".[29] On the other hand, the earlier newspaper report suggested that the Garden Pit was one of Landshipping's "most extensive pits", and "has been worked for the last two years".[30]

Whatever the truth of these details, in the months and years that followed, the Landshipping accident acquired an astonishing accretion of myths and legend. Most versions agree that the management of the colliery was harsh and unbending, to the extent of almost forcing the men to go down, even after warnings had been received about a threat to the mine from a rising tide. Other versions dwell on the proximity of the mine workings to the river, and imply not only that the mine surveying and planning were inadequate, but also that the workings were so close to the river bed that miners beneath could hear the dipping of oars from boats passing above![31] At least one report suggested that boys aged eight and ten were amongst the dead, but when the inquest took place on 27 February 1844, it emerged that the only person killed who might have been under age was a lad variously stated as being aged 10 or 11. No action appears to have been taken in respect of the 1842 legislation, which followed the Children's Employment Commission Report.

As the Landshipping disaster occurred in the days before comprehensive public enquiries, the reasons for it are still open to debate. The lack of reliable plans of mine workings was often a cause of difficulty in Pembrokeshire, and the Landshipping accident may be attributed to poor surveying as well as some negligence on the part of the management. Although the incident increased concern about flooding in mines, it cannot be said to have produced any immediate response in the form of either prosecutions or new legislation. In 1848, however, following mishaps elsewhere in Wales and in other coalfields, a Select Committee on Dangerous Accidents was set up. This committee produced its report on 1 August 1849, and its observations contributed to the passing of the Coal Mines Regulation Act, 1850. This legislation not only covered the retention of mining plans, but also provided for the appointment of regional inspectors of mines, with powers to go underground. The powers and duties of these inspectors were further refined in an Act of 1855.[32] Close attention to the evidence of the early Mines Inspectors will reveal much about the health and safety of those employed in the Pembrokeshire coalfield.

Herbert Mackworth was the first Inspector of Mines with responsibility for the South Wales area. His initial report, made in November 1852, noted just one mining fatality in Pembrokeshire in the years 1851 and 1852, but it nonetheless contained some scathing criticism of mining practice in the county, part of which was mentioned in chapter four:

> I found several boys underground who were 10 years of age, and there appears to be a general neglect of the physical and moral condition of the mining population. The ventilation of the collieries is very inadequate, plans are often wanting, and I had occasion to make numerous objections to insecure machinery and other arrangements. There is comparatively little firedamp. Isolated cases occur of men being burnt severely, which a little attention to the distribution of air would have prevented. There is hardly an instance of the employment of artificial ventilating power throughout the year, and in collieries wherein I measured the quantities of air, it was this summer less than half that required for the health and vigour of the miners.[33]

After such forthright comment, it might be supposed that Mackworth would have wanted to follow up on his observations. Apart from the formal recording of fatalities, he does not appear to have done so. In the years 1856 and 1857 Mackworth was responsible for inspections in South East Wales, whilst Thomas Evans was given responsibility for inspections in South West Wales. In his report for 1857 Evans indicated that little had changed in Pembrokeshire. Although he had not personally found females working underground, he was sorry to say that "boys of a tender age ... are to be found in very many collieries; this is in direct violation of the [1842] Act of Parliament. Mr. Tremenheere, the Commissioner appointed under this Act has during the past year obtained convictions against the owners of mines and parents of children which will in great measure have the effect of preventing the repetition of such offences." Unfortunately this optimism was misplaced, because a year later he had to report that "a large number of very young children are still working in the collieries of this district, and the attention of ... Mr. Tremenheere ... has been directed to it".[34]

It is clear that many people associated with the coal industry in Pembrokeshire were deeply reluctant to change their ways. This seems to have been as relevant to their use of old equipment as to their employment policies. In 1861 Thomas Evans was moved to mention a particular instance of poor ventilation at a Pembrokeshire pit which had a furnace intended to draw air through the workings. He wrote:

> I have known the ventilation most defective, almost at an explosive point near the furnace. The responsibility of working such a colliery has been pointed out to the manager, and now they are under notice of arbitration ... Whatever may be the result of the arbitration, it cannot fail to ensure better ventilation, greater safety, and the responsibility will be fixed upon the owner.[35]

Thomas Evans' concern was entirely justified, because the number of fatalities in this small coalfield was alarmingly high, and accidents involving more than one death seemed to be increasing. In 1853 boys aged 14 and 15 died at the Engine Pit at Little Milford when winding gear slipped over a hook, causing them to fall down the shaft. In 1854 there were four deaths arising from three separate incidents, two of which took place at the Trevane (Trefrane) colliery near Nolton Haven. The third was at Thomas Chapel, and as has been noted in chapter four, was a somewhat unusual mishap in that two men were drowned by floodwater entering mine workings through old pits and an adit level.[36]

In 1855 the Inspector noted six accidents causing seven deaths. Two of the latter occurred in Dr. Read's colliery at Little Haven, and the remainder at pits at or near Kilgetty owned by the Pembrokeshire Coal & Iron Co. Three of the deaths happened during the sinking of the massive shaft of the Grove colliery at Stepaside, and they were followed by two more deaths in one accident in August 1856.[37] Another two deaths took place at this company's pits near Kilgetty in 1857, but so far it is not clear whether these also were at Grove. Although 1858 and 1859 appear to have been much better years, seven deaths were recorded in 1860, arising from five separate mishaps. The worst of these took place at Moreton, near Saundersfoot, on 20 October 1860, when three men died in a gas explosion due to poor ventilation. This accident and the Inspector's damning comments on its causes, have been noted already in chapter four.[38]

Negligence and incompetence were not confined to Moreton colliery. In 1861 there were two accidents in the Nash & Sprinkle pits in Llangwm parish, near Haverfordwest. In the first, three colliers were killed when a large bucket fell down a shaft on top of them. The inspector noted that there were no guides in the shaft and that it was very badly fitted up. Four months later, on 21 July, an engineer died when he became entangled in winding machinery; an exasperated inspector declared that "the shaft is still without proper guides". Matters were no better at the nearby Hook colliery. On 26 April 1861, a year or so after a man had been killed by a bucket falling down a shaft, a collier fell from a bucket and was killed. Once again the inspector observed tersely that the shaft was "badly fitted up".[39]

The dubious quality of the equipment and perhaps management at both these pits appears to have continued for some time. In 1865 there was another fatality at Nash and Sprinkle, and in the following year a further death at Hook. Although there were some improvements in Pembrokeshire in the middle of the nineteenth century - most notably the provision of some miners' safety lamps at some pits - mere possession did not guarantee good use. This was indicated clearly by the two court cases in 1864 (one arising at Nash and Sprinkle) already noted in chapter four. Whilst it might be supposed that increased familiarity with such equipment would ensure greater safety, in practice it was very difficult to legislate to protect the naïve or foolish. On 16 September 1886, for example, a sixteen-year-old lad at Bonvilles Court colliery was killed by an explosion of firedamp, when he removed the gauze from a lamp, even though he was aware of the presence of firedamp.[40]

Almost twenty years earlier, in 1867, the seriousness of firedamp does not seem to have been understood by a reporter working for the *Haverfordwest and Milford Haven Telegraph*. If he had had any experience of the coal industry he surely would not have begun by writing:

> On Saturday last a slight explosion of firedamp occurred at (Hook) ... colliery by which one of the men got severely burnt about the hands and face. It speaks well of the officials, workmen and supervisor of these collieries that no lives have ever been lost there by accidents arising from the cause.[41]

In 1864 Thomas Evans was succeeded as Mines Inspector by the well-named Thomas Wales. In 1866 he reported on a fatality at Bonvilles Court colliery, Saundersfoot, already mentioned briefly in chapter four. This demonstrated clearly some of the everyday risks encountered by all those going underground. The dead man was Willam Parsell, a very experienced engineer with considerable knowledge of this pit. At the inquest it emerged that Parsell and a collier named Gwyther had been descending the shaft astride a wooden stage called a "mare", measuring only about 4 feet by 3 feet. There was an unexpected jerk on the rope, and Parsell was thrown off and fell to his death. The jury returned a verdict of accidental death. Bonvilles Court would seem to have been one of the better mines, because this mishap was said to be the first ever fatal accident at the colliery.[42] In the following year a young collier was killed by a fall of roof in an underground heading, but arguably this was due to one of the inherent hazards of the work rather than some neglect on the part of the management.

The only first hand account of daily life underground at Bonvilles Court at this period is provided by Billy Howells. As a youngster he encountered severe bullying from his "big boy", but declared that most regarded him as the "best small boy in the heading". He declared:

I was always down first rope in the morning and every day had done several trams before my big boy had come in, yet this went for nothing with him ... Many times have I had pieces knocked off my back and was not allowed to make a groan and being obliged to work with our boots and stockings off have kicked the tops off my toes against stones or coals ...[43]

At the age of fifteen Billy Howells left Bonvilles Court and went to work at Moreton Colliery and found it to be different, but no more pleasant. At Moreton he asserted:

The work itself was not so hard, nor the hours so long as they were at Bonvilles Court – there was also more room. We should finish work every day from two to four o'clock at the latest. The sufferings here however were from another source. The workings were so wet that the misery one worked in was beyond description. Before we would be at work for ten minutes the water would be running out of our boots, and every thread of our clothes would be as wet as if we had fallen in the tide. This was not the worst part of it for this water getting into my boots and the small coal would make then as "raw as a piece of beef" and the burning pain something awful.[44]

Moreton colliery was not only wet, but also relatively dangerous. On 30 September 1870, there was an explosion here which caused the loss of two lives, eight other men suffering burns. Thomas Wales subsequently reported:

On the day after the explosion I made an examination of the colliery, and found its condition very bad, and the evidence at the inquest went on to show that gas had been allowed to accumulate in the workings proceedings were instituted against thee acting owner, Mr. Williamson ... And a fine of £20 being the full penalty, was inflicted.

The *Pembrokeshire Herald* simply noted that the explosion had been caused by gas coming into contact with naked lights.[45]

The lack of improvement at Moreton was matched by a lack of progress at Hook. On the morning of 22 November 1871, there was a serious explosion of firedamp at Hook colliery resulting in two deaths and injuries to about twelve others. A local newspaper managed to include a rather inaccurate account of the accident in an issue which went to press on the same day.[46] In contrast, Thomas Wales later stated that he had "received no official report of the accident until the Monday after it had occurred". His report continued:

Next day I went to Hook colliery, and made an examination of the workings where the explosion had taken place. I measured the quantity of air passing, and found it from 5,000 to 6,000 feet per minute. I do not consider this a large quantity of air, but I believe it would have been sufficient to carry off all the gas, if it had been properly applied; but this was not done. The quantity of air which really reached the face of the workings was very small indeed, and I found, as might have been expected, gas accumulated where the men were at work. That in my opinion was clearly a breach of the first general rule. Men ought never to be allowed to work, not even with a safety lamp, where gas is lodged.

Observing that it was his duty to recommend proceedings against colliery owners in breach of the regulations set out in the Coal Mine Acts, he began proceedings against the manager of Hook colliery. Haverfordwest magistrates duly imposed a fine of £20.[47]

Unfortunately the wretched recital of death did not decrease significantly in the 1870's. Between 1861 and 1870 there were eleven recorded fatalities in Pembrokeshire, and between 1871 and 1880 another ten.[48] After 1871 there were three consecutive years without fatalities (1872-1874), three other years with only one death (1876, 1877, 1879), and three more when two deaths were recorded (1875, 1878, 1880). The fatalities in 1878 and 1879 all occurred at the rather remote Southwood colliery, in Roch parish. One of the deaths in 1880 was in the course of pit sinking at the Moreton colliery.[49] Thereafter the numbers did diminish, with only four deaths between 1881 and 1890, and just two in the decade following. The diligence of successive Mines Inspectors in trying to combat the casual attitudes so often encountered in

West Wales eventually began to show some significant results. Indeed a letter written in August, 1886, by J. S. Roberts of the Hook Colliery Company to the then Inspector of Mines, Joseph S. Martin, shows clearly how management had learned to pay more attention to the Inspectorate. Referring to a complaint made by Martin over ventilation, Roberts acknowledged the problem, and added: "we have now ceased working in the said place till the ventilation is made good by cutting through from the level". On a separate complaint concerning steam gauges Roberts declared that "your instruction [has been] carried out with regard to the valves". His letter ended on a note of almost abject contrition: "We therefore beg to apologise that on your first visit you should have had reason to complain; trusting that it will not happen in the future."[50]

What had happened to bring about such a change? The early Mines Inspectors appear to have been both brave and determined, fully committed to the legislation they were asked to enforce. A succession of successful prosecutions must have made a powerful impression on the mine owners, especially when they may have supposed that their remoteness in Pembrokeshire might be some protection. However, the Mines Inspectors were also helped at this period by Parliament's recognition that the law needed tightening up in numerous respects. In 1855 and 1860 Acts were passed relating to the inspection of mines, and following an appalling accident at Hartley colliery in 1862, there was legislation making it compulsory for every colliery to have at least two shafts or means of access or escape. The latter was certainly pertinent in Pembrokeshire where proprietors were frequently criticised for the inadequacy of their attempts to brattice (divide) single shafts. The reports of Thomas Evans referred to this issue on several occasions, and in 1861 and 1862 he implied that the problem was encountered more often in Pembrokeshire than anywhere else in South Wales.

In 1872 Parliament passed the Coal Mines Regulation Act, a comprehensive piece of legislation designed to regulate methods of working underground. In 1880 this was followed by an Employers' Liability Act, imposing greater responsibility on mine owners for the welfare of their men. A further Coal Mines Regulation Act in 1887 widened the scope of the 1872 Act. All too often, though, the legislators were reacting to mishaps or mine owners' attempts to evade the law. It cannot be said that their legislation was always sufficient. This was especially so in the important matter of mining plans. Although the need for reliable underground plans was recognised by 1850, it took many years to achieve. A government report of 1927 reviewed the history of this issue, and made these observations:

> Between the years 1850 and 1887 plans were only required to be made up half yearly. The smaller mines were in many cases surveyed by Mining Surveyors visiting the mines only at the time of the survey, and having little personal knowledge or information of the course of the workings in the intervening period. Clearly the risk of errors of omission from the plans was much greater than it is today, when quarterly surveys are required and most of the larger collieries have their own surveying staff. It is seldom that records have been preserved to enable old plans to be checked or verified. Under these circumstances we think plans made prior to 1887 should not be treated as indicating the actual positions of workings, but must only be treated as evidence that old workings existed in the neighbourhood.[51]

Another danger encountered in coalmining in Pembrokeshire was that of accidents arising during the movement of coal and culm. In 1842 R. H. Franks learned of numerous mishaps underground involving mine transport, usually causing fractures or crush injuries. Similar hazards existed with surface transport which, as will soon be seen, gave rise to three deaths in the Edwardian period. Even away from the colliery there were some dangers, especially with regard to shipping, and the next couple of pages will examine this aspect of the coalfield's safety.

Accidents to coal shipments can be attributed to two main causes – either the forces of nature or human error and ignorance. Around the rocky and deeply indented coastline of Pembrokeshire the natural hazards were, and are quite obvious. Instances of shipwreck amongst vessels carrying coal and culm were numerous, and a couple of examples may suffice.

On 18 December 1853, the MARY was working within Milford Haven when a westerly gale developed. Her captain sought shelter in the lee of the land near the entrance to the Haven. Unfortunately during the night the gale moved around to the southeast and the MARY's protection was lost. When her anchor cables broke, she was blown out to sea and driven towards the notoriously dangerous Jack Sound between Skomer Island and the mainland. The vessel was dashed onto rocks, but mercifully the very shaken crew of three managed to land on a small island and were duly rescued.[52]

The unpredictability of the weather was a major factor in the loss of the 20-ton sloop TRUE BESS. On 25 October 1859 the vessel was beached at Broad Haven when conditions deteriorated suddenly. The captain could do nothing until the incoming tide lifted his vessel off the beach, but by then a north-easterly gale was blowing so fiercely there was no prospect of sailing north as intended to Porthclais or Solva. The captain realised that he would have to go south to Milford, in spite of the dangers of Jack Sound. In the event the sloop was wrecked on rocks west of Little Haven, with the loss of the crew of three. This storm was subsequently described as "The Great Gale", a storm of such intensity that over 100 craft were lost around the Welsh coast on the same day.[53]

Human error as a cause of mishap could take many forms. Arguably instances of overloading can be attributed to the profit motive as well as simple error. Perhaps the best known case of the overloading of culm occurred with the smack RECHABITE. On 4 September 1861, this 19-ton vessel was struggling north through the waves and currents off Ramsay Sound, when clearly low in the water and heavily laden. To the consternation of those watching ashore, the bows of the RECHABITE dipped to a wave and then disappeared. The smack promptly foundered in front of them with the loss of the two-man crew. The moral of this melancholy event was articulated soon afterwards by the *Pembrokeshire Herald:* "The untimely fate of these men should be seen as a warning to masters of coastal vessels, against taking in too large a cargo."[54] Whether the fundamental reason was greed, or desperation to make a modest profit, is not entirely clear. What is known is that the Merchant Shipping Act of 1876, promoted by Samuel Plimsoll, sought to regulate the loading of vessels, and prevent such accidents. In time this legislation had a beneficial effect, but even in September 1880 the smack ALICE was lost off Pembrokeshire when overloaded with limestone. It emerged that this vessel, also often used to convey culm, frequently went to sea with a crew of only one man, notwithstanding the difficulty even a very experienced sailor would encounter in trying to handle the sails on his own. Although officially the sinking was attributed to overloading, the fact that the vessel's master was alone must have contributed to his death.

Errors of navigation could be equally serious. On 18 October 1879 the 21-ton sloop COURIER was approaching Porthclais with a cargo of culm from Little Haven when she failed to alter course for the harbour entrance, and so ran onto rocks. The vessel was wrecked, but the two-man crew were extremely fortunate to survive.[55] If a vessel was a total loss the position was clear to everyone. If, however, a vessel was damaged and deemed repairable, matters could become much more involved. The papers of Harvey and Co. of Hayle, Cornwall, include correspondence relating to damage suffered by Harveys' sailing vessel the PROVIDENCE in December 1833. This ship ran aground on Laugharne sands near the entrance to the Towy river, but the crew escaped. The ships' pilots at Tenby evidently regarded Carmarthen Bay as their domain, and it seems that a pilot cutter managed to move the stranded vessel into a safer position. Correspondence then ensued between Harvey and Co. and Hugh Wilson of Cresswell Quay, who was clearly an ally, and very possibly a local agent for Harveys. After a postal delay, he visited the PROVIDENCE to report on its condition and was joined by one Daniel Warren, who advised on its repair. Although the damage seemed to be considerable, local shipbuilders suggested that £200 would make her seaworthy. Warren asserted that £300 would put the vessel into a better condition than when she left Hayle. There was indecision over repairs and the option of sale was considered. The last letter available suggests that the ship's future was still unresolved.[56]

Generalisations can be hazardous, but broadly speaking it may be said that by 1887, legislation and the Mines Inspectors had checked the very worst kinds of carelessness and neglect. After this date, it must be admitted, there were some tragic and spectacular lapses in South Wales and elsewhere, but most of the essential principles of health and safety in the coal industry had been established. Additional regulations were introduced in the ensuing years, and mine officials faced increasingly rigorous examinations and tests of competence. The era of inexperienced and under-qualified managers came to an end, and supervision was made much more effective by the appointment of many more Mines Inspectors. Indeed, with the passing of the comprehensive Coal Mines Act of 1911 the total number in the United Kingdom was increased to 90, and different grades were established. The Pembrokeshire coalfield was small, though, and is believed to have remained under the cover of one inspector. In the 1890's this man was Joseph T. Robson.

The Inspectors' Reports were now notable for the amount of detail provided. Not only did they record fatal accidents, but they also included a brief description of each working colliery, specifically mentioning matters pertinent to safety like methods of ventilation and the use or otherwise of naked lights below ground. In 1891, for example, the relatively large Kilgetty colliery was still worked with naked lights, as were the smaller pits at Trefrane Cliff and Begelly. Both naked lights and safety lamps were employed at Bonvilles Court colliery, and only Hook colliery was said to be worked exclusively with safety lamps.[57] Furthermore, only the West Park pit at Hook and Bonvilles Court colliery were equipped with powered ventilating fans, the larger one at Bonvilles Court dating from 1863, and noteworthy as the first Waddle ventilating fan ever installed in a colliery. Further details may be found within Figure 22.

By now the coal industry in Pembrokeshire was in sharp decline. Although the total number of collieries in work did not vary greatly in the 1880's and 1890's – usually between seven and nine – the mines that closed in the 1880's were replaced in the lists by small pits employing fewer people. In the report of the Children's Employment Commission in 1842 some 661 men, women and children, we have noted earlier, were said to be at work in six mines. R. H. Franks gave no figures in respect of two other collieries mentioned, and it is very probable that several other smaller pits were in production at the same time. Accordingly the total number of people employed in 1842 is likely to have been at least 800, and possibly as high as 1,000. In contrast, in 1894 601 people were employed in the eight mines then recorded, whilst in 1899, 402 people were said to be employed in 12 mines, several of which were clearly very small. Suffice to say that the reduction in the numbers employed must have assisted the fall in the deaths and injuries reported. Indeed, J. T. Robson happily appears to have had no need to report any coal industry fatality in Pembrokeshire between 1893 and 1903. Furthermore the one death in 1904 occurred above ground, when a young clerk at the Freystrop colliery attempted to jump onto the footboard of a locomotive, but slipped and was crushed by a wheel.[58] Two years later there was an accident on a self-acting incline at Bonvilles Court colliery. The inspector's report does not indicate if the incline was above or below ground, but simply states that a chain broke and trams ran free, killing a 14-year-old boy.[59] On 30 November 1909, at Bonvilles Court the victim was an under-manager rather than a youth. He died six days after slipping when getting out of an empty tram in which he had been riding.[60]

In spite of improvements in training, management and practical operation, collieries in Pembrokeshire remained relatively backward in their practice, and the men were always vulnerable to the risk of injury. Prior to the First World War, Hook colliery had more than its share of mishaps. In 1907 a miner dismantling steampipes at a disused shaft in West Park was struck on the head by a pipe and suffered severe concussion.[61] At the time the construction of the Margaret pit was getting under way, with all the hazards that such work entailed. In February, 1912, soon after it opened, there was an explosion whilst the night shift was at work. In the words of the *Haverfordwest and Milford Haven Telegraph*:

The colliery at Hook has only just been opened out. There are three shifts at work, and the explosion occurred during the night while the third or last lot of men were down. It appears that the men were working with open lights. Three men were burnt more or less seriously.

After describing the men's injuries, the report noted that "work resumed the following day as usual". As a postscript, it added that the following night another man "was struck by some falling debris underground, and sustained a couple of fractures".[62] Hook's unfortunate record at this period was not improved when a 64-year-old miner named James Brock was killed at the Margaret Colliery in August 1913. In 1917 Hook is believed to have experienced some flooding, but at 4 am on 14 September 1935, "water burst through from an old working, and the main Margaret pit filled rapidly". Fortunately the miners had received some warning and were able to wade out, but nine pit ponies were drowned.[63] In spite of these incidents, Hook colliery was considered good by Pembrokeshire standards.

The Crosspark pit at Broadmoor provides an illustration of how primitive and dangerous conditions could be, even as late as 1926. Owen Gwyther worked at Crosspark as a young man, and described the experience at length many years later:

The pit was approximately seventy feet deep. I was 14 years of age, and it was my first job ... The pit had obviously been sunk some years before, and then abandoned. It was reopened in 1926 by the family who owned the land, a father and three sons by the name of Williams. They carried it on for a few months, and then it was financed by James Williams of Narberth, a firm of brewers who were obviously finding great difficulty in finding coal for their industry. The pit was served by a small vertical Boiler, which provided steam for the water pumps, the coal was carried in wooden skips (which I was employed to pull) and pulled up the pit by a beam which was manipulated by two men: The seam of coal was of reasonable quality, and about 2½ to 3ft. thick, however it pitched so steeply as to be nearly on its edge, which meant that the road had stone on each side, and coal top and bottom. It was the wettest place I ever knew. Streamers of water cascaded from the roof for the full length of the road, which was about 50 yards, it was so wet that we were saturated to the skin in about ten minutes. This we had to endure for the whole shift, the only relief was, some of the men had carried old jackets which were hung around the boiler. About every hour we sent our saturated jacket up, and replaced it with one off the boiler. It was of course never dry, but at least it was warm for a short time. After I had been there a few months, they took on another miner. His name was Sid Thomas. He had been working in the Welsh Valleys, but because of the strike, he had been turned out of his house, so with his wife and nine children, he came down to Pembrokeshire, and had a little cottage at Gumfreyston near Tenby. We had by this time started working two shifts, mornings and afternoons. It was his first afternoon, we were now three underground, two miners and myself. The other one was Fred Williams who although a first class miner, was stone deaf. We were using candles for light, but because of the streamers it was impossible to carry it, so if a dry spot could be found, one was placed at about 20 yard intervals. We had been underground a few hours this particular afternoon. Sid was working at the furthest face, while Fred was alone 20 yards back starting a new tophole. Fred said to me 'come on lets go see Sid and have a smoke', so being the only dry spot in the place, we squatted down for a small natter and a smoke. It was while we were talking, that somewhere between us and the pit, a terrific fall occurred. Fred being stone deaf did not hear it, and Sid having great trouble trying to converse with Fred seemed not to know what to do. However in a few minutes another fall occurred. This time I was greatly alarmed, thinking we were locked in, so I practically dragged Fred out to see what had happened. To my amazement not a stone was seen to have fallen. This really terrified me, and I had an awful premonition that something terrible was about to happen. However with my inexperience, I had no idea what. I was soon to find out however. I had just returned with an empty skip, and was just passing Fred's place, when there was a terrific tremor, a gust of air which extinguished the candles, and gushing water everywhere. Naturally I took off for the pit bottom. I arrived a second or so before Fred, I put the Bar (which was our means of ascent) between my legs and started to shout 'pull up.' It seemed an eternity before someone came to the pit top, and in the meantime the water was lifting Fred and I off our feet. We had seen nothing of Sid. We climbed unto the first square of timber in the pit, and was eventually pulled up. The water rose 36 feet up the pit, and of course everyone concluded that Sid had drowned. A crowd soon collected around the pit, dozens of helpers rushed pumps etc. and in a short time, a platform made, pumps put into operation, and by nine o'clock next morning, the water was mostly out. Volunteers were asked to go down to get the body, when a weak voice came from the bottom. It was a miracle. Sid had been saved by an air lock. The water had come in from where Fred had been working, he had cut through to the bottom of an old pit, the roads from which ran above ours, the full length, and were responsible for all the streamers soaking through on us. Incidentally my wages for all that was 12s.6d equivalent today to 62½ pence.[64]

At Crosspark clearly little had changed since the days of Robert Franks or even George Owen! The accident took place on 30 November 1926, and a week later T. Walden of Neath carried out an inspection. On 10 December the Inspector wrote to James Williams insisting on compliance with the Coal Mine Act, 1911, requiring either that the shaft be fitted with cages, or that a slant be driven.[65] Williams was not in a position to comply, and Crosspark was abandoned formally in February 1927.

Despite the inherent hazards in such primitive work places, there seems to have been a remarkably fatalistic willingness in South and West Wales to accept the very obvious dangers involved. Given the poverty of the time this now seems extraordinary, but a story from the early 1930's illustrates the point. A miner named Joe Bell was injured underground at Hook, and when he was brought out of the pit he was carried home on a stretcher by four of his workmates. As they went along the bus from Haverfordwest arrived, and Mrs Bell stepped off. She saw Joe on the stretcher and exclaimed "Blessed God! And how much compensation do I get?" In a period when an income was as vital as an income-earner, this was not callous as might be supposed now. Fortunately Joe Bell recovered to work again.[66] The remarkable acceptance of danger even extended to a curious reluctance to use better safety equipment when it became available. This disturbed Thomas Ashley, the Mines Inspector for the Swansea division of the Inspectorate in 1934:

> I regret to report that there is no enthusiasm generally on the part of workmen in this Division to use protective equipment. In other coalfields large numbers of workmen are using protective equipment in some form or other, and it is disappointing to find that there has been so little response in this Division.[67]

Part of the Inspector's problem was persuading colliery companies to bear part of the cost of the equipment. As the accident rate in South Wales was generally higher than elsewhere, it was plainly needed.

Just as the Landshipping disaster of 1844 constituted the most serious accident in the nineteenth century and was accordingly examined at length, like treatment will be accorded the tragedy at the small Loveston colliery on 26 May 1936. This was the most serious accident in the Pembrokeshire coalfield in the twentieth century. Twenty men were working below ground on a fine calm day, and no one suspected anything was amiss until thirteen of them emerged from the drift soaked to the skin, and clearly shocked. In one of the headings a collier had broken through into the long abandoned workings of the nearby Breeches Pit, and a torrent of water had burst out into the Loveston workings. Seven men were drowned; one of them would have escaped had he not made the brave but mistaken decision to go back to help his younger brother. Indeed the survivors were all fortunate, because the floodwater wedged a loaded tram across the roadway, blocking the exit to the foot of the drift. Several men owed their lives to Owen Gwyther who managed to keep his light above the water, and guided his colleagues over the obstacle. Owen Gwyther's own remarkable personal account of the disaster and its immediate aftermath is given in Appendix H. Figure 33 illustrates Loveston colliery and

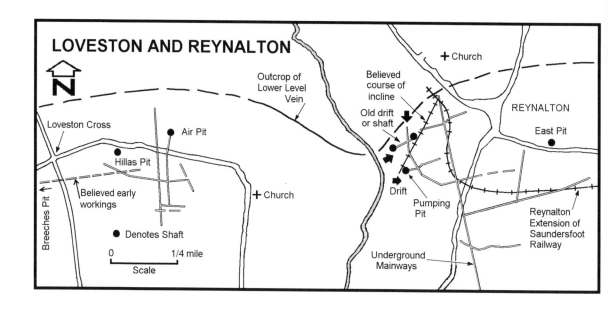

LOVESTON AND REYNALTON

N

Outcrop of Lower Level Vein

+ Church

Believed course of incline

Old drift or shaft

REYNALTON

East Pit

Loveston Cross

Air Pit

Hillas Pit

Drift

Breeches Pit

Believed early workings

+ Church

Pumping Pit

Reynalton Extension of Saundersfoot Railway

● Denotes Shaft

0   1/4 mile
Scale

Underground Mainways

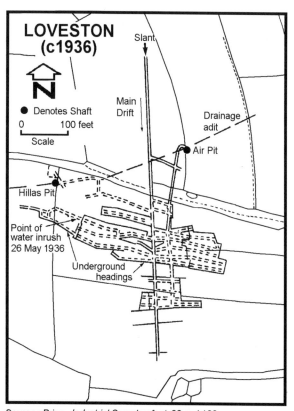

LOVESTON (c1936)

Slant

N

Main Drift

Drainage adit

● Denotes Shaft

0   100 feet
Scale

Air Pit

Hillas Pit

Point of water inrush 26 May 1936

Underground headings

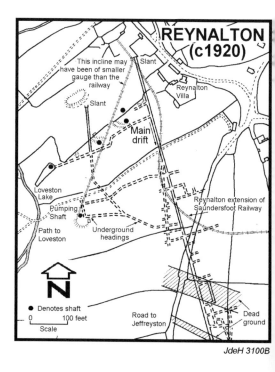

REYNALTON (c1920)

This incline may have been of smaller gauge than the railway

Slant

Reynalton Villa

Slant

Main drift

Loveston Lake

Reynalton extension of Saundersfoot Railway

Pumping Shaft

Path to Loveston

Underground headings

N

● Denotes shaft

0   100 feet
Scale

Road to Jeffreyston

Dead ground

JdeH 3100B

Source : Price, *Industrial Saundersfoot*, 98 and 100

Figure 33

its workings and also the small short-lived colliery at Reynalton (1914-1921).

The implications of the Loveston accident were greater than was generally realised. At the inquest the verdict of "accidental death" was returned on all the victims, but the jury added a rider to the effect that all old workings in the district should be surveyed before any new pit was opened.

After so many instances of flooding in Pembrokeshire this was a sensible and reasonable proposition, although not one that could be put into practice without immense expense. Furthermore, following the disaster a conference was held at which representatives of the Pembrokeshire owners, of the South Wales Miners' Federation, and also the Overmen's Association, met with officials of the Mines Department, and they agreed to form a Pembrokeshire Water Dangers Committee. According to the 1937 report of Inspector Thomas Ashley, the committee met four times in its first year, although no information about their deliberations was given.[68]

What is clear is that the three collieries active at this period were in locations that had been heavily worked in previous generations. Hook colliery had experienced some flooding from old workings in 1932, 1935, and 1937, and although there had been no mishaps at the reopened pits at Broom and Kilgetty, Broom in particular was considered to be a wet pit. Ironically, according to the Mines Inspector's Report for 1935, both Broom and Loveston collieries were granted exemptions from the requirements of regulation 2 of the Coal Mines General Regulations (Rescue) of 1928.[69] After some debate in the Pembrokeshire Water Dangers Committee, it seems very likely that the Department of Mines decided that enough was enough. Although there was some public reference to economic and geological difficulties at Broom and Kilgetty, it seems very probable that the potential risks of working at these sites was a factor in their closure early in 1939. Hook, the last significant colliery in the county, again experienced flooding from old workings on 19 May 1947. The report of the Inspector, T. A. Rogers, was not published until 1949, and it seems to suggest that this inundation caused the colliery's closure. In fact some work resumed, but further flooding in March 1948 put an end to it, and the colliery was abandoned formally in April 1948. In all the circumstances the case for closure on safety grounds was probably justified, even if it was never explicitly stated.[70]

Many years later, when old miners reflected on their days in the Pembrokeshire coal industry, invariably they referred to issues of health and safety. Early in the twentieth century cuts, grazes and bruises were accepted as an inevitable and daily consequence of such working conditions, not to mention afflictions like callouses and "beat knee" brought on by the unavoidable scrabbling about below ground. The utterly inadequate lighting in many mines made colliers prone to an eye condition known as nystagmus, and the repeated inhalation of coal dust could cause some serious respiratory disorders. Although these had been recognised before the time of the Children's Employment Commission, they were not studied in any systematic way in any coalfield until the twentieth century. It was not until 1922 that the Committee on Occupational Diseases amongst mine workers was formed, and a few years later the Mines Department appointed their own Medical officer. At the same period there was pressure for a government inquiry to study the condition known as "Anthracosis", to which anthracite miners were especially susceptible. In December 1930, it was agreed to refer this issue to the Medical Research Council.[71] These concerns had the strong backing of the miners' unions, and the struggle for compensation has been described in the autobiography of Arthur Horner, a leading union official of the 1930's.[72] The improvements which were made as an eventual result, were good and necessary. However most of these reforms appeared far too late to be of much help to the colliers of Pembrokeshire, who had laboured long in some of the worst conditions ever encountered in the British coal industry.

[1] N.L.W., Great Sessions, 4. Pembrokeshire Gaol Files, 813/4, concerning J. Hugh.

[2] N.L.W., Great Sessions, 4. Pembrokeshire Gaol Files, 813/5, concerning W. Thomas.

[3] N.L.W., Great Sessions, 4. Pembrokeshire Gaol Files, 817/1, concerning T. Evan.

[4] N.L.W., Great Sessions, 4. Pembrokeshire Gaol Files, 817/1, concerning J. Harry.

[5] N.L.W., Great Sessions, 4. Pembrokeshire Gaol Files, 817/3, concerning L. David.

[6] N.L.W., Great Sessions, 4. Pembrokeshire Gaol Files, 817/3, concerning R. Hendy.

[7] N.L.W., Great Sessions, 4. Pembrokeshire Gaol Files, 817/3, concerning R. Rees.

[8] N.L.W., Coleman MS, 445.

[9] N.L.W., Coleman MS, 449.

[10] N.L.W., Coleman MS, 451. The Children's Employment Commission Report, 1842, Appendix A, 492, includes a list of inquests held before J. S. Stokes, one of the Pembrokeshire coroners, and records 18 colliers' deaths in the years 1839-1841. The most notable relates to a female collier "smothered in a pit".

[11] *The Cambrian*, 4 April 1840. The accident occurred on 28 March 1840.

[12] *The Cambrian*, 16 June 1841. The Freystrop colliery was not one of those visited by R. H. Franks in 1841, possibly because it had been put out of action by this accident. It is thought to have reopened later.

[13] *Children's Employment Commission Report,* 1842.

[14] *Children's Employment Commission Report,* Part 2, witness 442, Lionel Brough, 578.

[15] *Children's Employment Commission Report*, Part 2, 471.

[16] *Children's Employment Commission Report*, Part 2, witness 431, Robert Brough, 575.

[17] *Children's Employment Commission Report*, Part 2, witness 419, M. Whittow, 572.

[18] *Children's Employment Commission Report*, Part 2, witness 420, Lewis Wilson, 572.

[19] *Children's Employment Commission Report*, Part 2, witness 433, Richard Hare, 576.

[20] *Children's Employment Commission Report*, Part 2, witness Thomas Stokes, 579.

[21] *Children's Employment Commission Report*, Part 2, Captain Child's remark is recorded as part of the evidence of Robert Brough, the manager of his Begelly colliery, witness 431, 575.

[22] *Children's Employment Commission Report*, Part 2, witness 420, Lewis Wilson, 572.

[23] *Children's Employment Commission Report*, Part 2, witness 431, Robert Brough, 575.

[24] *Children's Employment Commission Report*, Part 2, witness 430, Hugh Owen, 574.

[25] *Children's Employment Commission Report*, Part 2, witness 432, Samuel Singleton, 575.

[26] *Children's Employment Commission Report*, Part 2, witness 428, James Bowen, 574: and witness 429, Richard Buckley, 574.

[27] *Children's Employment Commission Report*, Part 2, witness 441, Thomas George Noote, 577.

[28] *Carmarthen Journal*, 16 February 1844.

[29] *The Times*, 19 February 1844.

[30] *Carmarthen Journal*, 16 February 1844.

[31] According to Galloway, *Annals of Coal Mining and the Coal Trades*, Vol. 2, 144, A person closely associated with the case asserted that "only about four feet of rock and sixty feet of sand intervened between the mine workings and the river bottom". A subscription was started for those who had suffered some loss, and soon raised £400.

[32] According to Roy Church, *The History of the British Coal Industry*, Vol. 3, 1830-1913, 423, "the origins of the legislation embodied in the first Mines Act in 1850 were to be found in a series of explosions, beginning at Haswell in 1844, and Jarrow in 1845, the combined effect of which was to galvanize public opinion and government. Seymour Tremenheere, the architect of the 1850 Act, interpreted the explosion at Risca in 1846 as the prelude to many more." In brief, the Garden Pit disaster does not appear to have been a significant factor in shaping this legislation, even though its benefits were to be experienced in Pembrokeshire and many other coalfields.

[33] P.R.O., POWE 7/1.

[34] P.R.O., POWE 7/2.

[35] P.R.O., POWE 7/4.

[36] P.R.O., POWE 7/1.

[37] P.R.O., POWE 7/2.

[38] P.R.O., POWE 7/4.

[39] P.R.O., POWE 7/4.

[40] P.R.O., POWE 7/22.

[41] *Haverfordwest and Milford Haven Telegraph*, 17 April 1867.

[42] *Haverfordwest and Milford Haven Telegraph*, 6 August 1866.

[43] Billy Howells' unpublished reminiscences, c1891, "A Debtor to Grace", 36. I am grateful to Roscoe Howells of Amroth for giving me the opportunity to study these reminiscences. There are brief references to conditions at Stepaside and the Kilgetty Ironworks at this period in "The Journal of Daniel Williams, 1848-1852", held at the Library of Brigham Young University, Salt Lake City, Utah, USA. I am grateful to Roscoe Howells for drawing my attention to this source.

[44] Billy Howells, "A Debtor to Grace", 39.

[45] *Pembrokeshire Herald*, 21 October 1870. The report related to the inquest held into the deaths of Owen Richards of Norchard (aged 14) and Thomas Jones of Jeffreston (aged 13). Eight others suffered burns. Also P.R.O., POWE 7/6.

[46] *Pembrokeshire Herald*, 22 November 1871.

[47] P.R.O., POWE 7/7.

[48] *Haverfordwest and Milford Haven Telegraph*, 4 February 1880. This issue carried a paragraph headed "accident at Moreton Colliery", and briefly described how James Willams of Wooden "was on the scaffold in the sinking pit, about 200 yards from the bottom" when he fell off and was killed. Given the depth mentioned, "the sinking pit" was the Moreton upcast shaft which for a few years, until 1887, was the deepest working shaft in any Pembrokeshire colliery. Pit sinking was always dangerous, but there were fewer fatalities at Moreton than at Grove colliery during its sinking in the 1850's, also P.R.O., POWE 7/16.

[49] P.R.O., POWE 7/22.

[50] Pembrokeshire Record Office, D/RTM/HPO/290.

[51] P.R.O., POWE 8/123. Report of the Water Dangers Committee to the Secretary for Mines, 8 July 1927, 6.

[52] Peter B. S. Davies, *Deadly Perils* (St. David's: Merrivale Press, 1992), 11.

[53] Ibid., 13.

[54] Ibid., 124 and 26.

[55] Ibid., 29.

[56] Cornwall County Record Office, Truro: Harveys of Hayle MS DDH 1/7/301 and DDH 1/7/311.

[57] P.R.O., POWE 7/27. This record is belied by both the report on the accident at Hook in 1912, and the recollections of Owen Gwyther, who worked at Hook colliery in the 1930's using naked lights.

[58] P.R.O., POWE 7/40.

[59] P.R.O., POWE 7/42.

[60] P.R.O., POWE 7/45.

[61] *Pembrokeshire Herald*, 27 December 1907.

[62] *Haverfordwest and Milford Haven Telegraph*, 12 February 1912.

[63] *Pembrokeshire Almanack, 1936.*

[64] Letter to the writer from Owen Gwyther, received on 13 January 1984. Owen Gwyther died in January 1986, aged 74. His text has been lightly edited for ease of reading.

[65] P.R.O., POWE 7/60.

[66] This story was given to the writer by Owen Gwyther on 1 May 1984.

[67] P.R.O., POWE 7/68.

[68] P.R.O., POWE 7/70.

[69] P.R.O., POWE 7/69.

[70] P.R.O., POWE 7/73. The Inspector stated simply: "The coal available had been practically exhausted and the colliery has necessarily been abandoned."

[71] P.R.O., POWE 8/149.

[72] Arthur Horner, *Incorrigible Rebel, The life of Arthur Horner* (London: 1960), 140-145.

Mining Transport

Canals and Inland Navigation

The canal age in Wales began with the construction of Kymer's Canal in the Gwendraeth Valley of Carmarthenshire in 1769.[1] This work was soon followed by others at Llanelly, Swansea and elsewhere in Glamorgan and Monmouthshire. Even so, it was 1792 before any attempt was made to build a canal in Pembrokeshire to assist the movement of coal. In that year Lord Milford endeavoured to construct a canal between his pits at Merrixton Bottom (Stepaside) and his shipping place on the beach at Wiseman's Bridge, a distance of just over a mile. This effort appears to have been unsuccessful. In the words of the well-known land agent of the time, Charles Hassall:

> Lord Milford has lately made part of a small canal near his coal works at Kilgetty. The country is indebted to my Lord for this first attempt at this valuable sort of improvement; which, I am told, was planned by his Lordship and executed (so far as it has gone) by his own colliers. It seems to be universally agreed among the skilful in the art that canals near the coast intended to reach a certain point inland, should begin at the highest level the ground will admit of, in order to reach as far as possible upon one line. Unfortunately the construction of Lord Milford's canal does not accord with this established principle; and is got so much under level before it arrives at the colliery it was meant to serve, that the benefits it would otherwise have produced, are in great measure lost. The undertaking, however, must be allowed its due share of merit; and is, upon the whole, better executed than could have been expected.[2]

Charles Hassall was in no doubt that the provision of canals would reduce costs substantially. He based his calculations upon figures he obtained for shipments of coal and culm from Pembrokeshire in 1792. The total shipments that year amounted to 60,523 chaldrons, and Hassall accepted that half of this amount had come from pits so close to the relevant shipping place or quay that no improvements could be made to benefit them. However the remainder came from collieries situated some distance from the sea in parishes like Jeffreston, Reynalton, Begelly and Yerbeston. On the basis that two Pembrokeshire cartloads made one chaldron, Hassall reckoned that 60,523 cartloads were taken to the various shipping places in 1792. At an average price per load of 1s.6d., the total cost of all this activity was over £4,500. If canals were built for the movement of this coal and culm, he calculated, transport costs could be reduced to a fifth of this total- that is to say, about £900. Given such a huge potential saving, he believed that coal shippers should and could find sufficient capital to build the canals required. Whether such optimism was totally justified is difficult to assess now, because it is debatable whether Hassall fully grasped the extent of the engineering needed not only to build the canals themselves, but also to provide the reservoirs and watercourses necessary to supply them. However he was clearly confident that canals would be of as much benefit to Pembrokeshire as to other areas of Britain. In the 1790's, we have observed, poor harvests caused high prices for corn and considerable unrest; Hassall's hope was that when the agitation died down, canal construction could resume and that "monied men will be glad to subscribe towards such undertakings in Pembrokeshire; whose collieries are yet extremely rich but want the application of proper machinery to render their proper profits".[3]

Another advantage in canal navigation, he believed, was that it would bring about a significant reduction in the number of people employed in carting work, releasing them to go back to farming, which he felt was much neglected. Sadly his visionary ideas were not acted upon. As late as 1815 the writer Walter Davies declared that Pembrokeshire "is indebted more to Nature than to Art for its inland navigation". He asserted that a canal linking Cresswell Quay, on a branch of Milford Haven, with Saundersfoot on Carmarthen Bay, "could not fail of highly improving the value of the collieries in that tract of country".[4] With all the advantages of hindsight there can be little doubt that both Davies and Hassall were correct; it was Pembrokeshire's misfortune that none of the landlords or coalowners was prepared to invest in such a desirable project.

The one canal which was attempted - Lord Milford's canal- appears to have been narrow as well as short. In the early 1960's the few remains then visible were inspected by an experienced industrial archaeologist who concluded that the canal had been built to a width of 10-12 feet, without locks, and was sufficient only for tub boat traffic.[5] The water supply appeared to come from colliery drainage adits spilling into a stone-lined channel coming down the valley beside Kilgetty colliery, although this flow may also have been used to turn a water wheel. By the 1990's the alignment of the canal up the eastern side of Pleasant Valley was almost completely lost, and the small canal basin at the top of the beach at Wiseman's Bridge had been filled in.

Although no effective use was made of canals in Pembrokeshire, they were built with considerable benefit in the counties of Carmarthen, Glamorgan and Monmouth. Indeed their development to provide links between inland collieries and the sea was essential to the growth of the South Wales coal industry and contributed to much more intense competition in the coal trade generally. By way of example, the 1790's saw the opening of both the Swansea Canal and the Neath Canal in their respective valleys. In the words of Colin Baber: "As early as 1801 the Swansea Canal carried down 54,225 tons of coal for transhipment and in 1810 the Neath Canal ... transported 90,000 tons down to Neath ... In 1820 the Swansea Canal carried 150,000 tons."[6]

In Pembrokeshire the River Cleddau was used in one important respect like an inland navigation, namely for the purposes of rafting. This epractice arose from the need of local collieries to have a regular and substantial supply of pitwood. Workmen were employed to cut and raft timber from wooded locations along the river, most notably from the Slebech estate. Trees were felled, roughly trimmed, and then rolled or hauled to the water's edge. There the rafters would rope and chain the timbers together to form a compact raft of perhaps 6 tons weight. Buoyancy was improved by the addition of 4 barrels, one tied at each corner. When fully assembled a rope from the raft would be attached to a ring on the stern of a two- man rowing boat ready for towing the raft towards Hook or Little Milford on the Western Cleddau.[7]

As much of this timber originated on the Slebech estate it was common for rafts to be assembled at or near Blackpool on the eastern Cleddau. When the tide was falling the boatman would row the raft down to Picton Point, where it would be anchored until the tide turned again. As the river was filling the raft would be moved up to Hook or one of the other small quays on the western Cleddau. The raft would then be dismantled and the timber carted to the pit head. The practice was a feature of life on the Cleddau right up to the time Hook colliery obtained its own rail connection to the main line system in 1930. Thereafter it became much easier to bring timber from distant parts of Wales, England or even Scandinavia.

For many centuries the main traffic on the Cleddau was coastal shipping and as this constituted the vital means of moving coal to distant customers the significance of shipping from Pembrokeshire will be discussed in a separate chapter.

Roads and the carriage of coal

Carting by road was undertaken either to take the coal and culm to inland customers, or to enable it to reach the various shipping places around the South Pembrokeshire coast. The carts customarily used for the work were long and narrow, with a capacity of rather less than one ton. Charles Hassall explained that because of the narrowness of the roads, cart builders were "obliged to make the body of the cart too long for the breadth, which is found very inconvenient in an uneven country; and can only be remedied by a general widening of the roads through the united efforts of the magistrates and landowners".[8] Walter Davies writing in 1815 also believed that trade was hampered by the size and weight of these carts, although by this time some larger and wider carts, with a capacity of up to two tons, were being brought into use.[9] The capacity of the carts clearly had a bearing on the economics of the activity, and generally speaking, according to J. U. Nef, in the eighteenth century the cost of transport normally prohibited any considerable sale of coal by land at a distance of more than 15 miles from the mine. The cost of coal normally doubled with every two miles that it was carried and, as a rule, the expenses of carrying coal 300miles by water was no greater than that of carrying it 15 to 20 miles by land.[10]

Hassall's concern about the way carters neglected farming was deeply felt. He observed that:

> As this business employs the country people during all the spring and summer months, they pay very little attention to the cultivation of the ground. It is a kind of dissipated life, which the carters become fond of; affording frequent opportunities of tippling, and having fewer hours of labour than the steady works of agriculture.[11]

According to the Crop returns of 1801 too, there could be no doubt that mining had an adverse effect upon farming. After referring to collieries in the parish of Lawrenny this point was made:

> It is a general observation in this county that in the neighbourhood of collieries tillage is much neglected, and the farmers are very slovenly in dressing their lands. The quantity of potatoes planted is very little indeed, and chiefly in the cottagers' gardens.

In the parish of St.Issell's, Saundersfoot, the amount of corn sown was reduced by the requirement to use land "for grazing the teams of cattle that convey the coal and culm to the shore". Similarly little corn was grown in the parish of Begelly because:

> The parish lies in the midst of coal works, and the landholders, whose farms in general are small, are chiefly engaged in leading coal and culm to the shore, which they are bound to do by a covenant in their leases. Depending principally upon this business for their livelihood they greatly neglect the cultivation of their farms. Many keep a team of two horses and two oxen, and some keep two teams, who do not sow a sufficient quantity of corn for their own families.[12]

In Hassall's day this combination of horses and oxen for haulage was a feature of the coalfield. He declared that "the expedition these teams use in conveying coals to the ships on our shores, which must always be loaded on one tide, never fails to strike with equal wonder and compassion, a bystander not used to such rapid driving as is always exhibited upon these occasions". At Cresswell Quay where there was only enough water to move loaded lighters for about four hours per high tide, the carters' driving is said to have been especially frantic, and truly alarming for anyone in the vicinity.[13] Mrs Mary Morgan, who visited her brother at Hook in 1791, went in awe of the oxen, but at least considered that the carters were in full control:

> I am afraid ... to go in the road where there are carts laden with coals that are drawn by teams of bullocks to and from the vessels that lie at the quays in unremitting succession. It is extremely frightful to encounter the branching horns of these prodigious beasts every minute, though they are in harness and in perfect subjection to their drivers, and in themselves are as gentle as dogs ... and those they drive here are some of the handsomest I ever saw.[14]

That Mrs Morgan does not mention horses is a reflection of their relative scarcity in West Wales at this time. They were much in demand both for transport and for operating horse gins, but hiring horses appears to have been especially costly. In 1787 Harcourt Powell wrote of Hook:

> We are obliged to hire horses to work the colliery at very great expense having no land to keep horses of our own. By taking a sufficient number of horses we should save considerably, by the amount I believe of about £100 per annum. [15]

Having reached this conclusion, Harcourt Powell advised Colonel John Colby to refer the matter to their agent, the ever reliable and capable Thomas George.

To say the least, Mrs Morgan was not impressed by local roads. She wrote: "Our journey to this place (Hook) was attended by many alarms to me, the roads being infinitely worse than I ever saw or could conceive."[16] There could be no doubt that the conditions of roads in the county was appalling. Outside the towns few if any had any kind of prepared surface, and the unfortunate traveller had to contend with potholes and deep mud in winter, and with bone jarring ruts and choking dust in summer. Walter Davies believed that the damaged state of the country roads was very largely due to the traffic in coal, culm and lime wearing deep ruts which were rarely repaired.[17] On the other hand, Hassall, writing earlier, in1793, claimed that roads had much improved in the second half of the eighteenth century because they had received the attention of "certain gentlemen of the County". He noted that a society had been established for receiving voluntary contributions towards the repair of Pembrokeshire's public roads. Unfortunately the task was so immense that this body had been quite inadequate for the purpose. Eventually an Act of Parliament was passed turning several main roads into turnpikes, and in 1792 four more Acts were obtained creating turnpike trusts to supervise the significant roads in South Pembrokeshire. In the event the funds raised appear to have been applied primarily to the principal roads between Haverfordwest and Milford, and Pembroke Ferry, leaving the rest little improved. Furthermore, in Hassall's opinion, the new roads "discover a lamentable want of exertion, and the parochial and cross roads, which are not included in any of the turnpike acts of this county, require particular attention".[18]

Although limestone for road making was available from the extensive outcrops north and south of the coalfield, not enough use was made of it in the eighteenth century. At the time of Dr.Collins' journey from St.Clears to Saundersfoot in 1806 his chaise had to travel by way of Tavernspite and Templeton, as the shorter and more direct route was impassable for a light vehicle. Even so, his journey was rough and, in his view, likely to be difficult in winter because the road consisted of a "very soft, slaty rubble stone which soon slacks in the air and becomes stiff clay. This was particularly the case after we passed the limestone ridge ... and then came into the stone coal country."[19] On the coal measures much less use was made of limestone for road construction, and roads were especially bad, except as Davies observed, "where collieries were worked with spirit". In effect he suggested it was otherwise where coal proprietors were willing to make investment both in their pits and in local roads.[20] Such instances were not numerous. In mining areas the fundamental problem was the sheer volume of traffic between the pits and the shipping places: the coal shipping season – broadly the summer months — saw carts moving to the shore in quick procession. Under the circumstances some colliery owners were willing to make contributions towards road maintenance. In 1787, for example, a number of concerns in the hinterland of Cresswell Quay paid 6d per hundred on all culm carried.[21] In 1800 the Landshipping colliery made a payment of £3.19s.4d. towards the upkeep of local roads in the previous two years, but in 1801 the company's contribution for the year dropped to just 15s.8d.[22] In 1808 a payment of 1s.0d. per hundred was made towards the upkeep of the roads on loads carried to Cresswell Quay from the pit at Brince, over a mile away.[23] The accounts of Thomas Bowen for the Begelly colliery in 1820 itemised an allowance of £12.19s.5d. for repairing roads while those for the year to 1 January 1822 listed payments both for carriage and "extra carriage and turnpike to Tenby, £20".[24]

The most notable road improvement in South Pembrokeshire in this period was made at the behest of the government. In 1814 the Royal Navy's dockyard at Milford was moved to a new site at Pater, or Pembroke Dock. As the roads to Pater were deplorable, a House of Commons select committee was asked to consider the issue. Their deliberations led in 1827 to the famous road builder Thomas Telford receiving a request to survey the overland route to the new dockyard. In due course he recommended both the amalgamation of existing turnpike trusts, and the building of a more direct route to Hobbs Point at Pembroke Dock, which he considered an appropriate site for a quay for shipping to Ireland.[25] The principal portion of Telford's route ran from St. Clears in Carmarthenshire westwards by way of Red Roses, Killanow and Kilgetty to Kingsmoor common. Here it linked up with a road maintained by the Tavernspite Trust, and this trust was given the task of building the next section of the Pembroke Dock road west from Kingsmoor through Broadmoor and Redberth.

Construction of the new road did not begin before about 1833, and as Telford died in 1834 it is doubtful whether he did any more than make the original survey and offer his expert advice. Even so, it is more than probable that the road was built in accordance with Telford's methods, involving the provision of substantial foundations and a carefully laid surface. In several places, for example Killanow and Broadmoor , the road ran close to, if not over, existing coal workings, and the major engineering feature was the bridge across the valley at Stepaside, just south of Kilgetty colliery. This structure was built with separate arches for the stream, the recently opened Saundersfoot Railway, and the minor road adjoining. Unfortunately when the bridge was partially reconstructed in 1978-79 a single concrete span replaced the latter two arches. In its original form the bridge and the completed road to Pembroke Dock, were first used by the mail coach on 6 April 1839.[26] The turnpike trusts improved the standard of Pembrokeshire's principal roads, but they were not popular with many users. In a very impoverished corner of Wales the tolls imposed by the trusts were resented by small farmers and dealers in culm and limestone. The setting up of additional toll gates in the 1830's only added to their sense of grievance, and in 1839, feelings boiled over in an attack upon the toll gate at Efailwen, near Clynderwen. This assault marked the start of the Rebecca riots, a series of disturbances and attacks on toll gates in West Wales which by 1843 concerned other grievances also.

As a result of the Rebecca riots a commission of enquiry was set up to look into these deeply felt grievances. Hearings began in the autumn of 1843, and some of the evidence clearly demonstrated the difficulties. James Summers, clerk of the Pembroke Ferry Trust (covering the road between Haverfordwest and Pembroke Ferry), declared that:

> It is a coal and culm country that lies between (Haverfordwest) and Pembroke Ferry and there are a great number of donkeys employed in carrying coal; the people fancied it a great grievance to pay 1d for a donkey, and the trustees have made a resolution to lower it to $^1/_2$d; the tolls are let up in December, but it would be carried into effect then.[27]

When hearings were held at Narberth, the Reverend Benjamin Thomas described the problems faced by a neighbour and himself when they tried to collect culm from a pit at Broadmoor near Jeffreston, a distance of seven miles from their homes. They had to pass through Plaindealing gate, owned by the Whitland Trust, a gate at the bottom of Narberth hill, another gate at Catershook, and a fourth at Begelly Bottom. He said: "In the summer the toll is $4^1/_2$d at each gate for a cart with three horses … and if I fetch lime at any time between the latter end of November and March they tell me that my cart breaks the road during these months more than in the summer, and I have to pay a double bill."[28]

In addition to carting, the roads from Freystrop and Johnston to Haverfordwest displayed another feature which continued until the late nineteenth century. This was the custom of colliers' wives leading donkeys which could carry numerous canvas bags of culm strung over their backs. As the collier's wife headed towards Haverfordwest she would sell the bags to anyone who could be induced to buy. *The Telegraph Almanack* of 1929 recalled this custom and the "wonderful power of persuasion" exhibited by the women towards any potential customer.[29]

Although the mining community of Hook was only a couple of miles east of Freystrop, there was no direct road between the two villages before the twentieth century. For many years anyone wishing to go from Hook to Haverfordwest either had to go by boat, or had to walk along the muddy track hugging the bank of the Western Cleddau to Little Milford, and then up the lane past Freystrop church to join the road into Haverfordwest. The lack of a proper road was a continual source of complaint, and a matter of serious concern to the colliery company, which was only too well aware of its total dependence on shipping. After several years of fund raising, work on the road was able to start in 1921. When it opened in February 1922, it was a cause for immense local celebration. At long last the people of Hook felt that they had a real link with the outside world, and road transport became a possibility for local coal and culm traffic.[30]

In the middle of the eighteenth century a wealthy landowner named Thomas Kymer lived at Robeston Hall, near Walwyns Castle, south west of Haverfordwest. His estate included land near Nolton Haven on St. Bride's Bay. As we have seen, in 1769 he was the pioneer of canal construction in Wales when he built Kymer's canal in the Gwendraeth valley in Carmarthenshire, but at the same period in Pembrokeshire it is thought that he built an early wooden tramway to move coal and culm from pits on his estate to the coast at Nolton Haven. Unfortunately no documentary evidence for this tramway has come to light, and it remains the stuff of rumour and legend. All that can be said is that Kymer was a man of ability and enterprise and the belief that he created such a tramway is in keeping with his character. He moved to Carmarthenshire from Pembrokeshire before 1770.[31]

Kymer's landholding was on the south side of the village of Nolton, and if his tramway was completed it would appear to have run no more than three quarters of a mile inland near the South Nolton Brook. However a separate tramroad of slightly later date does appear to have been built on R. P. Laugharne's estate between pits at Folkeston and Simpson, and Nolton Haven. Since the eighteenth century there has been a near level track from the north side of Nolton Haven running inland just below Nolton Farm and past a building long known as "The Counting House". Francis Green has noted that by a deed of 15 April 1769, a mason named James Matthias agreed to build a pier and quay at Nolton for £300 for the local landowner Roland Phillips Laugharne. These works were to be completed by 31 July 1770, the timber being supplied by Laugharne. It was also agreed that a certain George Roch should pay half the cost of these facilities and that he should then have the right to use them. It was understood that any profit arising from the use of the pier and quay should be divided between Laugharne and Roch.[32] Whilst it is believed that these works were carried out, the pier does not seem to have had a long life, because it is not to be seen in early printings of Ordnance Survey maps for the district. However a level area which is thought once to have formed part of the quay is still to be seen at the top of the beach on the north side of Nolton Haven. Without additional evidence the extent of the operation and its duration will remain a mystery.

The earliest Pembrokeshire tramway which can be dated confidently was constructed at Landshipping, on the estate of the Owens of Orielton. In 1800 Colonel Colby, as trustee of the estate, initiated fresh investment in the Landshipping colliery, the works including the building of a new embankment and bridge across Landshipping Pill and a new quay on the south side of the Pill.[33] Ten years later, in 1810 and 1811, tramways were added to these structures, linking them with the main pits comprising the Landshipping colliery.[34] In its original form this tramway was a plateway, that is to say it ran on L-shaped cast iron plates laid on stone blocks. At the time of writing it has not been possible to ascertain the precise gauge of the plateway, but some stone blocks and sections of plateway rail have been seen which bear comparison with those on 4 foot-gauge plateways in the Llanelly area. It is thought that these plateways went out of use either before or at the time of the Garden Pit accident at Landshipping in 1844. When the coal industry in this district received some new investment in the 1860's it is believed that the tramway then in use had edge rails. Unfortunately this reconstructed tramway seems to have been abandoned after a halt in mining activity in 1867.[35] The tramways are depicted in Figure 8 although not all lines were in use at the same time.

At Freystrop and Little Milford the coal works were inspected in 1805 by Edward Martin, a well-known coal viewer of Swansea. One of his recommendations was the building of a tramroad from the colliery to the Cleddau at Little Milford quay.[36] This involved the construction of a ropeworked incline about 400 yards long, dropping downhill to the quay. The term 'tramroad' used by Martin implies the building of a plateway with L-section rails, but it is not known if building began at once. Whilst the line was probably constructed as a plateway, in the event of construction being delayed for several years, it might have been given edge rails from the outset.[37] At all events, by the 1850's the line is believed to have been an edge railway, and it had been extended by the provision of two or three short branches to nearby pits, the most significant serving coal pits at Maddox Moor. The fortunes of this little system doubtless fluctuated with the fortunes of the coal industry, and the last reference to it appears on a plan accompanying the sale of the Freystrop colliery and adjoining land in 1882.[38] The Little Milford tramway is shown in Figure 34.

In the Saundersfoot district the first proposal for a tramway was made by the mining engineer John Curr of Sheffield, a noted authority on tramroads. In advising the proprietors of Moreton colliery on the possibilities for improving their works, he advised the building of a tramway in accordance with his own methods and principles.[39] Nothing happened however, and when Dr. Charles Collins of Swansea visited the district in 1806 he noted that there were no railroads or canals in use.[40] In the same year John Curr reiterated his proposal, linking it to the recommendation that several coal owners in the area should combine to form a single major concern to work the deeper seams.[41] Again, so far as is known, nothing was done, although it has been suggested that the Lord Milford, as the largest landowner, was unenthusiastic. As Lord Milford derived a useful income from coal royalties he might have been expected to welcome improvements, but it is noticeable that there is no evidence of any new tramway scheme in the Saundersfoot district until after his death in 1823. In December 1824, the Begelly coalowners Sarah Child and James Mark Child obtained a licence to lay down a tramway from their collieries over Lord Milford's estate to the shore at Saundersfoot, with additional authority to construct store houses there.[42]

A ledger formally belonging to the Tenby and Begelly Coal Company has survived, and includes a reference to a payment made on 31 December 1825 "to the Rail Road", and on the same date there is also mention of Morgan Hughes of Saundersfoot putting goods on the Rail Road at a cost of £2.19s.7d.[43] Unfortunately no further references to this line have come to light, but it may well have been one and the same railway and tramway as that known to have been built inland from the beach at Coppet Hall, prior to the construction of the Saundersfoot Railway. According to a map of the Hean Castle estate dated 1845, the line was then considered an "old tramway", thus implying that it had a very short career.[44] This plan suggests that the line was laid entirely on Hean Castle estate property, and did not run much further west than coal pits at Cants and Stonecross, sites now long obscured, but no more than 400 yards west of St. Issell's church, and a similar distance north of the later Fan Pit of Bonvilles Court colliery.

Such a limited length of line might have been of benefit to the owners of the Hean Castle estate (who presumably funded it) but of far less value to the Child family at Begelly, unless their intention in 1824 was to extend it close to their pits. To achieve this they would almost certainly have required a rope-worked incline to gain height, perhaps partly on the alignment of the minor road from St Issell's church towards Stonecross and Kingsmoor. The precise course of events may never be known, but if the Childs did not have an interest in this line it is not at all clear where their "Rail Road" could have been. Suffice to say that the section of line on the Hean Castle estate is said to have been laid with edge rails and worked by horses. Today the route of the tramway between Coppet Hall and St. Issell's church survives as a footpath known as the Black Walk, and the tramway itself is sometimes described as "the Black Walk Tramway". This tramway and the later Saundersfoot Railway are shown in Figures 4 and 35.

West of the Cleddau at Hook, a deed of 20 February 1837 gave consent to "lay down a railway or tramroad from the three coal or culm pits now sunk in the deep vein at the said colliery called Hook colliery ... at the head of the Pill in the said parish of Llangwm".[45] It also stated that the land taken for the railway or tramway should not be more than 15 feet wide. Although this document also refers to the making of a wagon or cart road across fields north of Hook Pill, the tramway described seems to have been simply the first section of a small network of tramways created in the middle of the nineteenth century between the Pill and a number of pits at Hook. The original main line of the tramway appears to have been about half-a-mile long from the Pill to the Commons Pit, sunk in 1840, with extensions onwards to the Slide Pit, Winding Pit and the Aurora Pit and the Green Pit. Before long it was extended as far

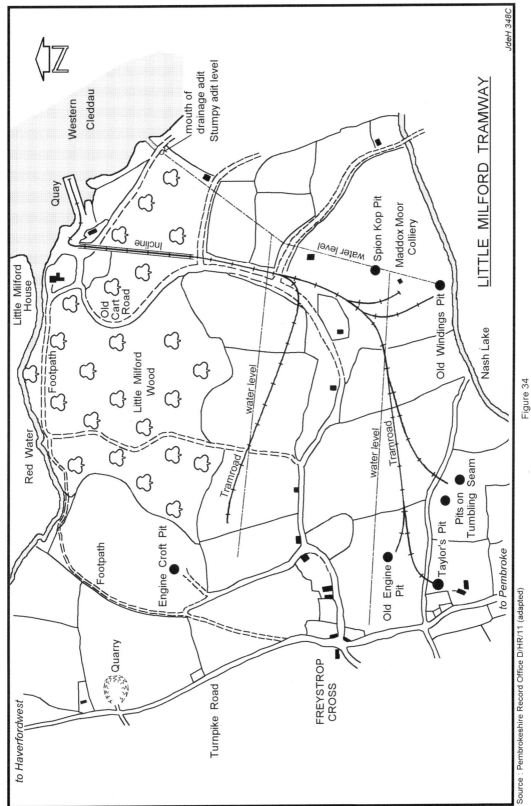

LITTLE MILFORD TRAMWAY

Western Cleddau

Quay

mouth of drainage adit
Stumpy adit level

Incline

Little Milford House

Old Cart Road

water level

Spion Kop Pit

Maddox Moor Colliery

Old Windings Pit

Nash Lake

Red Water

Footpath

Little Milford Wood

Tramroad

water level

Water level

Tramroad

Footpath

Engine Croft Pit

Pits on Tumbling Seam

Taylor's Pit

Old Engine Pit

to Pembroke

Quarry

Turnpike Road

FREYSTROP CROSS

to Haverfordwest

N

Figure 34

Source : Pembrokeshire Record Office D/HR/11 (adapted)

JdeH 348C

- 127 -

as the escarpment overlooking the Western Cleddau above Hook quay.[46] The 1st Edition Ordnance Survey map gives evidence that there was a tramway on the escarpment by the 1880's although by that time the tramway between the Commons Pit and the Pill had been abandoned. The precise sequence of events is not certain, but the explanation may well be that improvements to facilities at Hook quay made it a far better shipping place than Hook Pill.

Early in the twentieth century Hook Slope Pit (otherwise known as Boggy Pit) was linked to the tramway at the top of the escarpment by an aerial ropeway.[47] Nicknamed "The Aerial", coal and culm were conveyed in buckets by this means before being tipped into trams at the top of a tramway incline down the escarpment to the quay. Boggy Pit closed during or shortly before the First World War, and "the Aerial" was dismantled.[48]

After this time the only working tramway to Hook quay was a 770-yard narrow gauge tramway from the West Park colliery due north to the quay. Much of the material for its construction in 1888 was provided by McMaster's timber yard in Haverfordwest.[49] There were five bridges over or under this line largely built of wood, and the final 300 yards comprised a steep rope-worked incline dropping down to the quay. D. J. Lewis has recalled this incline in operation and described it thus:

> There was a single rail track on a very steep hill, and half way up there was a double rail track. Three loaded trams were brought to the top by a horse; these were fixed by a cable off a winch drum and a man worked a brake on the winch. The three full trams were let down and at the same time, these pulled three empty trams from the quay well up the steep hill. Half way up, at the double track, points were set and the full and empty trams passed. No power was needed for this job, just a brake drum, and it trundled pretty fast. The man in charge could see the full length of this track.[50]

One other tramway was built in the neighbourhood of Hook. In 1854 a proposal was put forward to develop a colliery at Nash, just south of Hook Pill. According to a report of July 1854, the surveyor preparing the project "has also planned out a railway from the colliery to Llangwm Pool which ... will be commenced immediately". In the event the colliery company was not incorporated until August 1858![51] The tramway was little more than ½-mile-long, running near the southern shore of Hook Pill to Sprinkle quay. It is believed that it was horse-worked, and operational from about 1858 until the Nash and Sprinkle collieries closed in 1866.[52] The routes of these tramways are shown in Figures 36 and 37.

The Saundersfoot Railway and Harbour Company

On two occasions the present writer has written at length about the origins and development of this company and a further very detailed history seems unwarranted.[53] Indeed as more is known about this concern and its association with the coal industry around Saundersfoot than is known about most other mining enterprises in other districts, a heavy emphasis upon it might be considered a distraction from developments then taking place in other parts of the coalfield. That said, the Saundersfoot Railway and Harbour Company was an important undertaking in the context of Pembrokeshire. As it developed it metamorphosed from early tramroad into true railway, and by so doing was, in transport terms, a pivotal enterprise. Furthermore it was the earliest example in Pembrokeshire of an idea pioneered in South Wales - the planning of a railway and harbour as a single combined undertaking. This idea had its earliest expression at Llanelly in 1802 with the authorisation of the Carmarthenshire Railway or Tramroad.[54] Similar schemes were promoted at Porthcawl in 1825, and again at Llanelly in 1828, before the Act authorising the S. R. & H. Co. was passed by Parliament in 1829.[55] This account will provide an outline of the company's history.

With the coal trade in mind, the Act of 1829 authorised the construction of a new harbour at Saundersfoot and a railway linking it to pits at the hamlet of Thomas Chapel, north west of Begelly and some 4¾ miles inland. Two branches were also approved - the first from Ridgeway

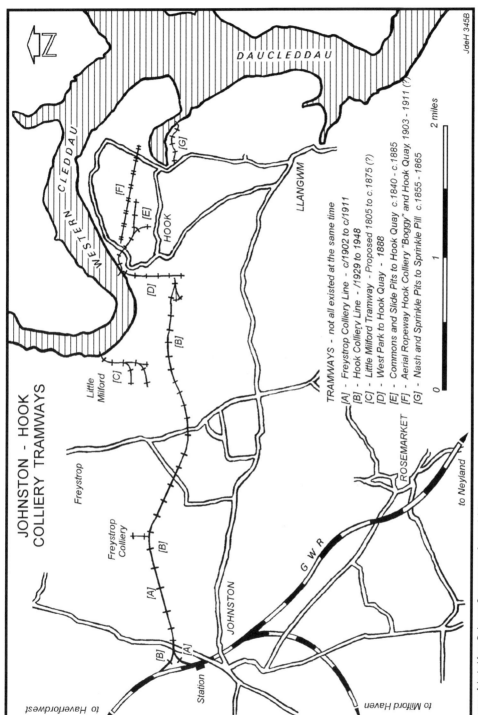

JOHNSTON - HOOK
COLLIERY TRAMWAYS

WESTERN CLEDDAU

DAUCLEDDAU

LLANGWM

HOOK

[F]

[E]

[G]

[D]

[B]

Little Milford

[C]

Freystrop

Freystrop Colliery

[B]

[A]

[B]

[A]

[B]

Station

JOHNSTON

G W R

ROSEMARKET

to Neyland

to Milford Haven

to Haverfordwest

TRAMWAYS - *not all existed at the same time*

[A] - Freystrop Colliery Line - c/1902 to c/1911
[B] - Hook Colliery Line - /1929 to 1948
[C] - Little Milford Tramway - Proposed 1805 to c.1875 (?)
[D] - West Park to Hook Quay - 1888
[E] - Commons and Slide Pits to Hook Quay c.1840 - c.1885
[F] - Aerial Ropeway Hook Colliery "Boggy" and Hook Quay, 1903 - 1911 (?)
[G] - Nash and Sprinkle Pits to Sprinkle Pill c.1855 - 1865

0   1   2 miles

JdeH 345B

Figure 36

Source : Adapted from Ordnance Survey maps of several dates

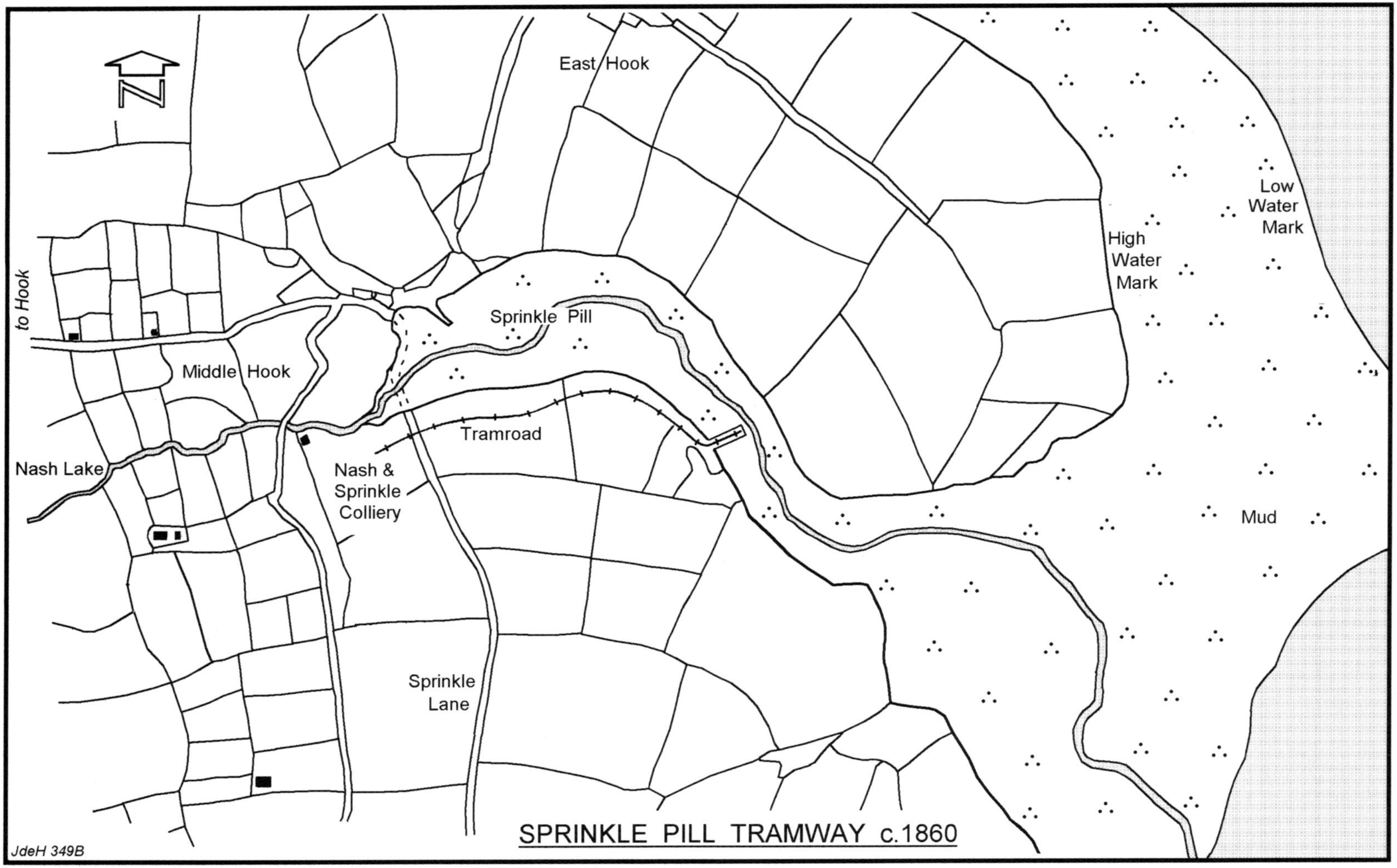

SPRINKLE PILL TRAMWAY c.1860

Figure 37

JdeH 349B

Source : Adapted from the Ordnance Survey

Low Water Mark

High Water Mark

Mud

East Hook

Sprinkle Pill

Tramroad

Nash & Sprinkle Colliery

Sprinkle Lane

Middle Hook

Nash Lake

to Hook

N

near Saundersfoot due west to Moreton (then often known as Merton), a distance of about a mile, and the second running north along the coast from the harbour to Wiseman's Bridge. According to the Act the company could not extend the branch to Wiseman's Bridge "until such time as the Harbour at Saundersfoot shall have been made and rendered fit for the reception of ships and vessels of the burthen of 20 tons". Given that coal exporters were then using the beaches of Coppet Hall and Wiseman's Bridge for shipping, this clause in the Act was probably designed to ensure that alternative facilities were available before construction of the branch railway along the coast began. The total cost of all the works proposed under the 1829 Act was estimated at £17,214.10s.4d.[56]

In its original form the Saundersfoot Railway was an edge railway but akin to a tramroad, in that the company existed to provide a transport facility, and it obtained its income by allowing approved stock (trams and wagons) onto its line on payment of certain tolls and charges. Such a line was an entirely logical development from the era of canals and turnpike trusts, but it was only adequate when traffic was not continuous, and haulage was by horses or oxen. Even though the Act permitted the use of steam locomotives, the company seal depicted drams being drawn by a horse. The line was built with fish-bellied rails laid onto stone blocks, and had an official gauge of 4 feet, although other reliable sources refer to the gauge as being in practice 4ft 0³/₄ inches.[57]

The principal subscribers were Sir Richard Philipps, of Picton Castle, Charles Ranken and William Evans. In keeping with the optimistic mood of the times, a glowing prospectus was issued on behalf of the company in May 1830, predicting that it could have a total annual revenue of £2,900. This document had the support of the contractors, William Bevan and Son of Morriston, Swansea, but rather surprisingly no later reference to this firm has been found. The first recorded minutes of the S. R. & H. Co. taken a year later state that the acting engineer was R. W. Jones. At this first minuted meeting he informed Sir Richard Philipps and William Evans that he had begun work on the railway at Kingsmoor, and also near the site of the proposed harbour at Saundersfoot. He was asked to continue "with all possible expedition" and given authority to proceed with land acquisition.[58] By January 1832 he had been given permission to buy cast iron rails, and by June the rails were in position between Coppet Hall and the harbour, and stone and spoil from the railway construction work were being transported to the harbour site for use in the new breakwater. Although in the same month R. W. Jones was given the grand title of "Principal Clerk, Clerk of the Works, and Receiver of the Tolls",[59] within two years he had moved from Saundersfoot to New Quay on Cardigan Bay where his civil engineering skills were used in the reconstruction of that harbour.

By late 1833 on average two vessels a day were being loaded at the harbour, although it was still not safe in stormy weather. Nevertheless the S. R. & H. Co began trading officially with effect from 1 March 1834.[60] The railway was then complete between Begelly and the harbour including a 400-yard tunnel at Kingsmoor, and a rope-worked incline half a mile inland from the harbour. The remainder of the line to Thomas Chapel was completed soon after, and that from Coppet Hall to Wiseman's Bridge is said to have been finished by June 1834. Unfortunately rock falls and broken rails interrupted the use of this branch, and it is doubtful if at this stage it saw any significant use at all. Before long both the branch and the harbour had suffered storm damage, and as regards the latter it was decided in 1837 to extend the north pier and reduce the entrance to give more protection to the vessels within.[61] With some difficulty efforts were made to excavate the floor of the harbour, and a reservoir with sluice gates was constructed behind it to enable the water in the reservoir to scour out the harbour from time to time. At this period the harbour was designed to accommodate vessels weighing up to 300 tons. Eventually it enclosed an area of 3 acres with ballast and landing quays totalling 425 yards in length. The initial three loading shutes were increased to five, for the benefit of different colliery companies making use of S. R. & H. Co. facilities.[62]

Although in 1840 the company treasurer could say that the railway and harbour were doing better than his "most sanguine expectations",[63] no work had been done on the branch line to

Moreton. Accordingly when the company obtained another Act of Parliament in 1842 it renewed powers to build this branch, and obtained authority for the reconstruction of the Wiseman's Bridge branch, and for its extension to Lower Level colliery at Kilgetty. The same Act also authorised a new branch from Kingsmoor to Broadmoor and Masterlands, although this was dropped in little more than a year.[64] Once again the Moreton branch was the subject of discussion rather than action, and nothing was done, beyond the apparent purchase of land. The line to Wiseman's Bridge was rebuilt on a slightly altered alignment, and at a slightly higher level beneath the cliffs north of Coppet Hall; the extension to Kilgetty, engineered by Francis Giles of London, gradually steepened over its final mile until it reached a gradient of 1 in 32 on the approaches to Lower level colliery.

Traffic was not confined to coal and culm. The colliery companies using the Saundersfoot Railway all required pit timber, and those contemplating any further development required limestone, bricks and building materials. In 1843, Mr. Stokes of the Hean Castle colliery was importing limestone, but breaking it up to move by road rather than rail. The Begelly company tried to avoid paying tolls to the S. R. & H. Co, and carted so much timber over parish roads that they became badly cut up. The S. R. & H. Co had to contribute to highway rates like other users, and so decided to amend its own rates to encourage these collieries to make use of the railway.[65] The bye-laws for the Saundersfoot Railway and Harbour Company, as revised in 1857, are reproduced in Appendix J.

The collieries situated inland from Saundersfoot with access to the railway faced an obstacle in the form of the self-acting incline half a mile from the harbour. This did not deter the proprietors of Bonvilles Court colliery, which was established in 1842 with shafts to the east and west of the through line to Begelly and Thomas Chapel. For the purposes of coal traffic on the incline, the weight of loaded trams descending enabled empty trams to be hauled up. When trams loaded with stone or timber had to be taken up the incline it could only be done by a horse hauling up individual trams. As inward traffic increased, the path adjoining the incline was damaged, causing the S. R. & H. Co to erect a winch to pull up the loaded trams. By the summer of 1844, the company had the idea of using Thomas Chapel as a railhead for Narberth, four miles beyond, and they considered building a warehouse for such traffic at Thomas Chapel.[66] However, events beyond Pembrokeshire soon moderated these expansionist dreams.

By 1845 railways had seized the public imagination so comprehensively that there was a huge surge in proposals for new railways, some practical, but many utterly implausible. This was the era of the Railway Mania, and the optimism and excitement extended to the furthest corners of the Kingdom. The shareholders of the S. R. & H. Co were particularly stirred by the plans of the South Wales Railway, which was authorised in 1845 to build a 7 ft gauge line from Chepstow to a point on the North Pembrokeshire coast near Fishguard, by way of Swansea and Carmarthen. The scheme included a branch line from Whitland to Pembroke Dock, crossing the coalfield in the parishes of Reynalton and Jeffreston.[67] The thought of such a line running within a couple of miles of Thomas Chapel immediately inspired the idea of building another railway to link it to both Saundersfoot and Tenby. Very soon a company was formed with the imposing but cumbersome title of the Tenby, Saundersfoot and South Wales Railway and Pier Company, and by October 1845 it was endeavouring to buy out the S. R. & H. Co for £40,000 in order to include the Saundersfoot Railway within its route. An agreement was reached for this purpose, and the ambitious new company obtained an Act of Parliament for its plans in 1846.[68]

Before long, though, all the hard work came to nought. Famine in Ireland, followed by mass emigration, severely reduced hopes for any lucrative Irish traffic, and the SWR's plans for railway construction in Pembrokeshire were halted. Eventually, in 1852, it was decided to build the SWR to a terminus at Neyland on Milford Haven opposite Pembroke Dock, and to dispense completely with the proposed Pembroke Dock branch from Whitland. By that time the T. S. & S. W. R. P. Co. had had to abandon its intentions, leaving the Saundersfoot Railway to do its own more modest job for the coal industry in the Saundersfoot district.[69]

Even this was not easy. There were financial problems caused by an economic recession in the late 1840's, and even the opening of an ironworks near the line at Kilgetty in 1849 did not do much to improve the fortunes of the railway. Indeed as a railway dependent chiefly upon coal and culm (although with some traffic in stone, timber, firebricks and iron), traffic fluctuated according to the state of the local economy. Although from 1850 there was an iron foundry and a firebrick works at Woodside near Wiseman's Bridge,[70] in time some collieries closed down and the number of independent operators on the Saundersfoot Railway diminished. By the 1860's the dominant figure in the company was Charles Ranken Vickerman, who enhanced his influence when he took over Bonvilles Court colliery in 1863, by then the most productive colliery in the area.

In the same year, 1863, the locally promoted Pembroke and Tenby Railway opened to traffic between the two towns in its title, and in the following year this company obtained powers to extend its line north from Tenby over the coalfield to Whitland to meet the South Wales main line. C. R. Vickerman had some interest in converting part of the Saundersfoot line to the P. & T's standard gauge of 4ft $8^1/_2$ inches, but although the P. & T. R. Act of 1864 provided for a possible connection, in the event nothing was done about it.[71] Instead, to C. R. Vickerman's dismay, the rival Moreton colliery was given a siding directly into its site, whilst the Saundersfoot Railway had to be content with an inadequate coal drop for the exchange of traffic between the two railways close to the point where the P&T line passed over the Saundersfoot Railway's tunnel at Kingsmoor. In 1868, after numerous protests, the P&T's Saundersfoot passenger station was moved from Moreton to a site close to the Saundersfoot Railway's coal drop. Bonvilles Court colliery, only four hundred yards from the new line, was still denied its own siding[72].

From 1869 C. R. Vickerman was in complete control of the Saundersfoot Railway,[73] and it was worked as an integral part of his industrial interests in the area, most notably the Pembrokeshire Iron and Coal Company, which comprised the collieries at Bonvilles Court and Thomas Chapel as well as the pits and ironworks at Kilgetty. As a result of serious financial problems the P. I. & C. Co. was reconstituted in 1873 as the Bonvilles Court Coal and Iron Company, the Saundersfoot Railway being a subsidiary of this new concern. For a short time consideration was given to building a standard gauge line from Kilgetty station on the P&T route dropping down the hill to the Kilgetty Ironworks, but for either legal or financial reasons the scheme did not proceed. Instead, in October 1873 it was decided to relay the railway for locomotive use from Saundersfoot Harbour to Lower Level colliery, effectively ending the tramroad era on this part of the line. In April 1874 an 0-4-0 saddle tank engine built by Manning Wardle and Co. of Leeds was delivered to Saundersfoot.[74] Initially named the BONVILLE it soon became ROSALIND or ROSSLYN, after C. R. Vickerman's daughter. Horses were retained to work the portion of line from the harbour to the incline, and also from the top of the incline to the exchange siding at Saundersfoot station. The failure of collieries at Thomas Chapel, and the decline in mining at Begelly, meant that by this date traffic worked through the Kingsmoor tunnel was negligible.[75]

The Kilgetty Ironworks closed as a result of a labour dispute in 1874, and by the end of 1876 it had gone into liquidation. Being by far the largest creditor, C. R. Vickerman managed to retain control and reform the concern in 1878 as the Bonvilles Court Coal Company. However traffic was now reduced, and by 1887 the track beyond Kingsmoor tunnel was lifted as an economy measure. In 1889 and 1890 the line from the harbour to the foot of the incline was relayed for use by ROSALIND.[76] Notwithstanding a spectacular accident on the incline in 1869 when a set of trams ran away and crashed at the bottom, no funds seem to have been available to modernise the incline or to relay the line above it. In 1893, after many years of eloquent pleas by C. R. Vickerman to the directors of the Pembroke and Tenby, a standard gauge siding was laid between the P&T and Bonvilles Court colliery.[77] Thereafter use of the exchange siding at the station ceased. Traffic to the harbour now comprised no more than coal and culm from the surviving collieries at Bonvilles Court and Lower Level. The closure of

Lower Level in 1900 meant that the only trains over that branch were to the company's workshops adjoining the old Kilgetty ironworks, or for the purpose of taking Stepaside and Kilgetty colliers to and from work at Bonvilles Court colliery. These trains, which by reversal at the harbour, worked to the foot of the incline, and were much photographed by visitors to Saundersfoot. Whereas they would refer to the train as *The Miners' Express* local people referred to it as *The Armour*. This was on the grounds of a perceived resemblance to armoured trains used by the British in South Africa during the Boer war; somewhat illogically the unkempt and blackened miners aboard the train were described as "the Boers"![78]

The promotion of the New Reynolton Anthracite colliery in 1913 soon offered the prospect of fresh traffic on the Saundersfoot line.[79] Agreement was reached between the colliery company and the S. R. & H. Co. for relaying the railway to Thomas Chapel, and the building of the 1^1/$_2$-mile-extension westwards to the reconstructed colliery at Reynalton. The colliery company ordered a remarkable locomotive to work this line, an 0-4-0 saddle tank only 6 feet high, allowing a mere 6 inch clearance when it was passing through the Kingsmoor tunnel. Built by Kerr Stuart and Co. of Stoke on Trent, and named BULL DOG, it was delivered in March 1915, by which time the line had been in use for several months worked by horses. Unfortunately after a few years it became apparent that the coal at Reynalton was unreliable, and the pit was increasingly unprofitable. Early in 1921, mining was halted by a labour dispute, and the workings were inadvertently allowed to flood.[80] Production never resumed, and the colliery closed. In June 1922, an auction of recoverable colliery plant and equipment took place at Saundersfoot station, as a result of which the locomotive BULL DOG and most of Reynalton's iron or wooden-bodied coal drams were transferred to the Saundersfoot Railway. The locomotive was put to work shuttling between Bonvilles Court colliery and the top of the incline. In 1923 about 1,000 yards of track at Reynalton were removed for use elsewhere on the line.[81] Although the revival of Reynalton colliery was short lived, the period of its operation saw numerous improvements in the general condition of the Saundersfoot Railway. The plan of the railway provided in Figure 35 includes the Reynalton extension.

Thereafter the story of decline in the coal industry was matched by decline on the railway. In April 1930 Bonvilles Court colliery closed down, and for some time the line was out of use, with BULL DOG and ROSALIND languishing in their respective engine sheds. The reopening of Broom and Kilgetty collieries in 1933-35 brought both back into service, with BULL DOG operating between Broom colliery and the top of the incline, and also to the coal screens at Bonvilles Court, which had been retained in working order. ROSALIND again operated below the incline. Throughout their existence at Saundersfoot, it is believed that the two engines met only once, when the BULL DOG was lowered down the incline and hauled to the workshops at Kilgetty for overhaul and the removal of the cab roof to increase the comfort of the engine crew.

Following the closure of both collieries early in 1939, the Saundersfoot Railway remained in use for clearing coal stocks until May. By July the BULL DOG had been sold for further service to the Llanelly steelworks and removed by the GWR over the Bonvilles Court standard gauge siding – one of the very last occasions the siding was used. Most of the remaining stock was life expired and only fit for scrap. By August dismantling of the railway was underway, the first portion to be lifted being that from Bonvilles Court to Broom. Some track around the harbour and on the Kilgetty line remained intact until 1940, but then track, trams and the ROSALIND were broken up to assist the World War II scrap drive. The last wooden sleepers were removed from Railway Street (now known as The Strand) in Saundersfoot in 1955, and most of the route was then converted into a public footpath.[82]

The Freystrop Colliery Railway

West of the Cleddau there was no serious attempt to build a new railway to serve the coal industry until the very end of the century. After a couple of years of preparation and planning the Freystrop Colliery Company was formed in July 1900 to take over and redevelop the site

THE SAUNDERSFOOT RAILWAY

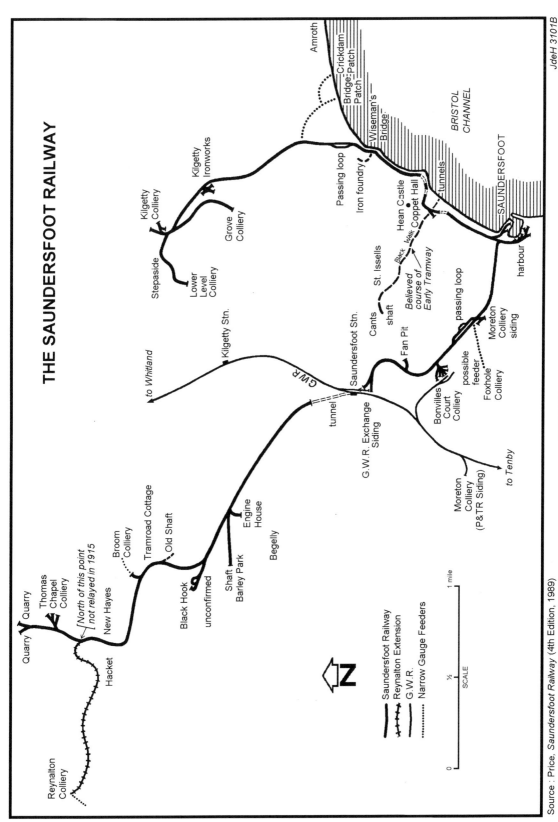

Figure 35

of the former Cardmakers' Pool at Freystrop.[83] The reconstruction of the mine took some time, but it became obvious that the anticipated output would make the previous practice of carting coal and culm either to the quays on the river or to Johnston station quite impractical. As the colliery was only one and a half miles east of Johnston the natural solution was the construction of a rail link between the colliery and the Great Western Railway at Johnston. Initial surveys of the terrain were somewhat discouraging, because much of the land consisted of marsh and bog. Nevertheless the work was put in hand and according to the *Pembrokeshire Herald* in September 1901, construction "will be proceeded with at once so as to enable the company to run their output to Milford Haven".[84] The job took almost two years, and in the words of the *Pembrokeshire Herald* "in spite of tremendous difficulties ... their efforts were eventually crowned with success". The newspaper went on to enthuse that "now it is possible for the wagons belonging to the company to be filled under the huge screen, five at a time, with different qualities of coal". After loading, the company's engine would move the wagons to the sidings at Johnston "for removal to any part of the country in a very short time". At the time of this press report in October 1903, it was said that production amounted to 400 tons of coal and culm per week, but that output was expected to increase considerably.[85]

The most notable shareholders in the Freystrop company were David Evans and John Glasbrook, well-known Swansea coal owners and coal shippers.[86] The Milford Docks Company also had a financial stake in the concern, and were often represented at meetings by two of their directors, C. E. Newbon and F. Brocklebank. As a result of their involvement, the junction with the main line at Johnston was laid facing south towards Milford Haven, in anticipation of sizeable quantities of coal moving in that direction for shipment. Indeed, according to a newspaper report in January 1903, "two vessels are being loaded with this coal at Milford Docks by means of the powerful new crane, capable of lifting ten tons".[87] In 1905 the colliery encountered geological problems which halted production for several months. Company correspondence dating from April and May 1906 included the assertion: "in consequence of the mine having been opened in disturbed ground we were obliged, at least temporarily, to discontinue using the pit in August last, and to open another, at some distance away, clear of the fault". Mining resumed, but the difficulties continued, and work ceased again in 1907.[88] Eventually it was decided to abandon the enterprise and accordingly, after a period of disuse, the line was closed officially in 1911. In its brief career it had been worked at different times by two tank locomotives. The first cannot be identified now, but the second was an 0-4-0 saddle tank built in 1905 by Andrew Barclay and Co. of Kilmarnock.[89] The locomotive shed was situated about 300 yards from the junction at Johnston, facing towards Freystrop. Figure 38 depicts this short-lived colliery line.

The Hook Colliery Railway

The Margaret Pit was sunk at Hook in 1910, and initially coal was moved to Hook quay in small trams over the narrow gauge railway built in 1888 to serve the older West Park colliery. This was an endless rope-worked tramway, driven by a stationary engine at the colliery. The side tipping trains on this line were not grouped together as a train, but spaced out about thirty yards apart along the line. This space was needed to give time for the loaded trams to be knocked off when they reached the incline, and the empties hooked on. This was a job involving good timing and some skill in connecting (or disconnecting) the hook and chain fitting into a "y" shaped bracket on the endless rope.[90] At the quay the coal had to be transferred to barges which were then worked down to Llangwm Pool for loading into sea-going vessels. Later the river was dredged in the vicinity of Hook quay to allow small coasters to come alongside for loading, but this system of transport was still slow and labour intensive, and a handicap to the colliery.

By 1919 the need for a rail link to the main line at Johnston was obvious. A document proposing the reconstitution of the Hook Colliery Company in 1920 observed that "but for

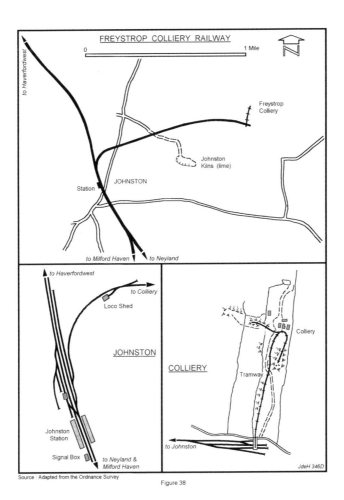

FREYSTROP COLLIERY RAILWAY

0   1 Mile

to Haverfordwest

Freystrop
Colliery

Johnston
Kilns (lime)

JOHNSTON

Station

to Milford Haven   to Neyland

to Haverfordwest

to Colliery

Loco Shed

JOHNSTON

Johnston
Station

Signal Box   to Neyland &
Milford Haven

COLLIERY

Colliery

Tramway

to Johnston

JdeH 346D

Source : Adapted from the Ordnance Survey

Figure 38

the lack of railway facilities, the Pembrokeshire coalfield would not have been undeveloped for so long". Even so, nothing was done until 1929 when it was decided to rebuild the old Freystrop colliery railway, extending it westwards to the West Park and Margaret Pit at Hook.[91] Work began in November the same year, the contractors Davies, Middleton and Davies of Cardiff using a vertical boilered steam crane to assist in the civil engineering and the laying of the track. The estimated cost of the work was £40,000, and this time the junction at Johnston was laid facing north to allow direct running towards Haverfordwest and Carmarthen thereby speeding up the delivery of Hook coal and culm by rail. Pembrokeshire County Council raised an objection to the level crossing over the main road near Johnston (one of five such crossings on the line) but eventually the problem was resolved. A siding for the use of the nearby Johnston brickworks was also provided. A permanent connection with the GWR main line was made on 13 November 1930, and the railway opened to traffic.[92] The track was mostly flat bottomed rail bolted to wooden sleepers; the line was just 4 miles long. The contractors' locomotive, D.M.D.Ltd No 10, an 0-6-0 saddle tank built by Peckett of Bristol, was retained, but another engine said to have been at Hook, an 0-4-0 saddle tank built by Hawthorn Leslie, was transferred to Davies, Middleton and Davies at Caerphilly. A small locomotive shed was provided at Hook Colliery.[93]

Following the closure of Bonvilles Court colliery at Saundersfoot, we have noted that Hook was able to capture some of that colliery's markets. In 1934 some 35,000 tons of coal and culm were dispatched from Hook by rail, and by that time the colliery railway had acquired an engine from the Mersey Docks and Harbour Board, an 0-6-0 saddle tank built by Avonside of

Bristol in 1910. The company also owned a modest fleet of open wagons to assist the distribution of their coal, these being marked "to be returned to Johnston". Loaded wagons were picked up from the sidings at Johnston by GWR freight trains. The Margaret Pit was flooded accidentally in 1935, but by then production was focused on the newer West Drift. Even so, output fell to just 20,000 tons by 1939, although it increased somewhat again during World War II. There was an additional boost to traffic at the Johnston end of the line by the setting up of an Admiralty Mines Filling Depot next to the now closed Johnston Brickworks. Under an informal agreement the Admiralty was allowed to store empty wagons at the colliery, and have the use of the colliery locomotive for 12s.6d per hour.[94] By the time of the nationalisation of the coal industry in 1947 it was clear that Hook colliery did not have much future. As we have seen, the mine experienced flooding in 1947 and 1948, and it was abandoned. Because the closure was so sudden, some new pit props were actually delivered to the colliery by rail after the event.[95] After the clearance of coal stocks and the removal of some equipment by rail, the colliery railway finally closed in July 1948. Much of the track was still in position as late as the summer of 1951, but it was all removed by the end of the following year. The Hook colliery line is depicted in Figure 39.

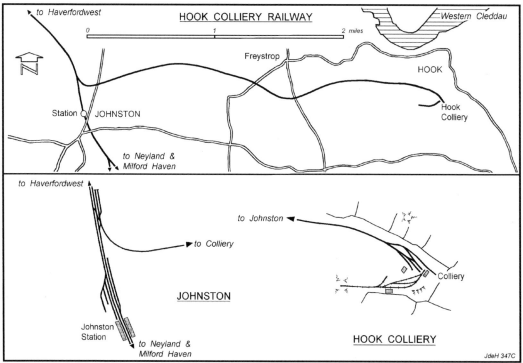

Source : Adapted from the Ordnance Survey

Figure 39

The Milford and St. Bride's Bay Light Railway

Following the failure of the Freystrop Colliery Company, the Milford Docks company did not lose interest in handling Pembrokeshire anthracite. As early as 1865 a proposal had been made for the building of a railway between the GWR at Johnston and pits on St.Bride's Bay at Little Haven and Nolton Haven, but no action was taken to make it a reality. The possibility of making such a line was raised again in 1911, inspired primarily by the desire of some Lancashire coal owners to develop the coalfield on St.Bride's Bay, by reconstructing old pits near Nolton. No doubt aware of the difficulties experienced by the short-lived Trefrane Cliff

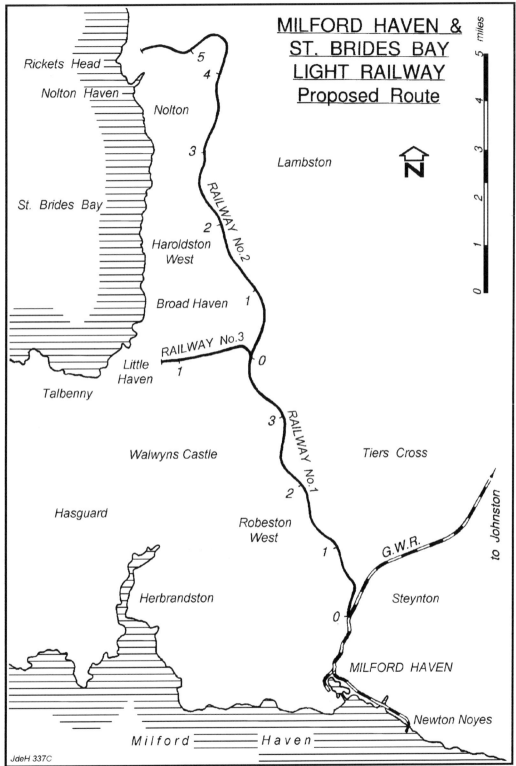

MILFORD HAVEN &
ST. BRIDES BAY
LIGHT RAILWAY
Proposed Route

Rickets Head

Nolton Haven

Nolton

5
4

3

Lambston

St. Brides Bay

RAILWAY No.2

2

Haroldston
West

Broad Haven

1

RAILWAY No.3

0

Little
Haven

1

Talbenny

3

RAILWAY No.1

Walwyns Castle

Tiers Cross

2

Hasguard

Robeston
West

1

G.W.R.

to Johnston

Herbrandston

0

Steynton

MILFORD HAVEN

Milford   Haven

Newton Noyes

JdeH 337C

Source : Pembrokeshire Records Office - Plans & Sections of Light Railway
Figure 40

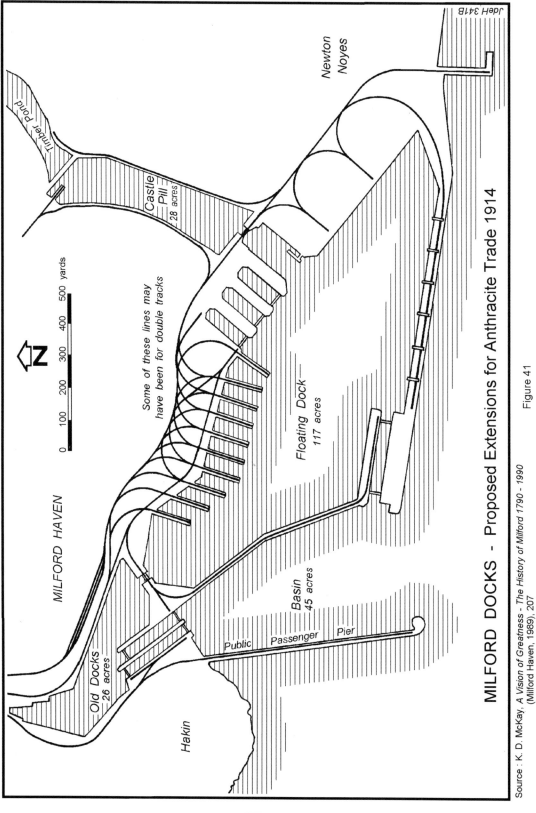

MILFORD DOCKS - Proposed Extensions for Anthracite Trade 1914

Figure 41

Source : K. D. McKay, A Vision of Greatness - The History of Milford 1790 - 1990
(Milford Haven, 1989), 207

colliery nearby in having to rely upon coal carts hauled by traction engines, the promoters of this scheme had more ambitious ideas. Their original plans contemplated the building of a pontoon for shipping purposes in the middle of Nolton Haven, coal being carried to the pontoon by an aerial ropeway.[96] The early surveys of coal reserves were very encouraging and left the Milford Docks Co. in no doubt that a railway to their docks would be a better way of handling the sizeable tonnages of anthracite anticipated. Indeed, the company duly opposed the proposal for a pontoon at Nolton Haven and produced their own plan not only to build 11 miles of railway between Nolton, Little Haven and Milford at a cost of £90,000, but also to enlarge the docks at Milford by the construction of a series of loading jetties between the existing docks and Castle Pill.[97] It was envisaged that these would be protected by two new breakwaters, one built south from Hakin Point, and the other west from Newton Noyes. The route of the proposed railway is shown in Figure 40, and the grandiose plan for the docks is indicated in Figure 41. Such ambitious proposals did not escape some local criticism and considerable opposition from the owner of the Stancombe estate at Nolton, but eventually the company obtained a Light Railway Order for building the line in 1916. By this time, however, attention had shifted to the business of the docks in wartime, and there was far less willingness to invest in such an optimistic project. Although the company was still interested in proceeding after World War I, the continuing objections of the Nolton landowner appear to have deterred any action.[98]

Motor Transport

World War I gave a massive boost to the building of motor vehicles of all kinds, and in the 1920's the use of road vehicles for the transport of both passengers and goods increased quickly. Whereas coal merchants were usually to be found in railway goods yards, motor vehicles allowed them to develop coal yards wherever circumstances might suit them. By the second World War, for example, an established coal merchant like Messrs Raymond of Letterston was using small lorries capable of carrying 3-ton consignments.[99] If Reynalton colliery had been developed at the end of the war rather than just before, it must be debatable whether an extension of the Saundersfoot Railway would have been built to serve it. Both Broom and Kilgetty collieries were reopened within sight of the Saundersfoot line, but the small colliery at Loveston relied entirely upon motor transport, and indeed a photograph exists showing a Great Western Railway lorry at this mine. Although Hook had its road by the 1920's, the decision to build the colliery railway was based on the hope of achieving a much larger output, as well as the likely ending of the colliery's reliance upon shipping. When Wood Level, Kilgetty, went into production in 1944 the manager, Edgar Howells, soon acquired four lorries to distribute culm all over Pembrokeshire. Loads were taken regularly to destinations as diverse as Haverfordwest, Crymmych Arms, Meidrim and Pendine.[100]

Endnotes for Chapter Seven

[1] An account of Kymer's Canal is given in Charles Hadfield, *Canals of South Wales and the Borders* (Newton Abbot: David & Charles, 1967), 31. Additional detail is given in R. E. Bowen, *The Burry Port & Gwendraeth Valley*, Vol.1, *Canals & Tramroads* (Usk: Oakwood Press, 2001).

[2] Charles Hassall, *General View of the Agriculture of Pembrokeshire* (London, 1794), 59.

[3] Hassall, *General View of the Agriculture of Pembrokeshire*, 59-61.

[4] Walter Davies, *General View of the Agriculture and Domestic Economy of South Wales,* Vol. 2, 409.

[5] Hadfield, *Canals of South Wales & the Borders*, 44. The lack of competent canal engineers was a limiting factor in canal construction in West Wales.

[6] Colin Baber, "Canals and the Economic Development of South Wales" in C. Baber and L. J. Williams (eds.), *Modern South Wales: Essays in Economic History* (Cardiff: University of Wales Press, 1986), 35.

[7] Dorothy and Betty Phillips, *Local Study – Hook,* unpublished account of 1953. For many years these ladies were schoolmistresses at Hook Primary School, and noted numerous facets of local life which might otherwise have gone unrecorded. In the twentieth century, until the 1930's, some rafting took place aided by small motorised craft. In the 1980's the rotting remains of two such vessels could still be seen – the MARY EYNON, lying west of Hook Quay, and the JANE, lying in Millin Pill, on the opposite side of the Western Cleddau.

[8] Hassall, *General View of the Agriculture of Pembrokeshire,* 30.

[9] Walter Davies, *General View of the Agriculture and Domestic Economy of South Wales,* 220-21.

[10] Nef, *The Rise of the British Coal Industry,* Vol. 1, 103. To judge from leases imposing a duty on lessees to cart coal, this principle applied in Pembrokeshire. In any case, Pembrokeshire being a peninsula county meant that most settlements were within a few miles of navigable water.

[11] Hassall, *General View of the Agriculture of Pembrokeshire,* 58.

[12] Williams, "The Acreage Returns for Wales 1801."

[13] Hassall, *General View of the Agriculture of Pembrokeshire,* 19. The reference to frantic driving is slightly surprising. Although there was urgency to load vessels to sail on the next high tide, the roads were poor and oxen would have been disinclined to hurry.

[14] Mrs Mary Morgan, *A Tour to Milford Haven in the year 1791* (London: John Stickdale, 1795), 230-231.
   Pembrokeshire was not the only area to suffer from a shortage of horses. According to A. H. John, "Iron and Coal on a Glamorgan Estate 1700-1740", *Economic History Review,* Vol. 13 (1943), 98; in the eighteenth century the Llansamlet colliery at Swansea had a complement of between 150 and 200 horses. Oxen were used to meet the scarcity of horses.

[15] N.L.W., Owen and Colby MS 2276.

[16] Mrs M. Morgan, *A Tour of Milford Haven in the year 1791,* 224.

[17] Walter Davies, *General View of the Agriculture and Domestic Economy of South Wales,* 221. It is very probable that some of these roads came into being primarily for coal traffic – the numerous roads converging on Cresswell Quay would appear to provide examples, although there are also some disused cart roads in Jeffreston parish. A nineteenth-century map of Little Milford actually shows an "Old Cart Road" to the quay; presumably this became obsolete with the building of a tramroad after 1805.

[18] Hassall, *General View of the Agriculture of Pembrokeshire,* 31.

[19] Diary of Charles Collins, published in *Narberth Weekly News,* May 1934.

[20] Walter Davies, *General View of the Agriculture and Domestic Economy of South Wales,* Vol. 2, 366.

[21] N.L.W., Owen and Colby MS 1137.

[22] N.L.W., Owen and Colby MS 2052.

[23] Pembrokeshire Record Office, D/POW/H/91.

[24] Carmarthenshire Record Office, Museum MS 438.

[25] D. Williams, *The Rebecca Riots* (Cardiff: University of Wales Press, 1955), 181-2.

[26] Williams, *The Rebecca Riots.*

[27] *Royal Commission of Enquiry for South Wales. 1844,* Evidence of James Summers, 174. Summers was also clerk to the Tavernspite Trust.

[28] *Royal Commission of Enquiry for South Wales. 1844,* Evidence of Rev Benjamin Thomas, 201-02.

[29] *The Telegraph Almanack,* 1929.

[30] Dorothy and Betty Phillips, *Local Study - Hook.* The opening ceremony was performed on 9 February 1922, by Mrs Joseph Roberts of Little Milford, wife of the then proprietor of Hook colliery. The Colliery Company contributed £100, and the principal local landowners, Mr Harcourt Powell and Col L. Phillips, contributed £200 each. The remainder of the money was raised from donations from the workmen and farmers of the district at a time when miners in Hook were earning little more than £1 per week.

31 Thomas Kymer is discussed in some detail in Bowen, *The Burry Port and Gwendraeth Valley Railway,* Vol.1.

[32] N.L.W., Francis Green MS. Vol. 6, 185. I am indebted to the late Terry Driscoll of Roch for advice regarding Kymer's landholding at Nolton.

[33] N.L.W., Owen and Colby MS 2052.

[34] N.L.W., Owen and Colby MS 2073.

[35] The writer holds photocopies of private correspondence relating to mining operations at Landshipping 1864-1867 which terminated on 10 July 1867, when funds were utterly exhausted. Although there were several later attempts to work coal at Landshipping most were on a small scale, and all were short lived.

[36] Hereford and Worcester Record Office, Pakington MS BA 4416(ii). The "Fraystrop (sic) colliery" was advertised for sale in *The Cambrian* of 26 October 1805. Whilst reference was made to a shipping place at Little Milford, there was no mention of an

operational or a proposed tramroad. There is a local tradition that prior to the building of this tramroad coal was moved to Little Milford Quay on sledges – rather than carts – hauled by oxen.

[37] It is possible that the Little Milford Tramway was built, or rebuilt, by Messrs Bowen & Whittow who worked the colliery from 1825. By this date a newly constructed line would almost certainly have had edge rails.

[38] A tithe map of 1840 at NLW shows the line running to, and just beyond, Maddox Moor colliery, no more than a half a mile from Little Milford Quay. The 1882 plan shows the later branches to other pits, it was annexed to the sale documents when the Pakingtons disposed of their holding at Freystrop in 1882.

[39] N.L.W., Gogerddan Papers (uncatalogued): letter of J. Curr, 12 May 1797.

[40] Diary of Dr. Charles Collins, 1806, published in *Narberth Weekly News*, May 1934.

[41] N.L.W., Gogerddan Papers (uncatalogued): Report on Moreton colliery to Edward Loveden, 1806.

[42] N.L.W., Picton Castle MS 4098.

[43] Pembrokeshire Record Office, HDX/951.

[44] The Hean Castle estate map is displayed in the Estate Office at Hean Castle. I am grateful to T. O. Lewis, owner of the Hean Castle Estate, for permission to inspect this and other papers.

[45] Pembrokeshire Record Office, D/POW/H/66.

[46] The alignments of some of these tramways can be traced in fields at West Hook. Fieldwork in June 2001 revealed that sections had been ballasted not only with colliery waste but with stone not local to South Pembrokeshire. Almost certainly this derived from ships coming to Hook in ballast to collect coal or culm.

[47] *Pembrokeshire Herald*, 20 August 1903, includes a report mentioning the construction of the aerial ropeway.

[48] The precise date of closure of this pit is not certain. POWE 7/46 at the P.R.O. shows that Hook Pill slope pit was abandoned in 1910, but this may refer to a subsidiary working nearby. Locally "Boggy" is said to have been busy before World War I.

[49] *West Wales Guardian*, 17 April 1987.

50 D. J. Lewis, *Dai The Mill* (St. Davids: Merrivale Press, 1995), 20.

[51] Public Record Office, BT/31/356/1299.

[52] The year of closure may be discerned from photocopy private correspondence in the present writer's possession indicating that on closure the manager of Nash & Sprinkle applied for a similar post with a new company at Landshipping.

[53] M. R. C. Price, *The Saundersfoot Railway* 4th edition, (Oxford: The Oakwood Press, 1989); M. R. C. Price, *Industrial Saundersfoot*.

[54] 42 George III Cap IXXX, The Carmarthenshire Railway or Tramroad.

[55] 10 George IV Cap.108, 1829.

[56] By the time the Bill was considered by the House of Lords, the estimate had increased to £17,364. 12s $3\frac{1}{2}$d: House of Lords Record Office, House Committee Book, 22 May 1829.

[57] T. R. Perkins, "The Saundersfoot Railway", 273.

[58] Pembrokeshire Record Office, S R & H C Minutes, 16 May 1832.

[59] Pembrokeshire Record Office, S R & H C Minutes, 11 January 1832 and 4 June 1832.

[60] Pembrokeshire Record Office, S R & H C Minutes, 2 June 1834.

[61] Pembrokeshire Record Office, S R & H C Minutes.

[62] Pembrokeshire Record Office, S R & H C Minutes, 19 September 1834.

[63] Pembrokeshire Record Office, S R & H C Minutes, 1 June 1840.

[64] 5 Vic., Cap 35, 1842.

[65] Pembrokeshire Record Office, S R & H C Minutes, 14 February 1844.

[66] Pembrokeshire Record Office, S R & H C Minutes, 3 June 1844.

[67] Pembrokeshire Record Office, S R & H C Minutes, 3 November 1845.

[68] Pembrokeshire Record Office, S R & H C Minutes, 10 August 1846. Royal Assent to the Act was given on 27 July 1846.

[69] Pembrokeshire Record Office, S R & H C Minutes, 3 June 1850. It was reported that there would be "little prospect now" of the harbour improvements for which the T.S. & S.W.R.P. Co. had got powers.

[70] Price, *Industrial Saundersfoot*, 154, provides a description of the Woodside Foundry. The adjacent Woolsons colliery at Wiseman's Bridge is described on page 88ff.

[71] Records of the Pembroke & Tenby Railway, 1859-1897, are held at the Public Record Office, Kew under reference RAIL 559. Railways 4 and 5 in the 1864 Act provided for standard gauge links with the Saundersfoot Railway.

[72] The writer has described C. R. Vickerman's struggle to obtain a siding connection to Bonvilles Court colliery in some detail in his article "The Saga of Vickerman's Siding" in *Archive* No.34 (Lydney, Glos: Lightmoor Press, June 2002). By the 1890's the Bonvilles Court Coal Co. owned at least fifteen standard gauge wagons to aid the distribution of its output. Ten of these wagons were supplied by the Midland Railway Carriage & Wagon Co., who also leased eleven or twelve wagons to James Vaughan, coal merchant of Milford (Pembrokeshire Records Office, D/RTM/JAV/74).

[73] C. R. Vickerman had a majority shareholding in the S.R.& H.Co from 1863, but in August 1867 the Court of Chancery put the company into receivership, with C. R. Vickerman acting as one of two sureties to allow the company to continue trading. In 1869 the Court discharged the receiver and put the S.R.&.H.Co into Mr. Vickerman's hands. This was challenged by Edgar Disney, another debenture holder, and the dispute was settled only when C. R. Vickerman bought out Mr. Disney.

[74] *Tenby Observer*, 30 April 1874.

[75] For greater detail see Price, *Industrial Saundersfoot.*

[76] Hean Castle estate report and accounts, 16 July 1891, in the privately-owned Vickerman papers.

[77] The Pembroke and Tenby Railway was absorbed into the great Western Railway on 1 July 1897. For the history of this line see M. R. C. Price, *The Pembroke and Tenby Railway* (Oxford: Oakwood Press, 1986).

[78] *Telegraph Almanack*, 1951.

[79] P.R.O., BT31/21832/132153. The spelling of Reynolton, like Jeffreston, was subject to local variations.

[80] The writer has given a detailed account of this concern in "The New Reynalton Anthracite Colliery Company", in *Archive*, No 23 (September 1998), published by Lightmoor Press, Lydney, Glos.

[81] Pembrokeshire Record Office, S.R. & H.C. minutes 5 June 1922, and 4 June 1923.

[82] Price, *Industrial Saundersfoot*, 178. In the late 1990's the highway authority laid a parallel line of bricks into the road surface of part of the Strand, to commemorate the fact it had once been the route of the Saundersfoot Railway

[83] P.R.O., BT/16426/664452.

[84] *Pembrokeshire Herald*, September 1901.

[85] *Pembrokeshire Herald*, 23 October 1903.

[86] P.R.O., BT31/16426/66452.

[87] *Pembrokeshire Herald*, January 1903.

[88] P.R.O., BT 31/16426/66452. The writer has been informed by elderly local residents that an additional reason for the failure of this colliery was the refusal of the owner of the Clareston estate, south of Freystrop, to grant a mineral lease to the company.

[89] John de Havilland (ed.), *Industrial Locomotives of Dyfed and Powis* (London: Industrial Railway Society, 1994), 202. A field visit to this site in October 1996, revealed infilling taking place at a recently collapsed shaft. At that time it was possible to trace the short abandoned incline from the colliery down to the overgrown sidings area.

[90] Description given to the writer in1986 by the late Douglas Jones of Haverfordwest, who formerly worked at Hook Colliery. A brief description of operations at Hook Quay appears in Lewis, *Dai the Mill*, 20. Lewis' reference to the use of horses presumably relates either to a period prior to the introduction of the endless rope or to a time when it was halted for repairs.

[91] Pembrokeshire Record Office, D/EE/7/256.

[92] de Havilland (ed.), *Industrial Locomotives of Dyfed and Powis*, 204.

[93] Ibid.

[94] Advice given to the writer by the late Douglas Jones of Haverfordwest in 1986.

[95] *Herald of Wales*, 10 June 1948.

[96] Pembrokeshire Record Office, HDR/HT/2/10.

[97] Pembrokeshire Record Office, D/MDC/5/5/11.

[98] Pembrokeshire Record Office, HDX/467/74.

[99] I am indebted to Terry Driscoll for this information, which was given to him by Thomas Raymond of Letterston.

[100] Information given to the writer by a former employee at Wood Level, H. Beynon, Kilgetty, on 23 April 1990.

Aberystwyth Castle c.1920 – built with Pembrokeshire limestone mortar, fired by Pembrokeshire culm
M.R.C. Price Collection

Cresswell Quay c.1910. This appears to have been a coal shipping place for six or seven centuries
T. Lloyd Collection

Saundersfoot Harbour, 1883

R. Howells Collection

A coal tram is end tipped on a coal shoot at Saundersfoot Harbour, c.1925

Mrs A. Williams

Saundersfoot Harbour, tram being tipped on coal shoot, c.1936   W. Griffiths

Tenby harbour c.1910. The steamer appears to be loading culm, but by this date such shipments from Tenby were only occasional   M.R.C. Price Collection

Bonvilles Court Colliery   W. Griffiths

Bonvilles Court Colliery, Fan pit   G. Davies Collection

Wisemans Bridge: Railway below cliff at Hean Castle   Mrs D. Evans

Wisemans Bridge: Iron foundry workers   Mrs F. Lawrence

Crickdam: tunnel in cliff exposed by rockfalls, 1990   M.R.C. Price

Amroth: in the early twentieth century there was housing backing onto the sea, just out of view, to the right. The small coal pits in this area were in the valley inland, to the left.   R. Howells Collection

View of Stepaside and Kilgetty colliery

R.E. Bowen Collection

Entrance to Kigetty Colliery, c.1979 showing weighbridge (left) and engine houses

M.R.C. Price

Engine house at Grove
Colliery, 1978
M.R.C. Price

Lower Level Colliery
Mrs D. Evans

"Bulldog" in its original condition   Mrs D. Evans

Saundersfoot Railway bridge over former main road at Begelly   Mrs D. Evans

Locomotive "Bulldog" minus cab roof at Broom colliery   Mrs D. Evans

Site of Broom Colliery, 1978   M.R.C. Price

Thomas Chapel: overgrown engine house at Hacket, 1979   M.R.C. Price

Thomas Chapel: ruined building near site of former Thomas Chapel Colliery, 1979

M.R.C. Price

Reynalton: bridge formerly used by the Saundersfoot Railway, 1963   M.R.C. Price Collection

Reynalton: Contractors using narrow gauge tramway to open mine 1912   M.R.C. Price Collection

Edgar Howells,
manager at
Loveston and later
manager of Wood
Level, Kilgetty
A. Lewis

Colliery staff at Loveton, 1935   R. Howells Collection

Cresswell Quay: views towards the Cresselly Arms from the coalfold north of the river, 1996

M.R.C. Price

Cresswell Quay: decayed quays on both sides of the Cresswell river, 1996   M.R.C. Price

Landshipping Quay: washed out remains of the quay, 1981. The Garden Pit was situated about 100 yards behind the camera, and it is thought that in 1844 the accident occurred when water broke into workings only about 40yds north of the Quay.   M.R.C. Price

Landshipping Quay: Pill and bridge, from the former quay. Former Colliery offices to the left and managers house to the right, 1981   M.R.C. Price

Landshipping Quay: Plateway point on beach by Landshipping Quay, 1981   M.R.C. Price

Landshipping: Westmeadow Colliery spoil heap, 1975   M.R.C. Price

The eastern Cleddau: Hook Quay lokking towards Little Milford, 1982   M.R.C. Price

The Eastern Cleddau at the Folly, approaching Haverfordwest   M.R.C. Price Collection

The Quay, Haverfordwest   M.R.C. Price Collection

Coal barge at Haverfordwest   M.R.C. Price Collection

T. W. Harcourt Roberts,
proprietor of Hook Colliery,
as a young man
        M.R.C. Price Collection

Workmen at Hook Colliery, c.1900   M.R.C. Price Collection

Pit sinking: the traditional "druke and beam", said to be at the Margaret Pit, Hook, 1907
M.R.C. Price Collection

Pit sinking: more substantial work at the Margaret Pit, c.1909   M.R.C. Price Collection

Aerial ropeway serving "Boggy", or Hook Pill Pit, in the Edwardian period   M.R.C. Price Collection

Believed to be the Roberts family at the Hook Colliery pithead
Mrs E. Roberts / Pembrokeshire Record Office D/HR/9

Engine house remains at Hook Pit, 1989   M.R.C. Price

Magazine near Hook Pill Pit, 1989   M.R.C. Price

Engine house and winding house for the Slide Pit, Hook, 1984   M.R.C. Price

Hook Colliery, c.1933   M.R.C. Price Collection

Hook Colliery Screens, 1947   M.R.C. Price Collection

Hook Colliery Screens, 1983   M.R.C. Price

Hook Colliery West Drift winding house and power house, 1983　　　　　　　M.R.C. Price

Saddle tank Locomotive in engine shed, Hook Colliery, 1950　　　　　　　R.J. Doran

Hook Anthracite Colliery coal wagon. Note the mis-spelling of "Pembrokeshire", and the reference to W.H. Essery, Swansea, as sales agents M.R.C. Price Collection

Hook Colliery railway was often used as a public thoroughfare – on this occasion apparently by a family in their "Sunday best" Mrs E. Roberts / Pembrokeshire Record Office D/HR/9

Newgale beach, seen from a point near Southwood Colliery site, c.1930   M.R.C. Price Collection

Newgale beach, looking south. Numerous small pits were opened on the hillside, behind the beach in the distance, c.1930   M.R.C. Price Collection

Trefrane Cliff Colliery, near Nolton, 1978   M.R.C. Price

The coastline between Trefrane Cliff and Ricketts Head, 1988   M.R.C. Price

Nolton Haven, c.1950. It is thought that in the era of coal shipping the levelled area above the beach (to the left) was a coal stockyard or "coal fold"   M.R.C. Price Collection

Nolton Haven, 1910. Note the remains of a small sailing vessel. St. Brides Bay was notoriously dangerous
M.R.C. Price Collection

Broad Haven beach, 1910. There were small pits in the valley behind the village
M.R.C. Price Collection

The Slash Pond, Broad Haven, excavated by opencast coal mining in the middle of the nineteenth century
M.R.C. Price Collection

The Isabel loading culm on the beach at Little Haven   M.R.C. Price Collection

Little Haven, c.1950. As at Nolton the pits were inland from the beach   M.R.C. Price Collection

Left: Freystrop: red water spilling from an adit near Stumpy Corner, 1987. The rails in the foreground formed a tramway to facilitate removal of rubbish from the adit.

M.R.C. Price

Below: Freystrop: remains of shallow coal workings south of Freystrop Wood, 1987

M.R.C. Price

It will be clear that the story of the Pembrokeshire coal industry is in large measure the story of its access to shipping places and shipping. Indeed, as has been noted, the earliest reference to coal is the reference to the shipments from Tenby and Creswell Quay to Aberystwyth in 1282. In the circumstances it seems more than coincidental that in 1328 Edward III gave authority for shipping dues to be levied for the construction of a stone-built pier at Tenby. This was duly built and was one of the earliest constructed in Wales. Given the quantity of coal apparently being handled at Cresswell, it is possible that it had a quay at an even earlier date.

The initial development of the inland (Daucleddau) region of the coalfield undoubtedly occurred because of the existence of sheltered water in Milford Haven and the tidal reaches of the River Cleddau. As has been seen, coal mining was established in most parts of the coalfield by the sixteenth century, but the area of greatest activity was in the parishes of Jeffreston, Loveston, Reynalton, and Begelly - arguably collectively a little Rhondda of the Tudor period. Not surprisingly, proprietors of coal and culm tended to look west to the Cleddau for safe shipping, rather than east to the open beaches of Carmarthen Bay. Cresswell Quay, as the nearest point on navigable water, became the focus for much of this activity. A little further north, however, the logical place for the shipment of coal and culm from the parish of Martletwy was Landshipping Pill. On the opposite shore Sprinkle Pill provided the closest water to the Great Nash Estate at Hook, although there were a couple of small quays on the Western Cleddau. Upstream, Little Milford on the Western Cleddau was the nearest point to the principal coal pits at Freystrop, and nearby Blackhill was the closest access to water available to Lord Milford's pits at Freystrop.

Prior to the eighteenth century the coal industry on St. Bride's Bay was small-scale and localised. The area was very remote, with an exposed and dangerous coastline, and very little protected water. The earliest attempt to create a shipping place, we have noted, appears to have been at Nolton in the year 1770. It is believed that a sizeable embankment was formed on the north side of this little bay, giving access to a timber pier built on rocks jutting out into the haven.[1] In the summer months this might have sufficed, but when a westerly gale was blowing in off the Atlantic in winter it was another matter. The timber pier did not last long, and its destruction was sufficiently complete to discourage thought of rebuilding it. As a result the only harbour on St. Bride's Bay in any way useful to coal shippers was at Solva, several miles north of Nolton Haven, and at least 3 miles beyond the northern outcrop of the coal field at Newgale. To the modern mind such distances are trivial, but in an age when the best roads in the county were deeply rutted cart tracks, the prospect of trying to haul carts over the hills to Solva was not at all appealing. Indeed it was not attempted with any regularity before the 1890's when the short-lived Trefrane Cliff colliery employed a traction engine for such haulage. Instead most considered it easier to cart culm the greater distance inland to Haverfordwest.

The reason the coalfield on St. Bride's Bay was never developed properly was quite simply because this district never had a satisfactory shipping place. In August 1808, a diarist in the Newgale area noted that "Mr Harries of Trenicol found so many difficulties attending the shipping of coal that it deterred him from raising any more except for the use of the Country. He only shipped two small cargoes, one of which went to pieces on the sand and all was lost."[2] In 1813 a proposal was made that a proper harbour should be built at Newgale. Mr R. Bright, then agent for the Southwood estate, responded by saying:

I am fearful that howevever highly desirable it would be to have a place of protection for Vessels on Newgol [*sic*] sands it is not possible to construct such a pier as would be sufficient for the purpose without an expense far beyond the value of any use it would be either to the public or to the proprietors of the adjoining lands.[3]

The difficulties were not confined to coal shipping; it also had a significant bearing on the ability of collieries to receive equipment, materials and other supplies to maintain their operations. On more than one occasion pitwood was offloaded close to Newgale beach in the belief that it would be washed ashore. In fact currents carried it down the coast or out into the bay and very little was recovered in usable condition.[4]

Conditions on the east side of the county, on Carmarthen Bay, were somewhat easier. The beaches at Saundersfoot, Coppet Hall, Wiseman's Bridge and Amroth were all used for coal shipping in calm weather. According to Dr. Charles Collins, although there was no quay at Saunderfoot in 1806, a great many small vessels visited to load "stone coal and culm", which had been carried down from neighbouring collieries and stored in bunkers or coal yards on the shore. "They contrive if possible", he noted, "to have such a stock ready as to load the vessels between tide and tide, as the bay lies much exposed to the eastward. The expedition with which they do this is surprising …".[5] Saundersfoot Bay was certainly hazardous in a south easterly gale and numerous fatal accidents occurred in the vicinity. According to an account published in 1820: "on one occasion five vessels were laid on the beach on a fine autumnal morning. By the time they were afloat in the afternoon a storm had arisen which drove four ashore of which two were beat to pieces."[6] In such adverse weather conditions vessels would often shelter at Tenby or in the lee of Caldey Island. Inevitably there were delays. In March 1829, the schooner ELIZA had to wait at Tenby for a fortnight before loading culm at Saundersfoot. Owing to the strong easterly winds then prevailing, Captain Griffiths of the ELIZA could not "lay the vessel on the beach at Saundersfoot to take it on board".[7]

By the eighteenth century (if not before) Milford Haven and the Cleddau was at least an "A" road, if not the M4 of the age. The traffic in small sailing vessels was constant. In 1748 Lewis Morris feared for the future of the coal trade because ballast had been tossed overboard without any regard for the navigable channel which was supposedly maintained at a depth of three fathoms.[8] As a result it seems that ballast banks were established on the shore line at Lawrenny and, on a small scale at Cresswell Quay, in the second half of the eighteenth century. A ballast quay was built at Hook in the 1790's following a court case in which a ship's master was convicted for throwing his ballast into the river.[9] Even in 1803 Fenton expressed concern for the waterway, but he admired the Cresswell River saying that it showed "a scene remarkably pleasing and lively from the small craft perpetually on the wing, either coming up or going down to and from Cresswell".[10]

Coal Handling

Throughout the long history of the Pembrokeshire coal industry the basic implement for moving coal was the shovel. Whilst horses or oxen might be used to haul carts or coal trams, once at the shipping place the shovel and manual labour prevailed. This was never more necessary than when a sailing vessel had to be loaded on an open beach. When Dr. Collins witnessed such a scene at Saundersfoot in 1806, he provided the earliest detailed account of loading methods:

I have frequently seen five or six vessels loaded in a day, most of them small craft from 30 to 60 tons, but many brigs of 100-200 tons. The coal and culm are brought down separately to the different yards just above high water and when a vessel arrives, all the carts are engaged to carry it down to the vessels, and when the carts get to the side of the vessel, the coal is shovelled out of the cart into her if a small one - otherwise a good platform hangs halfway down, and men and women heave it with great quickness.[11]

The "good platform" mentioned was presumably a cradle lowered down the side of the vessel to receive the coal or culm, and raised up to the deck whenever loaded to enable the contents to be transferred to the hold.

The main coal shipping quays from the eighteenth century are depicted in Figure 42. Most of the early quays on Milford Haven and the Cleddau were relatively small, and did not stand very high above the water. Lower Hook Quay, built by Caesar Mathias in about 1790, initially suffered considerable subsidence, and the repairs cost several hundred pounds.[12] Although at low tide it might be possible to load culm onto a small smack or ketch by a wooden shute, at high tide the hulls of these vessels might well stand higher than the quay. In such circumstances at Hook the usual solution was to set up a long plank, gently graded, to enable the mineral to be barrowed up, and tipped into the hold.

Hook, unlike Saundersfoot and Cresswell Quay, does not appear to have had extensive "coalfolds", or coalyards, behind the quay to help to expedite the loading of ships. A visitor to the district in 1777 provided an explanation: "we passed by several wharfs almost surrounded with culm pits, and so excellently placed as even to effect the shipment of the coal from the very mouths at the pits".[13] Even so Mrs Mary Morgan on her visit to Hook in 1791, was perturbed by the loaded coal carts going down to the quays in "unremitting succession".[14] In the same way there is no obvious evidence today of former coalyards at nearby Little Milford, although there would seem to have been sufficient space. Half a mile further north, at the long-abandoned and overgrown Blackhill Quay, there are walls which could have formed a coalyard, with the ruins of a house or office on the bank above overlooking the old quay.

At Nolton, on St. Bride's Bay, a levelled area was created above the beach on the north side of the Haven which may well have served as a small coalyard, initially perhaps in conjunction with the quay of 1770. After the quay had gone, incoming vessels would have been obliged to tie up to one of the substantial wooden mooring posts on the beach, and the old method of loading from horse-drawn carts brought alongside was resumed. Such was the desire to make the maximum use of the time available between tides that the first cart might be taken out to the waiting vessel when the water was still three feet deep beside it. A similar procedure was followed with vessels awaiting cargo at nearby Little Haven. Fenton succinctly summarised the activity here: "Little Haven affords shelter for small country vessels frequenting it in the summer to ship culm raised near this place in great quantities and of particularly excellent quality, an officer of the Customs being stationed to clear them out."[15]

Before 1755 Cresswell Quay had no less than five quays in different ownership.[16] It was a particularly interesting location because normally it could not accommodate vessels of more than 60 or 70 tons burthen.[17] Even then such craft had to time their approach or departure from Cresswell with considerable care to avoid running aground. As the waterway was and is funnel shaped, the river at Cresswell naturally fills and empties rapidly with the changing tides. Accordingly as a shipping place Cresswell was much better suited to serving lighters, barges and the smaller boats in the Welsh coastal trade. If larger sea-going vessels did arrive for a cargo they had to anchor in deeper water at Lawrenny whilst coal and culm was conveyed to them by lighter. As there were coalyards behind the main quay at Lawrenny, and yet no collieries in the immediate vicinity, it seems probable that some of the coal and culm from Cresswell was landed and stored at Lawrenny. Not surprisingly coal shippers were advised to charter smaller vessels for any shipments from Cresswell. In 1816 the agent at Cresswell Quay, Hugh Wilson, declared that if small vessels were employed "there is a certainty of having the coals in a larger state," because "the coals are tipped out of the carts into the vessel", whereas "larger vessels are obliged to lay about three miles down the river and the coals are sent in lighters to them which undoubtedly occasions some breakage".[18] To a much lesser extent Lawrenny also received coal and culm brought by lighter from Carew Quay, a shipping place off the coalfield, but apparently sometimes used when Cresswell was crowded, or when one of the not infrequent disputes prevented a shipper using Cresswell.[19]

The conventional wisdom regarding transhipment is that barge and ship would have lain

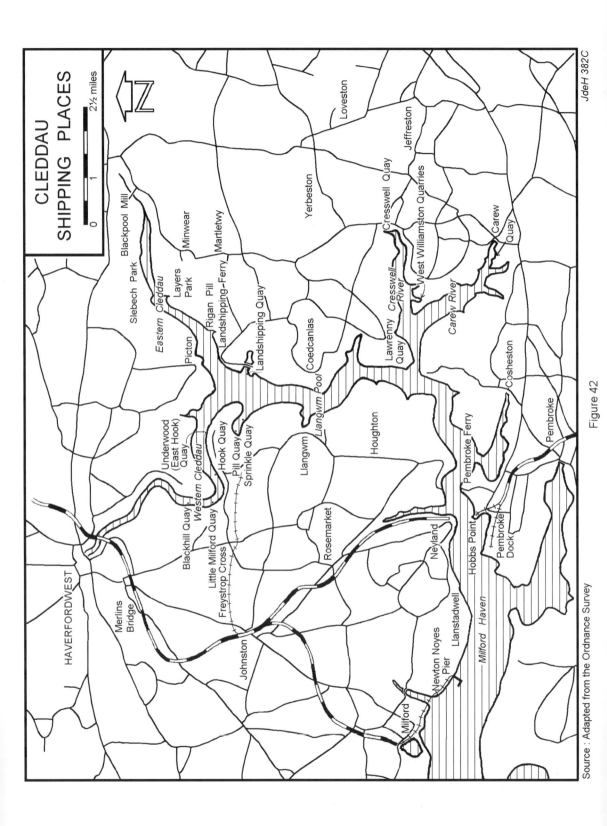

CLEDDAU SHIPPING PLACES

N

0 1 2½ miles

HAVERFORDWEST

Merlins Bridge

Slebech Park

Blackpool Mill

Eastern Cleddau

Layers Park

Minwear

Picton

Martletwy

Rigan Pill

Landshipping-Ferry

Landshipping Quay

Yerbeston

Loveston

Jeffreston

Cresswell Quay

West Williamston Quarries

Lawrenny Quay

Cresswell River

Carew River

Carew Quay

Coedcanlas

Llangwm Pool

Houghton

Cosheston

Pembroke

Pembroke Ferry

Llangwm

Underwood (East Hook) Quay

Western Cleddau

Hook Quay

Pill Quay

Sprinkle Quay

Blackhill Quay

Little Milford Quay

Freystrop Cross

Rosemarket

Neyland

Johnston

Hobbs Point

Pembroke Dock

Newton Noyes Pier

Llanstadwell

Milford Haven

Milford

JdeH 382C

Figure 42

Source : Adapted from the Ordnance Survey

-148-

alongside one another in mid-stream off Lawrenny, where the coals or culm would have been manhandled into the larger vessel. The method used might have been "whipping out", whereby a group of men clutching a rope would jump from a temporary staging on the ship and so use their weight to hoist up a barrel or basket of coal secured to the other end. Alternatively on occasions transhipment might have been achieved simply by men carrying baskets of coal up ramps. Even though the technology available was very limited, it would be a mistake to underestimate the ingenuity of practical men, and they surely gave much thought to these issues which had such a bearing upon their time, convenience and financial reward. It is clear enough that in its eighteenth-century heyday, Lawrenny was almost always busy. At that period the wharfage extended for three hundred yards, and the problem of ballast accumulating in the waterway may have been made worse by coal and culm spilled in the process of transhipment. No doubt the same difficulty arose at Llangwm Pool, which in busy periods was the site of some transhipment of coals and culm from Hook and, before 1801, some from Landshipping. Under normal circumstances on a rising tide the coastal shipping of the period could reach Haverfordwest on the Western Cleddau, and Blackpool on the eastern Cleddau, and the numerous small quays in between.

Culm was usually handled much more freely than coal. The ratio of coal to culm produced was seldom less than 1 to 5, and sometimes more than 1 to 20 as we have noted. Accordingly anthracite coal was a prized commodity, and it attracted a price to match. As there was every reason to avoid breakages, it seems entirely logical to suppose that some element of containerisation by barrel or sack would have been employed during shipping. The difficulty for the historian is that nowhere has such a practice been described. It is well known that the traditional measure for coal and culm in Pembrokeshire was a volume measure - the barrel - but the only other suggestion of containerisation comes in a letter from the Board of Customs to the Collector at Milford in October 1729. In this the Collector is told to ensure that the meter employed to check the quantity of coal or culm loaded onto a vessel should be supervised by a superior officer and "take care that they certify the number of bags, carts or other carriages used in the shipping of coals".[20] In the absence of more solid evidence, some surmise seems justified. At Cresswell Quay, for example, the loading of lighters had to be achieved rapidly between high tides. If these small craft were sitting on the mud as the tide receded it is likely that they could be loaded from above by shovelling culm down a shute. However shipments of coal, although less frequent, required more care. Given the need to tranship the coal again at Lawrenny the case for using barrels or bags or sacks is surely overwhelming. The writer would suggest, without proof, that in the eighteenth and nineteenth centuries, at least, sheer legs or some other lifting device was in use at Cresswell Quay. It is worth bearing in mind that when Thomas Kymer set about developing the coal industry of the Gwendraeth Valley in the 1760's he provided for the use of coal boxes in the canal boats and barges taking coal and culm down to the sea near Kidwelly.

The quay at Landshipping, together with the bridge over the Pill, was constructed in 1800-1801.[21] By 1810 a tramway had been laid from the colliery pithead across the bridge and out to the head of the quay, where the wider dimensions of the quay suggest the provision of two or three parallel tracks to accommodate trams of culm awaiting shipment.[22] Whilst no description of the quay in its working heyday has been found, the logic of what is known points towards the provision of some kind of simple coal-tipping apparatus at the quay head. Given that the quay was situated very close to the notorious Garden Pit, inundated by the accident of February 1844, it is a little surprising that no description is available. Although the disaster halted mining activity for some years, it is known that further investment was made in the tramway and coal handling facilities in the short-lived attempt to revive the industry at Landshipping in the 1850's and 1860s. Accordingly some aids to coal shipment at that period seem especially likely.

The economics of the coal industry in general, and shipping in particular, were remarkable: the unfortunate colliers received a pittance for their labour; many landlords claimed a royalty of a fourth or even a third of all that was sold, in addition to a ground rent, wayleaves and wharfage, the carters had to be paid for taking it to the quay; storing, loading and transhipping the coal or culm all had to be paid for; the lightermen required remuneration, and senior customs officials as well as the coal meter would have to be satisfied. Before coal and culm ever left Pembrokeshire a remarkable number of people received some payment for some task they had performed in the process.

The role of the ship's master in this protracted process depended on his relationship with the coal owner and exporter. As will be seen, there were a few instances of a coal owner having a financial interest in a vessel employed in the coastal or ocean going trade; there is no doubt that the coal proprietors shipping from Cresswell Quay had an interest in the lighters moving their product to Lawrenny.[23]

In some cases the ship's captain appears to have been the owner of his own small craft, and free to take decisions in his own interest. In other instances, where a master was given charge of a larger vessel, his position could be of vital importance to the success of the whole enterprise. As a matter of necessity by the late eighteenth century he needed to be literate and numerate, and authorised to take commercial decisions in respect of his cargo by the ship-owning company or partnership.[24] Accordingly once the ship's master had received and signed a bill of lading, the coal shipper was paid in respect of it. In this way the risk passed to the man responsible for the next stage of the journey from the colliery to the customer. If the business was done promptly, a ship's captain could expect a gratuity given in proportion to the freight charge on the cargo.

Coal Shipping and Customs

Numerous scholars have examined government methods for the monitoring of coastal shipping from the Tudor period onwards. As the usual intention was to be able to impose duty on goods for export, and sometimes on coastal shipments, the concern was to keep track of all cargoes which might be dutiable. In *The English Coasting Trade*, T. S. Willan summarised the main ways in which this was done, and referred to the use in various circumstances of the sufferance, the transire, and existing duty receipts to exempt consignments from duty. He went on to say:

> The movement of cargoes by sufferance, transire and import duty receipt had this in common
> – they demanded no coquet or bond. But where goods were of such a nature that they might be
> surreptitiously sent abroad, and thus evade customs payment, bonds had to be deposited against
> the discharge of a cargo at an English port. These bonds were released upon presentation of
> certificates that the goods had been duly landed at an English port, but they were forfeited if no
> such certificate was forthcoming.[25]

According to J. U. Nef, who was referring to the Newcastle coal trade, the size of the bond payable had to be "equal or more than equal to the full amount of the export tax on their cargoes".[26] Willan argues that "on the whole the amounts of the bonds correspond more closely to the value of the cargo than to any export duty".[27] Having mentioned several cases in which the bond exceeded the value of the cargo, he notes that between June 1709 and June 1710 there were 51 instances of 15 to 20 chaldrons of culm being shipped from Milford under a bond of £20. Clarity as regards intention and practice is made more difficult by the fact that the "duty on coals exported in British ships was abolished in 1709, and even though it was reimposed in the following year, it was only at the rate of 3s. per chaldron".[28] In any case there were periods when duties might be levied on coastwise coal and culm cargoes, and such shipments could also be subject to a bond.

By the seventeenth century the loading of coal and culm took place in the presence of an official called a meter, who was required to record the quantities being shipped, primarily for the benefit of the customs authorities. In 1729 the Board had reason to doubt whether the work was being done properly at Milford. They alleged that officers supervising the shipment of coals coastwise did not certify the real quantity shipped by at least one fourth of the quantity actually delivered, and so directed that a senior officer should check their work.[29]

Satisfactory supervision of loading appears to have been an ongoing challenge. Within the Port of Milford the task of the Customs was made especially difficult by the long and indented coastline, and by a shortage of men to cover the many shipping places. In Pembrokeshire it appears to have been common for tidesmen and boatmen, who assisted shipping as required, also to act as coal meters. At busy times it might be necessary to hire other men to stand in as boatmen for them, but in 1733 the Board decreed that established tidesmen and boatmen should concentrate on those tasks, and instead some other proper persons should be appointed to serve as coal meters.[30] The number of men so recruited may have been insufficient, because in 1738 a boatman, Griffith Sommers, was told to continue "to inspect the shipping of coals and culm at Cresswell Key, by taking the number of the carts at the key which are to be first measured and marked in the presence of the colliery surveyor". It was also directed that "when any vessels be at Lawrenny to lade coals and culm from Carey Key one of the said boatmen are to go up to the said Key and take the number of carts". However the Collector at Milford was told that "John Luntly, who commands the Boat" should keep "an exact account of the number and burthen of boats laden on the ships at Lawrenny from Cresswell and Carey Keys as a cheque [sic] upon the officers at those keys".[31]

Once a record had been made of the quantity to be shipped the amount would be certified by the issue of a coal coquet at the Customs House. When the shipment was intended for a foreign port the ship's master had to make oath in respect of both his cargo and his proposed destination, and then pay the relevant duty before a certificate was issued, and he was allowed to set sail. If the voyage was to be coastwise, it was customary for the master to give a bond to that effect, which might include the payment of a deposit in respect of any dues or duties which might be payable. In the unfortunate event of a ship intending to sail coastwise meeting bad weather, and being blown to a foreign port, the ship's Master was required to show that the circumstances amounted to a genuine case of distress. Otherwise the coast bond would be forfeit, and the Master might be liable to pay both the overseas rate of duty and a penalty.

The eighteenth-century correspondence between the Board in London and the Collector for Milford includes numerous references to such incidents. Some were accepted as genuine – for example on 6 March 1745 the Collector was advised to accept overseas duties for coal carried on the BLESSING OF SCARBOROUGH, James Coope, Master, after he had been forced overseas with coal intended for shipment coastwise.[32] In 1757, though, officials in Pembrokeshire were exercised over the activities of Michael Raymond, Master of THE INDUSTRY of Solva. He had loaded culm at Milford for Solva but took it (so it was believed) to Ireland. Raymond himself said he had been blown off course, and obliged to discharge the culm in Anglesey, but this was refuted by customs officials in the Port of Beaumaris.[33] The officials in Pembrokeshire described Raymond as "a noted smuggler", and "the author of all the late schemes at Solva for defrauding the Revenue", and asked that he be "prosecuted with rigour to deter others from such illicit practice".[34]

The authorities undoubtedly had a problem with coastal shipping in St. Bride's Bay. In June 1757, Griffith Coytmore, the Customs Surveyor at St. David's, reported that he had seized 12 chaldrons of culm landed at Solva which had been taken on board the sloop NANCY at Milford without the necessary paperwork, or payment of any duty. Accordingly Coytmore had stopped the sloop until the Board's wishes were known.[35]

By now such incidents had become too common, because the Collector at Milford informed the Commissioners of Customs and Excise:

> We have been credibly informed that a great many vessels have come lately into the Harbour of Milford, and under protection of being bound to Solva ... And have taken on board cargoes of coals and culm without ever coming near the Custom House and proceeded therewith to Ireland, and to some other by Creeks in Wales where no officers have been stationed ... all vessels going from Milford Haven to Solva are for a considerable time at Open Sea as they go round St.Anne's

Head, but that being a Creek of this Harbour they have never hitherto given any security as the law directs nor paid his Majesty's Duty at unshipping their coals at Solva aforesaid.

In an effort to find out who was exploiting the situation, the Collector had asked ships' masters to take out certificates or sufferances on the loading of culm at Milford for delivery to the officer stationed at Solva. Unfortunately they refused to cooperate because, in Mr Coytmore's view, "most of the small vessels of that Creek [Solva] are often employed in the above illicit trade".[36]

In 1760 a difficult situation was not much helped by the passing of another Act of Parliament, 33 George II, cap. 15. This Act recognised that the cost of carrying culm from Pembrokeshire in small vessels had become very expensive, and the legislators intended to ease the shipping of culm coastwise to neighbouring counties. This appears to have been a veiled way of saying that many Pembrokeshire people disliked the formalities, and some were inclined to ignore them. At all events, a procedure was laid down whereby anyone using a vessel not exceeding 30 tons burthen to ship culm from Pembrokeshire to any other place in the counties of Pembroke, Carmarthen, Cardigan and Merioneth might apply for a sufferance to be issued, upon which the officer supervising the loading would note the quantity being shipped, and require the Master or owner to pay duty at the rate of one shilling per chaldron. On the issue of a certificate of payment the vessel was cleared to sail. Plainly anticipating possible evasions of the law, the Act included a provision for a fine of up to £5 on any master fraudulently changing either his own name, or the ship's name, in an attempt to conceal his activities.

Then as now, well-intentioned legislation could have consequences not foreseen by those who approved it. This Act overlooked the fact that there had been a local trade in culm within Pembrokeshire, free from duty, for many generations. Customs officers in the county must have been disinclined to interfere, because until December 1766, no attempt was made to levy dues on shipments within the Port of Milford. Doubtless prompted by the Board, duties were levied then on local shipments from Tenby and Little Haven. By June 1767, the response in Pembrokeshire was so negative that the Collector wrote to London to say that:

> The gentlemen of this county threaten us with prosecution for these proceedings, intimating that we have no right to insist on the duties; that the same are not due by law on coals and culm carried from one part of a port to another part of the same port.[37]

The commissioners of Customs and Excise sought expert legal opinion, and advised that culm shipped at Little Haven and Nolton for Solva and St.Davids could be considered liable for duty. Griffith Coytmore informed local traders, who then claimed "a prescriptive right and privilege enjoyed since time immemorial" in respect of shipping culm by water on these short routes "to burn lime to manure their ground". Furthermore, any interference by customs would bring an immediate prosecution of the customs officers concerned for detention or damages. The threat was real enough to Coytmore, who admitted:

> I am intimidated from executing your orders without a manifest prejudice to myself and family being unable to defend or contest such suit with the whole country, and further I beg leave to mention that if I once lay my hand upon such a vessel or culm at the place of lading or discharging it would be impossible to secure the same.

Poor Coytmore! Unhappily he represented government in a district too remote to take government very seriously. To add to his discomfiture, the Commissioners insisted that these duties be paid, although it may have been some relief to learn that neither the vessel nor the culm could be liable to seizure under the provisions of the 1760 Act.[38]

The limited options available to customs officials may have prevented the issue coming to a head, but on St.Bride's Bay they continued to have instances of culm shipments disregarding officialdom. By then the correspondence with London tended to emphasize the need for more manpower to meet the requirements of the 1760 Act. One letter of November 1767 is especially interesting, in that it lists seven officers authorised to attend the discharge of coal or culm, and eight officers authorised to attend its loading. After almost thirty years Griffith Summers had the title of "Waiter and Searcher" at Cresswell, whilst Griffith Coytmore, junior, enjoyed the same post at Little Haven and Nolton. The other "Waiters and Searchers" were at Black Tar (Llangwm), Little Milford (Hook), Landshipping, Saundersfoot, Hillsend (Amroth), and within the Port of Milford itself (possibly meaning Lawrenny).[39] The list is a fair indication of the importance of these shipping places at that period.

The opening of Saundersfoot Harbour, together with the improvements carried out in the ensuing years, not only enhanced Saundersfoot's status as a shipping place, but also brought about a rapid increase in the volume and range of coal and culm shipments. An example of a Bill of Lading for a coal shipment to Kent in 1837 is provided in Appendix K. Saundersfoot's advance soon challenged both the business and the standing of Tenby and Cresswell Quay. The latter had been in decline for some time, but Tenby's attractive location gave it the potential to become a significant resort for visitors. Most of its shipping was local to the Bristol Channel, with occasional sailings for Cornwall or South Devon. The customs report book for 1858 does not record any vessel visiting Tenby from a foreign port, whereas it does list eleven vessels arriving at Saundersfoot from overseas, eight being from France, one from Antwerp, one from Jersey, and one from Dantzic(sic). The last was the only one not to arrive at Saundersfoot in ballast, clearly indicating that the others had come for cargoes of coal and culm. In the same year seven vessels visited Milford from foreign ports, only one of which arrived in ballast. Two of these were from Quebec, and one from Norway.[40]

Six years later in 1864, the same pattern broadly prevailed. Of ten vessels visiting Saundersfoot from overseas ports nine arrived in ballast, and of the nine vessels from abroad sailing to Milford five arrived carrying other cargoes. In 1864 one sailing from France to Hook is recorded, and one from Guernsey to Tenby. Whilst it is clear that the longest voyages were usually made by vessels visiting Milford, the precise destination within the Haven is rarely stated. In 1859 it is recorded that a ship sailed from Cherbourg to Landshipping and in 1861, 1865, and 1867 mention is made of one arrival from overseas at Llangwm. In 1868 a similar reference arises in relation to Cosheston, but curiously no mention is made at any time of Lawrenny, despite the evidence from other sources of Lawrenny's prominent role in coal and culm shipping.[41] In the circumstances it is surmised that the names "Milford" and "Lawrenny" were synonymous, or that if a vessel acquired a cargo by transhipment, without touching a quay or beach, it was deemed to be simply a shipment "from Milford".

By 1858 it seems clear that Saundersfoot saw many more trading vessels than Tenby, where the main commercial activity was fishing. At all events it was proposed that the customs officer at Tenby should move to Saundersfoot, but this removal was delayed by the lack of suitable accommodation in Saundersfoot. The Collector at Milford made his own enquiries, and concluded that the difficulty in obtaining suitable premises has arisen "from a desire among the inhabitants that the officer should not become a resident amongst them".[42] Evidently little had changed in this respect since the eighteenth century, and customs officials were still regarded without enthusiasm! Even so, in October 1859, the customs authorities in London were notified that the Customs Officer had moved to Saundersfoot, and accordingly they were asked to maintain travelling allowances to enable the officer to visit Tenby at least twice a week to clear the steam vessels then trading to Bristol and Ilfracombe, and to other villages to prevent "petty smuggling between the villagers and crews of some vessels trading with coal and culm to the adjacent bights and inlets".[43]

Anxiety over smuggling persisted for many years. In April 1880, the correspondence from Milford to London referred to the local trade in providing provisions "for windbound vessels at anchor from all parts", in Milford Haven. This was thought to offer potential for a considerable amount of petty smuggling "were it not for the fear of being overhauled by the Pembroke Dock boat".[44] Arguably the problem was diminishing, because in 1880 the total number of vessels coming to Pembrokeshire from foreign ports was down to eleven, less than half the number seen in 1868.[45]

Given the coal industry's reliance upon coastal shipping it was inevitable that a shipbuilding industry would develop to serve it. By the Elizabethan period it is known that shipbuilding was taking place around the shores of Milford Haven. There were no shipyards in the modern sense - merely temporary slipways across beaches where there was enough space above the high watermark to allow for ship construction. The shipwrights usually favoured local oak, often to be found on the tree-lined banks of the Cleddau, although some imported timber might also be used. Ropes, sails and other fittings are believed to have been made locally, although some might be brought in from a more substantial port like Bristol. It is thought that an organised team of shipwrights comprising 15 to 30 men could complete a typical vessel in anything from eight months to a year.

Up to the eighteenth century, local sailing ships seldom measured much more than 20 tons, and depending upon the style of rigging, were usually described as sloops or smacks. However, as early as 1566 Sir John Perrot of Carew owned a fifty-ton barque, named PERROTT, which traded with Newfoundland. By the end of Elizabeth's reign in 1603 the largest ship sailing regularly from Pembrokeshire was the LION OF MILFORD, a 100-ton vessel which is known to have made voyages to France and Newfoundland.[46] These were quite exceptional at a time when local shipbuilding was struggling to keep up with the seventeenth-century expansion in trade. In the event the local industry could not meet the challenge, and Barbara George has shown that whereas 54 per cent of all trade was conveyed in local ships in 1617, by 1680 the figure was down to a mere 13 per cent.[47]

Several scholars have studied shipbuilding in Pembrokeshire up to the nineteenth century, most notably Barbara George and Robin Craig. Barbara George gleaned much information from the shipping registers for Milford and Pembroke Dock from 1815, which not only noted newly built vessels, but other local ships extant from the eighteenth century. By further painstaking research Robin Craig managed largely to reconstruct the shipping registers for several ports in West Wales from 1786, the year when the general registration of coastal shipping was required by statute. Although their work overlaps, Craig has provided more information on vessels built prior to 1800.[48] George recorded only two vessels actually built on the Pembrokeshire coalfield in the eighteenth century, namely a 32-ton ship built at Lawrenny in the 1780's, and a 48-ton vessel built at Black Tar (Llangwm) in the same decade.

Examining the evidence now available, Mark Matthews has concluded that in Pembrokeshire "the single largest ship constructing area was Milford, which built 21 per cent of the total tonnage constructed in the county in the thirty year period from 1800 to 1830".[49] Whilst vessels used in the coal and culm trades could be built at any site, it is likely that those actually constructed on the coalfield were intended for use in shipping coal, culm or limestone. Of shipbuilding locations on or adjacent to the coalfield, Lawrenny was by far the most significant. In the first decade of the nineteenth century it produced four vessels, and in the second decade another eight, measuring on average 68 tons. In ensuing decades the ships appear to have become smaller but more numerous: 17 were built in the 1820's, 18 in the 1830's, and 13 in the 1840's. One more of 28 tons was built in the 1850's. Curiously construction at Lawrenny then ceased, but Cosheston, about 400 yards away on the south side of the waterway, became a ship-building centre. There four vessels totalling 88 tons were built in the 1860's, three more totalling 201 tons in the 1870's and another of 27 tons in the 1880's.

In comparison with shipbuilding at Lawrenny and Cosheston, work at other coalfield sites was almost occasional. Tenby produced one vessel in each of the first three decades of the nineteenth century, and then four in the 1840's. Saundersfoot built three in the 1840's, three more in the 1850's, but only one in the 1860's. The two ships built there in the 1870's seem to have been the largest, totalling together 107 tons. At Landshipping two vessels, totalling 203, tons were built in the 1810's, but no more until the 1830's, when six were constructed totalling 298 tons. One vessel of 69 tons was built at Hook in the 1810's, and one of 30 tons at Cresswell Quay in the 1830's. It seems that shipbuilding was not attempted on the coalfield on the most exposed part of St. Bride's Bay, but between 1790 and 1840 ten vessels were built at nearby Solva.[50]

The sloop must be considered the vessel most typical of the Pembrokeshire coal and culm trade. They were generally no more than 40 feet long, broad in the beam, and built with a flat bottom to enable them to sit upright on West Wales beaches. They carried cargoes weighing anything from 20 to 50 tons. Their design meant that as sailing craft they were ungainly, and relatively slow to respond to the helm. As they could not sail close to the wind, they were obliged to tack alternately to port and to starboard to make progress into the wind. Even so, some of these cumbersome craft served for an amazing length of time . The ANN AND MARY, for example, a 15-ton sloop built in 1762, was lost in April 1873 off St. David's Head whilst carrying culm or limestone from Milford to Abercastle.[51]

Another distinctive Pembrokeshire craft was the lighter. This was a flat- bottomed barge-like river craft with a shallow draft and bluff, rounded bows. They were able to move at most states of the tide, and could reach the shallowest shipping places around the Haven - most notably Cresswell Quay, Landshipping Pill, Garron Pill, and the limestone quarry inlets about West Williamston. Their usual cargoes were culm, limestone and gravel. They were moved by means of a single large square sail, or by long oars with wide blades known as "sweeps". According to one source they were nicknamed "willy boys", although the reasons for the term are now lost in the mists of time. It was quite common for a lighter to carry a small cabin to provide rudimentary accommodation for the usual crew of two men and sometimes they would sleep on board. This was not without hazards, as was indicated by a report in *The Cambrian* in 1840: "On 13 February 1840, Isaac James of Landshipping, lighterman was left in charge of a barge belonging to the Landshipping colliery with a cargo of culm for Haverfordwest. About 3 am he went to sleep in the cabin, in which there was a fire. His companion found him about 7 o'clock in the agonies of death."[52]

On the River Cleddau lighters were mainly used to convey culm on the Cresswell river and on the Eastern Cleddau about Landshipping. Consignments from Cresswell Quay would be taken by lighter to Lawrenny for transhipment into sea- going vessels, whilst prior to the construction of Landshipping Quay a similar operation was often undertaken at Llangwm Pool almost opposite Landshipping. As navigation to Haverfordwest on the Western Cleddau could be difficult except at high tide, lighters were also used to transport minerals and agricultural products to the county town. Although proposals for improving the Western Cleddau were put forward in 1843, nothing was done.[53] One famous photograph shows a round-nosed lighter aground at Haverfordwest in the early years of the twentieth century. The use of lighters on the Cleddau may have been of very early date; in 1530 John Leland noted lighters at work on the River Towy moving goods into Carmarthen from the then limit of ordinary navigation at Green Castle, three miles to the south.[54]

As mentioned, the registration of coastal shipping was not required by law until 1786. Even then the Act did not compel the registration of vessels measuring under 15 tons, and so many smaller craft went unrecorded.[55] Another Act passed in 1795 provided for the registration of such vessels, although this legislation was rescinded in 1837.[56] A register of vessels on the River Cleddau was drafted by John Gwynne, clerk of the peace in Haverforwest, under the 1795 Act. The register provides the names of the owners and ships' masters, together with a note of the type of vessel, her tonnage, the number of crewmen, and the "line and extent of navigation" of each vessel. Somewhat surprisingly, 37 of the 40 vessels registered in 1795 were described as lighters, and only two as sloops. The others were simply said to be a boat. Every vessel was said to employ two men including the ship's master, with the sole exception of a lighter owned by Thomas George, and named THOMAS, which had a three-man crew.[57]

Mark Matthews has calculated from this list that the average tonnage was around 18 tons, with most vessels measuring between 14 and 20 tons. The lighter THOMAS appears to have been the largest vessel registered, measuring 28 tons. These vessels together gave employment to 81 sailors or lightermen on behalf of 30 registered owners. The most important of the latter was Hugh Barlow who owned eight 20-ton lighters for the purpose of moving coal and culm between Cresswell Quay and Milford Haven. These were numbered 4 - 11 in the fleet of lighters used at Cresswell; no. 1 was owned by Sir Hugh Owen, and nos.2 and 3 by Harcourt Powell. The next largest shipowner in 1795 was also a shipwright, John Daniel, who operated two lighters and a sloop. These were all of 14 tons and also worked in the Cresswell River. Accordingly it may be surmised that they were also engaged in moving culm or limestone.[58]

It is thought that in the era of the enterprising Colonel Colby at the beginning of the nineteenth century, the Landshipping Colliery not only had a lighter for its own use on the Cleddau, but it also operated one or two sailing vessels as well. One is believed to have been the schooner LANDSHIPPING, again mentioned in Chapter Nine: both its name and its availability suggest ownership by the colliery company. Another example of a colliery company owning larger vessels is provided by the Tenby and Begelly Coal Company. As early as the 1820's this undertaking acquired two vessels in an effort to gain some control over the despatch and distribution of their own output. The sloop PEGGY with a capacity of 20 tons was employed primarily in serving local customers around Carmarthen Bay. It seems that the PEGGY seldom went west of Tenby, but on occasions might sail as far east as Swansea. Voyages of greater distance were made by the 100-ton brig MARY ANN which regularly sailed to ports in the West Country and Southern England, and often returned with consignments of timber, bricks or limestone.[59] The company paid all the expenses of both vessels - including the wages of the captain and crew, their victuals, disbursements and gratuities, depending upon the nature and duration of the voyage. Naturally the company had to pay for the ships' maintenance and any repairs required.

Rather surprisingly there are no other references to a coal company owning its own shipping for many years, although there can be little doubt that many of those who invested in the Pembrokeshire coal industry also invested in coastal shipping. In 1848, for example, there is a record of the good ship LADY PHILIPPS sailing from Saundersfoot to Pembroke with culm from Kilgetty Colliery.[60] The name and spelling of Philipps implies a link with the Philipps family of Picton Castle, then proprietors of Kilgetty Colliery. Much later, in January 1884, the sale of certain assets at Hook colliery included a 20-ton vessel said to be in good order.

By the nineteenth century there were numerous instances of sailing vessels being owned outright by individuals. For instance, in 1853 the MARY of Milford, a 44-ton sloop, was owned by John Rowe, a coal merchant of Pembroke Dock.[61] Some years earlier, in October 1837, Michael James of Solva, a farmer and merchant, had the misfortune to lose his 28-ton sloop JANE in Jack Sound off the North Pembrokeshire coast. Less than two years later, in May 1839, James's replacement vessel, the smack INDUSTRIOUS, was wrecked in the same area.[62] Not all the shipowners were male: in 1825, for example, Martha Morgan was the owner of the 17-ton sloop ANN AND MARY and in 1866 Eliza Merriman owned the 21-ton Milford-registered sloop EXLEY.[63] It was a statutory requirement at this time for the ownership of vessels to be divided into 64 shares, even though the shares might be owned by no more than two people. In 1829 , for example, the 24-ton sloop WAFT was owned by two Tenby seafarers, David Rees holding 43 shares and Thomas Lloyd holding 21 shares.[64]

Decline in Shipping

As popular enthusiasm for railway building turned into the Railway Mania of the 1840's, *The Shipowners and Shipmasters' Directory to the Port Charges ... Great Britain and Ireland* was published in London. Quite apart from the charges listed, it provides a fascinating glimpse of shipping practice and procedure of the period. The section relevant to coal shipping through Pembrokeshire ports is included in Appendix L. When this directory appeared shipping had no real rival for the transport of coal and culm from the county. In the second half of the nineteenth century this changed considerably, and the decline in shipping was due largely to the expansion of the railway system. The 1850's witnessed the development of Neyland, sometimes known as New Milford, as the western terminus of the South Wales Railway. In April 1855, a year before the new line to Neyland was opened, the S.W.R.'s engineer I. K. Brunel was said to be supervising the provision of coaling jetties for his huge ship, the GREAT EASTERN. By February 1856, he was advocating the construction of coal shipping stages like those built by the S.W.R. at Briton Ferry, and by 1859 the then S.W.R. engineer, W. G. Owen, was reporting that the hydraulic machinery for lowering railway trucks from the pier to the deck of the pontoons at Neyland were operating in a convenient manner.[65] Unfortunately, after all this activity, considerable difficulty was encountered in attracting shipping to Neyland, and it is debatable whether the coaling facilities were very much used, other than for bunkering steamships working passenger and cargo ferry services to and from Ireland.

At the same period similar difficulties were being experienced a few miles to the west, at the town of Milford Haven. Its development as a port was long hampered by the lack of a deep-water berth with a rail connection. By an Act of 1860 the Milford Haven Railway and Dock Company was authorised to build a line about two miles long from the terminus of the Milford Railway to Newton Noyes, where a pier was to be built into the haven.[66] Financial difficulties delayed construction, but eventually it was thought to be ready for freight use in the autumn of 1868. In 1869 a prospectus was prepared seeking a lessee to work Newton Noyes pier. In due course two cranes were erected at the pier and some stress was placed on the pier's potential as a place of export for coal and iron. It was pointed out that vessels bound for Swansea, Cardiff and Newport frequently had to seek shelter in Milford Haven and such delays could be avoided if the coal was despatched by rail to Newton Noyes. Although these observations were fair, they were premature because the pier was completed before the connecting railway line was entirely fit for use. By the time contractors had made good an embankment carrying the line across the entrance to Castle Pill, the railway had to be relaid from the broad gauge to the standard gauge following the elimination of the broad gauge in South Wales in 1872. Further delays attended the development of Milford Docks and the Newton Noyes line fell into disuse. When it was reopened in January 1882 a special train was run from London right through to the 900-foot-pier at Newton Noyes to enable a party of influential business men and journalists to inspect the facilities, including those for the handling of coal.[67] Although the new arrangements were described enthusiastically in *The Times*, the pier did not attract much attention.[68] When the main dock development of Milford Haven was completed in 1888 it lapsed into obscurity once again. Although some shipments of coal were made through Newton Noyes it was never developed properly for this purpose. Whilst the Freystrop colliery scheme of 1898 to 1905 envisaged regular shipments by way of Newton Noyes, the failure of the colliery meant that actual shipments were very few.[69] The great irony of Newton Noyes pier was that it was possibly Pembrokeshire's least successful shipping place, and yet it was the one with the most modern equipment for coal handling!

In the 1870's an effort was made to modernize the role of the traditional lighters by the introduction of steam barges. Never very numerous, these had the familiar task of taking transhipped cargo from seagoing vessels and carrying it up river to Haverfordwest, or occasionally Blackpool on the Eastern Cleddau. They were primarily intended for general cargo rather than coal or culm, although it is believed that bagged coal or culm was sometimes carried. The best known of these steam barges was probably the CLEDDAU. She was built at Pembroke in 1879, and measured 55 tons. She was operated, with others, by John Bacon & Co of Liverpool. In May, 1906 the CLEDDAU was holed accidentally near Haverfordwest and lost her cargo. The vessel was subsequently sold.[70]

The steam barges were succeeded by a small number of motorized barges. One of the best known of these was nicknamed "Abby Folland's lighter", after its Master, Absolam Folland, who used it regularly to convey culm from Hook Colliery to Rowland's coalyard at Haverfordwest. According to the recollections of Reg Phelps, late of Hook, the barge was built in the same way as Llangwm fishing boats, that is to say, butt built, caulked with oakum, pitched and tarred. The barge had a broad flat bottom, perhaps 40 feet long and about 12 feet in the beam. There was a small low cabin at the front and another at the rear. When loaded the vessel could carry 30 to 35 tons of culm. [71]

The Hook Shipping Companies

During the 1890's there were regular coal shipments from Hook to Singapore for tin smelting. According to T. W. Harcourt Roberts large five-masted sailing vessels measuring 5,000 to 6,000 tons were employed for this purpose, but because of their size they had to be loaded from barges in the deeper water of Llangwm Pool.[72] This laborious process may well have been a factor in a contemporary proposal for a new wharf to be provided for the colliery. Although the proprietors Messrs. Roberts and Canton had done well to win this trade, the landlords declined to support the idea. In a letter of 31 May 1895, their advisers pointed out that the existing colliery would be exhausted when the lease expired in 1905, and with such a limited life expectancy it was deemed inadvisable to contribute to the cost of a wharf or a road to the mine.[73]

Doubtless this was a disappointment to Messrs. Roberts and Canton, who must have been very well aware both of the inadequacy of their shipping facilities and their isolation from the national railway system. Whilst the life of the colliery was extended by the sinking of the Margaret pit in 1908-1910, the shipping quay remained of limited use for anything more than coastal traffic. Before World War I a rail link to the Great Western Railway had been suggested, but initially nothing was done, and then wartime conditions made such a link to Hook impractical. Even the well-developed plans of the Milford Dock Company for a line from Milford Haven to collieries on St. Bride's Bay had to be abandoned in 1916. By then Hook colliery anthracite found it increasingly difficult to compete in the home market, and the colliery company felt obliged to try to develop its foreign trade. The only option was the acquisition of shipping to enable Hook coal and culm to be carried to foreign customers as promptly as possible.

The first Hook Shipping Company was formed in 1917 with a nominal capital of £5,000 in £1-shares.[74] This was later increased to £10,000, although to the modern mind the figures still seem ludicrously low for the purchase and operation of small ships. Two vessels were acquired - the HALDON and the ELIZABETH DREW - both built as schooners, but altered to being auxilliary motor vessels. For whatever reason, this company was not a success, and went into liquidation early in 1920, with T. W. Harcourt Roberts, the main proprietor of Hook Colliery, as liquidator.

The Hook Shipping Co (1920) Ltd. was formed as a result of a reconstruction agreement relating to the earlier company. The new company undertook to pay the liquidator £6,396 in cash, and to allot to his nominees 564 fully paid £1- shares in the capital of the new concern. The nominal capital of the 1920 company was a much more realistic £50,000 in £1-shares. By October 1920, £16,509 shares had been issued for cash, and another 7,232 shares paid up other than in cash.[75] According to a report by Edward Daniel and Co. of Swansea, dated 6 October 1920, the new company owned six vessels. There were four motorised sailing vessels, namely, the ELIZABETH DREW(180 tons, valued at £3000), the HALDON (180 tons, valued at £6,000), the PORTLAND (80 tons, valued at £1628) and the CAMBORNE (200 tons, valued at £6,000). There were also two sailing vessels, the MARGARET HOBLEY (200 tons, valued at £2,750) and the ELIZABETH BENNET (260 tons, valued at £4,750). According to the report:

> These boats take shipments of coal to the north French ports and bring back general cargoes, so generally freightage is earned both ways. We have come to the conclusion ... that this company is constructed on sound lines and is likely to develop into a very lucrative undertaking.

Edward Daniel & Co. undoubtedly had experience in the coal trade, but their advice to the company was not sound. Even in 1920 their valuations on the Hook company's vessels were high; by 1921 there was a severe world-wide recession in the shipping industry and valuations slumped. Too many ships were available for too few cargoes, and freight rates fell to the point where numerous Welsh shipowners could not continue. Such a dramatic change in the commercial climate naturally had an impact on the Hook Shipping Company, and matters were not helped by the CAMBORNE repeatedly experiencing engine trouble. In an era of low freight rates the very purpose of the company was in question, and at a board meeting held on 10 May 1922 it was proposed that the shipping company should be amalgamated with the Hook Anthracite Colliery Co Ltd. This does not seem to have taken immediate effect because it was not until 6 January 1923 that another meeting was held to approve the winding up of the 1920 company. Once again T. W. Harcourt Roberts was appointed liquidator.[76]

The demise of the Hook companies signalled the end of any direct involvement in shipping on the part of the Pembrokeshire coal industry. Although coal and culm shipments continued to be made until 1939, in the age of the steam- and diesel-powered coaster very few vessels were owned in South Pembrokeshire. John George of Trevine in North Pembrokeshire was possibly the best-known local shipowner at this period. He operated the THOMOND (127 grt) from 1911 to 1919, and the BEN REIN (158 grt) from 1921 to 1936.[77]

William Burgess, Saundersfoot harbourmaster 1965-1983, could recall these ships, and indeed activity at the harbour at the time of World War 1. Many years later he noted that most of the vessels calling for coal were ketches of perhaps 100 tons, with a few square rigged vessels and some small steamers. He added that

> Many of the sailing ships were without auxiliary engines and to get under way they were warped from one buoy to another. There was one buoy in the centre of the Harbour, large rings on each side of the Harbour Mouth, and a buoy some distance outside the Harbour, and by this time with a favourable wind the Ships were under way. At this time Ships used to bring limestone from North Pembrokeshire to Saundersfoot and take a cargo of coal away. The limestones were burnt in a kiln at the back of what is now Jones and Teague Chandlery, the lime being used by farmers and local people for white-washing their houses and walls.[78]

After the war sailing ships became scarce, and visits by foreign vessels were more frequent. Several Dutch motor ships came to Saundersfoot, often carrying the captain's family as crew. Amongst other vessels loading coal and culm in this era the DRUMLOUGH was owned in Cardigan, and the HARPAREES at New Quay. The FOAMVILLE and its sister ships were owned by J. Monks & Co. of Liverpool, and the CASTLE COMBE and other COMBE-named coasters were owned by the Ald Shipping Company of Bristol. A number of vessels of French, Dutch, German and Irish registration were also involved in the trade.

Endnotes for Chapter Eight

[1] Harry, *The Pembrokeshire Coalfield*, 71.

[2] M. Walters, notebook of the 1840's, incorporating R. Bright's much earlier diary notes, 17. The writer was allowed to make a full copy in 1985 by the then owner, the late J. McBrearty of Pelcomb, near Haverfordwest.

[3] M. Walters, notebook of the 1840's, incorporating R. Bright's much earlier diary notes, 21.

[4] M. Walters, notebook of the 1840's, incorporating R. Bright's much earlier diary notes, 2, "The cutter waited at Solva three weeks for favourable weather, and of ninety pieces thrown into the water to be hauled ashore, only five were saved the others being driven to sea." This occurred in the year 1791.

[5] "The Diary of Charles Collins, 1806", reproduced in *Narberth Weekly News*, May 1934.

[6] *An Account of Tenby* (London, 1820), cited in Edwards *A Study of the Daucleddau Coalfield*, 51.

[7] Cornwall County Record Office, Truro: Harveys of Hayle muniments, DDH 1/2/67.

[8] Lewis Morris, *Plans of Harbours, Bars, Bays and Roads in St. George's Channel* (London: 1748).

[9] N.L.W., Owen & Colby MS 2095.

[10] Fenton, *An Historical Tour through Pembrokeshire*, 150.

[11] "The Diary of Charles Collins, 1806", *Narberth Weekly News*, May 1934.

[12] N.L.W. Owen and Colby MS 2095. In July 1791 a suggestion that Lower Hook be made into a ballast quay was rejected. It is not entirely clear from this source whether the quay was the main quay serving Hook colliery or the smaller quay about three-quarters of a mile lower downstream at Underwood, which served some small pits at East Hook. The main Hook Quay was enlarged in the nineteenth century but at this period these loading arrangements applied at both.

[13] H. R. Wyndham, *A Tour through Monmouthshire and South Wales, 1777* (Salisbury: 1781).

[14] Mrs M. Morgan, *A Tour to Milford Haven in the year 1791*.

[15] Fenton, *An Historical Tour through Pembrokeshire*, 91.

[16] Thomas Lloyd of Freestone Hall, Cresselly, owns a conveyancing plan of 1755 showing five quays, a coal yard and three culm banks, and two small structures identified "accompting house".

[17] East Kent Archives, Whitfield, Dover, E/KU 1453 B5/4/1261: Letter of Hugh Wilson to Messrs. Cobb and Son, Margate, 9 August 1816.

[18] Ibid., lighterage involved extra expense. In relation to Lawrenny, Wilson remarked that "the additional 6s. 0d. per hundred is for the lighterage from hence and invariably charged by us on all cargoes shipped at that place".

[19] P.R.O., CUST 75/5,89. The correspondence refers to "Carey Key" rather than Carew, but there can be no doubt it refers to Carew.

[20] P.R.O., CUST 75/5 p1: letter dated 16 October 1729.

[21] N.L.W., Owen and Colby MS 2052.

[22] N.L.W., Owen and Colby MS 2073.

[23] Pembrokeshire Record Office, D/LLW/300: Boatmans Accounts, 1807. Seven boatmen are listed at this date.and also forty-two ships' masters assisted by them. Of these, seven masters made three or more visits to Lawrenny/Cresswell in 1807, and fourteen made two visits. Also, D/POW/H/96 indicates Mr. Powell's ownership of a lighter in 1822.

[24] The important role of the ship's master is discussed in Simon P. Ville, *English Shipowning during the Industrial revolution: Michael Henley and Son, London Ship owners, 1770-1830* (Manchester: Manchester University Press, 1987), 67 et seq. Whilst the emphasis of this work is on a large London-based company, it has much to say about the shipping industry of the period and the coal trade between North east England and the capital.

[25] T. S. Willan, *The English Coasting Trade, 1600-1750* (Manchester: Manchester University Press, 1928), 2-5. Despite the title of this book, references to England also include Wales.

[26] Nef, *The Rise of the British Coal Industry*, Vol. 2, 236.

[27] Willan, *The English Coasting Trade*, 6. Willan refers to an Act of 1662, 14 CarII, c.11, which gave formal authority to the system of coquets and bonds, but effectively endorsed existing practice.

[28] Ibid., 7.

[29] P.R.O., CUST 75/5, 1.

[30] P.R.O., CUST 75/5, 32. The main legislative authority followed at this period appears to have been I Wm and Mary, Cap 22 and 9 Anne, Cap 15.

[31] P.R.O., CUST 75/5, 89. "The Boat" presumably means the Customs' own cutter, whilst "boats" relates to the lighters moving between Cresswell and Carew and Lawrenny.

[32] P.R.O., CUST 75/5, 224. These cases were occasional rather than regular. The next, somewhat similar case noted, was a year later, in March 1746.

[33] P.R.O., CUST 75/1, 233. The Collector at Beaumaris shared the concerns of the Collector at Milford, and observed: "we are under some apprehension that vessells frequently load culm at Naulton[sic] and Little Haven and slip away with it over sea without entering in the Custom House, and if they happen to put into a port coastwise which is sometimes the case the Masters pretend they were forced off the coast for the preservation of their vessels. However as there is reason to think that by this means frauds are often committed, direction is given to all officers in this Collection to seize all boats and vessels with their cargoes if they shall come in without despatches or any pretence whatsoever."

[34] P.R.O., CUST 75/1, 233.

[35] P.R.O., CUST 75/1, 232.

[36] P.R.O., CUST 75/1, 231.

[37] P.R.O., CUST 75/2, 81.

[38] P.R.O., CUST 75/2, 119.

[39] P.R.O., CUST 75/2, 102.

[40] P.R.O., CUST 75/29.

[41] P.R.O., CUST 75/29.

[42] P.R.O., CUST 75/3, 476: letter of 23 April 1859.

[43] P.R.O., CUST 75/3, 495: letter of 24 October 1859.

[44] P.R.O., CUST 75/4, 450: Letter of 26 April 1880.

[45] P.R.O., CUST 75/29.

[46] George, "Pembrokeshire Sea Trading before 1800", 33.

[47] Ibid., 37.

[48] Summary sheets relating to Robin Craig's work on the shipping registers for Cardigan, Pembroke and Milford are deposited at the Pembrokeshire Record Office, HDX/1190.

[49] M. D. Matthews, "Mercantile shipbuilding Activity in South-West Wales, 1740-1829", *Welsh History Review,* Vol. 19, No.3 (June 1999), 414.

[50] George, "Pembrokeshire Sea Trading before 1900", Table 12.

[51] P. B. S. Davies, *Deadly Perils*, 36.

[52] *The Cambrian*, 22 February 1840. The traditional dress of the lightermen was a long sleeved fustian waistcoat with cream coloured fustian trousers tied below the kness with strings, sometimes called "yorks".

[53] N.L.W., Haverfordwest Deeds, 1466-1498, covering the period 1842- 1846.

[54] John Leland, *The Itinerary in Wales, in or about 1536-1539*, 112.

[55] 26 Geo III Cap. 60.

[56] J. Geraint Jenkins, *Maritime Heritage* (Llandysul: Gomer Press, 1982), 84.

[57] Matthews, "Mercantile Shipbuilding Activity in South West Wales, 1740-1829," 407.

[58] Ibid.

[59] Pembrokeshire Record Office, Tenby & Begelly Coal Company ledger, 1833-1838, HDX/951.

[60] Carmarthenshire Record Office, John Francis Collection: Lewis of Henllan, 20.

[61] Newspaper advertisement reprinted in *Where the River Bends - an illustrated History of Hook* (Haverfordwest, 1996), 10.

[62] Davies, *Deadly Perils*, 13.

[63] Ibid.

[64] Ibid., 9 and 36.

[65] P.R.O., RAIL 640: South Wales Railway Engineer's Half- yearly report, 30 August 1859.

[66] Construction proceeded in 1864 on the authority of 27 and 28 Vict., Cap 256, although an earlier Act of 1860 had approved the building of Newton Noyes pier.

[67] J. F. Rees, *The Story of Milford* (Cardiff: University of Wales Press, 1954), 79.

[68] P.R.O., RAIL 1075/169; *The Times*, 19 January 1882.

[69] *Haverfordwest and Milford Haven Telegraph*, 10 August 1898. Initially it was supposed that local coal might be used by the steam trawler fleet based at Milford but according to the *Pembrokeshire Herald*, 23 October 1903, trawler owners were not anxious to use anthracite as they were fearful of an effect on fire bars.

[70] Account of the barge CLEDDAU was published in the *Western Telegraph,* 15 December 1999.

[71] R. Phelps, "We lived by the River", *The Pembrokeshire Magazine*, No.22 (April/May, 1984), 2.

[72] Pembrokeshire Record Office, "The Hook Coalfield, Pembrokeshire", Brief notes by T. W. Harcourt Roberts, c 1952.

[73] Pembrokeshire Record office, D/EE/7/293.

[74] P.R.O., BT 31/23796/ 148263.

[75] P.R.O., BT 31/257668/ 165952.

[76] The brief history of this company is contained in the BT31 file mentioned above. The Hook Anthracite Colliery Co. is recorded under BT 31/32463/ 171980.

[77] R. S. Fenton, *Cambrian Coasters* (Kendal: World Ship Society, 1989), 106.

[78] Letter from William Burgess to the writer dated 16 July 1985. The late Clem Scourfield of Sardis, who knew the harbour well at the same period, informed the writer that the largest Dutch vessel to call was named WILHEMINA.

The Coal and Culm Trades

A comprehensive study of the Pembrokeshire coal trade from the thirteenth century to the twentieth would be an immense undertaking. It would involve extensive research into the records of customers in Britain and Ireland, as well as those of the coal owners and producers in Pembrokeshire, and a detailed examination of prices, duties and the many aspects of trading practice in each period. Fascinating as these matters might be, they go beyond the essential focus of this thesis, namely, the Pembrokeshire coalfield and the industry based upon it. This chapter is simply intended to give insights into how that industry endeavoured to serve its customer by providing glimpses of the trade at different moments between the eighteenth and twentieth centuries.

As indicated by the chapter heading, the Pembrokeshire coalfield effectively had two distinct commodities to offer - coal and culm. Coal invariably attracted a much higher price than culm, although culm was produced in much greater quantity; the ratio could be as high as one to ten, or even more. Similarly coal often attracted heavier duties than culm. The markets for these commodities often differed: coal was much preferred by brewers and maltsters, and those using stoves for domestic heating, whilst culm was quite adaptable for lime burners and those making "balls" of culm and mud for use in the hearths of humbler homes in South and West Wales. The way that these commodities were handled was also quite different; because coal was much more expensive the customer was always concerned to ensure that he received exactly what he had ordered. It was essential that the coal was riddled to remove both culm and rubbish, and it was also desirable to handle it with care to avoid the breakage which could reduce it to culm. Lastly, most of the coal was shipped to ports in England, or Ireland or even abroad; contrariwise, whereas some culm was shipped coastwise to other west coast ports there was a significant trade in culm within the port of Milford itself.

As mentioned in Chapter Two, in the sixteenth century the port was considered to be the entire Welsh coast from Worm's Head on the Gower peninsula to Barmouth on Cardigan Bay. In 1684 the port of Llanelly was created, and the eastern most limit of the port of Milford then lay just to the east of Saundersfoot. Later still a port of Cardigan was created, covering the coastline north of St.David's Head. These changes are of some significance because at certain times there were different duties imposed on shipments from one head port to another ("inter-port") to those levied upon shipments within the same port ("intra-port"). At some periods the latter might be permitted free of duty. In any event it was usual for different levels of duty to be payable upon coal and culm. A brief outline of this complex and technical topic is given in T. S. Ashton and J. Sykes, *The Coal Industry of the Eighteenth Century* (Manchester, 1964) Appendix D, 147.

The Coal Trade

By the eighteenth century trade in coal and culm had been continuous for at least five hundred years. However, during this century there is good reason to believe that the volume of trade increased markedly. Such an inference may be drawn from the following table, listing numbers of ships operating within South Wales ports in 1701 and 1796 respectively, albeit without the precise cargoes carried by these vessels being specified.[1] Indeed, it indicates that over three times as many ships were operational within the port of Milford and Pembroke in 1796 as were active nearly a century earlier:

PORT	1701		1796	
	NUMBER OF SHIPS	TONNAGE OF SHIPS	NUMBER	TONNAGE
Chepstow (inc.Newport)	28	744	33	1,401
Cardiff (with its creeks)	11	218	30	1,069
Swansea (with Neath)	37	1,468	85	4,929
Llanelly	-	-	63	2,081
Milford & Pembroke (including Tenby)	36	1,092	119	4,838

As the Port Book records end in 1714, useful figures for coal shipments from Pembrokeshire in the eighteenth century are rare. Even so, there is a record extant of coal and culm shipments from Sir John Pakington's Freystrop colliery for the six months from 1 February 1714. This remarkable survival constitutes the earliest known account of shipments from a particular colliery, and shows that Freystrop then had a particular trading link with the Appledore district of North Devon. Of 137 shipments made from Little Milford Quay no less than 66 went to Appledore, with five others to Clovelly, and single shipments to Bideford and Northam. Nine other cargoes were dispatched to Fowey (1), Plymouth (2), Dartmouth (4), Poole (3), and Christchurch (1). Six more cargoes went to Ireland, namely to Dublin (3), Waterford (2), and Wexford. Within Wales, Little Milford made 33 shipments to Haverfordwest and ten others to ports from Pembroke to Cardigan and Aberystwyth. Only 13 shipments included any quantity of coal, and 9 of these were dispatched to Appledore. As regards the vessels involved in this trade, the HAPPY RETURN of Haverfordwest went to Little Milford 21 times, and on 27 June 1714, actually made the trip twice. Looking beyond Milford Haven, the TWO BROTHERS of Appledore made six voyages to and from Little Milford, and five other Appledore vessels made the trip on four occasions. The largest cargo carried by the TWO BROTHERS comprised 6 hundreds and 2 carts, whilst the HAPPY RETURN carried 8 carts only. The largest cargoes of all were one of 7 hundreds and 6 carts sent to Dartmouth in the MARY MAGDALEN in April 1714, and another of 7 hundred and 5 carts dispatched to Ireland in May in the WILLIAM AND SARA of Waterford. Not surprisingly, the most valuable cargoes included coal and were shipped to Poole on 25 May 1714.[2]

In the ensuing years, contemporary observers testified to the bustle of activity. Defoe noted that much coal was being shipped through Tenby, and that "its inhabitants are principally traders in sea coal". The commerce in Milford Haven was even more important, with Defoe describing Pembroke as "the largest, richest and ... most flourishing town in South Wales except Carmarthen".[3] Pembroke at that time was the home port for nearly two hundred sailing ships. A couple of decades later, in 1748, Lewis Morris was to report of Tenby that "they ship off yearly here between coal and culm from seven to eight thousand chaldrons".[4] Morris's evidence of an expanding shipping industry connected with coal and culm is substantiated by the following table giving figures for coal shipments to London in the period 1745-1765:

Coals brought into the PORT of LONDON from the SOUTH WALES COALFIELD in each of the Following years							
Years	Milford	Tenby & Haverfordwest	Carmarthen	Swansea & Neath	Llanelly	Cardigan	Total Quantity
	Tons	Tons	Tons	Tons	Tons	Tons	Tons
1745	1,516	298	43	-	-	-	1,857
1746	1,308	319	9	-	-	-	1,636
1747	2,175	448	32	-	-	-	2,655
1748	1,864	50	21	-	-	-	1,935
1749	2,727	124	-	-	-	8	2,859
1750	2,439	116	-	38	-	3	2,596
1751	2,091	287	32	57	-	-	2,467
1753	1,753	1,101	-	119	-	-	2,973
1754	2,867	890	89	16	-	-	3,862
1755	2,517	-	124	186	-	-	2,827
1756	3,031	453	176	21	-	45	3,726
1757	2,862	570	224	17	637	-	4,310
1758	2,020	206	-	63	-	-	2,289
1759	1,777	151	11	11	-	-	1,950
1760	2,964	405	53	-	-	-	3,422
1761	2,636	117	117	21	-	-	2,891
1762	2,221	631	13	-	-	-	2,865
1763	3,840	369	369	-	-	-	4,578
1764	2,544	599	151	79	-	-	3,373
1765	3,122	807	119	45	-	-	4,093

Source: *Royal Commission on Coal in the United Kingdom,* Report of Committee E, Statistics of Production, Consumption and Exploitation 1871. C435-2. (No figures given for 1752).

Taking the years 1745, 1755, and 1765, it may be seen that whereas in 1745 1,516 tons were shipped from Milford, and 298 tons from Tenby and Haverfordwest, in 1755, 2,517 tons were shipped from Milford alone. Ten years on, trade had increased further, and no less than 3,122 tons were dispatched from Milford, and 807 tons were sent out from Tenby and Haverfordwest – figures more than double those of twenty years earlier. Throughout this period the Pembrokeshire ports clearly dominated South Wales' trade with the capital, presumably because the special qualities of Pembrokeshire anthracite were not to be found in bituminous coal shipped from other areas.

Given that London was only one destination for coal shipment, and not necessarily the most important, growth on this scale is compatible with Charles Hassall's assertion that in 1792 a total of 60,523 chaldrons (approximately 120,000 tons) were exported or shipped coastwise from Milford.[5] Although some have questioned his figure, there can be little doubt that he knew many of the coal owners and shippers of the day, and kept in touch with their activity. That said, comparison of figures requires considerable care to ensure that like is compared with like. Not only were a range of different measures in use in West Wales in the eighteenth century, as described in Appendix A, but the student must always be alert to the distinction between coal and culm, and shipments overseas and shipments coastwise. Hassall's figure is clearly a global figure for all shipments of coal and culm, the coal element of the total being a little over one sixth, namely 10,756 chaldrons, of which 409 chaldrons were exported.

The next figures available appear to make 1792 a good year for the coal trade. In 1796 it was decided to create an entirely new district head port of Pembroke, to cover the eastern and southern shores of the Cleddau and Milford Haven, as well as Saundersfoot Bay. No doubt this seemed to be a good idea at the time, but by 1823 the decision was reversed with the port of Pembroke being absorbed back into the port of Milford. At the start of this period, in 1797 and 1799, figures exist for coal shipments from both Pembroke and Milford. These were included in a Parliamentary report on the state of the coal trade in 1800, and are stated to represent coals actually exported. On this basis in 1797 Pembroke exported 254 chaldrons 18 bushels, and Milford exported 102 chaldrons, the combined figures being significantly less than that for 1792. On the other hand 1799 was much better, with 478 chaldrons 22 bushels being exported from Pembroke and 125 chaldrons from Milford. In the light of these figures, Hassall's assertions for 1792 are entirely credible. The same source provides figures for the 1790's in respect of Pembroke alone, expressed largely in Winchester chaldrons (with some in Newcastle chaldrons) and these support the same conclusion. On this evidence 1794 was an outstanding year for the coal trade with exports from Pembroke of 547 chaldrons 18 bushels (Winchester measure), and 12 chaldrons 44 bushels (Newcastle measure).[6] Unfortunately no global statistics survive from the early years of the nineteenth century, the next figures available relating to the years 1816 to 1818. In this case, the figures are given in tons, but coal and culm shipments have not been separated, and their value is somewhat reduced by the absence of any figures for coastwise shipments from Milford. Despite these limitations, the following table incorporates the figures:

Year	PEMBROKE SHIPMENTS		MILFORD SHIPMENTS
	Coastwise	Ireland & Foreign	Foreign
	Tons	Tons	Tons
1816	27,532	271	316
1817	21,956	3,333	1,310
1818	28,970	3,462	269

Source: *Royal Commission on Coal*, Appendix to the Report of Committee E, 1871.

Fortunately, for most years from 1819 to 1850 useful figures for coal and culm shipments are available under the single heading of "Milford", and these are reproduced in Figure 43[7] It is clear that tonnages of culm generally far outstripped those of coal and that the high point of culm shipments came in the early 1840s. Against this background an attempt will be made to illuminate the nature of the trade by examining letters and sales records of various colliery owners and agents from the eighteenth century onwards. It must be noted that some small proprietors as well as large landowners were anxious to get involved in the coal industry.

In the late eighteenth century the Cresswell colliery comprised numerous distinct pits, and records have survived showing output for numerous years between 1770 and 1830. As these indicate something of the experience of those working coal and culm for shipment, the output figures from the various active pits are reproduced in Appendix M, together with other information in respect of coal and culm output from the county prior to 1830. It is clear that culm was always the main commodity produced and that only small amounts of culm were sold at the pits, the remaining coal and culm being shipped. Furthermore, these records demonstrate how in the eighteenth century a colliery might be understood to be a group of small, sometimes tiny production units yielding only very moderate amounts of coal and culm and, as already noted, worked by several lessees or partnerships with a relatively small labour force. Such a concept of a colliery was clearly very different to that prevailing by the twentieth century, when most had substantial buildings, elaborate pit head-gear, and a labour force numbered in hundreds.

A sales book relating to Hook colliery has survived, covering the period between October 1785 and October 1786, providing another indication of the nature of the trade. In customary

COAL AND CULM SHIPMENTS FROM MILFORD - 1819 TO 1850

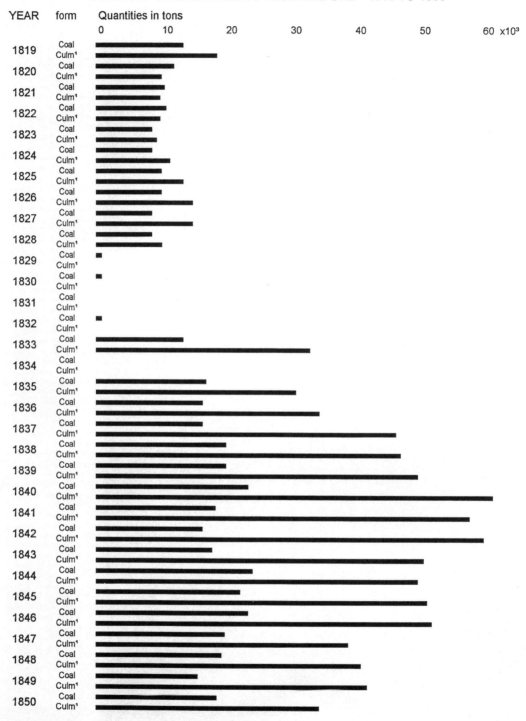

Note : ¹ = Report has 'Culm or Anthracite'
Source : Royal Commission on Coal, 1871

JdeH 358B

Figure 43

Pembrokeshire fashion, the figure are expressed in hundreds and barrels, the terms chaldron and bushel being preferred by customs officials and dealers in London. During this period there were sales of 82 hundreds of coal and 635 hundreds of culm. The range of trade from Hook colliery is shown in diagrammatic form in Figure 44, but much of the culm was sold around the shores of Milford Haven or along the coast of North Pembrokeshire. Larger quantities were consigned to towns like Haverfordwest, Fishguard and Newport (Pembs) and some was shipped up the coast as far as Anglesey. With the exception of Appledore in Devon, only small cargoes were dispatched to ports in Cornwall and Devon. There were few shipments to Ireland.[8] In contrast a record of coal and culm shipped from the open beach at Wiseman's Bridge in a six-week period in 1789 shows that it was all destined for ports around the Bristol Channel.[9]

In 1789 and 1790 we are given a glimpse of the coal trade at Landshipping in surviving correspondence between Benjamin Williams, a corn and coal dealer of London, and David Wilkins, agent to the Landshipping and Clyne collieries. On 16 November 1789 Williams wrote to Wilkins to tell him of the safe arrival of Captain Boston with his cargo, of which he had sold 70 chaldrons at 57s.6d. per chaldron. As he expected to sell the rest that week he recommended that one or two more vessels be engaged to load immediately at Landshipping. In short, although it was late in the year, and out of the main shipping season, trade was good.[10] Three days later Benjamin Willams wrote direct to John Colby and confirmed the desirability of sending more cargoes immediately. He added that:

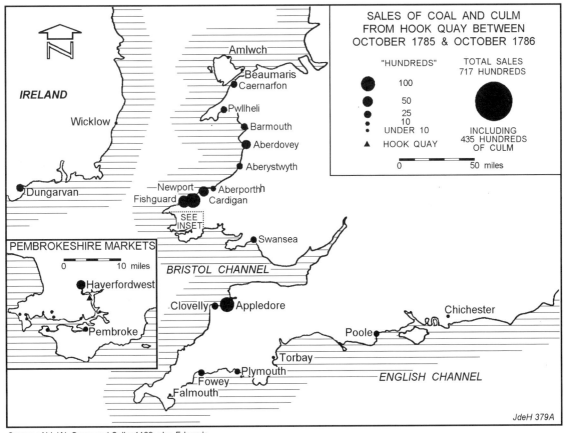

Source : N.L.W. Owen and Colby 1139, also Edwards

Figure 44

I think our market will keep up for some time but for the unavoidable delays we experience from the meters or bargemen, there should be no time fixed for discharging. Boston would have been near cleared by this time could we have got a meter, but the quantity of ships with coals from Newcastle that arrived here last week and with whom the meters are engaged will prevent us from beginning till tomorrow morning.[11]

In effect the coal trade was obliged to operate subject to certain procedural constraints as well as the obvious vagaries of the weather and the tides.

On 19 January 1790 Benjamin Williams had mixed news. First he was pleased to hear that Wilkins had a sizeable vessel loading at Landshipping, and observed: "the sooner you can dispatch her the better". Secondly, he enquired about other vessels loading for the London market and informed Wilkins: "I am just told there is one arrived at or near Milford to load 300 chaldrons. She belongs to one of the Newcastle boat dealers, and will be sold by him - but I hope it is not true, as they always hurt our market." The coal producers and shippers of Newcastle and Sunderland dominated the coal trade of London and the East coast which was essentially a bituminous trade; Williams' words point to one of the Newcastle dealers intruding in another area, and indeed, another trade - the anthracite trade.[12]

A week later Williams wrote to say that his correspondent in Dublin: "Had engaged the OAK of about 90 tons or 100 tons burthen Geo. Maumary, Master, that the vessel had sailed for your colliery where I suppose you have seen her before this." However as Wilkins had doubted that they would have enough coal for dispatch, Williams declared "we shall be under the necessity of procuring her a freight from some of your neighbours, which I hope you will be under no difficulty in doing, but shall be glad to know by return of post if the vessel is arrived, and what you can do for her, for unless we get her a freight the owners will come on me for not fulfilling my agreement".[13] These letters make it plain that this trade was heavily dependent upon close co-operation between the shippers in Pembrokeshire and the dealers in London, and else-where. It was also dependent upon a postal service of remarkable frequency and efficiency, some fifty years before the introduction of the penny post.

After the lapse of another week, Williams was still anxious to ensure that Captain Maumary of the OAK could obtain his cargo quickly. He wrote to Wilkins: "I shall be much obliged by your trying to prevail upon the Captain to proceed to Tenby pier where I shall engage him a loading from Mr. Hy. Phelps of Norchard ... he will there meet with no detention if he will go." Williams also expressed concern about a Captain Rees, who had behaved strangely:

> but think he will deliver his cargo safe. However have given orders for £50 insurance being made – if the policy comes in time, will give you the account in this. Hope shall see him soon as Coals are now a good Sale. I yesterday sold two Cargoes at 60s.(per chaldron) and engaged another in the River at same price.[14]

A couple of comments need to be made with reference to this last communication.

First, marine insurance began in the Tudor period, and by the late eighteenth century was commonplace both for ships and for cargoes, whether carried on coastal or ocean voyages. Whilst doubtless employed at an earlier date, this letter is the earliest seen so far making mention of insurance in relation to Pembrokeshire's coal trade. Secondly, in spite of the reported heavy demand for coal, the commodity was subject to significant fluctuations in price. Early in April 1790, Williams advised Wilkins that he had sold thirty chaldrons from a cargo just received at the price of 55s. per chaldron.[15] According to the colliery accounts for the year to 31 December 1790, the total output for the year was 698 hundred 5 carts, of which only 46 hundred 2 carts was actually coal. Little wonder David Wilkins had difficulty in meeting his orders! Wilkins, incidentally, was paid an annual salary of £30 as agent to the Landshipping and Clyne collieries. At this period the lessee of these pits was John Boston, almost certainly a relative of John Boston mentioned as sailing to London in November 1789.[16]

A decade later this trading link with London appears to have been broken. Although John

Boston & Co at Landshipping sent numerous consignments to Chichester, Arundel and Shoreham, there is no evidence of any going to London, albeit a large coal shipment of 45 hundred went up the east coast as far as Sunderland. On the West coast the most northerly destination was Maryport, although there were many shipments to ports around Cardigan Bay, and particularly to Caernavon, Pwllheli and Aberdovey. There were also some significant customers in Ireland, notably at Wexford and Dungarvan. A cargo of 7 hundred 10 carts of culm was shipped as far as Barbados![17] The range of trade from Landshipping colliery in 1801 is shown in diagramatic form in Figure 45.

During the 1790's the very gradual inflation which had begun in the middle of the century began to accelerate as a consequence of the conflict with France. The combination of inflation with growing competition challenged coal producers everywhere, and certainly put pressure on those in Pembrokeshire. Indeed, events which might now appear to have marginal importance then had even greater significance. By way of example, in 1798 and 1802 legislation was passed allowing coal shipped from Newport to the east of Flat Holm and Steep Holm to be carried free of duty.[18] The effect was to give Newport an immense advantage in shipping coal to Bridgwater, Bristol and Gloucester. It created a real problem for those at Swansea and Neath who were also shipping bituminous coal, and also a difficulty for those shipping anthracite from Pembrokeshire. Trade was lost to Newport, and after a few years Welsh coal owners west of Newport petitioned Parliament for some relief. By this period

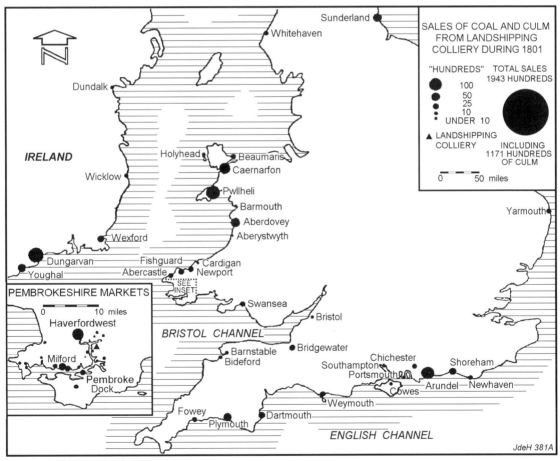

Source : N.L.W. Owen and Corby 2310 and Edwards

Figure 45

Pembrokeshire had a relatively small coal trade with the three English ports, and a culm trade only with Bridgwater. However, between 1808 and 1809 coal shipments to Bridgwater fell from 242 chaldrons to 148, to Bristol from 317 chaldrons to 294, and those to Gloucester dropped from 1068 chaldrons to 777.[19] Had it not been for the particular qualities of Pembrokeshire coal it is likely the trade would have been cut further. Nevertheless Newport seems to have retained favourable trading conditions until duties were ended in 1831. Arguably there was an element of relief in that profits tended to rise with prices. Michael Flinn also saw a positive aspect when he wrote: "Up to the peak of prices in the second decade of the nineteenth century, coal prices rose less steeply than other prices, and … in the post war deflation, coal prices showed a greater resistance to decline than other prices."[20]

Further glimpses of the coal trade at Landshipping can be gained from surviving correspondence between the colliery proprietors and Messrs. Cobb, brewers and maltsters of Margate. The first batch of letters is dated 1824, at which time the lessees of the colliery were Messrs Morgan & Johnstone. On 24 March 1824, prices were low, because stone coal was quoted at 12s. per hundred or £2 per chaldron. Messrs Morgan & Johnstone wanted to encourage buyers, and made the point that "we have a tolerable stock in hand, so that any vessel you may send will have good dispatch".[21] Six weeks later 120 tons of coal were offered for shipment on board the WILLIAM, captained by Moses Cormack of Solva. On 7 May 1824, the vessel was in Ireland, but it was expected within three weeks. The coal was available at 18s. per hundred, free on board, and Morgan & Johnstone admitted: "we think this is rather high, but you could get one of Deversons of Sandwich to come here at a less freight". Deverson was a master mariner and shipowner from Thanet, who would have been well known to Messrs. Cobb in Margate. The very next day, though, Morgan & Johnstone wrote to Messrs. Cobb offering to obtain a vessel to ship coal to Margate at 15s. per hundred, with the ship's master apparently required to pay his own duties in London. This was agreeable, and the vessel was duly chartered. The latter may have been the CHARLOTTE of Cardigan, Capt D. D. Williams; at all events the CHARLOTTE was soon at the centre of a controversy over the quantity shipped. On 30 June 1824, Morgan & Johnstone declared that the CHARLOTTE and D. D. Williams, master, had taken twelve hundred of over measure:

> We calculated and we are sure he had on board 108 tons. We have often loaded him with culm from Ireland when he was not deeper in the water than when he had your coal on board, and he has always made out and received his freight for 108 tons. We have often had a whole cargo of our coal weighed out and then have invariably made out 9 tons to the hundred.[22]

Messrs. Morgan & Johnstone may have been overcharging, but in any event, within a year they had given up their lease to Sir John Owen. On 5 July 1825, W. G. Allen, on behalf of the colliery, wrote to Messrs. Cobb to inform them that:

> The colliery is now worked by Sir John Owen Bart.MP.; reduced price to £8.0s.0d. per hundred of 6 London chaldrons, which with charges of quay etc, will cost f.o.b. £8.12s.9d. As you used to deal at this colliery with Messrs. Morgan & Johnson I beg to solicit a continuance of your orders …[23]

Allen's invitation to continue trading with Landshipping must have been effective, because several of his letters to Messrs. Cobb sent in the ensuing eight years still exist. On 31 August 1827, he was concerned about the brig MARY, as nothing had been heard since she had sailed. He asked that on her arrival in Kent the master should write to him if he could not get a full freight at Margate, or thereabouts. In that event the vessel might go to Poole and take a cargo of clay to Swansea, and at Swansea load another consignment for Landshipping. This letter brings out the commercial importance of having a full cargo in both directions: all too often vessels plying in the coal trade had to return to their port of loading in ballast.

There was a tendency amongst shippers to exaggerate the level of demand and activity to give a good impression to their customers and to help maintain their interest. Whilst the demand does appear to have been real at this period, loading and dispatch were often quite protracted, either because there was a shortage of good coal, or a shortage of good people to carry out the work quickly. On 4 August 1830 W. G. Allen told Messrs Cobb that the demand had been so great vessels were having to wait for their turn to be loaded. However the schooner LANDSHIPPING would be loaded in a few days when it was hoped to send them invoice of coal and butter. Evidently they saw no problem in sending a consignment of dairy produce at the same time as a bulky, dirty cargo like coal! The same combination occurred again in the same vessel in October 1830, when six pots of butter were shipped to Margate along with eleven hundred of Pembrokeshire coal.[24]

Landshipping was not the only place to experience delays in shipping. Hugh Wilson, who managed the quays at Cresswell, appears to have acted as agent or adviser to Messrs Harvey of Hayle, Cornwall, in respect of the agricultural and coal trades in Pembrokeshire. On 27 March 1829, he informed them that Captain George Griffiths had had to wait for two weeks at Tenby until the easterly wind abated and it became safe enough to beach his vessel at Saundersfoot ready for loading.[25] On 13 August 1829, Wilson wrote again and after providing comments on the state of the crops in his locality, he added: "I have just heard from George Griffiths of the schooner ELIZA and I beg to say he is now on his return from the Isle of Wight, and intends loading culm for your works at Hayle immediately on his arrival."[26] George Griffiths clearly came regularly to Pembrokeshire for Messrs Harvey, because on 2 April 1830, Wilson reported that Griffiths had told him that their latest order for culm would soon be on its way to them.[27]

By 1831 competition with coal producers in Carmarthenshire and Glamorgan had increased significantly. On 29 November 1831, William Webb, a coal shipper of Llanelly, demonstrated his desire to capture a customer from Pembrokeshire shippers when he forwarded a speculative cargo of twelve weys of Bushey Vein coal for use at the Hayle Foundry. He asked Messrs. Harvey to ensure that "you will give our product a fair trial", and he hoped "that this may be the commencement of much good business between us".[28] Pembrokeshire shippers had to defend their position, and some acted in a similar fashion. In May 1831, William James of the Hean Castle colliery at Saundersfoot, having heard from Captain Deverson that Messrs Cobb used a considerable quantity of stone coal for malting, offered to send nine tons, otherwise seven chaldrons, of excellent quality at the reduced price for trial purposes of £6.10s.0d per hundred. Unfortunately it is not clear if either of these approaches led to regular orders being won.[29]

By 1832 there is every indication that Landshipping could not produce enough coal to meet the demand. In writing to Messrs. Cobb on 27 September 1832, W. G. Allen acknowledged that "vessels here have not waited so long for freight for the last ten or twelve years". On 13 November he wrote again, saying that there had been delays from six weeks to two months in loading vessels, but "now a new pit is at work we load vessels much faster". However it was late in the year, and he pointed out that there would now be some difficulty in freighting as many vessels "are laid up for the season or are already gone on the grain trade to Ireland".[30]

By 1835, W. G. Allen's duties at Landshipping were being performed by William Butler. Early in the year he conferred with others trading regularly between Haverfordwest and London with regard to shipping coal for Messrs. Cobb, and he concluded that he could charter a vessel for 10s. per ton. On 15 March, 9 hundreds 4 carts of coal at £8.4s.0d. per hundred were loaded at Landshipping on the sloop AURORA, James William, Master, and Messrs. Cobb were advised that she would sail on a favourable wind.[31] The fortunate survival of the Landshipping colliery sales book for 1835 shows that this was the only sailing for Margate that year. Other English destinations for coal shipments included Ross, Barnstaple, Newquay, Scilly, Plymouth, Weymouth, Poole, Winchester, Portsmouth, Hythe, Dover, Sandwich, Whitstable and Faversham. Two particularly noteworthy orders came from London buyers. Messrs Cory and Scott of London were sent four shipments of coal totalling 137 hundreds, 10 carts, one shipment being the largest single consignment of the year-47 hundreds 8 carts of coal. Edmund Lucas of Westminster also received four shipments, these amounting to 113 hundreds 6 carts. All in all, approximately 88 per cent of coal produced at Landshipping was dispatched to England.

There was also a market for coal in Ireland, and the 1835 sale book records twenty shipments, almost all to Dundalk or to Wexford. Ten shipments were sent to assorted traders in or near Dundalk, whilst the largest single shipment went to Messrs Breen and Devereux of Wexford (15hundred 6 carts of coal). In fact Breen and Devereux received four cargoes and Thomas Brenan of Wexford received three. Coal shipments to Ireland were equivalent to about 8 per cent of the total from Landshipping.[32]

Although the records reveal plenty of traffic at Landshipping, it seems clear that the colliery was finding it harder to attract shipping when it was required. On 13 February 1836, Butler admitted he could not get a vessel to ship coal to Messrs. Cobb. He had offered 10s.6d. per ton for a charter but the master would not take it. In exasperation he declared: "the difficulty lies in these small vessels being almost insanely obliged to return in ballast". Put another way, a paying cargo in one direction only was hardly an economic proposition. Facing the same difficulty in September, he confessed to Messrs. Cobb that he was unable to charter a vessel. Instead he recommended that Messrs. Cobb should charter a ship from his port "as the only means by which you can be sure of a cargo".[33] Matters were no better in 1837. Sir John Owen himself wrote to Messrs. Cobb from London on 29 November 1837 to say that there was a cargo at Landshipping, "but no tidings of a vessel to take it away".[34]

There was more to Landshipping's troubles than the frequency with which vessels were sailing in ballast in one direction: As we have emphasized, this was a common problem for every Pembrokeshire coal shipper. After the long delays in the early 1830's for vessels loading at Landshipping, there may well have been some reluctance on the part of shippers and ships' captains to call at Landshipping quay. However, the most important factor was surely the opening in 1833 of Saundersfoot Harbour, creating a much better berthing place close to the collieries at the eastern end of the coalfield. In 1833 it is recorded that 11,497 tons were shipped through Saundersfoot.[35] The sheltered quays along the Cleddau and the upper reaches of Milford Haven now faced competition from a harbour, not just a quay, purpose built for the rapid loading and dispatch of ships carrying coal and culm. The changed circumstances for Landshipping are well illustrated by the fact that in October 1837 the Kilgetty Colliery Co. shipped an estimated 130 tons of stone coal for Messrs. Cobb on board the good ship THE BROTHERS, loaded at Saunderfoot Harbour. The Bill of Lading for this consignment is depicted in Appendix K and it should be noticed that on delivery Messrs. Cobb & Co considered that they had received 117 tons. In Pembrokeshire there was evidently a strong desire to go on using the traditional measures, rather than the then modern imperial weights despite the risk of disputes.[36].

In this era the coal trade to London was of immense importance to the capital, and the subject of considerable Parliamentary concern. The Report of the Select Committee on the Coal Trade, 1838, included evidence indicating the high value accorded to Pembrokeshire anthracite. An experienced coal factor, James Bentley, informed the Committee that the price of Swansea best stone coal was 14s.6d. per ton on board ship, and the second quality was 13s.0d. In contrast the equivalent price of Milford stone coal was 19s.8d., and the price of the Saundersfoot coal was from 16s.0d., to 17s.0d. per ton. He also quoted prices for some bituminous and other coals, which were all significantly cheaper. However he noted that prices had risen, and whereas in 1835 Merthyr coal had been 8s.6d. per ton, in 1838 it was 11s.0d. per ton, and Llangennech coal, shipped at Llanelly, which had been priced at 10s.0d. per ton in 1835, now fetched 11s.0d per ton.[37] The high price of Pembrokeshire anthracite may well have reflected not only its undoubted quality, but also the distance it had to be conveyed and any perceived difficulty associated with its shipping. Another witness before the Select Committee declared that: "the delay in loading coals, at the Welsh ports particularly, has been from five to six weeks frequently, which of course adds very considerably to the amount of freight".[38] Given the intense competition that had arisen in the market, it is remarkable that

Pembrokeshire coal retained a share in the trade, despite the problems. As mentioned in an earlier chapter, price-cutting made conditions even more challenging in the 1840's. By July 1843 the Kilgetty colliery faced closure, and the difficulties were summarised by T. S. Heptinstall of the colliery company in a letter to Sir Richard Philipps. Having mentioned that a decision on closure had been postponed until September, Heptinstall expressed his concern at the probable loss of jobs, and added:

> The reduction in prices, the want of sale and our heavy payments and imports will render a stoppage unavoidable in case we cannot obtain relief or assistance to meet the crisis.[39]

Clearly Heptinstall was hoping to win concessions from Sir Richard Philipps as landlord, but in the autumn the colliery was closed. The pit re-opened in the era of the Pembrokeshire Iron & Coal Co., but in the late 1850's the newly-sunk Grove pit became the main shaft in this locality.

The Culm trade

Almost all the evidence so far considered has related to the coal trade, but in Pembrokeshire most collieries, as has been emphasised, produced far larger quantities of culm than coal. In an age when lime burning was an activity basic to both agriculture and building work, providing a steady supply of culm to fuel limekilns was a significant business. The importance of this trade was reflected in the passing of an Act in 1760 to simplify the shipment of culm from the port of Milford to destinations in the counties of Carmarthen, Cardigan and Merioneth, as well as Pembroke, subject to a standard rate of duty.[40] The shipping implications of this Act are discussed in Chapter Eight. Suffice to say that it did not impress Pembrokeshire people. In 1794 the land agent Charles Hassall spoke for many when he declared that all coastwise duties on culm should be abolished.[41] Besides this concern there was a feeling amongst some culm producers that the price of their product should be raised. In February 1772, J. Harcourt Powell and John Colby discussed calling a meeting of colliery agents in Pembrokeshire for this purpose.[42]

In the meantime the trade in culm extended not only around the Welsh coast, but also into Somerset, Devon and Cornwall. Between 1785 and 1799, the brigantine ALBION made many voyages from Cresswell (or more likely Lawrenny) to Dartmouth in South Devon. Michael Nix has studied the available records of these voyages, and his observations reflect the inflationary effects of the 1790's:

> Between 1785 and 1799 the purchase price of one hundred of culm rose from £2.10s.0d. to £3.10s.0d. The steepest increases occurred in 1793, at the beginning of the French Revolutionary War, and in 1797, a year of deep economic and national gloom. Freight rates doubled from almost £2.10s.0d per hundred, to over £5. Profits also rose markedly. During 1785, the gains made from five culm voyages ranged between £22 and £34. By 1794 this had risen to between £58 and £70.[43]

On the basis that the ALBION might make four culm voyages in an average year, Nix assessed the annual profit to be approximately £226.

The ALBION was owned in Bideford, a port with long established trading links with Pembrokeshire. In the seventeenth century and eighteenth century prior to the French Revolutionary War, over 80 per cent of the culm received into Bideford and Barnstaple was dispatched from Tenby, and most of the rest came from Pembroke or Carmarthen. Whereas in the years 1791 to 1793 there is no record of Swansea contributing to the culm trade with Bideford and Barnstaple, within fifteen years 40 per cent of the shipments came from that port. In the years 1810 to 1812, Swansea's share grew to 80 per cent, and Tenby's was reduced to just 9 per cent! According to Nix, in 1792 the aggregate of all coal and culm shipments from Pembrokeshire exceeded those of Swansea, but by 1816 Pembrokeshire's shipments coastwise were less than a twentieth of those of Swansea.[44]

In brief Bideford, and doubtless Barnstaple and Ilfracombe, witnessed a remarkable change in direction in the culm trade. The main reason was the construction of the Swansea Canal in the 1790's. It was well known that canals could reduce transport costs dramatically, and the completion of the Swansea Canal gave this advantage to the coal proprietors of the upper Swansea valley. For the first time they could offer culm to buyers in North Devon on favourable terms, and furthermore the construction of canals inland from Torrington and Bude early in the nineteenth century greatly enlarged the hinterland able to benefit as a result. With Pembrokeshire losing its leading position in the trade with the West Country, its shippers were obliged to concentrate on selling culm around the western coast of Wales and to Ireland.

The organisation of the coal and culm trades with Ireland was unusual. Dealings in most, if not all, other commodities were controlled by contacts between merchants on both sides of the Irish Sea. In the case of coal, according to L. M. Cullen, "control of the trade was in fact in the hands of the masters of vessels from the colliery ports". He went on to argue that although the ships' masters often held only a small shareholding in the vessels they commanded, their position gave them effective control. The masters, he asserted, "shipped their coals without knowledge of conditions at the Irish ports other than what they had picked up from the masters of colliers returning in ballast". Against this background, Cullen declared that "this absence of any regulation of the trade encouraged the periodic glutting of the Dublin market", and resulted in the coal trade being throughout the whole of the eighteenth century distinctly an unprofitable business.[45]

These comments are open to question. J. V. Beckett, referring to this trade in the middle of the eighteenth century, said that "the fear was always present that Cumberland would lose its competitiveness by comparison with other English, Welsh and Scottish coalfields enjoying coastal proximity to Ireland. In fact these problems did not prove to be serious, and in 1750 West Cumberland still provided some 70 or 80 per cent of the coal sold in Ireland."[46] For his part, Cullen paid proper attention to the substantial trade from Whitehaven, and also took an interest in the trade between Ayrshire and Ireland. However it seems that he did not study the trade from South Wales closely, and was content to dismiss it as "small". In relation to Dublin undoubtedly it was small – Whitehaven provided house coal, and completely dominated the market. Pembrokeshire, though, regularly shipped anthracite coal and culm to numerous smaller ports from Drogheda in the North to Youghal and Cork in the south, usually at the behest of Irish merchants. Possibly the demand for culm rather than coal was more predictable; certainly the sea crossing (and therefore communications) between Pembrokeshire and places like Wexford and Waterford was somewhat shorter than that between Whitehaven and Dublin. At all events, the majority of vessels involved in the trade with Pembrokeshire originated from Ireland and came to Wales in reliance upon their masters' knowledge of demand in their own locality. The general pattern was for most culm shipping to take place between March and October, and in Pembrokeshire one of the signs of Spring was the arrival of what was jokingly referred to for generations as the "Irish Navy". Although no doubt there were periods when trade was less profitable, but the "Irish Navy" would not have returned year by year were there not a worthwhile market for anthracite on the east and south coast of Ireland.[47]

By the nineteenth century there can be little doubt that the culm trade with Ireland was profitable. Although Paul O'Leary does not appear to have paid close attention to the Pembrokeshire coal trade, he has observed that:

> There was keen competition between Welsh ports for the Irish market, forcing companies to provide extremely generous measures in order to maintain their market position. At the western extremity of the coalfield trade with Ireland picked up markedly in 1809, accounting for approximately a quarter of all the vessels out of Llanelly ..."[48]

In 1808 the Llanelly coal proprietor, Alexander Raby, had advised his landlord that over-measure was a necessary aspect of the trade with Ireland,[49] but it is not clear if Pembrokeshire coal shippers took much part in these practices. The rapid erosion of Pembrokeshire's market share at this period seems to suggest otherwise.

Unfortunately, surviving records do not always make it possible to distinguish precise figures for coal and culm raised. Such was the case at Begelly. A ledger for the period 1833-1838, when the colliery was worked by the Tenby & Begelly Coal Co., provides a record of payments for coal and culm from different customers, rather than a record of the volumes sold.[50] George Edwards made a close study of this book and calculated that in 1835 "of the 16,232 tons raised at the colliery, 12,040 tons was shipped from Saundersfoot and the remainder sold locally". These sales "to the country" mostly went to destinations within a few miles of Begelly, but sizeable amounts were conveyed over local roads to Mynachlog-ddu in the north and St. Clears in the east. Almost all of these loads would have been culm.[51]

Similarly, much of the larger volume shipped through Saundersfoot Harbour was culm destined for the farms and limekilns around the coast of Carmarthen Bay, and of Pembrokeshire south of Milford Haven. Although Begelly had some customers on the west coast of Wales, broadly speaking this colliery (and very possibly others near Saundersfoot) was serving a different local market to that served by Landshipping, Hook and other pits within Milford Haven. Begelly made no shipments to Ireland in 1835, but a few small consignments were exported to Wexford and Waterford in 1834.

Begelly had no foreign customers at this period, but a small amount of coal was dispatched to London, and most other customers for coal were in England. Cargoes were sent to Exeter, Winchester, Littlehampton, Arundel and Brighton. There were also numerous shipments closer to home, many probably culm, including cargoes ultimately destined for Bridgwater, Taunton and Torrington. This suggests a modest recovery of trade, after the extraordinary switch in trade from Pembrokeshire to Swansea at the start of the century.

Culm undoubtedly constituted the greater part of Begelly's output, and, in 1835, the same was true at Landshipping. In this case there are figures to show that the ratio was one hundred of coal to nearly four hundreds of culm, and typically whereas most of the coal was shipped to England, most of the culm was sold in Wales. Whilst culm sales to England amounted to 91 hundred, and to Ireland about 60$^{1}/_{2}$ hundred, the remaining 1,627 hundred found a market in Wales. In 1835, Landshipping culm was less than half the cost of the coal, being priced at £3.6s.0d. [52]

Culm found a ready market around the coast of Cardigan Bay. Although single shipments are noted to ports as far north as Beaumaris, Caernavon, Pwllheli and Portmadoc, Landshipping appears to have enjoyed a particularly good trading association with Aberdovey. Vessels from Aberdovey seem to have called at Landshipping in groups - for example, when the culm shipping season started in late March 1835, ten Aberdovey ships visited Landshipping between 27 March and 3 April. Six lesser groupings of Aberdovey shipments may be discerned, ending with the visit of six vessels at the close of the season, between 9 October and 13 October. In total fourteen Aberdovey ships are mentioned in the sales book, of which three made six visits and two made five visits. Barmouth, Llangranog, Aberporth and Cardigan are noted as destinations for shipments, but strangely there is no reference to the Cardiganshire ports of Aberystwyth, Aberaeron and New Quay. Sales records from individual collieries are not plentiful, but further research might reveal whether other Pembrokeshire pits enjoyed links with these ports in the way Landshipping appears to have been associated with Aberdovey.

Quite apart from the Cardigan Bay trade, Landshipping did some steady business in culm in Pembrokeshire, most being shipped to ports and pills within Milford Haven and the Cleddau. In this sheltered area the shipping "season" had much less meaning, and even in winter the colliery had dozens of customers. In 1835, the most notable was Messrs Edwards & Roch of Pembroke. This firm received no less than 295 consignments of culm amounting to 228 hundreds 4 carts. Most of their shipments were quite small - often less than one hundred - but very frequent, especially in the first half of the year. Between July and December Messrs. Edwards & Roch received just 74 shipments, whereas in the same period a newcomer, Henry Morgans of Haverfordwest, received 79 consignments. These were mostly heavier in the early months, so that in the second half of the year the colliery had dispatched 144 hundreds, 3 carts, to Morgans, making him the largest customer in this particular period. Unfortunately it is not clear why his business with Landshipping developed so quickly, although it may be surmised that he had turned to Landshipping as an alternative to some other supplier. The relative decline in shipments to Messrs Edwards & Roch is also unexplained, although the fact that other merchants - for example Charles Parry of Pembroke – took numerous consignments during the summer months may have had a bearing on their business.

It is clear that some of those who traded on a regular basis were selling culm to their own localities. The sales book of 1835 makes frequent mention of Nicholas Morris of Pwllcrochan, J.Huzzey of Pembroke Ferry, Samuel Mason of Underhill and John Seale of Brownslate. A few appear to have been publicans (and possibly maltsters) – for example, Mr Llewhelin of the Porters Arms, Haverfordwest. Others were landowners – Sir R. Philipps of Picton, Baron de Rutzen of Slebech and of course the owner of Landshipping, Sir John Owen of Orielton, and his kinsman, Col. Owen, MP., of Llanstinan. Lastly the sales book mentions about forty local residents who sent carts to the colliery to collect culm, mostly when farming was quiet. Many of these sales were very small, and doubtless intended only for personal use. However, a Mr. Davies of Coedcanlas collected three hundred by cart, and a few others purchased over one hundred.

Most of the culm sold "to the country," to local people, would have been intended for farmers' limekilns or for the slow burning fires which were such a feature of ordinary domestic life. For generations, culm for lime burning was shipped on a seasonal basis, and according to a nineteenth-century writer, the price of lime was influenced by the price of culm. Most of the lime and culm used in Devon came from south or west Wales, and a study of the seasonal patterns for both trades in 1806 revealed an obvious correlation between the two, with the season for both beginning in late February or early March, and ending in late October or early November. The peak period of activity was always between June and September, which happened to coincide with the time when wheat fields were being prepared for winter sowing. In 1806, according to Nix, no less than 104 cargoes of limestone and 88 shipments of culm were noted in the Port Book at Bideford.[53]

Thus far no evidence has been given in respect of the culm trade from St. Bride's Bay. In February 1848, James Higgon acquired the Folkeston colliery at Nolton, and fortunately the Nolton Haven Shipping Book for that year has survived. In spite of the minimal facilites at Nolton, the colliery shipped a sizeable quantity of culm in the summer season. In the thirty-two days between 31 May and 1 July at the height of the shipping season, twenty-one cargoes of culm were dispatched. The Shipping Book, uncharacteristically for Pembrokeshire, refers to tonnages and to big and small coal - even though the price for the commodity was always the standard 6s.3d. per ton for culm. Only one shipment was to a destination well beyond the boundaries of the port of Milford, and that was a cargo of 61 tons (the largest in this period) carried in the London-registered BREW BESS from Nolton to Chester. On 31 May 1848 two vessels left Nolton for Borth, near Aberystwyth, and a couple of other smaller vessels visited Nolton twice during the ensuing month. The WILLIAM of Milford sailed to St. Davids (Porthclais) on two occasions in June with loads weighing twenty tons, and the ELIZA ANNE set sail for Solva on 16 June and 1 July with cargoes of 23 tons on each occasion. In total there were five shipments to St. David's, five to Solva and two to Fishguard, with single sailings to Abercastle, Aberporth, Dale, Llannon and Newport (Pembs).[54]

With regard to both coal and culm shipments, it was decidedly the case that Saundersfoot Harbour quickly came to dominate trade after its establishment in 1834. In September 1837, it was decided to add two new loading shutes to the three initially installed. In 1839 two more were proposed, and the Saundersfoot Railway & Harbour Co. consulted a notable civil engineer, Thomas Dyson, on their ideas for improving the harbour.[55] We have seen that Landshipping quay and others along the Cleddau felt the competition posed by the purpose-built harbour. It was thus reported in February 1840 that the Broadmoor company, which hitherto had shipped through Cresswell Quay, now intended to ship through Saundersfoot –

a change symbolising the long term decline of Cresswell Quay, and the advance of the newly-built harbour.[56] Indeed the annual report of the SR & H.Co, dated 30 May 1840, was both enthusiastic and optimistic: "the success at this place has far exceeded the sanguine expectation of last year, and the increase in shipping during the last five months, and the extent of the preparations now being made by several collieries ... affords good prospects of the future shipments far exceeding those of any former year".[57]

In 1842 the picture changed. There was a widespread depression in the coal and culm trades and some collieries – Landshipping and Broadmoor, for example - had dropped their prices to retain their customers. Their action, it was said, "had hurt the Begelly and Kilgetty companies, who could not compete with such cuts".[58] The basic problem was the glut of anthracite on the market "at almost nominal prices at the instigation of Carmarthenshire rivals".[59] Understandably receipts fell, although in June 1843 John Longbourne, the company treasurer, said that he expected "a much more serious deficit judging from the dreadful state of depression under which trade of every description has laboured in the past year". He went on to stress the "horrible competition" which had arisen between local owners shipping from Saundersfoot, and those who were shipping from Llanelly and Swansea and other ports. Looking to the future, he hoped for a considerable increase in orders and observed that foreign trade was developing: four cargoes of culm had been shipped to Alicante, and a sample cargo of coal was about to go to Prussia.[60]

In February 1844, John Longbourne observed that low freight rates had induced coal shippers in Llanelly, Swansea and Cardiff to send speculative cargoes to all the markets favoured by Saundersfoot producers, causing almost every port to be glutted with anthracite. Higher freight rates, he believed, would cause consumers to resort to the best, and the maltster was likely to return to the district for coal. In the circumstances he regretted the fact that Mr.Myers, of the recently-opened Bonvilles Court Colliery, was also sending speculative shipments because "it would destroy all chance of unanimity and mutual cooperation". This was needed, otherwise it would be harder for a colliery like Thomas Chapel to compete, "because Myers ships his coal with a transit over the railway of $1^1/_4$ miles, and excludes the Thomas Chapel Co. who are paying for a transit of $4^1/_4$ miles". Plainly it was in the interest of the S R & H Co to see that the Thomas Chapel company remained in business![61]

After the extremely successful 1830's, Saundersfoot itself was now being squeezed by shippers at ports in Camarthenshire and Glamorgan. In June 1844, though, encouragement was derived from the way in which Irish buyers were returning to Saundersfoot for culm because they found it stronger than that from Pembrey, Llanelly or Swansea. Matters would be better it was thought, if Saundersfoot shippers did not compete with each other:

> a jealous avidity to sell (even to over-reach and thereby to obtain the customers of their neighbours) on the part of the shippers prevents us availing ourselves of our advantages in dealing with coal merchants. The consequence is that merchants are cautious in giving their order, relying as they do on the last party applying to them reducing his price below that of the party who preceded him.[62]

In 1845 trade at Saundersfoot improved, and the chief concern of the S R & H Co became the possibility of being connected to a major new railway then recently authorised - the broad gauge South Wales Railway. Although it reached Haverfordwest in 1854, and Neyland, on Milford Haven, in 1856, a branch was not built towards Saundersfoot and Tenby. The eastern side of the coalfield had no long distance rail link until the opening of the Pembroke and Tenby Railway in 1866. Even then, as a standard gauge line, it was of limited value for coal traffic until the broad gauge main line across South Wales was converted to the standard gauge in 1872. With the exception of Moreton colliery, which was provided with a siding on the P & T line from the outset, the other collieries remained dependent upon shipping by sea until the 1890's and beyond. In the circumstances it is a remarkable fact that there was no significant movement of coal by rail from Pembrokeshire before 1866.

Even after the South Wales main line was converted to the standard gauge, Pembrokeshire coal owners had to face the fact that railway freight rates from the county were hardly competitive with those offered to anthracite producers in the larger Carmarthenshire coalfield. Even so, in 1879, many of the Carmarthenshire collieries were finding the economic climate difficult, and on the premise that cooperation would be better than competition, C. R. Vickerman of the Bonvilles Court Coal Co. tried to establish an understanding with two anthracite businesses in Camarthenshire – Messrs. Norton of Cross Hands, and the Gwaun-cae-Gurwen company at the head of the Amman Valley. On 31 December 1879, C. R. Vickerman wrote to Howard J. Norton at Llanelly, and after enquiring if Nortons intended "to continue your ruinously low prices for another season," he got to the point:

> on all hands ... I am told that our anthracite collieries are insane on our returns, looking at the small number of producers of the best qualities. If you, and Gwaun-cae-Gurwen Co and myself could come to an arrangement we would not fear the others - but most probably one or two more of 'the next best' would join us – when they were assured that we had arranged among ourselves. Now is the time, before entering into the contracts for another year, to see any deeds which we can or cannot 'arrange'- and for each to shape his course accordingly. Will a meeting be of any avail?[63]

Unfortunately C. R. Vickerman went on to seek some commercial information, a move not guaranteed to endear him to another hard pressed colliery proprietor. Whilst ready to share information himself, his tendency to raise such questions was probably seen by others as betraying the weakness of his own position. In a letter dated 9 March 1880, appealing to the London coal merchants Charrington Sells and Co. for orders, he asked misguidedly for the names and addresses of their regular customers. The reply has not survived, but in his next letter C. R. Vickerman went out of his way to be conciliatory. He also offered to give a favourable rate for a cargo of coal he could load onto the SWIFT, a vessel then due to sail to Rochester. The response is not clear, but in early May, Charrington, Sells and Co. offered to take 1,000 tons of Kilgetty vein coal. This was far less than C. R. Vickerman would have liked, but he did not hesitate to accept.[64]

Meanwhile, in spite of further correspondence with Messrs Norton, it appears that little progress had been made towards the "understanding" C. R. Vickerman had sought. After his unsatisfactory experience in trying to form alliances with competitors, in February 1892 C. R. Vickerman adopted a different strategy. Representing the Bonvilles Court Coal Co., he and E. J. Harvey were founder members of the Association for the Promotion of the Use of Anthracite Smokeless Coal. The purpose of this body was to consider matters affecting the interests of anthracite owners, separately or collectively, and to encourage the general consumption of anthracite in London as the "only real and effective cure for black fogs". Unfortunately this association appears to have been less weighty than its title, and little was achieved.[65]

Competition in the coal industry generally was becoming more intense, and coal proprietors had to do all they could to find new uses for their product. In the anthracite area of South Wales several men worked on the problem of trying to make anthracite a suitable fuel for iron smelting. As early as 1837, George Crane of Ynyscedwyn iron works in the Swansea valley believed he had succeeded by applying a hot blast to the smelting process. Nevertheless the particular characteristics of anthracite caused some problems. Although in theory these could be overcome with care, in practice other grades of coal worked better for the purpose, and the further use of anthracite in ironworks was limited. In the context of Pembrokeshire it is interesting to note that C. R. Vickerman and his friends promoted the Pembrokeshire Coal and Iron Co. in the mid 1840's, when enthusiasm for Crane's method was still strong. By the time the works opened, this sentiment was subsiding, and the Kilgetty Ironworks was never the success that its promoters anticipated.

As a domestic fuel anthracite culm worked well in the "stummin," or mixed balls of culm and mud long used in homes in West Wales. Unfortunately anthracite was not a great success in other domestic settings. In an open grate it often burned with difficulty, and sometimes could be extinguished by the use of a poker. From time to time ingenious engineers designed and duly patented domestic stoves intended to consume anthracite, but none was able to make this coal truly popular. For household fires other grades of coal were cheaper or more effective, and only when its smokeless quality was valued was there much incentive to adopt it. Similarly manufacturers usually favoured anthracite when its smokeless quality was especially prized, as in the brewing and malting industries. Apart from specialised functions as a fuel used in the making of saddlers' ironmongery, and in heating agricultural hothouses, the markets for anthracite in the second half of the nineteenth century were essentially the same as those in the first half of the century – that is to say for hop drying, malting, and lime burning.[66]

Given such limited usage, and given the expansion of the anthracite industry in Carmarthenshire, where costs were usually lower, it is not surprising that in the late nineteenth century the Pembrokeshire coal and culm trades were in decline. In an age of main line railways those coal producers still dependent upon shipping inevitably faced a constant struggle. Although railways could speed up the delivery of anthracite to customers around the kingdom, they could also bring other grades of coal into Pembrokeshire from elsewhere. The development of quays and docks at Neyland, Milford and Pembroke Dock encouraged coal traffic to come into the county for the bunkering of steamships. Naturally Pembrokeshire producers wanted to be involved in this market, but they did not find it easy. Whereas in the 1860's they had been encouraged by the news that Queen Victoria liked the smokelessness of anthracite and had ordered that Bonvilles Court coal should be used aboard the Royal Yacht,[67] the reality was that this coal burned with an intense heat which could damage fireboxes and firebars. For practical purposes it was often thought necessary to blend anthracite with steam coals from Glamorgan or Monmouthshire, and week by week steam coal arrived by rail and sea. By the end of the century there was sufficient demand for different types of coal for local coal merchants to have established wharves at larger stations like Haverfordwest, Milford Haven and Pembroke. In the twentieth century this trend continued until even small stations like Clynderwen, Kilgetty and Manorbier had their own coal sidings. In brief the railways had the effect of making the coal trade truly national, and no longer local.[68]

In the Edwardian era the coal traffic in and out of Pembrokeshire was significant. In 1906 Milford imported 21,016 tons by sea alone. In the following year the equivalent figure was only 656 tons – a dramatic change most likely largely due to the removal of the Irish ferry service from Neyland to Fishguard, a port to which bunkering coal might more easily be sent by rail. Even so, substantial amounts of bunkering coal were used within the port of Milford - no less than 96,635 tons for vessels sailing to foreign ports, and 2,197 tons for those sailing coastwise. Although it has been reported that in this period Hook colliery was dispatching sizeable amounts to Singapore, in 1907 the exports of coal to foreign parts totalled only 300 tons. Shipments coastwise amounted to 21,353 tons, most of which was undoubtedly culm. As the total output of coal and culm in Pembrokeshire in 1907 was 49,694 tons it is evident that well over half the coal passing through came from collieries elsewhere.[69]

In the twentieth century the output of the Pembrokeshire Coalfield was puny in comparison with other coal mining areas of Britain. In South Wales, by 1913 the Rhondda alone boasted 53 pits, with a total output of over 9.5 million tons of coal. Pembrokeshire output for that year was a mere 55,000 tons! Appendix N provides figures for total output in each year between 1876 and 1948, and also figures for production from individual collieries extant after 1912, which underline the small output over these years as a whole. What is more, it was clearly the case that from the end of the nineteenth century a significant fall in output occurred. Reference is made elsewhere in this thesis to the belated and mostly unsuccessful attempts to revive or redevelop the coal industry in the twentieth century. Arguably the greatest achievement was increasing the volume of trade between Pembrokeshire and France in the 1920's and 1930's. The available records show that in 1927 there were nine shipments to Rouen of cargoes ranging from 300 to 450 tons.[70] At the same time there were a dozen smaller shipments to Ireland. By 1934, there were thirteen sailings to Rouen, and just one to Dublin, and in the following year nineteen shipments to Rouen, one to Le Havre, and three to Irish destinations.[71] The export trade came to an abrupt end in 1939 with one shipment to Rouen, and a final shipment from Saundersfoot to New Ross in Ireland on 8 May 1939.[72]

Endnotes for Chapter Nine

[1] *Cambrian Register, 1796.*

[2] Hereford and Worcester Record Office, BA 2309/ 55. I am grateful to Ian Cran, Caloundra, Queensland, Australia for drawing my attention to this reference and allowing me to see his unpublished paper entitled "Little Milford Colliery".

[3] Daniel Defoe, *A Tour through the Whole Island of Great Britain* (London, 1769 ed), Vol.2, 368.

[4] Morris, *Plans of Harbours, Bars, Bays and Roads in St. George's Channel,* 17

[5] Hassall, *A General View of the Agriculture of Pembrokeshire,* 60

[6] *Report of the Select Committee on the State of the Coal Trade,* 1800. Appendix 42 - an account of the coals exported from the ports of the United Kingdom between 1 January 1790 and 1 January 1800.

[7] *Report of the Royal Commission on Coal, 1871,* Appendix to the Report of Committee E

[8] N.L.W., Owen and Colby MS 1138.

[9] N.L.W., Picton Castle MS 7082. This document is unusual in showing more coal (20h 1c) than culm (16h 8c) being dispatched.

[10] N.L.W., Owen and Colby MS 2106. Williams was also the London merchant acting for Hook colliery. On 28 October 1789 he wrote to John Colby to say: "Good coals are much wanted, and such as those from Hook would be selling at 55s. per chaldron ... I have this season sold about 400 ch. from Hook." N.L.W. Owen and Colby MS 1951.

[11] N.L.W., Owen and Colby MS 1952.

[12] N.L.W., Owen and Colby MS 2107.

[13] N.L.W., Owen and Colby MS 2108.

[14] N.L.W., Owen and Colby MS 2109.

[15] N.L.W., Owen and Colby MS 2110. According to Robin Craig "Carmarthen vessels in deep sea trade 1785-1825", *Carmarthenshire Antiquary,* XXXVI (2000), Joseph and Benjamin Williams were sometime corn factors, apothecaries and general factors of several successive London addresses. For a time Benjamin Williams was in partnership with a Mr. Jackson, and they had links with shipowners in Carmarthenshire as well as Pembrokeshire.

[16] N.L.W., Owen and Colby MS 2308.

[17] N.L.W., Owen and Colby MS 2310. As regards overseas coal trade, the leading firm of the period in South Wales was Messrs. Summers and Clibborn.

[18] 37 Geo III, c 100 and 42 Geo III, c 115.

[19] *Report of the Committee on the Petition of the Owners of South Wales Collieries,* 1810, Appendix 6: Accounts of coal and culm imported into Bridgewater, Bristol and Gloucester in 1808 and 1809.

[20] Flinn, *The History of the British Coal Industry,* Vol. 2, 311.

[21] East Kent Archives, Whitfield, Dover, Cobb MSS EK/U 1453 B4/1540. I am grateful to R. S. Craig for drawing my attention to these records and the further references from the Cobb MSS at the East Kent Archives.

[22] East Kent Archives, Cobb MSS EK/U 1453 B4/1540.

[23] East Kent Archives, Cobb MSS EK/U 1453 B4/1501.

[24] East Kent Archives, Cobb MSS EK/U 1453 B4/1501.

[25] Cornwall County Record Office, Truro, Harveys of Hayle, MSS DDH1/2/67.

[26] Cornwall County Record Office, Truro, Harveys of Hayle, MSS DDH1/2/145.

[27] Cornwall County Record Office, Truro, Harveys of Hayle, MSS DDH1/2/54.

[28] Cornwall County Record Office, Truro, Harveys of Hayle, MSS DDH1/2/170.

[29] East Kent Archives, Cobb MSS EK/U 1453 B4/1534.

[30] East Kent Archives, Cobb MSS EK/U 1453 B4/1501.

[31] East Kent Archives, Cobb MSS EK/U 1453 B4/1537.

[32] The writer is indebted to Mr. R.Weedon of Landshipping, for giving him an opportunity to study the 1835 colliery sales book.

[33] East Kent Archives, Cobb MSS EK/U 1453 B4/1537.

[34] East Kent Archives, Cobb MSS EK/U 1453 B4/1537.

[35] S. C. Hall, *The Book of South Wales* (London:

1861), 79. Although the S.R. and H. Co. did not begin to trade formally until 1 March 1834, the harbour was in use some months earlier.

[36] East Kent Archives, Cobb MSS EK/U 1453 B4/1536.

[37] *Report of the Select Committee on the Coal Trade*, 1838, Evidence of James Bentley, paras 1282-1284.

[38] *Report of the Select Committee on the Coal Trade*, 1838. Evidence of Robert Johnstone, coal merchant, para 1941.

[39] Carmarthen Record Office, John Francis Collection, Lewis of Henllan,19

[40] 33, George II, c15.

[41] Hassall: *A General View of the Agriculture in Pembrokeshire*, 62.

[42] N.L.W., Owen and Colby 2103.

[43] M. Nix, "North Devon Coal and Culm Trades, 1780-1830", *The Devon Historian*, October 1999.

[44] Ibid. 7.

[45] Cullen, *Anglo–Irish Trade, 1660-1800*, 122.

[46] Beckett, *Coal and Tobacco*, 39.

[47] Dorothy and Betty Phillips, *Local Study - Hook*.

[48] Paul O'Leary, *Immigration and Integration: The Irish in Wales, 1798-1922* (Cardiff: University of Wales Press, 2000), 23.

[49] M. V. Symons, *Coal Mining in the Llanelli Area* (Llanelli: Llanelli Borough Council, 1979) Vol 1, 329.

[50] Pembrokeshire Record Office, HDX/951.

[51] Edwards. *A Study of Daucleddau Coalfield*, 77-79.

[52] The writer is indebted to Mr. R. Weedon, Landshipping, for the opportunity to study the 1835 colliery sales book.

[53] Nix. "North Devon coal and culm trades, 1780-1830", 7. As regards the price of coal and lime, Nix quotes the nineteenth century work by R. Fraser, *General View of the County of Devon, with observations on the Means of its improvement*.

[54] Pembrokeshire Record Office, D/HIG/50. The remains of old lime kilns may be seen at numerous sites around the West Wales coast. A disused anthracite fired malting kiln still exists near the harbour at Trefechan, Aberystwyth.

[55] Pembrokeshire Record Office, Saundersfoot Railway & Harbour Co., minutes 26 February 1839 and 3 June 1839.

[56] Pembrokeshire Record Office, Saundersfoot Railway & Harbour Co., minutes 7 February 1840.

[57] Pembrokeshire Record Office, Saundersfoot Railway & Harbour Co., minutes 1 June 1840.

[58] Pembrokeshire Record Office, Saundersfoot Railway & Harbour Co., minutes 7 June 1841.

[59] Pembrokeshire Record Office, Saundersfoot Railway & Harbour Co., minutes 6 June 1842.

[60] Pembrokeshire Record Office, Saundersfoot Railway & Harbour Co., minutes 5 June 1843.

[61] Pembrokeshire Record Office, Saundersfoot Railway & Harbour Co., minutes 14 February 1844.

[62] Pembrokeshire Record Office, Saundersfoot Railway & Harbour Co., minutes 3 June 1844.

[63] Vickerman papers (privately owned), letter book, 1879-1884; see also M. R. C. Price, "A glimpse of the Pembrokeshire Coal Trade in 1880", *Archive*, No. 27 (Lydney: Lightmoor Press, 2000).

[64] Vickerman papers (privately owned), letter book, 1879-1884. Ironically Norton's Old Cross Hands colliery closed down in 1883, but the Bonvilles Court colliery eventually gained its own railway siding in 1893.

[65] N.L.W., Picton Castle MSS3887-8.

[66] Vickerman papers, Lewis and Bidder's Report, 1 February 1873.

[67] Vickerman papers (privately owned). Letter of C. R. Vickerman to C. H. Perkins, Sketty, Swansea, 5 August 1880.

[68] Local newspapers of the period often included advertisements for coal at goods yards - for example, in 1907, William Roberts of Haverfordwest advertised in the *Pembrokeshire Herald* the availability of coal in 6, 8 and 10 ton trucks. Even before main line railways became well established in the county there was some inward traffic in house coal by sea from, for example, Lydney, Gloucestershire.

[69] *The South Wales Coal Annual*, 1908.

[70] P.R.O., CUST 75, Overseas Clearances Register, Milford Haven 1927-1939.

[71] P.R.O., CUST 75/29. In terms of sailings to France, this was actually better than sixty years before. In 1864, there were just twelve shipments from Pembrokeshire to France, plus two to Quebec, two to Demerara, one to Norway, one to Portugal, one to Spain, one to Belgium.

[72] *The Western Telegraph* 11 May 1939.

Coal Society

For many generations the labouring classes in the Pembrokeshire coalfield spent their usually shortened lives in toil, poverty and squalor. They were constantly vulnerable to the unpredictability of landlords and mine owners, quite apart from the inherent risks of accident and disease. This shared experience of deprivation and danger made Pembrokeshire colliers (like those in many other mining districts) a close knit body, well aware that their survival might depend upon the skill, strength, courage or commitment of their colleagues and their neighbours. There were many times, though, when their poverty was so profound that their whole existence was devoted to the necessities of survival.

Benjamin Malkin, who visited South Pembrokeshire in 1803, adopted a dismissive attitude to miners' housing. He declared that "a stranger is much disgusted with the squalid appearance of the mud cottages, the undistinguished abode of the whole family, human and bestial".[1] Mrs Mary Morgan, who visited Hook twelve years earlier, was disarmingly honest about her own timidity. Even so, having declined a chance to descend into a coal pit, she did venture to crawl into a miner's hut. As she said:

> You cannot enter any other way than on your hands and knees. When in, you can only just stand upright near the middle of it, where there is a large fire of this country's coals, which are very different from ours. They emit a steam that is intolerable in a close place, such as I am now describing, where there is only one aperture in the top by way of a chimney. Though they eat in these huts, yet I saw no culinary utensils nor household furniture, not even a bench of turf round the hovel to sit down upon. The miners sit upon their hands, as the Indians do.[2]

Mrs Morgan made this depressing account a little more acceptable with her concluding comments, "You are to observe that these are only temporary erections where they eat, and take rest at intervals from their labour, or shelter from a storm. They have all cottages in the villages."

If these were typical structures situated around eighteenth-century coal workings, it is little wonder that none survives. In truth even the cottages where they slept with their families were no more than hovels, described in South Pembrokeshire as "clom" cottages - the term "clom" coming from a Nordic word meaning dirt. Although they were built on stone foundations, the side walls were seldom more than six feet high, and comprised layers of mud, clay, straw and bramble. This was cut, shaped and finished with a spade, and the same tool was used to cut out small windows. At one end of the building a wattle and daub chimney would be constructed, wrapped round with hayrope to ensure greater stability. Except in the warmest months of summer, the windows would be covered with sacking, and the only lighting within this gloomy abode would be provided by tallow or rush candles. Although the floors amounted to no more than flat stones and beaten soil, the occupants had a means to keep the interior reasonably dry.[3] Their method was to burn "stummin"- a local name (already noted) for compacted balls of culm and clay which were burnt on their domestic fires. These fires were kept going continuously, and could produce a surprisingly intense heat as well as unpleasant fumes. The combination of damp floors with a smoky, fetid atmosphere was a challenge to the constitution of the most robust resident. Such premises were plainly undesirable homes at all seasons, but especially so in times of torrential rain. When the era of clom cottages was over, some were rebuilt in stone, but many of the others soon deteriorated and collapsed. Right across the Pembrokeshire coalfield the sites of many former cottages have been lost. Edwards noted in 1950 that elderly residents of Stepaside could recall over forty "clom" cottages in their neighbourhood which by then had vanished.[4]

In the second half of the nineteenth century new housing was provided in the coal mining communities, but very little was built at the expense of the colliery companies. The Pembrokeshire Iron & Coal Co. erected a small block of cottages between Kilgetty colliery and the ironworks, and a few more were soon built by the Bonvilles Court company within half a mile of the colliery. At the same period some miners' cottages were also constructed at Broadmoor. As late as 1914 the isolation of the small village of Reynalton prompted the New Reynolton Anthracite Colliery Co. to construct a few cottages for their workmen. The improvements that had come about in cottage accommodation from the middle decades of the nineteenth century to the middle of the twentieth century were made apparent in a survey of housing in the area around Hook colliery carried out in 1946. At this date 65 per cent of those employed at the colliery lived in Hook, and another 25 per cent in the villages of Freystrop and Llangwm, within two miles of the pithead. The survey went on to say:

> Speaking generally, the type of house in this area is the two-roomed cottage with attics in the roof used as sleeping quarters. These cottages were erected 75 to 100 years ago by the owner of the estate, but within the last 20 to 25 years the estate was placed on the market for sale and the tenants were given the opportunity to buy their own homes ... every cottage in this particular area has a water tap. Very few however have bathrooms, which of course is a real necessity for a mine workers' home. It is stressed finally that lack of bathrooms in many of these small cottages is a great hardship on the mine workers concerned, because there are no pithead bath facilities at the Hook colliery.[5]

In spite of continuing poverty, it is clear that conditions for mining families had made some progress in the twentieth century. This was just as well. The wretched housing in the mid-nineteenth century was matched by the wretchedness of almost every other aspect of miners' lives. Many families were so poor they were obliged to scratch out a living in any way they could. Billy Howells, born in 1857, recalled in later life how he was raised by his mother, who left colliery work to try to sell sand gathered from Saundersfoot beach. As soon as he was old enough Billy had to help, collecting sand, and also chalk brought to the harbour as ballast by ships coming to collect coal. A mixture of sand and chalk evidently made an excellent scouring sand for cleaning tables, buckets and the like, and it was sold door to door in towns like Tenby.

In the 1860's, according to Billy Howells, Saundersfoot harbour had other attractions for the local poor:

> Not only would we children gather this scouring sand and chalk from the beach, but we used to go down to the pier when the tide was out and gather up all the small coals that had fallen down between the vessels and walls of the harbour while they were being loaded.... Anybody and everybody were allowed at that time to gather up and take away, and very many people would avail themselves of it, for there were more poor people about the village and neighbourhood besides ourselves. Indeed, so great was the rush for this small coal that unless one was sharp and there in good time, someone else would be there before us, and it was "first come, first serve" ... After gathering this coal we would carry it home in bags, and mix with some clay that we would get from some of the neighbouring fields, the owners of which having given us consent to dig it, and thus make it into "balls" [stummin].[6]

This need to gather in anything of the slightest value is underscored by Billy Howells' description of his household's poverty. As a young collier, frequently he went to a very hard day's work on no more than bread and water, and in the evening "very often we should sit down to nothing more but potatoes and salt, or a little vinegar. Fish (except shell fish that we gathered on holidays) 'flesh nor fowl' we rarely ever tasted unless it was given to us." Elsewhere in his reminiscences Billy Howells recalled the brutalised conditions in the collieries, and the utter inadequacy of his clothes for warmth or protection. Indeed stories have been handed down from this period of boys walking to work with sacking or rags wrapped round their feet for want of shoes. In the depths of winter such material could become frozen to the ground, compelling the child to urinate on his own feet in order to free them. Whatever the season, many boys worked underground barefoot, and indeed wearing little more than a shirt and pants. Tom Waters of Kilgetty worked in such a way in the 1890's, and many years later he recalled the experience:

> We used to be barefooted, and bare all down there, and a little shirt ... Knock your back and the blood would run down here in your eyes. And you would cut your feet on the coal, the coal that was anthracite, sharp as glass nearly, and at night my father would be there on the bed, with a tallow candle, tallow candles we used see, in the colliery, and dropping in the hot grease on the skin, and out with the coals from our feet – aye, it was hard times and no mistakes. [7]

Even in the twentieth century it was common for the men to go underground wearing rags, or a heavier material called "brattish", wrapped around their feet. Although by then many had boots, they were for Sunday best, or just for walking to work. In any case boots had to be made to last as long as possible. In addition the men usually wore trousers and flannel shirts, and perhaps a jacket with pockets big enough to carry some of their kit - the food tin, water jack, tobacco box, timber scribing knife and of course the very necessary candles or lamp.[8]

In an era when women worked below ground it seems that their attire was little better than that of the men and boys, and very few concessions were made to their gender. By the second half of the nineteenth century, though, the garb of the women was severely practical. Their clothing usually consisted of boots and black stockings, a long flannel dress and a large canvas apron.[9] The women who worked on the screens and spoil-banks were always anxious to protect their hair from coal dust, and so sought to protect it by tying scarves tightly across the forehead and down to the chin.[10]

In 1841, when R. H. Franks visited Pembrokeshire on behalf of the Children's Employment Commission, he was dismayed by what he discovered. Writing of the Begelly area, he said:

> The collier population of this district, more particularly the males, are dirty and drunken in their habits; the cottages they inhabit are low and ill ventilated; the drainage is bad, and their practice of living and sleeping in large numbers, in the same apartment, tends much to spread disease.[11]

Drunkenness was undoubtedly a problem. Arguably it helped to anaesthetise the senses of those living in such miserable conditions. On occasions it may even have been assisted by coal owners, because colliery accounts sometimes refer to an allowance of ale granted to labourers or carters. Certainly there was no shortage of places to buy drink. In Franks' time, for example, the rural parish of Martletwy, which included Landshipping, had two beerhouses and four other public houses.[12]

Similar observations were made by the Rector of Begelly, Revd Richard Buckby, in giving evidence to the Royal Commission on Education in Wales in 1847. He declared:

> The parish contains a mining population. Out of seventy marriages, in six only have the brides not been visibly enceintes. Seduction (which in these cases is much more condemnatory of the one sex than the other deserves) is generally followed by marriage if the woman conceives; not otherwise. The people are extremely cunning, but grossly ignorant, and with no real sense of their own interest. Families are often crowded together at night promiscuously, of all ages and sex. Underletting prevails to an extent which is highly injurious; the rent to the head landlord is mostly paid by this system. The average of life is very short – not above 33 years, as appears from the register. This may be accounted for by the personal dirtiness of the miners, who never wash their bodies. Weddings are times of great rioting and debauchery. The intended bride and groom live together for a considerable time previous to the marriage. They brew as much ale as they can, and sell it, without a licence, to their friends, who are expected to give more than the market price. This is one way in which they can raise money to begin the world with. There is also a similar custom called cuk-making, i.e. cake–making. The bride and her friends make cakes, which are sold on the night of the marriage in the same way as ale. All these customs are merely varieties of 'biddings.' The whole system works unmixed mischief. The population is mostly indigenous, not imported. The miners generally possess a small tenement on a holding of lives,

which has in former times been granted them for electioneering purposes by the landowners; and this prevents their fluctuating much. They are utterly careless about sending their children to school, and about most other things.[13]

Extreme poverty was the primary fact of life for many on the coalfield in the early nineteenth century, as the numerous critical comments made about the coal mining districts indicate. As the decades passed, though, the influence of Christianity clearly grew, and by the second half of the nineteenth century the lives of ordinary people saw some improvement. Indeed the increasing importance of religion in the lives of Pembrokeshire people can hardly be exaggerated, because even those who did not make a habit of worship still came under its influence indirectly. A newspaper report in August 1866 about a fatal accident at Bonvilles Court, concludes: "It appears that it is an old established custom among workers at the Bonvilles Court colliery to read prayers every morning at the three different headings, and to hold a general united prayer meeting once a month."[14]

The abysmal ignorance of poor labouring families, often referred to in the early nineteenth century, gradually gave way to a growing sense of spiritual awareness and self discipline. This advance began largely through the work of the Sunday Schools, which became a feature of the life of almost every Anglican church and non-conformist chapel on and off the coalfield. It is known, for example, that at the time of R. H. Franks' visit in 1841, the Revd Richard Buckby had started an Anglican Sunday School at Begelly which was endeavouring to impart some knowledge of the Gospel.[15] The Christian instruction of *adults* as well as the young had a prominent place in the work of the Methodist and Baptist leaders.[16] Indeed the Methodist interest in local mining communities began in the eighteenth century with John Wesley himself. In 1771 and 1777 he preached at Houghton, just south of the coalfield, near Llangwm, and in 1777 and 1781 he spoke at Jeffreston.[17] Accordingly the seeds of non-conformity were sown, germinating in later years in chapels which were not only places of worship and learning, but also centres for further social and musical activity for all the family. Through the influence of the chapels, too, those who gained the vote in the late nineteenth century would become radical Liberal in their politics. In the middle of the nineteenth century the emphasis in the chapels was often formal and evangelical in character; by the end of the century chapels and their Sunday Schools had tended to become less earnest, and more recreational, so that the social teas would no longer be followed by scripture tests, but by concerts or light entertainment, singing or recitations.

One of the highlights of the Sunday School year came with the Sunday School anniversary, often held on a public holiday rather than the exact anniversary date, in order to ensure the best possible attendance. In 1860, for example, the anniversary of the Independent Sunday School in Narberth was marked on Good Friday, and whilst it is not known if any of the teachers were directly involved in the coal industry, it is evidence of the culture of the times that this one Sunday School could muster 27 men and 9 women as teachers, and had at least 171 boys and 162 girls on the roll. A procession through the town to honour the anniversary was followed by tea and cakes, and an evening service.[18] In somewhat similar fashion, public holidays were favoured for the annual Sunday School treat, Easter Monday and Whit Monday being very popular dates. On these occasions the tea would be followed by games in a nearby field, or on a beach. Such were the arrangements made by the Broad Haven Baptist Sunday School on Whit Monday, 1887.[19] By the end of the century these occasions had often become opportunities for a trip to the seaside by horse and cart or pony and trap. In the summer of 1905, *The Pembrokeshire Herald* reported that the annual outing of the Narberth Church Sunday and Day school had been held on 14 July:

> Saundersfoot was the favoured spot, and upwards of 250 adults and children left the station in the morning, the GWR having made special arrangements for cheap tickets ... The special train back started from Saundersfoot at 8.30pm, and all reached home safely, having spent a most enjoyable day.[20]

The activities of the Sunday Schools were closely matched by those of the Temperance movement, organised in Pembrokeshire from the early 1840's by non-conformist ministers and their congregations. Soon the principal towns all became centres for temperance meetings, and the temperance message was given greater impact and colour by the Rechabite and teetotal societies in promoting teas, choirs and musical events. The evangelical fervour of some of these occasions did not suit every taste, but in April 1844, a *Pembrokeshire Herald* reporter acknowledged in relation to Tenby that "the total abstinence principle is greatly on the increase here, and its beneficial effects are already apparent on the lower classes of people".[21]

Numerous nonconformist chapels established branches of the Band of Hope to advance the temperance movement amongst young people. These became significant social gatherings for youngsters devoid of other organised activities. On 16 March 1860, for instance, the Narberth Band of Hope marked its anniversary with a procession around the streets of the town, supporters of the movement from Stepaside and Templeton participating with them. After tea and cake in the school room, the occasion concluded with recitations and singing. [22]

The temperance movement remained lively well into the twentieth century, and was especially strong in the coal mining village of Stepaside. Here the success of the cause was due in no small measure to the leadership of George Williams, who was holding outdoor temperance meetings at least as early as 1860.[23] Even in the 1930's one in four of the weekly guild meetings at Stepaside Wesleyan Chapel was devoted to the temperance cause, although by then support for the temperance ideal had begun to weaken.[24] Temperance was a vital part of the Primitive Methodist cause, and those Primitive Methodist chapels at Summerhill, near Amroth, Kingsmoor and Cresselly, set in the heart of colliery communities, would have seen members become strict teetotal and spend their social lives in chapel activities like Band of Hope meeting and outdoor camp meetings.

Just as the chapels were closely associated with the temperance movement, so they were also associated with the development of singing festivals, and those competitive cultural occasions known in Welsh-speaking districts as "eisteddfodau," a term sometimes used even in anglicised South Pembrokeshire. In September 1896, for example, the *Pembrokeshire Herald* noted that such an event was to take place at Saundersfoot, and similarly in April 1908, at Broad Haven Baptist Chapel.[25] In 1904 the annual eisteddfod at Saundersfoot proved to be a quite remarkable occasion, bringing together C. R. Vickerman's son and successor, and the noted trade union leader known as "Mabon."

> the annual eisteddfod ... proved to be a great success in every way. Beautiful weather favoured the event, and a good surplus will be available to swell the fund for improving the public lighting of the streets. The presidents at the crowded meetings were Sir Charles Philipps, Bt., Picton, and Mr C. H. R.Vickerman, JP of Saundersfoot. The conductor was Mr W. Abraham MP (Mabon).

Mabon, in his opening address, dwelt upon what the eisteddfod had done for Wales in the past in educating and elevating the nation.[26] The message was well known, and doubtless there were numerous eisteddfodau across the county at this period. The provision of such events on a regular basis spurred chapel choirs on to greater achievements, and aided the development of the powerful tradition of male voice singing. It must be admitted, however, that choirs from the mining areas of Pembrokeshire were not plentiful, and rarely possessed the number seen in the better-known male voice choirs of Glamorgan. A photograph of the Begelly Male Voice Choir in 1912 shows just nineteen men.[27] The Saundersfoot Male Voice Choir was founded in the Edwardian period and enjoyed a high reputation until disbanded in the 1950's.[28]

The growing appreciation of music encouraged men to learn to play an instrument, and for many this became possible for the first time when they attended classes run by local silver or brass bands. Such bands were never very numerous in Pembrokeshire, but they were usually set up by local fund raising and public subscription, and were sometimes sponsored by a chapel or teetotal society. Recalling the early years of the twentieth century, a Hook collier named Billy Bowen later described how he could not get into the Temperance band, and so had to turn to a town band nicknamed the "Beer and Bacco". Most of the men in this band had been barred from the Temperance one by their drinking habits; Billy Bowen declared that as a group they were deemed to be a disgrace to the chapel![29] This last observation serves as a reminder that only some of the miners were drawn into the chapels and their culture of temperance and self-improvement. Indeed, if recollections of violence in a Stepaside public house at the turn of the twentieth century can be taken as representative of colliery community life, then the ale house was a significant rival to the chapel.[30]

Pleasure fairs provided occasional entertainment for the residents of mining communities. The Portfield fair held in Haverfordwest in October of each year had a history going back to the 1690's, and attracted people for miles around. In the middle of the nineteenth century Saundersfoot was the setting for a fair held each May known as "France Fair." By the end of the century it appears to have changed into a children's sports day, but by then the village was visited for up to a fortnight each summer by Studts' travelling fair. In time this too faded from the scene, and was replaced by another travelling fair, Danters, which provided amusement each August right up to the 1960's.[31]

In the later decades of the nineteenth century there occurred in Pembrokeshire, as in other areas of Britain, a secularisation of leisure. For many generations sport had been the preserve of the gentry and the prosperous, and most of their activities were quite out of the reach of ordinary people. By 1870 though, questions were being asked about this social divide. In a letter to the *Pembrokeshire Herald* in July 1870, a blacksmith complained that the rules for rowing at the forthcoming Haverfordwest Regatta would exclude the very class of competitors most likely to guarantee a close race. He demanded: "Why should any young fellow because he is getting his livelihood by the sweat of his brow, be excluded from pulling?" Accordingly he asked that the organisers should reconsider the rules, and open the event to amateurs who were mechanics or artisans. On the day the regatta included what were described as "rustic sports", meaning competitions that were open to the lower classes.[32] Before long rustic and aquatic sports were a feature of the numerous regattas held around the Pembrokeshire coast, including the popular longshore sports and regatta held at Saundersfoot every August.

Before organised team games had had much chance to grasp the attention of ordinary workmen, towns and villages sometimes expressed their rivalry by putting on races between their respective champion athletes. In 1870 Saundersfoot's best sprinter, George Twigg, a smith by trade, was pitted against William Lewis, a shoemaker from Narberth, in a 100 yards race. To the surprise of Saundersfoot residents Twigg was beaten, but they were so confident of his ability that another race was organised, on Kingsmoor Common. To the dismay of Saundersfoot, Lewis won again.[33]

Doubtless watched by local colliers from the Saundersfoot and Begelly districts, this event cannot have escaped the notice of the local industrialist, C. R. Vickerman of Hean Castle. Whether it actually prompted him to take steps on behalf of Saundersfoot cannot be determined now, but as an enthusiastic sportsman himself, he certainly realised the benefits of sport. In the 1870's Vickerman was not only influential in starting the longshore sports, but he also set about draining the marshy ground behind Coppet Hall beach to create a sports field. In one of his most enlightened moves he helped to initiate an annual Saundersfoot sports day, which soon developed into a notable day in the village calendar.[34] In August 1893, the Saundersfoot athletic sports and pony races attracted spectators from Haverfordwest and Carmarthen, as well as the immediate locality.[35] In August 1899, it was estimated that the same event was watched by a crowd of almost 3,000 - in effect doubling the population for the day! [36]

In the 1880's C. R. Vickerman went one step further, and organised his own cricket team. As he was keen to have a good local pitch available he employed a number of local men to create a cricket oval out of a field at Harry's Tump near Sardis, and not far from the main gate of Hean Castle. Some games were played away from home. In September 1874, the *Tenby Observer* reported a cricket match played at Pembroke Dock on 29 August 1874. It was a single innings match between the 9th East Norfolk Regiment and Hean Castle, with both Vickerman, father and son, playing for the Hean Castle team.[37] Unfortunately the use of the Harry's Tump field does not appear to have outlived the Vickermans' ownership of the Hean Castle estate, but a field boundary on the site still shows evidence of the oval created in the nineteenth century.[38] Although there were one or two other teams of cricketers in the Saundersfoot district by the turn of the century, it was not until 1926 that the Kilgetty and Saundersfoot United Cricket Club was founded.[39]

By the late nineteenth century both rugby and association football were well established in the county, and by the 1880's there were rugby teams in (amongst other places) Haverfordwest, Llangwm and Tenby.[40] For a small village like Llangwm, though, there was a perennial problem in finding enough men to field a complete team. Most men had to work a solid six-day week right up to the time of World War I, and those who were unemployed were often obliged to move away to find another job. This difficulty became most apparent in 1920 when Llangwm and Kilgetty met in the semi-final of a cup competition. After Llangwm had won, it was alleged that three members of their team came from outside the district, and were ineligible. The claim was upheld, and Kilgetty went through to the final by default.[41]

In the 1880's Milford Haven was the main centre for association football, although there were several other teams in the county, including Tenby.[42] In the twentieth century this sport went from strength to strength in Pembrokeshire, and soon every town and village would boast of a team of their own. Even so, the old problem of trying to combine work and sport remained, although it eased somewhat after World War I when it became customary to allow colliers and other working men to have a half day on Saturday. Benjamin Waters of Kilgetty, whose family had long been associated with the coal industry, presented the Kilgetty & District Challenge Cup in 1926 to encourage the development of the game.[43] This was a successful move, and it was a feature of the inter-war years that football teams were fielded by a number of churches and chapels as well as small villages.

Some improvement came about, too, in the educational provision for the children of labouring classes following the Elementary Education Act of 1870. Intended to "fill the gap" in the old voluntary school system, new board schools were set up in those parishes where provision for all children could not be met by the undenominational British or (far more numerous) National (Church of England) schools. Despite the coming of compulsory education for children of up to ten, legislated for in 1880, and the provision of free schooling in 1891, Gareth Jones has rightly concluded that "the education provided in elementary schools for the mass of children remained restricted and mechanical".[44] At best, the regime of the three "R's" bestowed merely a modicum of literacy amongst working-class children. Many school buildings, especially voluntary ones which did not receive rate-aid (as did the board schools), remained dirty and ill-ventilated. Moreover, impoverished parents all too frequently looked to the earnings of their young children to keep the family solvent, and so were lax about sending them to school.

Although this system had obvious limitations, at least working-class children were made semi-literate, and given an educational foundation upon which to build. Arguably these youngsters gained greater assistance from the instruction in reading they received in the Sunday Schools which, in the case of non-conformist sects, were also open to adults. The opening decades of the twentieth century were to see the provision of opportunities for learning which serious-minded labourers, farm workers and colliers alike, could seize. After the belated establishment of the Pembrokeshire County Library at Haverfordwest in 1924, by January 1926 there were some fifty-four library centres in the county, mainly at elementary schools, as at the mining villages of Amroth and Stepaside. Aberystwyth University College, too, was to send tutors to Pembrokeshire each year from 1919, and in 1925 four classes were conducted at Haverfordwest, Pembroke Dock, Kilgetty and Tenby. In this way Kilgetty miners gained an opportunity to learn something of economics and history.[45]

Notwithstanding these changes from the late nineteenth century bringing some improvements to the lifestyle of Pembrokeshire miners and their families, the way of life remained essentially rural, and different to that prevailing in the more developed mining areas of Glamorgan. It seems remarkable now that only at Hook and Johnston were Miners' Welfare halls or institutes established, and then only at very late dates – 1921 and 1928 respectively. In the case of Hook, the institute did acquire features of the miners' institutes to be found on the main South Wales coalfield, with the setting up of a silver band, and the provision of a library and facilities for snooker and billiards.[46] The closest the Kilgetty area came to such a development was the establishment of the Free Gardeners Hall by public subscription. In due course it became a venue for social activities and amateur dramatics.[47] In such modest changes there was evidence of the move away from chapels and churches so apparent in the twentieth century. The chapel was the cradle for many aspects of local culture, but increasingly men felt that they had come of age to make their social life their own. Before very long, though, the coal industry in Pembrokeshire was dead, and men had to exercise their responsibility and judgement in other walks of life.

Endnotes for Chapter Ten

[1] B. H. Malkin, *The Scenery, Antiquities and Biography of South Wales* (2nd edition, London: 1807).

[2] Mrs M. Morgan, *A Tour to Milford Haven in the year 1791*, 235.

[3] Harry, *Living and Working in the Pembrokeshire Coalfield*, 69.

[4] Edwards, *A Study of the Daucleddau Coalfield*, 98.

[5] Ministry of Food and Power, *Regional Survey Report, South Wales* (1946), 214.

[6] Billy Howells, unpublished reminiscences, c1891 "A Debtor to Grace," 6. I am indebted to Roscoe Howells of Amroth for giving me the opportunity to study these reminiscences.

[7] Tom Waters was recorded on tape in the 1960's by Richard Keen when working for Pembrokeshire Museums, and is quoted by Harry, *Living and Working in the Pembrokeshire Coalfield*, 83.

[8] Description given to the writer by former miners, now deceased, and by David Jenkins of Hook, who was raised in a mining family.

[9] A. V. John, *By the Sweat of their Brow*, 184.

[10] Reminiscence of the late Mary Richards of Stepaside who, up to the time of her death in 1974, was the last survivor of the many women who had worked in the Pembrokeshire Coal Industry.

[11] *Children's Employment Commission Report*, 1842: Evidence of R. H. Franks, xvii.

[12] Robert L. Davies and Jane Nelson, *A River Never Sleeps* (Narberth: 1999), 38, 39.

[13] *Royal Commission on Education in Wales Report*, 1847, Part 1, xxvii, 421/2.

[14] *Haverfordwest and Milford Haven Telegraph*, 6 August 1866, concerning a fatal accident at Bonvilles Court. Colliery.

[15] *Children's Employment Commission Report, 1842*, Part 2. Several of the children interviewed by R. H. Franks said that they attended a Sunday School – at Begelly, for example, this was stated by James Davies (aged 8) and Mary Day (aged 11).

[16] Thomas G. Stickings, *The Story of Saundersfoot* (Tenby: 1970), 58. In 1846 the Moreton Wesleyan Chapel, established in 1844, had 62 pupils, whilst the Bethesda Chapel (Calvinistic Methodist) a mile further south had 55 pupils.

[17] H. J. Dickman, "Wesleyan Methodism in Pembrokeshire" *The Journal of the Pembrokeshire Historical Society*, No. 3 (1989), 92. Whilst the first Baptist chapel in South Pembrokeshire was established at Molleston, near Templeton, as early as 1731, English speaking Baptist chapels were rare in the county before about 1820.

[18] D. W. Howell, "Leisure and Recreation", *Pembrokeshire County History*, Vol.IV, *Modern Pembrokeshire 1815-1974*, (Haverfordwest: 1987), 440.

[19] Ibid., 443.

[20] *The Pembrokeshire Herald*, 21 July 1905.

[21] *The Pembrokeshire Herald*, 26 April 1844.

[22] *The Pembrokeshire Herald*, 30 March 1860.

[23] D. W. Howell, "Leisure and Recreation", 439.

[24] Ibid., 438.

[25] *The Pembrokeshire Herald*, 4 September 1896, and 24 April 1908.

[26] *The Pembrokeshire Herald*, 26 August 1904.

[27] W. R. Morgan: *The Story of Begelly*, 78.

[28] Stickings, *The Story of Saundersfoot*, 68.

[29] Reminiscence of the late Edward Green given to the writer in October 1986.

[30] W. R. Morgan, *The Story of Begelly*.

[31] Stickings, *The Story of Saundersfoot*, 76,78.

[32] *The Pembrokeshire Herald*, 22 July 1870.

[33] D. W. Howell, "Leisure and Recreation," 425.

[34] Stickings, *The Story of Saundersfoot*, 75.

[35] D. W. Howell, "Leisure and Recreation," 424.

[36] *The Pembrokeshire Herald*, 1 September 1899.

[37] *The Tenby Observer*, 3 September 1874.

[38] Account given to the writer by Mrs Dorothy Evans, daughter of Capt. J. F. Vickerman.

[39] D. W. Howell, "Leisure and Recreation", 426.

[40] Ibid., 429.

[41] Ibid., 431.

[42] Ibid., 430.

[43] Ibid., 433.

[44] Gareth E. Jones, "Education 1815-1974", in D. W. Howell (ed.) *Pembrokeshire County History*, VolIV, *Modern Pembrokeshire 1815-1974* (Haverfordwest: 1993), 398-402.

[45] D. W. Howell, "Leisure and Recreation", 453. The Central Labour College classes which were offered to miners in Glamorgan from the Edwardian period did not appear in Pembrokeshire. In the Rhondda such classes tended to stimulate militancy, but despite Pembrokeshire's poor working conditions such attitudes were never very evident.

[46] Description given to the writer by Dorothy and Betty Phillips, retired schoolteachers of Hook.

[47] I am indebted to Graeme Phillips, a former resident of Kilgetty, for this information.

Hook Colliery brass band

Miss D. Phillips

Conclusions

Viewed from the perspective of the twenty-first century, with all the contemporary concern for technology, efficiency and high productivity, the Pembrokeshire coalfield may well appear to be of marginal significance, and woefully backward through much of its recorded history. However as we have seen, this history was long – spanning seven centuries - and for at least half that period the light of knowledge illuminates the story very intermittently. The lack of evidence relating to the early centuries is frustrating, but what is certain is that the first and finest advantage of the Pembrokeshire coalfield was Milford Haven itself. A superb natural harbour, it was acknowledged as such in Tudor times. When writing the play "Cymbeline", Shakespeare asked:

> How far is it to this blessed Milford? And by the way
> Tell me how Wales was made so happy as
> To inherit such a haven.[1]

The Haven and its associated river system was essential to the early development of the coalfield. The coal pits of Freystrop, Hook, Landshipping, and Jeffreston were all close to suitable shipping places, and accessible to the small craft then available. In an era when roads were appalling, water transport was far cheaper than land carriage for bulky and heavy commodities like coal, limestone or timber – perhaps in the ratio of 1 in 12, or 1 in 16, depending on the condition of the relevant road. As Eric Kerridge has observed (following T. S. Willan): "Coal was carried by water wherever possible ... Coasting vessels, which were being much improved, provided the cheapest freights of all."[2]

The second advantage was the discovery at some early date that Pembrokeshire coal or culm was suitable for lime-burning. These two industries or activities grew together and eventually died together. Although it is not possible to identify an exact date when mining and lime burning began, it is quite clear that both were established in or by the thirteenth century. Certainly the record of coal and limestone shipments to Aberystwyth in 1282 is both fascinating and teasing. The order was substantial, but given that one ton of coal or culm was generally required to burn two or three tons of limestone,[3] the only slight surprise is that the order for limestone was not much larger. Arguably at least a thousand tons of limestone were needed. The traditional Welsh cart had a capacity of just under a ton, and if it is assumed that carts of this capacity were in use in the thirteenth century, the six hundred cart loads of coal ordered would represent about five hundred tons of coal or culm.[4]

Whilst the Aberystwyth order is the meagre sum of thirteenth-century documentary evidence, there is also some physical evidence to be considered. Limestone was burned with coal at Cilgerran, and probably at Roch, in this great era for the construction of castles. Indeed, most if not all, of these magnificent stone-built fortifications around the south and west coast of Wales date from the twelfth and thirteenth centuries. The period also witnessed the establishment of most of the region's monastic foundations, and the use of coal in the thirteenth century by monks at Neath and Margam is well attested. The religious life of the region was developing rapidly, and, in the words of R. R. Davies:

> The most visible expression of the transformation of the local church in Wales in three centuries was the building and rebuilding of its parish churches. Not a single surviving parish church in the country pre-dates the eleventh century or, for the most part, the early twelfth.[5]

In brief, these centuries saw a building boom, and by the second half of the twelfth century it was a boom assisted by the availability of tenacious, lime-based mortar. It was a boom inspired and driven very largely by the Normans, and in this era the Normans dominated Pembrokeshire.

These facts, and the implications arising from them, merit much closer consideration, but the writer believes that there must be a strong possibility, even a probability, that this building boom was linked to the availability of coal, culm and limestone in Pembrokeshire. Most castles, and many churches, were built close to navigable water. For military purposes such arrangements undoubtedly aided the delivery of foodstuffs, ordnance and other supplies, but in the first instance it assisted the delivery of building materials. In an age dependent upon the sea for the movement of bulky commodities this is surely significant. As there is no record of coal mining in Carmarthenshire before the Tudor period there must be a possibility that Pembrokeshire coal (if not limestone) contributed to the construction of Norman castles from Kidwelly westwards, with Aberystwyth being perhaps one of the more distant royal strongholds built with materials from Pembrokeshire. Setting aside the reasonable, but speculative possibility that in these early centuries Pembrokeshire coal and limestone may have reached Devon, Cornwall and Ireland, there are still grounds for supposing that there was a sizeable coal and culm trade in West Wales in the thirteenth century.

In the fourteenth century the building boom ended. In part this may be attributed simply to the fulfilment of most of the immediate needs for fortifications and ecclesiastical buildings and a period of greater peace in the fourteenth century. Doubtless extensions, enlargements and repairs were required with some regularity, but further study would focus on, for example, the availability of finance and a skilled workforce, as well as upon any perceived need for new construction. The whole question of competent labour surely came to the fore with the onset of the Black Death in 1349. As this grim disease did its deadly work, economic activity of all kinds must have been severely reduced, even if not curtailed. Documentary evidence relating to the Black Death in Pembrokeshire is slight, although John Howells has considered the matter in his contribution to *The Pembrokeshire County History*.[6] R. R. Davies notes that many contemporary accounts reveal reduced incomes from land, mills, tolls and fisheries, and give numerous references to abandoned land. He also observes that farmers in the lordship of Pembroke were allowed a remittance of £80 in their leases, because "of the deadly pestilence which lately raged in these parts".[7] In the absence of more detailed study the present writer would simply suggest that the disease may well have been a major factor in the coal industry suffering some decline. Certainly references to it in the fourteenth and fifteenth centuries are not plentiful.

In Tudor times, as in the thirteenth century, coal was being worked extensively in Jeffreston parish. Even then the industry had been busy for so long it was natural for local people to be concerned for its future, and even to the extent (as George Owen says) to welcome a fiscal restraint on coal exports. A century later, Defoe tells us, "coal had become the principal article of shipment from Pembrokeshire and Glamorganshire". He adds that, chiefly as a result of Milford's trade in fuel, Pembroke became the "largest richest and ... most flourishing town of South Wales, except Carmarthen. Neither Tenby nor Llanelly ... were far behind Milford Haven or Swansea Bay, in point of ships loading with coal."[8] Some years later, in 1748, J. H. Allen, owner of the Cresselly estate, expressed his concern for the future of the trade, and yet it still lasted for another hundred and fifty years in Jeffreston, more or less continuously! Although coal mining over this vast span of time was almost entirely manual, such a prolonged period of activity could be expected to have a noticeable impact on the landscape. A visit to the present day parish of Jeffreston soon makes it clear that the evidence still exists.

The best known area of such working is to be found in Underhill Wood, just north of Jeffreston Church. Here, in a stretch of woodland perhaps seven hundred yards long and two hundred yards across, may be seen deep trenches, pits and ponds on the northern outcrop of the Timber Vein.[9] A similar, slightly smaller area of very intensively worked ground is to be found just to the west at Quarrybacks, adjoining the minor road from Jeffreston to Loveston. However, south and west of Quarrybacks, behind tangled hedges, and well away from any modern highway, lies the secluded overgrown valley which was the centre of the Jeffreston coal industry. Forgotten cart tracks, sometimes ten feet deep, are concealed in the boscage, and everywhere there are signs of disturbed ground and old mining spoil. Half a mile south of Millards Farm large pools lie in the valley bottom, one with a wooded island of spoil near the north bank. To see this extraordinary site is to wonder at the sheer scale of the work undertaken in past centuries. From Broadmoor in the east, almost to Bishops Bridge, Cresselly, in the west – a distance of well over three miles – there is ample evidence of former mining. Simple observation suggests that in the thirteenth century the visible outcrop of the Timber Vein in this area must have been immense.

Documentary sources all point to the coal and culm from this huge and lengthy outcrop being moved through nearby Cresswell Quay. The river at Cresswell is muddy and shallow, and being near the tidal limit of a funnel shaped waterway, it fills and empties rapidly with the tide. The prompt loading of coal and culm here, without a quay, would have been immensely difficult, quickly cutting up the soft, grassy banks. Although there is no record of the construction of a quay in the medieval period, such a facility would have been essential. Given the record of coal shipment from Cresswell in 1282, it is reasonable to suggest that Cresswell may very well have been the site of Wales' first purpose-built coal shipping quay. As mentioned in Chapter Eight, by 1755 there were five quays at Cresswell, with a number of associated coalyards and counting houses nearby. Today, whilst one quay stands in good order, and one has vanished, the remainder can still be seen, albeit in an extremely decayed condition. Furthermore, north of the river, the walls of the coalyards still exist, together with the ruins of a small counting house, and there is enough still in place to understand the extent of activity at Cresswell in its heyday. Although restoration would be costly, the historic significance of this most fascinating spot demands that it should receive more care and attention.

For centuries the coal industry looked towards the shipping quays of the Cleddau and Milford Haven, but the census returns of 1801 indicate that the population of Pembrokeshire was densest between Saundersfoot Bay, Jeffreston and Reynalton, and also between Haverfordwest, Llangwm and Milford Haven. In brief there is evidence of a significant, but not total correlation between the populous areas and the coalfield. In the absence of earlier census returns it is very difficult to demonstrate the influence of the industry on population movement in the eighteenth century, but it is tempting to observe some connection between the fact that John Wesley visited Tenby in 1784 and found it largely derelict and deserted, whereas in 1781 he had encountered "a large congregation of honest colliers at Jeffreyston".[10] That said, Margaret Gilpin observed that up to 1841 "the population increased most where a parish had mineral wealth – limestone in Carew, and anthracite in Freystrop, Martletwy and Coedcanlas".[11] As her study was confined to parishes abutting the Cleddau and Milford Haven and excluded other mining parishes (even Jeffreston), it is not entirely clear if the population increase she discerned was due to more mining activity in general, or to a movement of mining families from one part of the coalfield to another in search of employment.

For many generations much Pembrokeshire coal mining had the air of a cottage industry – small scale and localized, and often involving several members of a family group. Although larger mines would function steadily throughout the year, even in the nineteenth century there were smaller mines in Pembrokeshire where employment varied with the seasons – Nolton and Begelly, for instance. Although there were parishes where coal mining had severely reduced the amount of land available for agriculture – St. Issells and Begelly for example – it seems that up to the twentieth century there were usually men willing to take leave from the colliery to give some seasonal assistance to local farmers. More than that, the fact that a considerable number of colliers held modest small holdings gave them a personal interest in the agricultural cycle, and not just an occasional role as a hired hand. It was their cottage gardens and smallholdings which enabled them to survive in the face of their very low wage levels and to ride out periods of industrial disputes rather better than the miners of the South Wales coal valleys. This is one reason why in this remote district they were less militant and usually more deferential than fellow workers to the east.

George Edwards does not discern any significant decline in the coal industry until the middle of the nineteenth century, and then sees it occurring in particular district – for example, Landshipping after the failure to resuscitate the industry in the 1850's and 1860's.[12] Much of his work can be said to have stood the test of time, but if he had given more attention to the coal industry prior to 1800 he might well have shared the present writer's view that the decline in the industry really began in the late eighteenth century. Thereafter the coal valleys to the east were to develop at an ever increasing rate from the mid-nineteenth century whilst Pembrokeshire, for its part, was not to share in such industrial expansion.

The reasons for the county's coal industry going into decline were numerous, but the first and most obvious factor was the very difficult geology. Contorted, fractured and unreliable seams were not easy to work at any time. A thin seam worked at shallow depth by a few men with picks and shovels and a windlass might be within the bounds of commercial possibility in the late eighteenth century, but such conditions could never sustain a substantial mechanised colliery. As has been seen, the historic coal workings in the parish of Jeffreston were almost worked out by the start of the nineteenth century, and the best coal had long gone. The Timber Vein in Jeffreston and neighbouring parishes was probably the best and most productive coal seam the county ever possessed, but it was taken very early, leaving little for the attention of Victorian capitalists. Thereafter good coal could only be found at depth, and it is no surprise that in the nineteenth century most capital investment took place either in the Saundersfoot district, where the deeper Lower Level and Kilgetty veins could be reached, or at Hook, where steam pumping engines made mining possible below sixty yards, the limit imposed by traditional adit drainage.

The structure and organisation of the Pembrokeshire coal industry was not conducive to much change. Landlords had become accustomed to receiving large royalties, and their leases encouraged lessees to work coal regardless of serious thought for the long-term development of their mines. When profits were being made in the eighteenth century they went to line the pockets of the gentry who were aware that their collieries must have a finite life, but who, for the most part, were curiously disinclined to do very much about it. By the nineteenth century costs were increasing and profits falling, and arguably by then many pits were not generating enough surplus to allow for significant capital expenditure. It was Pembrokeshire's misfortune that its excellent anthracite was unsuitable for early steam engines. Given both the capital cost of acquiring such engines, and the expense of importing appropriate fuel it is understandable that no one attempted the investment before Colonel Colby, and later Lord Milford. Although the belated allowance given by legislation in 1821 was a real help, by then the county had lost ground to rival producers.[13]

If these factors were not enough, the decline of the industry in Pembrokeshire was hastened by the building of canals elsewhere in South Wales, which had the effect of opening up hitherto remote and little-worked coal reserves. Not surprisingly, those canals constructed to reach into the anthracite producing districts above Swansea and Neath had the greatest bearing on the performance of the industry in Pembrokeshire. Smiths Canal of 1783-85 was short, linking collieries at Llansamlet with the River Tawe at Swansea, a distance of little more than three miles. In 1794, however, an Act was passed authorising the building of a canal from Swansea sixteen miles inland to Henneuadd, near Abercrave in Breconshire, and this, the Swansea Canal, duly opened in 1798. In the same decade the Neath Canal, authorised in 1791, was being built ten and a half miles up the Vale of Neath to Glyn Neath. It opened in 1796, but was extended to a better shipping place on the sea at Giants Grave in 1799. Similarly, further east the important Glamorganshire Canal between Merthyr Tydfil and Cardiff was opened in 1794, and extended to a sea lock in 1798. Rather later, in 1812, the Kidwelly and Llanelly Canal Co. was formed, and in due course it took over and extended Kymer's Canal in the Gwendraeth

Valley. By then there was also a clutch of short canals between the bituminous coal pits around Llanelly, and the nearby coast.[14] Accordingly, at the start of the nineteenth century the new canals meant that inland areas of the South Wales coalfield were ripe for development. Colin Baber had no doubts about the significance of canal construction, and observed:

> Canals made it economically viable to carry heavy, bulky materials to a wider market, thus increasing the possibility of a greater concentration of industrial activity on a regional basis. In many areas, therefore, canals made industrialization possible.[15]

If the last point be related to Pembrokeshire, it might well be argued that one reason why the county did not become industrialized was because it lacked any canals.

Although most canals had relatively short lives as effective commercial concerns, quickly losing traffic in the second half of the nineteenth century to the expanding railway companies, their arrival at the start of the nineteenth century transformed both the size and the pattern of trade. The impact made upon coastal shipping has been noticed in the chapter on the coal and culm trades. It is true that Pembrokeshire managed to retain some of its markets for some time, but with the overall demand for anthracite rising the county failed to increase its share of the trade to match, losing ground to newer rival producers. The need for change must have been obvious: Charles Hassall and Walter Davies were two who spoke up for it. Even so, most of the gentry and the monied middle class in Pembrokeshire (with the exception of Colonel Colby) were slow to respond, and arguably the coal industry survived the nineteenth century more by good fortune than good management.

The sheer age of the industry was clearly part of the problem. In 1800 the demand of maltsters and brewers for coal was little more than a century old, but the demand of the lime-kilns for culm was ancient beyond recall. In Pembrokeshire the winning and sale of culm had acquired a rhythm which matched the rhythms of agriculture and the seasons. If the landlords found it difficult to invest and to innovate, it seems that the ordinary inhabitants of the coalfield also found it hard to imagine any other way. George Owen spoke of colliers' attachment to obsolete festivals; in the nineteenth century they were plainly attached to their own measures, and loathe to abandon them for the bushel and chaldron, let alone for the new imperial weights. The coal mining community was deeply conservative, and ever reluctant to change.

The Saundersfoot Railway and Harbour Company was a bold, but rather belated attempt by Lord Milford and his advisers to try to catch up with developments in the main South Wales coalfield. In the 1830's it was very successful, and until the 1870's it did enough to retain a viable coal industry. The arrival of main line railways, the failure of the Kilgetty Ironworks, and the recession of the late 1870's however were challenges to which neither the S. R.& H. Co. nor C. R. Vickerman could respond adequately. The two financial reconstructions of C. R. Vickerman's Saundersfoot empire brought in substantial amounts of capital, but the fundamental problems remained. As traffic moved away from the sea and on to the railways Pembrokeshire became too remote to compete, and freight rates inevitably put the county's coal producers at a disadvantage in comparison with those further to the east. In 1897 for example, whilst the Great Western Railway charged $1^1/_2$ d. per-ton-mile for the first twenty miles coal was conveyed over its rails, and the Pembroke and Tenby Railway charged $1^1/_4$d. per-ton-mile, the Great Western rates for greater distances were much more favourable than those of the P. & T. R. The anthracite collieries in the Gwendraeth Valley and Mynydd Mawr areas of Carmarthenshire had the benefit of lower rates and shorter journeys for their consignments.[16] In the meantime, in Pembrokeshire, as an ancient mining area, collieries were not only at risk of encountering geological problems, but also at risk of meeting uncharted workings, and frequently mines were developed without sufficient continuity in policy and planning. By the twentieth century the underground workings from Bonvilles Court ranged from a point near the harbour in the east, to the vicinity of Broadmoor in the west. Although the anthracite was of excellent quality, and capable of commanding a high price from specialist consumers like brewers, it became increasingly difficult to raise coal at anything like an economic price.

During World War I all coal mines were under government control, and the emphasis was placed on production rather than on long-term planning. The labour disputes of 1921 and 1926 seriously reduced output, and weakened the Bonvilles Court Co.'s capacity to make new investment. By this time such expenditure would have made little difference. In Carmarthenshire the grouping of anthracite collieries into larger combines, leading to the total dominance of the trade after 1927 by Amalgamated Anthracite, intensified the competition for Pembrokeshire. In all the circumstances the demise of Bonvilles Court colliery in 1930 is not surprising. What was remarkable was the willingness of Capt. J. F. Vickerman and his colleagues (including Lord Merthyr) to make a fresh attempt to revive the industry at Broom and Kilgetty. Like most coal owners in Wales, the Vickermans were not very popular, but without doubt their willingness to carry losses and go on supporting their collieries kept the industry alive for longer than ordinary accountancy would have allowed. Even in the 1930's reopening Broom and Kilgetty must have seemed brave, but with hindsight it seems extraordinary. Notwithstanding the Loveston accident, and its implications, the Pembrokeshire coal industry had little chance of a long-term future. Figure 46 provides further details of collieries at work in the years 1921 and 1936.

The story of Hook in the 1930's and 1940's says much about the final phase of the Pembrokeshire coal industry. When the colliery was acquired by Watts, Watts and Co. in 1934 it was a development of apparent promise. The company owned pits at Ferndale in the Rhondda Fach where they were producing perhaps 2,000 tons per week. The purchase of Hook represented a diversification into anthracite mining at a time when the Welsh anthracite trade was dominated by the much larger Carmarthenshire collieries of the Amalgamated Anthracite combine. Watts, Watts and Co. undoubtedly expected to be able to boost production from a modest two hundred tons per week, and it is believed that the manager of the period was asked to double output. The minimum requirement was for the colliery to cover its costs. Between 1929 and 1932 the Hook Anthracite Colliery Co. had spent a considerable sum improving facilities on the surface – not least by the opening of the colliery railway in 1930, and by the provision of new screens in 1932. By then a new drift had been driven from the Rock Vein to the Timber Vein, where the coal was somewhat thicker, but subject to gas. In spite of this investment, the underground layout at Hook in 1934 was typical of an under-capitalised operation. For fifty years the top priority had been to produce coal, with organised development work a very secondary consideration. The plan of the mine at this period betrays the management's commercial anxiety, and their readiness to put day-to-day expediency ahead of the need to deal with areas of difficulty underground. Development had been inconsistent and messy, or, in the words of an extremely experienced mining engineer, "By guess, and by God ... !"[17]

As experienced coal proprietors, Watts, Watts and Co. must have been aware of the problems at Hook, but must have felt quite confident that they could surmount them. Initially they drove north, endeavouring to win the deeper Lower Level coal, where the seam was 3ft.6in. thick, with a far better roof and floor. The plan to drive to the deep was also intended to avoid old workings, but this hope does not seem to have been fulfilled. Whilst the company wanted to create a mine which was well laid out for systematic working, this appears to have been frustrated by encounters with early workings, faulting and thin seams. In 1936 the Margaret Pit was abandoned, and efforts were concentrated on the newer West Drift, which had been driven down to the Timber Vein lying to the west of the older workings.

At the surface Watts, Watts and Co. built a patent fuel plant in 1936 in the hope of being able to use it to make a more commercial product from culm.[18] Regular coal shipments from Hook Quay ended in 1936, and traffic was concentrated on the Hook colliery railway. Such changes could not disguise the fact that Hook was a small and failing colliery. The most able colliery managers naturally sought larger and more promising mines, and by the 1940's the quality of management at Hook was poor and working practices less than satisfactory. By way of example, miners had used naked lights in the Rock Vein workings of the Margaret Pit where

COAL MINES IN 1921 AND 1936

PEMBROKE, 1921

		Manager	Below ground	Above ground
Bonville,s Court Coal Co., Ltd., Saunders-foot, R.S.O.	Bonville's Court	Saundersfoot	D. Davies (2,811)	277	76
Canton, W. J., Nolton Haven, Broad Haven, Pem.	Nolton (Slant)	Nolton Haven	-	-	-
Hook Colliery Co., Hook, Haverfordwest	New Hook	Llangwm	Thos. Worthing (3,266)	58	39
New Reynalton Anthracite Colliery Co., Ltd., Radstock Coal Office, Radstock, Somorset	Reynalton (Pit & Slant)	Begelly	Jas. Steele (1,014)	79	24

Source : Welsh Coal and Shipping Manual, 1921

PEMBROKE 1936

			Manager	Under-Manager	Below ground	Above ground	Seams Worked
Bonville's Court Coal Co., Ltd., Saundersfoot, Pembrokeshire	1. Broom (Slant)	Kilgetty	H. D. Connick (1,011).	R. J. Williams (4,189; 1st).	126	102	Coal, A. Lower Level
Kilgetty Anthracite Co. Ltd., Saundersfoot, Pembrokeshire	2.Kilgetty	Ditto	Ditto	D. R. Morgan (3,063; 2nd).	11	9	De-watering
Loveston Colliery Co., Ltd., Gloucester Chambers, Swansea, Glam.	3. Loveston (Slant)	Ditto	E. Howells (2,023; 2nd).	.. ..	26	11	Coal, A. Lower Level
Watts, Watts and Co., Ltd., Regis House, King William Street, London, E.C.4.	4. Hook (Slant)	Llangwm	B. Spencer (2,540).	D. Williams (1,379; 2nd).	19	19	Coal, A. Rock and Timber
Ditto	5. West Park, Nos. 1 & 2.	Ditto	Ditto	Ditto	2	1	Coal, A. Pumping Abandoned 4/36

Source : P.R.O. POWE 7/70

Figure 46

JdeH 3119A

there was little gas; when attention turned to the Timber Vein a few men suffered injury before the practice changed.[19] Good production remained a struggle, and output never exceed the 42,000 tons achieved in 1934. When the West Drift flooded in 1947 the game was up. In spite of all the investment at Hook, it had proved impossible to extend its life or increase output. Although numerous relatively minor accidents occurred at Hook, with hindsight it was very fortunate not to have been the scene of a real disaster. The Gresford colliery at Wrexham witnessed a gas explosion in September 1934, which cost the lives of 266 men. Although a much larger colliery, and better organised, the inquiry into the Gresford accident revealed numerous irregularities and deficiencies.[20] Explosion, inundation, rock fall, or whatever, there were plenty of hazards at Hook, and arguably the underpaid colliers of Hook were more fortunate than they realised.

Loveston was bad enough, and undoubtedly caused officialdom to do some serious thinking. Both Broom and Kilgetty collieries had been reopened with reasonable investment, and Broom in particular was well laid out below ground. Even so, the fact that Broom and Kilgetty collieries closed so quickly in 1939, strongly suggests that the Mines Inspectorate recognised that they, too, faced a serious risk of flooding. The inrush at Hook eight years later only confirmed the view that it was time to end mining in Pembrokeshire, and the N.C.B., which had been established in 1947, duly closed Hook in April 1948.

For many years prior to 1934 Harcourt Roberts was manager of the Hook Colliery company, and although it is very doubtful if he ever saw the pit make much money, he was always an enthusiast for the Pembrokeshire coal industry. When the closure of Hook colliery was proposed, he urged the N.C.B. to examine two other locations with a view to developing a new mine to employ a workforce which had little alternative employment. His powers of persuasion must have been considerable because the N.C.B. did proceed with a trial pit at East Hook, which in George Edwards' words was "an undertaking which in any other part of South Wales coalfield might have been postponed".[21]

In 1950 the trial drift was put down in a field close to the Cleddau, but it had not been driven 300 yards before it flooded. The project was ended. After this costly failure the N.C.B. was disinclined to pursue Harcourt Roberts' other proposal, which was for a deep drilling survey for coal in the Newgale and Nolton area, to verify the existence of extensive untapped reserves. Confident that such a survey would be successful, Harcourt Roberts proposed the sinking of five new mines giving a combined output of 700,000 tons per year![22]

Whilst Roberts was right to point to the St. Bride's Bay district as an area with virgin coal reserves, his scheme was a flight of fancy. After many decades of decline, no one was going to risk the vast amount of capital required for such a speculative project. Figure 47 gives an indication of the number and range of abandoned coal mines in Pembrokeshire by the middle of the twentieth century. Even so, in 1953 the Pembrokeshire County Development Plan mentioned Harcourt Roberts' proposals for new colliery development in the Nolton area, and noted the possible requirement for a railway between the main line at Johnston and Druidston Cross, near Nolton.[23] As late as June 1955, George Price, a Sheffield mining engineer, together with Dr. R. H. Blundell, produced a report on the coalfield for the Milford Docks Company in which they advocated the sinking of boreholes in the Nolton area to establish the existence of workable coal.[24] Nothing appears to have been done, not only because the results of such operations were uncertain, but also because attention was turning now to the more exciting possibility of developing Milford Haven as a port for the oil industry.

The report by Price and Blundell was the final flourish on the part of supporters of the Pembrokeshire Coalfield. In later years several very experienced miners of the writer's acquaintance have all said that the one site in the county still worthy of development is in the open country north of Tiers Cross, between Johnston and St. Bride's Bay.[25] Here there would be no risk of meeting uncharted workings, and a real possibility of laying out a mine for modern working methods. Given the greatly reduced status of the coal industry in the twenty-first century, there seems to be no likelihood of anyone ever pursuing this idea.

Between 1903 and 1905 Sir William Thomas Lewis, then owner of Hean Castle, Saundersfoot, was a member of a Royal Commission examining the United Kingdom's coal supplies. As regards Pembrokeshire, he estimated that there were then 172,583,813 workable tons available, but also almost 131,000,000 tons which could not be worked. He also made a calculation about the likely quantities to be found under St. Bride's Bay, and under Carmarthen Bay, off Saundersfoot. Without attempting to distinguish precisely between the workable and the unworkable he estimated that there were 53,360,000 tons of coal under St. Bride's Bay, and an enormous 329,664,000 tons under Carmarthen Bay. In the years from 1905 to 1950 about 1,800,000 tons was mined in Pembrokeshire, so it may be fairly supposed that the considerable tonnage which remains will be for the foreseeable future one of the county's concealed assets.[26]

As a postscript to the history of the coal industry it should be mentioned that for a few weeks in the summer of 1990 anthracite was excavated at Kilgetty and sold commercially. The coal was found on the site of the new Stepaside Primary School, and extracted opencast by mechanical diggers. Some 4,700 tons were obtained in a month, giving a weekly production rate in excess of 1000 tons – ironically the highest ever achieved at any location in Pembrokeshire.[27]

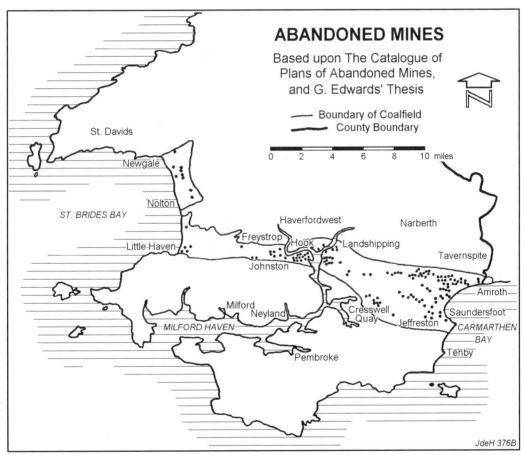

Source : Edwards

Figure 47

[1] William Shakespeare, *Cymbeline*, Act 3, scene 2. This play is set in the period of the Roman occupation of Britain, and in Act 4, scene 2, a Roman captain informs his general, Lucius: "To them the legions garrisoned in Gallia / After your will have crossed the sea attending / You here at Milford Haven with your ships.......".

[2] Eric Kerridge, *Trade and Banking in Early Modern England* (Manchester: Manchester University Press, 1988), 11, 12. Kerridge refers to T. S. Willan, *River Navigation in England, 1600-1750* (1964), 119 et seq., and *The Inland Trade* (1976), 1, 2, 21-22.

[3] George, "Pembrokeshire Sea Trading before 1800", 30.

[4] Edwards, *A Study of the Daucleddau Coalfield (Pembrokeshire)*, 47.

[5] R. R. Davies, *The Age of Conquest; Wales 1063-1415* (Oxford: Oxford University Press, 1987), 187.

[6] John Howells, "The Countryside", in R. A. Walker (ed.) *Pembrokeshire County History,* Vol II, *Medieval Pembrokeshire* (Haverfordwest: The Pembrokeshire Historical Society, 2002), 420, 421.

[7] R. R. Davies, *The Age of Conquest*, 425 and 426. The quotation is derived from the *Calendar of Fine Rolls, 1347-56*, 240.

[8] Daniel Defoe, *A Tour through the whole Island of Great Britain* (London, 1725), Vol.2, 85.

[9] Underhill Wood, Jeffreston, is now scheduled as a site of scientific interest.

[10] H. J. Dickman, "Wesleyan Methodism in Pembrokeshire" *The Journal of the Pembrokeshire Historical Society*, No.3 (1989), 96, 97.

[11] Gilpin, "Population changes round the shores of Milford Haven from 1800 to the present day", 23-26.

[12] Edwards, *A study of the Daucleddau Coalfield (Pembrokeshire)*, 83. Decline in the coal industry is seen here in terms of decline in the population of particular parishes.

[13] 1 and 2 Geo IV, Cap 67. (1821)

[14] For a history of all these developments see Charles Hadfield, *Canals of South Wales and the Borders*.

[15] Baber "Canals and the Economic Development of South Wales", 24.

[16] *South Wales Coal Annual, 1903*, 148. Freight rates changed little at this period, and the compiler of the *Coal Annual* appears to have overlooked the fact that the P.&T.R. ceased to exist in 1897, but the figures are presumed correct for that date. The Burry Port and Gwendraeth Valley Railway and the Llanelly and Mynydd Mawr Railway both charged 1.15d per-ton-mile for the first twenty miles, and much lower rates for longer distances.

[17] I am indebted to H. E. Nicholas, formerly Deputy Chief Inspector of Mines, for guidance on the interpretation of surviving Pembrokeshire mining plans.

[18] The ovoids produced at this plant by compressing coal dust and tar were all embossed with a small "hook" symbol. Unfortunately the plant suffered numerous breakdowns and lost money, and so was closed within four years. I am grateful to Edward Green of Hook for this information.

[19] Recollections of Owen Gwyther in a private letter to the writer, dated 1 December 1983.

[20] Michael Pollard, *The Hardest Work under Heaven: The Life and Death of the British Coal Miner* (London: Hutchinson, 1984), 160. For a more detailed account see Stanley Williamson, *Gresford: The Anatomy of a Disaster* (Liverpool: Liverpool University Press, 1999).

[21] Edwards, *A Study of the Daucleddau Coalfield (Pembrokeshire)*, 107.

[22] *Pembrokeshire County Plan*, 1953 (edited J. A. Price) 77 - 79. At the same period a brief attempt was made to work a small private mine – the Glywaran pit – near the former Nash and sprinkle colliery at Hook. The only licenced private mine in Pembrokeshire after nationalisation appears to have been Wood Level, Kilgetty, which was worked from 1944 to 1950

[23] Ibid., 80.

[24] Pembrokeshire Record Office: George Price and Dr. R. H. Blundell, *Report on the Pembrokeshire Coalfields* (June 1955).

[25] Although there were two or three unsuccessful applications in the 1980's for opencast coal extraction in Pembrokeshire, none consisistuted a serious long-term attempt to revive the coal industry. The coal miners consulted included the late Owen Gwyther and the late Osborne Evans of Kilgetty (died 1985) who as a boy had been into the Trefrane Cliff Colliery at Nolton with his father.

[26] *Report of the Royal Commission on Coal Supplies*, 1905: Final report, part 2, 9/55. Sir William Thomas Lewis defined the area to the west as "under the sea in St. Brides's Bay two miles beyond the high water mark, after allowing for necessary barriers and loss in working". The area to the east he defined as "under the sea in part of Carmarthen Bay from Saundersfoot to Kidwelly, one mile beyond high water mark, and after allowing for necessary barriers and loss in working".

[27] Advice given to the writer in September 1990 by Messrs. Richards and Goldsworthy, building contractors.

Appendix A

Weights and Measures

The student of the early coal trade quickly encounters many unfamiliar and obsolete measures: the sheer variety of measures which were once in use in different parts of the British Isles is nothing less than astonishing. The foundations for the study of this arcane topic were well laid by the mining historian J. U. Nef in his monumental work *The Rise of the British Coal Industry*, published in 1932.[1] For him the county of Pembroke represented only one small part of his work, but for the purpose of this present study it is necessary to take a further look at this subject. In addition to noting measures formerly used in Pembrokeshire, it is essential to try to understand them in order to be able to gain some idea of the coalfield's output and importance.

In the heyday of the Pembrokeshire coalfield, prior to the Industrial Revolution, figures for the production of coal and culm were not gathered in any systematic way. From the second half of the sixteenth century the Welsh Port Books provide some useful, but by no means comprehensive, evidence of coal shipments. Very few other sources are available before the eighteenth century. Even then references are scattered and figures insufficient to gain a very clear picture of the development of the industry. In this era, long before a common standard for weights had been established, coal and culm were measured by volume - usually by reference to the volume of the receptacle used for carrying or conveying coal in a given locality. This may seem quaint to the modern mind, but in the circumstances of the time was entirely reasonable. Standard volume measures could suffice for local purposes once there was agreement on the size of, say, a barrel (or any other container) required for moving coal. A deficient barrel could then be altered by a cooper or carpenter.[2] In Pembrokeshire the traditional measures employed were the barrel and the hundred.

The Hundred and the Barrel

In the Tudor period there appears to have been a dispute over measures employed in the Jeffreston district, and the resulting Special Commission of Enquiry of 1577 makes it clear that coal was measured by the barrel and the hundred.[3] Time and again witnesses testified that: "The hundred of sea-coale and colne doth contayne 60 barrells and not above." Furthermore several asserted that these measures had been in use for as long as they had known the industry (forty years in one case), giving the barrel and the hundred the status of traditional measures of very long standing.

Twenty five years later George Owen declared that in Pembrokeshire coals were sold by the barrel, "which is of Bristol band, or near about four Winchester bushels, and not by the chaldron, as is used in other parts of this realm." His reference to Bristol is especially interesting because it implies that the measure in use at Bristol, the focus of much maritime trade with South Wales, was also in use in Pembrokeshire.[4]

J. U. Nef ignores this point, and suggests that at Bristol there were 9 barrels to the ton, or possibly when a barrel was filled and heaped, a larger quantity. In his view, in Pembrokeshire "generally speaking there were about 7½ barrels of coal to a ton".[5] He offered no direct evidence about the size of the barrel employed in Pembrokeshire, although he did acknowledge a slight variation in the size of barrel used at different shipping ports. He also recognised that weight would be affected both by the quality of the fuel, and by the manner in which the barrel was filled. Accordingly his assessment of the weight of the barrel must be regarded as approximate, as must his view that the hundred weighed about 8 tons. However, these measures appear to have been used for virtually all purposes in Pembrokeshire until the time of the Civil War.

The Chaldron and the Bushel

Whilst J. U. Nef largely pioneered the study of weights and measures, several other writers since have had the resolve to address a subject made difficult not only by the need to recognise many local variations, but also by the challenge of having to rely upon limited evidence to try to attribute a weight to a volume measure. The importance and interpretation of the chaldron as a measure has occupied much of the debate. The term is thought to have originated in North East England in the fifteenth century, but before the end of the seventeenth century it was an official measure used in most of the ports of the United Kingdom.

The imposition of the tax of 5s. per Newcastle chaldron in 1599 evidently caused this measure to be used regularly in the north-west as well as in the north-east. Between 1600 and 1604, the content of this chaldron is reported to have been two tons at Liverpool, Chester, and Workington.[6] Thereafter Nef argues that the weight of the Newcastle chaldron increased significantly, whilst on the west coast the chaldron retained a weight of two tons - thereby becoming a distinct measure in itself. He admits that when the chaldron does appear in the Port Books in relation to Pembrokeshire this point is not mentioned, but observes that only two entries out of several hundred in respect of Milford and Tenby specifically refer to "London measure". Accordingly he argues that the west coast chaldron applied in Pembrokeshire, and that the use of the London chaldron was exceptional. The present writer consider this to be a fragile assertion; it could be argued just as easily that if the London measure was the measure invariably applied, the fact it is stated on only two occasions is hardly surprising.[7]

The earliest reference to the chaldron in Pembrokeshire was noted by the mining historian R. L. Galloway, who states that in 1617, 747$^{1}/_{2}$ chaldrons of coal were shipped from Milford. His source is said to be "the balance sheet of the farmers of coal taxes"; such taxes were introduced in Tudor times, and the chaldron was evidently the measure favoured by the supervising officials.[8] There is no indication that Pembrokeshire people adopted this measure at such an early date: it appears to have been a term primarily employed in the coal trade in London and Newcastle. Elsewhere local measures prevailed, and as T. S. Willan has emphasized, a port receiving coal shipped coastwise within Britain recorded the cargoes in the measure applicable in the port from which it was dispatched.[9] In 1632, for example, Exeter noted consignments of coal from Milford and Tenby in hundreds, from Swansea and Burry in weys, and only from London and Newcastle in chaldrons.

The earliest reference to the chaldron (or chalder) in the Port books for Milford and Tenby occurs in 1646-7.[10] In brief, there was a transition in the second half of the seventeenth century, probably caused by Crown decree or regulation, whereby for coal shipping purposes the chaldron or chalder displaced the hundred. The intention was to achieve greater clarity and certainty for fiscal and customs purposes, but as several versions of the chaldron were known in the coal trade this was not a simple matter.

John Hatcher argues that the London chaldron had a fixed capacity as early as the sixteenth century.[11] Ostensibly it consisted of four vats, each comprising 9 statute bushels, 36 bushels in total. That said, there was still scope for significant variations in measure. These might arise from variations in the specific gravity of coals of different kinds, the degree of weathering experienced by the coal, and, in addition, the size of the coal being measured, its moisture content, and the extent to which the person doing the measuring was both honest and careful. Furthermore an Act of 1664-5 stipulated that the bushels should be heaped up, a requirement effectively enlarging the capacity of the chaldron by a third, being equivalent to 46 levelled bushels.[12] Hatcher appears to say that this legislation was endorsing existing practice; but it also clearly indicated the potential difficulties in studying this topic.

Hatcher's reasoning with regard to the Newcastle and the London chaldrons may be followed in Appendix A of Volume 1 of the *History of the British Coal Industry*. Suffice to say that the writer accepts his case for a London chaldron of 28 cwt. as being normative in the period when volume measures prevailed. In 1810, however, a witness before the House of Commons Committee responding to the Petition of South Wales Coal Owners testified that "a ton and a half is generally reckoned equal to a chaldron".[13] His reasoning may have been related to the understanding that the anthracite coals of South Wales have a higher specific gravity than the bituminous coals.

The Hundred and the Cart

Around 1730 Pembrokeshire's traditional measure of sixty barrels to the hundred was displaced by a new measure for local use of twelve carts to the hundred. Reference to the "cart" was not entirely new to the county; as has been noted, the earliest known record of the Pembrokeshire coal industry in 1282 made mention of 600 cartloads of coal to be shipped at Tenby and Cresswell Quay. However, given such a period of time, there is no way of knowing whether the thirteenth-century cartload bore any resemblance to the "cart" of the eighteenth century.

The reasons for the change to the new measure are not clear. The thirteenth century reference suggest that carting was as old as the industry itself, although it is known that there were occasions when coal was being moved in panniers or other containers on pack animals. Arguably by the eighteenth century Pembrokeshire coal carts were of a sufficiently standard size to be themselves a reasonably reliable volume measure.

Another possibility is that the new measure provided an opportunity to advance the weight of the hundred. J. U. Nef argued that:

> the tendency everywhere was for the content of a given measure to increase, often because of the efforts of traders to diminish the burden of taxes on coal, and, again, because the receptacles in which coal was carried increased in size.[14]

Nef somewhat overstated this case, and, as we have seen, Hatcher has demonstrated that both the Newcastle and the London chaldrons were fixed for centuries. Even so, mining royalties, wayleaves, shipping dues and the like were often made by measure, and an increase in measure could relieve some of the burden of such payments. There is some evidence that in Pembrokeshire the measure was increased. In 1759, as A. H. John has noted, Sir John Philipps complained that his trade "is ruined by other persons underselling him and loading 12 carts, whereas I never load more than 10".[15] Evidently Sir John's policy was to continue to supply coal on traditional terms, whilst other traders apparently followed the trend towards increasing measures, and advanced the weight of the hundred. No doubt the effect was to increase their share of the market.

In the 1730's, in the period when the barrel measure was being replaced by the cart, the hundred was still equivalent to about eight tons. In 1805 the hundred was said to be equivalent to 10 tons. The evidence for the change appears in a report made that year by the noted coal viewer, Edward Martin. He advised the owner of the Little Milford colliery, Freystrop, that he could expect an output of "40 tons per day, called 4 hundred in Pembrokeshire and 4 wey at Swansea".[16] Although at first sight this statement seems precise, in reality precision in these matters was always difficult, and Martin's remark may be better read as a short generalised assertion. A letter written in 1831 to attract new business to Hean Castle colliery at Saundersfoot surely provides a more useful comparison of measures and weights. In it William James of Hean Castle colliery informed Frances Cobb of Margate that the colliery's "stone coal for malting" was of excellent quality. He added:

> our price is £7 per hundred, being about 9 tons, otherwise 7 chaldrons, but to encourage your giving them a trial I will advance the price 10s. per hundred which then will be only £6. 10s. 0d. I will warrant them to be as good as any you have had from my part of Wales.[17]

As these comments were intended to encourage an enduring trading relationship their reliability seems very likely, and the present writer takes the view that whilst the hundred may be equated with 8 tons in the first half of the eighteenth century, it was probably in excess of 9 tons by the nineteenth century. Indeed, on the basis of a London chaldron being about 28 cwt., seven chaldrons would be in excess of 9 ½ tons.

One further item of evidence may be noted. The 1820's and 1830's witnessed the transition in Pembrokeshire from volume measures to weights, and for some years transactions could be conducted in either way. This may be illustrated by what is now a somewhat enigmatic memorandum to a letter sent by Messrs. Cobb and Sons on 30 June 1824. The memorandum reads:

> Agreement for freight should be made should be made at per ton or at per chaldron of Cu. 29.1.gm. the weight being taken by the customs at 91 lbs per barrel according as made out in delivery either by weight or measure as may be required. If by weight, to be weighed per barrel, or an adequate draught to be allowed if weighed in a larger bulk.[18]

Whilst this indicates that both weights and measures could be used, unfortunately it does not clarify the actual procedures followed either on shipment or delivery. As weighing machines were not commonplace in Pembrokeshire at this period, it was natural for most coal shippers to continue to rely on the familiar measures. Further research on the coal and culm trades might help to cast more light on these matters.

The Long Hundred

The uncatalogued Gogerddan papers at the National Library of Wales include references to the Moreton colliery, near Saundersfoot, in the late eighteenth century. Amongst these papers is found the following intriguing note:

> 120 horses carry 60 barrels at 4 bushels/ barrel
> 36 bushels to the chaldron
> 7 chaldrons to the long hundred.

The significance of this note would appear to be threefold:

First: it points to the practice in the period of using packhorses as a means of moving coal. Thus, by implication, one horse could carry two bushels, usually understood as 168 lbs.

Second: it introduces another measure- the long hundred, comprising 7 chaldrons.

Third: the reference to four bushels per barrel corresponds with George Owen's statement about the barrel measure.

This appears in contrast with a quite separate note found in early nineteenth century papers relating to the Southwood colliery at Newgale which refers to a hundred being 12 carts, adding that "1 cart = 18 Winchester bushels, therefore a hundred = 216 Winchester bushels". The same paper also described the chaldron as comprising 36 Winchester Bushels, thereby implying that 2 carts were equivalent to a chaldron, and six chaldrons were equivalent to a hundred.[19] What this note does not say is that the bushels were intended to be heaped, thereby giving a significantly larger measure. Hatcher suggest that keeping the bushel increased the measure by as much as one third, which would effectively make 8 chaldrons equivalent to a hundred. This is not an adequate explanation for the discrepancy with the Gogerddan reference.

In so far as the chaldron was a measure only used in Pembrokeshire in relation to coal shipments, it must be assumed that the "long hundred" was a term bridging local usage with the terminology of coal exporting. As noted, by the end of the eighteenth century the London chaldron was deemed to comprise about 27 cwt.or 28 cwt, and six chaldrons about 8¾tons.[20] Accordingly a "long hundred" in Pembrokeshire comprising seven such chaldrons would weigh just over 10 tons, and correspond roughly with the advanced weight of the hundred at this period. In this way this note in the Gogerddan papers would appear to give additional evidence of the enlarging of the Pembrokeshire hundred in the eighteenth century.

Symons, writing about the coal industry at Llanelly mentions both the tendency to enlarge coal measures, and also a widespread practice of giving over-measure by perhaps five per cent.[21] This was done, he suggests, to compensate the purchaser at the time of delivery for the loss or breakage of coal in transit. No doubt honest coal owners and traders adopted this practice, but so many different people were involved in this trade from colliery to customer that the scope for fraud and deception was considerable. For this reason officials called coal meters were employed in many areas to see justice done between vendor and consumer. It is recorded that in 1829, nine coal meters were employed at or around Milford Haven.

Other measures mentioned in Pembrokeshire:

The Wey

This measure is first mentioned in relation to Pembrokeshire in the Welsh Port Books in 1585/86 in respect of a shipment of 18 weys from Milford. Curiously, there is no later reference to the wey at Milford, although it is noted on several occasions at Tenby in relation to shipments made between 1598-99 and 1604-05. Without specifiying his source, Nef asserts that at both Milford and Tenby, 10 weys made a hundred, and on the basis that a hundred then weighed roughly 8 tons, he maintains that the wey was equivalent to four-fifths of a ton.[22]

Nef quite rightly stresses that the Pembrokeshire wey should not be confused with the much more significant Glamorgan wey, which was substantially heavier. Furthermore it must be noted that the weys in use at Llanelly, Swansea and Neath were by no means identical in weight at all times. As has been noted, in 1805 Edward Martin declared that the Swansea wey and the Pembrokeshire hundred were comparable in size. At that period the wey at Llanelly is believed to have weighed half that of the wey in Swansea. Reverting to the seventeenth century, in view of the amount of maritime trade between South Pembrokeshire and Bristol it may be worth noting Nef's statement that "at Bristol before the middle of the seventeenth century, coal was sometimes measured by the waye, which appears from entries in the port books to have equalled about one ton". Although there is no direct evidence to suggest that the measure then used in Bristol was briefly employed at Milford and Tenby, there must be a possibility that trade with Bristol influenced the few references to the wey which do exist.

The Score

One reference has been found in the Gogerddan papers to the score. It is believed to have referred to twenty chaldrons, a usage similar to that employed in the coal trade in London.

The Skip

The Gogerddan papers include a report on Moreton colliery in 1778, by J. Woolstenhulme, who was not a local man. He states that the pit could produce 160 skips per day; it is doubtful whether the term "skip" was much used in Pembrokeshire.[23]

[1] Nef, *The Rise of the British Coal Industry*.

[2] In Derbyshire lead ore dishes were tested by filling them with grain measured from a standard dish. A carpenter could then alter the dish by lowering the rim to reduce volume, or by scooping out more wood to enlarge it.

[3] P.R.O., Court of Exchequer: Special Commission of Inquiry, E178/3493.

[4] G. Owen, *Description of Pembrokeshire*, Part 1, H. Owen (ed.) (London: 1892), 137-139.

[5] Nef, *The Rise of the British Coal Industry*, Volume 2, Appendix C, 372.

[6] Ibid., Volume 2, Appendix C, 370.

[7] In private correspondence to the writer, both Dr. David Hussey (1997) and Peter Claughton have doubted the existence of the West Coast chaldron.

[8] Galloway, *Annals of Coal Mining and the Coal Trade*, volume 1, 223.

[9] Willan, *The English Coasting Trade*, Appendix 3, 208.

[10] Nef, *The Rise of the British Coal Industry*, Volume 1, 380. The figures used by Nef were provided by E. A. Lewis.

[11] Hatcher, *The History of the British Coal Industry*, Volume 1, Appendix A, 567.

[12] 16 and 17. Charles II., Cap. 1.

[13] House of Commons Committee on the petition of the South Wales Coal Owners, 1810, Evidence of Henry Smith, 3.

[14] Nef, *The Rise of the British Coal Industry*, Volume 2. Appendix C, 367.

[15] A. H. John, *The Industrial Development of South Wales*, Appendix D, 188, quoting P.R.O. Court of Exchequer, E134, 7 Geo. I Mich. 17.

[16] Hereford and Worcester Record Office, BA 4416 (ii) 1, Report on Little Milford Colliery, 1805.

[17] East Kent Archives, Cobb MSS EK/U 1453 B5/4/1534.

[18] East Kent Archives, Cobb MSS EK/U 1453 B5/4/1540.

[19] Notebook and diary of M. Walters of Nolton, Pembrokeshire, c1800-1845 (privately owned).

[20] Evidence of Henry Smith noted in the House of Commons Report on the Petition of the South Wales Coal owners, 1810.

[21] Symons, *Coal Mining in the Llanelli Area*, 327.

[22] Nef, *The Rise of the British Coal Industry*, Appendix C, 373.

[23] N.L.W., Gogerddan Papers (Uncatalogued).

Abandoned early coal workings at underhill Wood, Jeffreston, 1998 Mrs T. Pearson

Appendix B

Shipments Prior to 1750

Up to the eighteenth century there are no figures available for either county or colliery output, although the Port Books do give some information about the number and size of coal and culm shipments. These figures are reproduced in the two tables below.

COAL SHIPMENTS FROM MILFORD TO IRELAND 1559-1603

YEAR	Shipments		Amounts (Tons)		Total
	Coal	Culm	Coal	Culm	(Tons)
1559-1560	26	25	143	90	233
1563-1564	4	5	12	11¹/₂	23¹/₂
1566 (¹/₂)	1	12	4	62¹/₂	66¹/₂
1566-1567	14	21	120	87	207
1585-1586	11	31	112	318	430
1586-1587	10	27	104	221¹/₂	325¹/₂
1587-1588	21	16	188	184	372
1593-1594	14	27	192	318	510
1598-1599	28	26	243	326	569
1600-1601	15	44	151	498	649
1601-1602	30	40	310	502	812

Source: E.A. Lewis (ed.), *The Welsh Ports Books, 1550-1603*.
NOTE: The legal port of Milford extended from Wormshead to Barmouth.

COAL AND CULM SHIPMENTS FROM MILFORD AND TENBY 1660-1710

YEAR	MILFORD				TENBY			
	Coastwise		Overseas		Coastwise		Overseas	
	Culm	Coal	Culm	Coal	Culm	Coal	Culm	Coal
1660 (¹/₂ year)	7,635	368	-	-	-	-	-	-
1661-62	-	-	763	1,172	-	-	-	-
1663-64	-	-	1,367	938	-	-	-	-
1665-66	4,792	302	1,182	889	-	-	-	-
1666-67	-	-	-	-	4,120	27	-	-
1668-69	-	-	2,442	1,133	-	-	40	-
1669-70	-	-	190	3,133	-	-	110	-
1670-71	12,868	2,508	-	-	-	-	-	-
1671-72	-	-	2,127	784	-	-	-	-
1672-73	8,564	442	-	-	3,884	208	-	-
1680-81	11,206	2,468	3,669	2,350	-	-	-	-
1682-83	-	-	-	-	8,010	1,288	24	52
1687-88	22,464	1,826	1,712	2,030	7,000	2,216	-	-
1709-10	10,188	557	1,990	194	-	-	-	-

All figures in tons based on: Hundred of 8 tons, Chaldron of 2 tons, Barrel of 2/15 ton.
Sources: E.A. Lewis (ed.), *The Welsh Port Books, 1550-1603*.
    J. U. Nef, *The Rise of the British Coal Industry*.

Appendix C

Prospectus of Bonvilles Court Coal & Iron Co. Ltd., 1873

Issue of 16,500 Shares of £10 each,

of

THE BONVILLES COURT
COAL & IRON COMPANY LTD

Incorporated under the companies' Act s 1862 and 1867, by which the liability of Shareholders is limited to the amount of their Shares.

SHARE CAPITAL £200,000, IN 20,000 SHARES OF £10 EACH.

of which 16,500 are now for Subscription.

Price of Subscription, Par – or £10 per Share, Payable as follows:

£1	per	Share ...	...	...	on Application
3	,,	,,	...	...	...	on Allotment
3	,,	,,	...	...	...	on 20th May, 1873
3	,,	,,	...	...	...	on 20th June, 1873

£10

Subscribers may pay up their Shares in full on any day on which an instalment is due, entitling them to discount at the rate of £6 per Cent. per Annum for such prepayment.

DIRECTORS

JAMES BEAUMONT, Esq., Merrow, near Guildford (late General Manager of The East India Iron Company).

WENTWORTH GORE, Esq., London and Lyndhurst, Hants.

FREDERICK LEVICK, Esq., 46 Belsize Park, London (late Managing Director of The Blaina Iron Company)

'The Honorable' HENRY WILLIAM PETRE, Springfield, near Chelmsford, Essex.

CHARLES RANKEN VICKERMAN, Esq., Hean Castle, near Tenby, and Thoby Priory, Essex.

BANKERS

THE LONDON AND COUNTY BANK, 21, Lombard Street, E.C., London

SOLICITOR

JOHN HOLMS, Esq., 34 Clement' Lane, London, E.C.

This Company is formed for the purpose of acquiring, working, and further developing the well-known extensive and valuable Coal and Mineral properties–portions of which have been in work from 40 to 50 years— known as the BONVILLES COURT COLLIERIES and the KILGETTY IRONWORKS AND COLLIERIES, situate at Saundersfoot, near Tenby, South Wales, together with rich Hematite deposits at Penally, South Wales

These extensive and valuable Works, upon which a very large sum of money has been expended, were formally owned by Mr. C. R. VICKERMAN, in conjunction with several relatives and friends, but in consequence of deaths and family arrangements, the whole burden of the undertaking devolved upon him exclusively, and, as he resides for the greater part of the year in a distant county, he determined to dispose of the Works to the present Vendor to this Company, accepting, however, a seat on the Board.

The Company will therefore have the benefit of his valuable experience and assistance, which his knowledge of the district, and his influence with the resident population enable him effectually to give.

The Company also acquire the Railways (about 7 miles in length) which intersect the property, connecting it and the neighbouring collieries and works with the Harbour of Saundersfoot, and the Company also become Proprietors of the Harbour of Saundersfoot, which is of considerable local importance, being the port at which Coals are shipped from the district.

The BONVILLES COURT COLLIERIES are well known throughout England, as they supply the special quality of Coal chiefly used for malting purposed, call "Myers' Malting Anthracite Coal", which commands very high prices, being specially suitable for the preparation of the best malt.

The area of the Estates as to which this Company possess mining rights is more than 7,000 acres, or 11 square miles.

They are held upon mining leases for long unexpired terms, at very low dead rents and moderate royalties.

The Mineral lands comprise numerous veins of Argillaceous Ironstone of proved good quality.

The present contents of the Coal Fields are calculated at 8,000,000 tons. The Coal is of the rarest quality, is absolutely free from sulphur and other deleterious ingredients, and approaches more nearly Charcoal than does any other fuel; and consequently commands very high prices at times.

By the improved process adopted at the Kilgetty Works, the "Culm" is utilized, by conversion into a superior quality of Coke, for use in the furnaces; and it is specially suited for the manufacture of Patent Fuel, for which there is great and continuous demand.

The deposits of Hermatite Ore are rich in quality, yielding over sixty per cent. of Metallic Iron. The extent of these deposits not having been ascertained, no estimate has been made of their probable yield, although doubtless it will prove a source of considerable revenue. About 1,000 tons have been raised and used.

The Kilgetty Ironworks are of a very complete character, comprising blast furnaces, cast house and hot-air stoves, gas apparatus, calcining kilns, coke ovens, engines and boilers, coal washing and grinding machinery, and all the requisites for the economical manufacture of Pig Iron, the existing furnace plant being capable of producing about 15,000 tons of Pig Iron per annum. It is intended to erect immediately additional furnaces, capable of treating a further 15,000 tons, thus increasing the total capacity of manu-facture of Pig Iron to 30,000 tons annually.

The Pig Iron produced at Kilgetty is of special excellence, and is much esteemed from its similarity to Charcoal iron, arising chiefly from the exceptionally pure character of the Coal used at the Works.

It is also specially suitable for the manufacture of Bessemer Steel, Armour Plates, Tin Plates, etc., and meets a ready sale in anticipation of production.

The Works also include plant for the manufacturer of "Patent Fuel".

Saundersfoot Harbour, with its quays, wharves, landing-stages, shoots etc., was constructed under Special Act of Parliament, by which tolls and duties are authorised to be levied. These will belong to the Company, which will also have the right of levying a railway toll on all goods and traffic.

The possession of the Harbour, among other advantages, places the Works in direct communication with Milford Haven, the Government Dockyard at Pembroke, and by the railway and sea with all parts of the kingdom. The saving in tolls and shipping dues alone averages from 1s. 8d. to 2s. 6d. per ton.

The Railways are about seven miles in length.

The purchase-money, payable by the Company for the entire properties, including the Railway, Harbour, etc. as a going concern, is £210,000, this amount being based on the Reports made by B. P. BIDDER, Esq., and LEWIS THOMAS LEWIS, Esq., F. G. S., jointly, and by Messrs, WILLIAM BIRD & CO.

As a proof of the confidence in the undertaking entertained by the Vendor, he has consented to allow the sum of £95,000 to stand as a deferred payment for five years, taking Mortgage Debentures bearing Interest at 6 per cent. per annum for such sum, the balance—namely, £115,000—being payable in cash.

This arrangement may be looked upon as a very favourable character, as the entire profits of the undertaking—after deducting the amount necessary to pay interest upon the Debentures (amounting to £5,700 per annum only)—will be available for division as dividends on the Share Capital of the Company now for subscription.

After such payment to the Vendor, there will remain the sum of £50,000,—an amount considered amply sufficient to provide for the purchase of the stocks manufactured and now at the Works,—to furnish the necessary working Capital,—to provide for the development of the Coal properties,—and for such an augmentation of plant as to enable the Works to produce 30,000 tons of Pig Iron per annum, without interfering with the supplies necessary for the maintenance of the present Coal trade.

In terms of purchase no addition has been made for the extremely valuable goodwill and brand, and the very valuable connection, extending throughout England and Ireland, both for Myer's Malting Coal, as well as the Kilgetty Iron, which is well known as a specially choice make.

The current prices for the coal delivered, f.o.b., in Saundersfoot Harbour is 27s. per ton. For Bessemer Pig Iron the price would be £8 10s. to £9 per ton; but as the present quotation may be considered, to a certain extent, as exceptional, the Directors have thought it safer to take, as a basis of their calculation, the estimates to be found in the following extract from the Report of Messrs. BIDDER & LEWIS, which, being based on an average of a number of years, may be considered normal:

> Dealing with an "output" of 200 tons of Coal and Culm per day = 60,000 tons per annum: at a cost of 8s. 6d. per ton; and assuming that one-half, or 30,000 tons, will be culm [to be converted into "Anthracite Coke," and consumed in the blast furnaces, in addition to what is consumed by the engines, and sold to the local trade at cost price], there will remain 30,000 tons, which, at the recent average selling price of 25s. per ton, would show a profit of 16s. 6d. per ton. But by allowing a further 2s. 6d., and not assuming any consequent increase in the selling price, there would still be a profit of 14s. per ton. £21,000

> The yield of four blast furnaces, at 150 tons each per week, would produce 30,000 tons, of Pig Iron per annum, which at present rates and prices, would show an actual profit of £2 to £3 per ton; but assume an average profit of 20s. per ton (which, for the special reasons already given, is fairly probable, and more likely to be increased than diminished), and the income from the four furnaces would give, per annum £30,000

£51,000

After providing for payment of Interest on the Debentures, the net profits would, according to these estimates, yield very large Dividends on the Share Capital of the Company.

An additional value is given to the position and extent of the property, and to the quality of the Minerals (before commented upon), but the very exceptional nature of the labour employed, as regards quality and permanence. It is drawn from the numerous class of small freeholders and occupiers of land, whose status forms a special feature of the district.

The Directors feel every confidence that the results of this Company will be highly satisfactory, the property being of a most complete character, offering a remarkable field for development in every branch of the undertaking.

Copies of the Reports and valuations of B. P. BIDDER, Esq., LEWIS THOMAS LEWIS, Esq., and Messrs. WILLIAM BIRD & CO., of the Agreement for purchase, and of the Memorandum and Articles of Association, can be seen at the Offices of the Solicitor.

In the event of no allotment being made, the deposit will be returned in full, without deduction.

Should a less number of Shares be allotted than applied for, the deposit will be made available towards the sum payable on allotment.

Applications for Shares must be made on the accompanying form, which must be forwarded, together with a deposit of £1 per share, to the Bankers of the Company, THE LONDON AND COUNTY BANK, 21 Lombard Street, London, or any of its Branches; or to the Secretary, at the Offices of the Company, 8, Great Winchester Street Build-ings, E.C., London, where the Prospectus and Forms of Application may be obtained.

By order of the Board,
JOHN ROBERTS,
Secretary.
OFFICES OF THE COMPANY,
8 GREAT WINCHESTER STREET BUILD-
INGS, E.C.,
LONDON.
5th April, 1873.

The following Contract has been entered into on behalf of the Company: 5th April, 1873.—An Agreement made between THOMAS LEVICK of the one part, and JOHN ROBERTS, as Trustee for and on behalf of the Company, on the other part.

Appendix D

Memorandum relating to Bonvilles Court Collieries – 1900

Source: Vickerman papers (privately owned)

Memorandum dated 26th November, 1900
(attached to notes on Mineral Leases)

SCHEDULE A
BONVILLES COURT COAL COMPANY

Brief description of the Mineral District Collieries, Harbour and Railways etc. belonging to the Company.

I LEASEHOLDS

The property comprises the entire mineral District surrounding Saundersfoot harbour producing Anthracite Coal or unequalled quality in addition of deposits of Argillaceous Iron Ore which yielded Iron scarcely inferior to Charcoal Iron and comprises about *4000 acres* equal to 6 *square miles* nearly.

The Collieries at present at work are two in number viz. *Bonvilles Court* and *The Grove* producing the noted Anthracite Coal called "Bonvilles Court" and "Kilgetty" commanding the highest prices in the Market.

Other Collieries not now at work but capable of being reopened at moderate outlay are 4 in number viz. *Old Kilgetty, Foxholes, Moreton, Hacket* and *New Hayes.*

The Leases and conditions under which all the above Collieries are held are detailed in Schedule C. N.B. It is in contemplation to reopen the Old Kilgetty Colliery which lies to the use of the Grove and Kilgetty Colliery and for this purpose to transfer the entire plant from the latter Colliery, which Colliery was closed a few months since. It was the coal from the Old Kilgetty pit which made the reputation of these Collieries 60 years ago and there remains a very large area unworked.

II Freeholds

1. The *Harbour* of Saundersfoot and *Railways* of about 7 miles connecting the collieries with the shipping Port, constructed and incorporated under Three Acts of Parliament viz. 10 Geo: C. 109 and 5 Vic c.c. 35 and 53 and entitled to charge the following *Tolls* and *Dues* viz. on coal and culm 2$^{1}/_{2}$d. p ton p mile Iron Ore 2$^{1}/_{2}$d. p ton p mile, corn shop goods etc. 8d. p ton p mile with 1d. p ton extra if conveyed in the Company's carriages.

Harbour Dues of 2d. p ton and shipping rates of 4d. p ton on Iron/10d. p ton and other dues as p Schedule to Act 5 Vic C. 53.

2. *One Third* share of *minerals* under *"Bickening Lands"* containing 18a. 2r. 30p. held on tenancy in common with the Owner of the remaining 2/3rds about 4 acres of Upper Vein have been worked.

III   Capital Expenditure on Works

Since the formation of the original "Bonvilles Court Coal & Iron Company Limited" in 1872-3 upwards of £44,000 have been expended in extensions and substantial and permanent improvements of the collieries, harbour, and Railways and Works, the details of which outlays are given in Schedule E.

Before any of this outlay has been incurred the works were valued by Messrs. Wm. Bird & Co. of Lawrence Pountney Hill, London on behalf and at the cost of Mr. James Carlton then an intending purchaser (who completed his purchase) at the sum of £225,000 as by their Report and Valuation dated 21st June, 1872.

IV   Goodwill

The *"Kilgetty Vein"* has been known to the market for 200 years and the Bonvilles Court Vein for 50 years and upwards. Both veins have always commanded the highest prices 2% or 3% p ton above the *next* best qualities Messrs Bass & Co. always take as much as we can spare them although they state that it costs them at their Maltings fully 5/- p ton more than "Gwaun-cae-gurwen" and other good Anthracites.

The Collieries have an old established connexion of very many years standing. The late Edward Chuck of Ware *then* the largest Maltster in England was one of their best customers, and put £10,000 into the collieries, on a change of ownership in order to "keep a hold" as he declared upon Kilgetty Coal.

The *"Bad debts"* during the past 7 years of depression have only averaged a loss between £9 and £10 per annum thus shewing the soundness of the business transactions.

V   Completion

The gradual acquisition by the present owner as opportunities occurred during a period of 40 years and upwards of the entirety of the *Mineral District* and of the Harbour and Railways has given him the command of the Local Labour Shipping and Sales Markets and thus is avoided the disastrous competition which exist when there were 6 or 7 independent collieries in the District raising the cost of production and of shipment and lowering prices on sales. It also enablers the owner to regulatethe "output" ... is of immense importance by diverting the "knocking down of prices" and the consequent difficulty of "getting them up again".

SCHEDULE D
SAUNDERSFOOT HARBOUR and RAILWAYS and Rolling Stock

Freeholds

Harbour with North and South piers of solid masonry of over three acres in extent with Ballast and Loading Quays 450 yards long.

Five (5) loading shoots with windlasses etc. etc.

There is sufficient depth of water for vessels of 500-600 tons burthen.

Reservoir (large) with double sluice gates divided from the Harbour by substantial stone wall. The Company have powers under the Acts for converting it into a *Floating Dock* and charging extra rates for its use.

Steam Crane for discharging Ballast etc. with Engine of one pair of $4\frac{1}{2}$in. Cylinders and 9in. stroke.

Railways
1. From Grove and Kilgetty Collieries to the Harbour $2\frac{3}{4}$ miles in length—4ft. gauge laid with rails 42lbs. per yard.
2. Connecting Bonvilles Court and Foxhill Collieries with the Harbour and also with Saundersfoot station on the Pembroke and Tenby branch of the Great Western Railway—about 2,200 yards—same gauge.
3. From Hacket to New Hayes Collieries to Saundersfoot Station about 2 miles, at present unlaid with rails.
4. Self acting incline—with Drum brake and powerful chains between Bonvilles Court Colliery and the Harbour.
5. Rails and pass-byes around the Harbour and Quays.
   Rates, Tolls and Dues chargeable under the Companys Acts of Parliament on
   Coal and culm $2\frac{1}{2}$d. per Ton per Mile
   Iron Ore
   Iron/10s. per Ton
   Harbour Dues in registered Tonnage   /2s. per Ton
   Shipping Rates on Cargoes   /4s. per Ton
   Floating Dock (when constructed)   6s. per Ton

Rolling Stock Locomotive Engine 4ft Gauge 8" Cylinders and 14" Stroke built by Manning & Wardle, Leeds.
15 Eight Ton Railway Waggons—ordinary gauge built by the Midland Railway Waggon Company.
75 Iron Colliery Loading Trams—4ft. Gauge.

Bickening Minerals one third share of Minerals under area of 18a.2r.30p (See Schedule A).

Capital Expenditure from June 1872 to June 1878

	Grove Colliery (including pumps etc.)	959	10	10
b.	do Steam Capstan	642	14	0
c.	Bonvilles Court Colliery including alterations at Ventilator	740	8	10
	do (20" Engine etc.)	567	17	8
	Railway and Harbour a/c including Locomotive and Steam Crane	8750	5	4
	Cottages	649	1	8
a.	Bonvilles Court Colliery Sinking shaft to win Kilgetty Vein	3318	9	3
	Stanley Minerals (freehold purchase)	325	0	0
		23743	19	4
	Expended by James Carlton under Agreements between 3,000 and 4,000 in 1872-73 (say)	3506	11	0
		27250	10	4

Further Capital Expenditure
from June 1878 to March 1889

a.	Bonvilles Court Colliery completing sinking pit to K, vein	3017	6	4
b.	Masonry Arching Roadway underground connecting Grove and Kilgetty collieries	1046	6	6
	Fox Holes Colliery—Sinking Shaft 62 Fathoms	3328	3	5
	Woodside Level Opening Work	334	6	11
b.	Grove Colliery New Piston etc. to In Engine	267	7	6
	Kilgetty Colliery—Nut coal Machinery	159	0	1
	Bonvilles Court Collieries Pullies No. 2 & 3 etc.	1245	1	-
		9308	1	9
	Add capital expenditure from March 1889 to September 1900	8009	0	0
Total outlay – 1872-1900				
		£44565	12	1

SCHEDULE F

COLLIERIES AND PLANT ABOVE AND UNDERGROUND

I   Bonvilles Court Colliery

Landing Shaft 85 faths x 11ft. x 10ft. with pithead Weigh House capstan etc.

Winding Engine 24" Diam. x 6ft. stroke in Stone built house with 2 flat wire ropes and 2 sheave wheels ft. Diam.

Pumping Engine 20" Diam. x 6ft. stroke in stonebuilt house with 85 faths. of pump rods—29 faths. of 10" pumps. 40 faths. of 11" ditto 18 faths of 5 ditto with poles polecases clack pieces etc.

Upcast Shaft 60 faths x 9ft. x 10ft. with Waddle Ventilating Engine 20" dia and Fan 16ft. diameter. Pit head pulley and guides complete.

Saw Mill and *Winding Engine* 16" dia. with circular saw pullies wire ropes, bells, winding drum etc. complete in stone built houses.

Engine Houses Carpenters and Smiths shops offices stores and Lamp Houses stone built and slated.

Large Iron Water Tank and Reservoir

Revolving and Shake Screens at pits mouth for separating the coal from the nuts, peas and small culm.

Weighing Machine One farm weighing machine—one cart ditto—2 pit carts ditto.

Railway   (4ft. gauge) to coal and culm works about 35 tons.

Boilers $25^{1}/_{2}$ft. x 20ft. galloway Tube Boilers

(9)   26ft. x 22ft. and 15ft. x 24ft. Tubular
$14^{1}/_{2}$ft. x 22ft. - 13ft. x 24ft. 14ft. x 25ft. $14^{1}/_{2}$ft. x 33ft. cylindrical
All fitted with the necessary steam and feed pipes safety valves water gauges injectors boiler feed etc.

Hay and Chaff House containing Chaff cutting machine worked by vertical engine $8^{1}/_{2}$" x 1' 8" stroke.

Underground

Engine Slant Underground. 14" Hauling Engine with about 1,200 yards of steel wire rope and sheave wheels and guides
One Tangyes' driven pump driven by a Priestmans Oil Engine
Pit and Drift to Kilgetty Vein Shaft 36 faths. and 11ft. dia fitted with Boiler and Engine Room containing one new cylindrical Steel Boiler $4^{1}/_{2}$ft. x 30ft. complete with fittings.

One pair of 12" *Winding Engines* Pit Head Steel wire ropes, 3 sinking Tubs, Water Tub etc.

64 yards of 3" steam pipes and 72 yards of 4" pumps in pit.

85 yards of $1^{1}/_{2}$" pipes 140 yards 2" pumps in slope.

Slope Drift 114 yards long for winding and also giving second access to Kilgetty Vein.

Rails about 95 tons @ 16lbs. to the yard underground and on coal culm and rubbish tops.

Underground	*Trams*	166
ditto	*Waterhaulers*	6
Screen Trams		9
Rubbish Top	*Carriages*	8

1 *Horse Box* and 2 pit cages

Colliers Tools

Smiths Ditto

3 horses 1 Pony 1 Donkey underground with Harness etc.

Stables for 10 horses   ditto

The Grove and Kilgetty Collieries

These Collieries are connected with each other underground by stone drift arched 870 yards in length the former taking water of and ventilating the latter. N.B. It is proposed shortly to transfer the machinery from these pits to the Old Kilgetty Colliery.

II   The Grove Colliery

Landing and Pumping shaft Bratticed in 3 divisions 105 faths. x 16$^1/_2$ft. x 12$^1/_2$ft. oval with pithead *40* feet.

Cornish pumping engine of 274 horse power 80˝ dia. x 10ft. stroke in house, and 8ft stroke in pit. (New piston and cylinder cover) working one 20" pole one 22" pole and one 12" pole with 105 fathoms of pump rods 15" square 35 faths. of 16" pumps 51 faths. of 18" pumps and 20 faths. of 12" ditto.

Winding Engine 30 horse power vertical 40" dia. x 3'6" stroke fitted with Drum 15ft. dia. 4$^1/_2$" wire ropes and 212ft. pullies.

Steam Capstan One new Loame's Capstan Engine. One pair of 12 engines and 120 faths. of 15" Hemp Rope.

Boilers 4 double flued 7ft. x 30ft. in stone boiler house with slate roof

        1 single ditto 5ft. 8" x 30ft.

        1 Cylindrical 4' 6" x 34' 6"

all fitted with necessary safety and water gauges Steam and feed pipes etc.

2 Pit Cages each holding 2 colliery trams.

3 Engine and *Boiler House* Smiths and Carpenters shops and Colliery stores substantially stone built and slated.

Incline (Self acting) fitting complete with Drum, incline ropes and *Carriages* each carriage holding

4 colliery trams 184 yards long—screens for separating coal and culm etc. etc. (114 yards double road and 70 yards single road)

Weighing Machine pit Bank and 1 Cart machine

Railway (4ft. gauge) to Coal Stocks and Colliery about 800 yards.

2 *Horses* and *Harness* underground

Stables for 10 horsed   ditto

2 Horses on surface with stables for same. Harness etc.

III   Kilgetty Colliery

This is a modern colliery and is fitted up with nearly all modern Engines Boilers etc.

It is connected underground with the *Grove Pit* by an arched heading of 870 yards long.

Landing Shaft 84 faths. x 9ft. dia. with pithead and Guides complete.

Winding Engines 1 pair of 14" x 3ft. in a substantial stone built house with $22^1/_2$" steel wire ropes 10ft. dia. sheave wheels and 2 pit cages 1 Air compressor for actuating underground pumps.

Slope Hauling Engine 16" x 3ft. fitted with about 1,000 yards of $2^1/_2$" steel wire ropes 2 sheave wheels 7ft. diameter and 29ft. ditto in a stone built and slated house. One 12ft. 6" x 24" *Tangyes* Special *Pump* with 700 yards of 4" pumps and 850 yards of $2^1/_2$" steam pipes.

2 *Weighing Machines* on Pit bank.

Screens for separating the coal and culm.

One revolving Screen Elevator and travelling belt for the manufacture of Nut coal and worked by a vertical 10" x 8" engine in house.

The whole covered in with corrugated iron roofing.

Engine Houses Smiths and Carpenters Shops Stores and offices.

Boilers   25ft. x 30ft. cylindrical

    (4)   25ft. 8" x 30ft. tubular

fitted complete with steam and feed pipes safety and water gauges etc.

Flooring Plates about 48 tons.

Storehouses and Workshops on Platform (by the Blast Furnaces) substantially built stone and slated houses comprising spacious offices, stores Carpenters Smiths and Fitters Shops containing

2 *lathes* (one very large and powerful) and 1 *saw mill* worked by *Engine* 11" x 30"

Stroke and Boiler 4'6" x 22'6".

Fitters and Smiths Tools.

Cast House Spacious and lofty. Stone built and corrugated iron 52ft. x 69ft. and 27ft. high.

V   Old Kilgetty Colliery

Engine Pit of 49 faths. x   10 feet diameter
Quarry Pit of 42   ”   x   8—
Sunk to Old Kilgetty Vein of which a large tract to the deep commanded by
a Bully driven from the Engine pit is still unworked.

VI   Thomas Chapel Colliery

These Collieries command an area of over *1,000 Acres* and consist of the
New Hayes Pit of 78 faths. x 10 feet diameter Sunk to the Kilgetty Vein of
which but little has been worked and the *Hacket Colliery* of 29 faths. to the
Lower Level Vein.
Coal of the finest quality has been worked to the rise from *Hacket Pit* but
large and important mining can be made by driving a slope to the deep—
or by a New Shaft at a spot indicated on the plan.

VI   Foxholes Colliery

This pit of 60 faths. x 9 feet dia. is sunk to the *Timber Vein* also inter-secting
the *Rock* and *Low Veins*.
It is connected on the surface with Bonvilles Court Colliery by a slope
tramway of about 350 yards.
One corrugated iron *Engine house* on stone foundations.
One 4ft. x 35ft. Cylindrical *Boiler* with steam feed pipes etc. com-plete.

VII   Moreton Colliery

Two Pits to *Rock* and *Timber Veins* of about *50* fathoms each.
One pit of about *150 fathoms* to *Lower Level* or *Bonvilles Court* Vein
Engine Houses etc.
      One 14” x 24” stroke *double winding Engine* with Drum and winding
Gear nearly new.

Former Bonvilles Court
Coal Co. cottages,
Stepaside, 1979
M.R.C. Price

Appendix E

Advertising Sheet for Auction of Plant and Machinery at Hook Colliery on 6 March 1900

Source: Pembrokeshire Record Office   Reference: D RTM/HPO/297

HOOK COLLIERY, NEAR HAVERFORDWEST.

Important Unreserved Clear-Out Ready Money Sale by Auction of Machinery, Boilers, Plant, &c., and a quantity of Old Iron.

J. LLEWELLYN DAVIES

Has been favoured with instructions from the Trustees of the will of the late Thomas Harcourt Powell, deceased,

TO SELL BY PUBLIC AUCTION

AT

HOOK COLLIERY

NEAR HAVERFORDWEST,

On Tuesday, March 6th, 1900

THE FOLLOWING

MACHINERY

BOILERS, PLANT, &C., &C.

CONSISTING OF

EAST PIT.—One 20" Cylinder Horizontal Engine, with Feed Pump, Pumping Gear, Slant Rods, Rocking Pillar and Pumping Beam complete; 45 Fathoms of 8" Rods formerly attached to Pumping Beam, with Strapping Plates and Bolts; One 12" Plunger and Case with Clack Pieces, Doors, Clacks & Snore Pieces; 20 Fathoms of 12" Pumptrees, and 25 Fathoms of 10" do., with all the necessary Joint Rings, Bolts and Nuts for joining same; Ten Fathoms of 13" Pumptrees, with Joint Rings and Bolts, Clack Pieces, Bucket Door Piece, Door and Snore Pieces, and spare Clack Seatings and Fittings; One 14" Horizontal Winding Engine, with a 10 feet drum on a second motion Shaft, with Feed Pump complete; Two Pit Cages with Chains and Props; the Sheerlegs on this Pit, with Screen, &c., &c. :

One 10" Cylinder Engine; One Coal Crusher with Pulleys; Two Spherical Ended Boilers, and one Cornish Boiler, with all their Grates, Dampers and Fittings, and all Steam and Feed Pipes attached to the Engines; One Old Boiler used as Feed Water Tank and Pipes, Two Crab Winches, Mortar Mill, Spanners, &c., &c.

WEST PIT.—One 8½ Vertical Engine with Feed Pump, Pumping Gear, Slant Rod, and Pumpimg Beam, and Balance Box; 25 Fathoms of 5" Rods, with Plates and Bolts; One 6" Plunger and Case, with Clack Pieces, Doors, Clacks, and Snore Piece; 26 Fathoms of 6" Pump Trees, withall neces sary Joint Rings, and Bolts; 15 Fathoms of 8" Pumptree with Joint Rings and Bolts. Clack Piece, Bucket Door Piece, and Snore Piece, and Clack Seatings; the Sheerlegs as fixed on this Pit with Screen; One Cage and Chain; One 14" Cylinder Diagonal Engine, with Drum on Second Motion Shaft, with Feed Pump; Old Boiler used as Cistern; One Ventilating Fan and Engine; Two Spherical Ended Boilers, with Grates, Dampers, and Fittings, with all the Steam and Feed Pipes to the three Engines; One Underground Force Pump, to work by Hand; One Crub Capstan, with Handles complete; Two Crab Winches, together with a quantity of Flooring Plates, 3¾-inch Pipes, Forges, Anvils, and Block Tools, &c., &c.

QUAY.—Two Weighing Machines, Five Tripping Cranes and Chains, Screen, Large Drum at top of Incline, &c., &c.

Sale to commence at 11 for 12 o'clock prompt.

The Auctioneer respectfully invites the attention of Colliery Proprietors, Engineers, and Metal Merchants to this Genuine Clear-Out Sale. The Colliery is situated within easy distance of the Banks of the Haven, and being connected by a Tramway to the Jetty (a distance of about 400 yards) at Hook Quay, Purchasers can easily have their purchases conveyed to the water side and taken away by vessel. About Three Miles from the Johnston Station of the G.W.R., and Five Miles from Haverfordwest, with which it is connected by the river.

Any further particulars may be obtained by applying to the AUCTIONEER at Cleddau Villa, Milford Haven, or to

MESSRS. EATON EVANS & WILLIAMS,

SOLICITORS,

HAVERFORDWEST.

Printed at the " Pembrokeshire Herald" Offices, Bridge Street, Haverfordwest.

Appendix F

THE MEMOIRS OF JAMES THAIN OF STEPASIDE, KILGETTY
(born 3 May 1870)

My first job in the mine was trapping, that is opening and closing doors for the men and horses with trains of cars as they passed to and fro. These doors are used to direct the ventilation of the mine and the health and sometimes the lives of the miners depend on these doors being kept closed. I well remember how the boss cautioned me in regard to this. There were two doors so that while one was open the other was closed. In this way the ventilating current was not greatly disturbed. I had other duties such as: watching the switches on the side-track and coupling the cars ready for the drivers. For this I was paid the sum of seven pence per day. I shall never forget the first day. It was the longest I ever experienced. After I had my trip or train of cars coupled I would sit at my inside door and listen for the driver. He had about a mile to go and I could hear the rumble of his cars almost from the times he left the inside parting or side-track for the reason that the roadway was arched with rock almost its entire distance. I trapped three days, but it seems like three months to me now. So many things transpired to make it eventful. On the third day the boss asked me to take a job in the interior of the mine. We worked this on a three shift basis; two of us on each shift of eight hours each. This was indeed very desirable more so because it gave me a raise of two pence making my wage nine pence (eighteen cents) per day. It also gave me a greater working knowledge of the working face or interior of the mine. The time passed more swiftly as we were kept busy and were interested in our little machine which was a novel yet simple affair. There was a large sump or well where the water collected, and after we had pumped it dry we could rest for an hour or more if we desired. But boy like, we wanted to see all that was going on around us and we often left our pumps to go see the boys and men that were producing the coal. We used to help the larger boys load their little cars or trams as we called them; anything to be doing something new. Sometimes the men would give us a pick and let us try to dig coal. The coal seam was only sixteen inches thick, so we had to lie down on our side in order to get between the roof and the floor. I used to fear that the coal would be all mined before I was big enough to have a share of digging it. However, they are still working that little coal seam though sixty years has passed since that time. Sometimes we would take our pumps apart in order to see their construction or as we used to say to make some repairs, which we felt they always needed. We continued at this job about six months until it became very monotonous. The odd hours deprived us of a good deal of the association and good times with the other boys. I especially rebelled against working Sunday. However, the time came as the workings advanced to higher ground, that the necessity of maintaining the pumps became unnecessary, and we boys were given different jobs in various parts of the mine. Some tramming or pushing or helping-up as we called the little fellows who with a little iron hook with a cross piece attached, hooked on to the empty cars to assist the larger boys in getting their cars to the top of the many steep grades. In coming down with their loaded cars they used sprags, often as many as four of the wheels were spragged or braked the declivity being so great. Those were stirring times in the life of us boys. We were very reckless in regard to the dangers that beset us and our fellows. Many times we used to race our cars down those little roadways at an alarming rate, heedless of the danger to anyone coming up. All of us boys were barefooted as to wear shoes would have been too great an encumbrance as, the roadways were only $2\frac{1}{2}$ to 3 ft. high. Many times, especially in the morning, have I knocked my back against the roof tearing the flesh off all along the backbone. The following day do the same thing, possibly half a dozen times, until our backs were kept raw, which was the price we paid for being so long legged. We used to be so stiff and sore in the morning before we warmed up. We called this soreness "growing ages." I presume it was. We were growing too big for our roadway. Many a good old cry I have had after knocking a fresh scab of my back. Then I would sit down awhile until I would hear the rumbling of the car of the boy in the next roadway and I would get up and hurry away to load my train so I would not lose my turn, which was considered a disgrace. We prided ourselves on the speed we could load and complete the trip. However, those were happy days in a way. We had lots of fun as we congregated at the side-tracks waiting to dump our cars. We thrashed out all the leading questions of the day at those stopping places. We had tests of strength, wrestling matches and fights galore. Time passed very swiftly and as we grew we took bigger jobs that required more muscle and experience.

At the age of nineteen I took a place with my foster brother, who was several years older than I, cutting or digging coal as we called it. I was now a man, a full fledged miner. My foster father had died in the meantime and my brother married leaving me the sole provider for my foster mother and a family of four. We were certainly in pretty hard circumstances when my brother took me with him to dig coal. This increased my wages from about one shilling and six pence to four shilling per day. I was so overjoyed the first payday that I could scarcely get home quick enough and poured it all in mother's lap. If I do say it, I always did that as long as she lived. She died when I was twenty two years old.

For three years I worked very hard. That coal was the hardest that I ever saw and the position in which we had to lie in order to dig it made it extremely laborious. The method of mining was what miners call the long-wall system. That is, all the coal was taken out and vacancy filled up with props and refuse. It didn't take much to fill up the space left as I said before the coal seam was only sixteen inches thick. Each pair of men were given about twenty-five feet of space as their part of the working space, so that there was a continuous open space or breast of several hundred feet. The man in the various stalls as we called them were within speaking distance of each other. Some of them allowed their places to lag behind, making the work face irregular, which often caused the roof to break and the coal to become set or much harder to dig, as the continued pressure on the working face had been disturbed. This called for many arguments and very often the manager or his assistant had to come in to settle the dispute. Then the men who had allowed their places to get behind were given a shorter working face until they had caught up with the fellows in the adjoining room as it was called. I remember an old fellow and his son worked to the left of us at one time. The old man had a bad habit of allowing the part of the working face near to me to hang behind, compelling me to work along in the solid, or cutting a rib as we termed it. I often remonstrated with him but without avail. One day I had my place worked in several feet ahead of him and he was working off some of the loose coal seemingly enjoying the fact that my efforts had made easy work for him. He had his pipe in his mouth taking a smoke and working at the same time. All of a sudden I heard a crash and I crawled as fast as I could toward him, at the same time calling for help from my brother and his son, (the old man's) who was some distance away. He was almost entirely covered up with large pieces of slate which had fallen from the roof. We released him from the debris that had covered him; he being unconscious we thought him dead, we pulled him out to the roadway and I told his son to fetch some water which he carried in his bucket or can. I didn't think he was dead now as I couldn't see any particular injury on him. I poured some water over his head and he revived immediately. I shall never forget the first thing he said when he opened his eyes; "where is my pipe?" I said you ought to be glad you are alive and take a lesson and don't let your place hang back again endangering the life of yourself and others. He looked at me kind of queer, but never said a word. However I think the experience did him some good. It is not necessary to relate the many incidents that occurred during the next two years.

We worked regularly as, whenever we had no cars to ship the coal it was dumped on the ground and stored against the time that business would pick up. We had several local strikes, one I shall never forget. There was a mass meeting called of all the miners in the community. After much oratory and discussion from the various leaders among the older men, it was decided that we go on strike for higher wages. However before the time of striking had arrived, a few of the leaders, who were among the most ardent advocates of a strike, made it their business to go around among the men and call it off, and the final outcome of it all was that we didn't stop work at all.

In the meantime I had with several other young men of my acquaintance made preparations to leave home for mines about 100 miles away, where they paid better wages and where the work was not so laborious. Mother being sick at the time did not want me to leave home. I was glad for her sake that I did not have to leave. Mother died shortly after this, and another strike among the boys a short time after her death decided me to leave home. It was the most wonderful time of my life as I had never been more than about ten miles from home before.

(I am indebted to Roscoe Howells of Amroth, Pembrokeshire, for bringing these memoirs to my attention.)

Stepaside, as seen from the bridge c.1930, Kilgetty Colliery to left   M.R.C. Price Collection

APPENDIX G

NUMBER OF MEN EMPLOYED 1891 and 1896

Name of Pit	1891			1896		
	Underground	Surface	Total	Underground	Surface	Total
Begelly Meadow	9	2	11			
Bonville's Court	128	41	169	154	41	195
Kilgetty Lower Level	104	59	163	115	52	167
Hook West Park	86	53	139	80	48	128
Landshipping				2	1	3
Trefrane Cliff	25	10	35	28	8	36
Yerbeston	6	10	16			
Cardmakers Pool				Not Working		
Llethr (Roch)				2	2	4
Meads(Jeffreston)				11	2	13

SOURCE: Report of H.M. Inspector of Mines, 1891 Ref. POWE 7/27 and 1896 Ref. POWE 7/32

APPENDIX G

NUMBER OF MEN EMPLOYED 1902 to 1950

Colliery \ Year	1902	1906	1910	1914	1918	1922	1926	1930	1934	1938	1946	1950
Bonvilles Court	240	301	330	384	307	350	306	293				
Hook	41	61	60	73	69	146	108	243	269	113	90	
Reynalton		11		48	72							
Freystrop	81	15										
White Park		24										
Kilgetty Adit Level	45	24	30									
Meads(Jeffreston)	23	12	2									
Masterland		5										
Langdon			7									
Broadmoor							14	12				
Loveston									48			
Broom									95	208		
Kilgetty										75		
Wood Level											25	20

<u>Source:</u> Edwards, *A Study of the Daucleddau Coalfield (Pembrokeshire)*

APPENDIX H.

THE LOVESTON ACCIDENT 26 MAY 1936.

An account given to the writer in 1983 by the late Owen Gwyther,
slightly edited for ease of reading.

Loveston colliery was started in the early 1930's, probably about 1932 or 33. It was started
by three brothers, Edgar, Newton, and Wallace Howells, together with their father and
stepbrother. First of all a pit was sunk down to the coal vein, they then went back some distance
to the north and started a slope. This was to be the main colliery, the pit later acting acting
as upcast for ventilation. Edgar had been working as under-manager in a colliery in the Welsh
valleys; his brother Newton also worked as a miner in the valleys. As work progressed they
started to employ extra labour; eventually the work force rose to over thirty employees
(however this was not until a few years after).

The enterprise was not without its difficulty. First of all there was the hazard of old outcrop
workings. But when they did strike the seam proper everything seemed set for success. The
slope was driven down, the seam of coal was twenty to twenty four inches thick and of very
good quality. Level stalls were there opened east and west, more miners were taken on, and
indeed for a while everything went well. However, as often happens, the stalls going east ran
into some geological disturbances, the seam of coal went down to a few inches thick, and
several had to be abandoned. It was around then that they ran into financial difficulty, and [the
colliery] was eventually taken over by a Frenchman, Edgar still carrying on as manager. The
seam of coal in the face of the slope was still good, and as it was driven forward, more stalls
were opened up. Success was enjoyed for a while but unfortunately the slope then ran into
difficulty. The seam reduced to a few inches, and it also went over much steeper. This meant
quite a lot of dead work following this small seam, to see if it would return to normal. After
twenty or thirty yards it did come back, but much higher - about five feet - and in the form of
"slash", a term we used when the coal was not the usual quality. The slope going through this
stage was much lower than normal because of the very hard rock top. It was also much steeper
but the slope was still being driven forward, and four or five stalls were being worked in the
slash. It was then on the fateful afternoon of 26 May that disaster struck.

On 25 May a few of us were working two shifts, alternative mornings and afternoons. It was
my week for afternoons. However on arrival at the colliery, I learned that my mate Albert Allen
was absent.

This meant working by myself in the stall, which was against regulations. On returning home
that night I was met by the manager who informed me that my mate had a poisoned hand and
would not be in work for some time. He then told me to double back the following morning
and work three in a stall with two miners named Keats Badham and Joe Phillips. I returned
the following morning and Joe decided he would rather me work in the face with Keats and
he would do the filling, tramming, cutting the posts etc. Everything went normal until about
two o'clock or just after. Joe had gone out to the deep with the last tram, while Keats and I
were posting up prior to leaving. Suddenly there was a kind of vibration. I faintly heard Joe's
voice from the mouth of the road shouting, and somehow I instinctively knew from the roar
that water had broken in. I was exceptionally lucky in so far as I had replenished my acetylene
lamp with some new carbide. (Being open lights we provided our own, therefore I had a good
light). We ran to the little companion deep which ended in our road and water was already

pouring down this. However we managed to get up above the water and out into the main deep. We could then see that the water was coming from the west side. The torrent was completely filling the road and it had carried a full tram across the main deep and jammed it cornerwise against the side. The water was then being diverted to the little deep and also over the top of the tram. About eleven miners were about forty or fifty yards below this down the deep. A pump was working by the side of the deep about forty yards down. This was driven by electric, and fastened to the timber was a heavy armour plated cable. We were now about six or eight feet above the water, and probably because I had the best light, I clambered over the tram with assistance and hanging on to the cable, I managed to get halfway down holding my light above the water and shouting encouragement to those coming from below. I am glad to say that eight out of the eleven made it. Unfortunately three of my best pals did not - that was Joe and Ernie Phillips, (brothers) and Jack Hilling; there was also Freddy Beynon, Tommy Lloyd, Bob Williams and Will Jenkins. The last three were killed when the water broke in. Will Jenkins we found at the time – he had been washed out to the main deep. The others were not recovered until a fortnight later. Joe my pal who had only left me a short while was later found pinned against the side with the tram which had been hurled across the deep. You can imagine the force of water when you consider that nine men including myself had clambered over that tram and the water was going over the top of it with such force that it was impossible to see or know. The water had of course been cut in from Breeches Pit which was about half a mile away to the south west.

(Figure 33 includes a plan of Loveston, noting the point of water inrush on 26 May 1936)

Loveston colliery
disaster 26 may,
1936. Men leaving
the drift after a
rescue attempt
Western Mail

APPENDIX J

SAUNDERSFOOT RAILWAY & HARBOUR CO. BYE-LAWS

BYE LAWS for regulating the Traffic and
Management of the Railway

1. No Waggon or Carriages to pass along the line unless of a proper size and make suitable to the road and the wheels of the same to be of the proper form and size—case hardened—in the true gauge of the road

2. All Waggons or Carriages to be passed over the Inclined plane in such number order and manner as the Officers appointed to superintend the same shall direct and no Waggon or Carriage shall be passed over the Inclined plane unless in the presence of the said Officer to whom two hours notice shall be given to attend for that Purpose.

3. All Trams or Carriages passing along the Railway laden or empty shall be driven and bought on to the Weighing Machine for the purpose of being Weighed at the desire or upon the requisition of the Harbour Master or Collector

4. When Waggons or Carriages meet on the Railway the empty or lightest shall retreat or turn back to the next pass-bye or parting and each Driver shall place the rail latches in such a position as will be required for his passing and so leave them and shall not drive along the Railway at a greater rate than five miles an hour, and no driver or other person or persons shall be allowed to ride on any Tram, Carriage, or horse or other animal

5. No driver shall leave his Tram or Trams upon the Railway and no incompetent person shall be permitted to drive on the Railway

6. If from any Cause a Tram break down or become incapable of passing along the Railway it shall be at once removed by the Driver to the side of the Railway so as to cause no obstruction to the Traffic and within twenty four hours afterwards the Driver or his Employer shall remove the Tram from off the property of the Railway Company

7. No Driver or other person shall haul any Tram or Trams off the Railway unless in case of accident

8. All persons not conforming to these Bye Laws or in any wise obstructing or molesting the Company's Officers in the execution of their duty shall be liable to all damages occasioned thereby and shallbe fined such sum as the Convicting Magistrate may think fit not exceeding £5 for each offence

9. All persons trespassing on the Railway will be prosecuted or otherwise dealt with as the Law directs And all Animals found straying thereon will be impounded

BYE LAWS for regulating Use of Management of
the Harbour, Quays etc

1. All Masters of Vessels and all Hobblers, or helpers of Ships acting as Pilots bringing Vessels into the Harbour with the Wind blowing W. to W.N.W. or outward from the Harbour, must come to an Anchor and warp the Vessel in, under the direction of the Harbour Master or his Deputy

2. All Masters of Vessels, Hobblers, or Helpers of Ships (in charge of the same for the time being) moving any Vessel in the Harbour, or taking any Vessel out of the Harbour under Canvas or otherwise shall be liable for whatever damage may be caused in consequence thereof to the Pier Wall, Jetties etc or to any Vessel, and be subject to a penalty not exceeding £5, in accordance with the Acts of Parliament relating to the Company

3. All Vessels within the Limits of the Harbour to be under the Control of the Harbour Master or his Deputy

4. All Masters of Vessels to stem and report the particulars of their Vessels upon their arrival within the Limits of the said Harbour

5. If any Vessel or Vessels cause damage to the Quays, Jetties or other Erections or to any of the Marks, Mooring Posts, Buoys or Works or to any other Vessel within the said Harbour the Owners and Masters thereof shall be liable for all such Damage whether through accident or otherwise in accordance with the Acts of Parliament relating to the said Company

6. All Booms, Yards, Spars and spare Anchors to be got in, peaked up and trimmed and all Ropes and Chains to be slacked at the Order of the Harbour Master or his Deputy

7. All Vessels to be in turn for loading and discharging in order that they shall be reported at the Harbour Office on arrival and entered in the Stemming Book kept there for that purpose but no Shipper to occupy more than one Coal Jetty at a time, provided other Shippers are ready to load

8. Should the Vessel on turn not be ready the next Vessel on turn that is ready shall have the turn, the first Vessel on turn taking a berth next in succession if ready

9. All Ballast to be discharged and taken in at and from the places and in such manner as appointed by the Harbour Master and none other and by Men appointed by the Company at the rates named at foot of these Bye Laws

10. No ballast to be thrown out within the limits of the Harbour except by permission of the Harbour Master

11. All Vessels with their Ballast or Cargo discharged and not going to load at the place of discharging, or not in turn for loading, and all laden Vessels, to move off from the Quays and Stages for others to discharge or load and all Vessels under the Jetties ready for taking in their Cargo or in course of taking in their Cargo shall move from one Jetty to another when required by the Harbour Master and in case of refusal or neglect the Harbour Master to send Men on Board to move the same at the expense of the Master or Owner
12. All Vessels waiting their turn for discharging, or loading to be moored and made fast at and to such places as the Harbour Master or his Deputy may direct and to move from one mooring to another when required be either of them to do so
13. Masters of Vessels shall keep sufficient hands on Board who shall hold themselves in readiness either to slack down their ropes or fastenings or move their Vessels as the Harbour Master or his Deputy shall direct
14. No Vessel shall lie waiting at a Jetty or Stage longer than one day Tide
15. On the rising of the tide, or as soon as any Vessel shall have completed her discharging or lading, the Consignee or Shipper or his or their Agent shall heave up the Shoots and properly secure the Machinery of the Jetty or Shipping place at which Vessel had been laden
16. Every Shipper or other person using a Jetty of Shipping place shall clear and remove from such Jetty or Shipping place or from the Platform of the same immediately after it shall have been used by him, all Coal, Culm Dirt, Rubbish or other Articles left thereon which shall be removed or deposited on obedience to the Orders and to the satisfaction of the Harbour Master
17. All Coal, Culm, Ore, or other goods or Merchandize of whatever description are to be placed and deposited on being landed accord-ing to the directions of the Harbour Master
18. All Coal, Culm, Ore or Goods of whatever description are to be removed by the owners or persons in charge of them from off the Harbour Quays or Jetties within Fourty eight hours after receipt of Notice from the Harbour Master to that effect And in default of compliance with such notice Rent will be charged from the expir-ation of the Notice—but such Notice not to be given within 14 days from date of landing And if such Goods shall be in the way of other Goods they will be removed by the Harbour Master as the expense and risk of the Owner or Owners to another part of the Harbour
19. No Rubbish or filth shall be thrown into any part of the Harbour or the Basins, Ponds or Water courses belonging thereto
20. No person or persons shall pick up and take away any Coal, Culm, chips or other Articles from the Quays, Jetties or Harbour or any part thereof or the roads or approaches thereto without the permission of the Harbour Master

21. All idle and disorderly persons and all persons not having business to transact are forbidden to trespass upon the Quays, Jetties or Har-bour or into the Storehouses or Yards or into the Office attached to the Weighing Machine or into any other Office—or in any other way trespass upon the property of the Company and all such persons who shall be detected so trespassing may be taken into Custody and upon conviction before a Magistrate shall be liable to the fine mentioned in Bye Law (No. 23) or otherwise dealt with as the Law directs And all animals found straying on any part of the Company's property will be impounded
22. No person shall obstruct or molest the Harbour Master or his Deputy in the execution of his duty
23. All Masters of Vessels, Hobblers, or other persons not conforming to these Bye Laws shall be liable to all damages thereby occasioned and shall be fined such sum as the Convicting Magistrate may think fit, not exceeding £5 for each Offence

Harbour Regulations

Rate for discharging Ballast
1d per Ton for Wheeling (on the Register Tonnage of each Vessel)
For each Man employed on Board as my be agreed

Pier Light and Signal

per Register Tons	to	30	Tons	3d
30	,,	to	50	,,	6d
50	,,	to	70	,,	9d
70	,,	to	100	,,	9d
100	,,	to	150	,,	1/-
150	,,	upwards		2/-

Rent: 1d per ton per week on all coal, culm, or other goods in accordance with Bye Law No.18.

APPENDIX K

BILL OF LADING FOR A SHIPMENT OF COAL FROM SAUNDERSFOOT TO MARGATE, OCTOBER 1837

Source: East Kent Archives, Dover   Reference: EK/U 1453/B5/4/1536

APPENDIX L

*James Daniel, The Shipowners' and Shipmasters'
Directory to the Port Charge of Great Britain and Ireland
(London, 1846), 110et seq.*

MILFORD HAVEN

This is one of the best harbours in Great Britain; its situation is admirably adapted for vessels taking shelter, and is of easy access.

PILOTAGE

Vessels from Sea into the Harbour of Milford, and up and down the said Harbour, on foreign voyages (vessels belonging to the port are exempt), levied under the Trinity Board, per Act 6 Geo.IV., cap.125.

From a line drawn from St., Anne's Point to Sheep Island, to any part of the harbour below a line drawn from Newton-Nose-Point to Martin's Haven, in addition, under 14 feet, 2s.; 14 feet and upwards, 2s 6d.

Additional Rates for Vessels boarded without the Entrance of the Harbour.
From a line drawn from Lenny Point to Skokhelm Island, 2s. per foot.
If to the southward of St. Govan's Head, 3s. per foot.
From Caldy Island eastward, or from the westward of Grasholm, or three leagues without Lenny Point, in addition to the harbour pilotage, £3.3s.; six leagues £4.4s.; ten leagues, £6.6s.
Vessels not having British registers pay one-fourth in addition to the above rate.

Rates for services and assistance performed in the Harbour.
1ˢᵗ - For a boat carrying an anchor of above six cwt. with a corresponding
hawser, if in Hubberstone Road (not exceeding, at the discretion of the
sub-commissioners, the sum of   £2. 2s.0d.
2ⁿᵈ- For a boat carrying an anchor of above six cwt. with a corresponding
hawser, if below Hubberstone Road and above the Stack Rock
(not exceeding, at the discretion of the sub-commissioners)
£2.12s.6d.
3ʳᵈ- For a boat carrying an anchor of above six cwt, with a corresponding
hawser, if in Dale Road, the anchor *from Milford*   £4.4s.0d.
If carried from Dale   £2.12s.6d.
For a boat carrying off an anchor of three cwt. and not exceeding
six cwt. with corresponding hawser, the boat and men to have
three-fourths of the above specified sums.
With an anchor of two cwt. and not exceeding three cwt. with a
corresponding hawser, the boat and men to have
one half of the above mentioned sums.
For unmooring a vessel drawing 14 feet of water and upwards,
and bringing her alongside the quay or to Hubberstone Pill from
the first situation above mentioned; for the pilot   £1.1s.0d.

If with a boat, an additional sum (not exceeding, at the discretion
of the sub-commissioners), of £0.10s.6d.
For unmooring a vessel drawing 14 feet of water and upwards,
and bringing her alongside the quay or to Hubberstone Pill, from
the second situation described; for the pilot £1.1s.0d.
If with a boat, an additional sum (not exceeding, at the discretion
of the sub-commissioners), of £0.10s.6d.
For unmooring a vessel drawing 14 feet of water and upwards,
and bringing her alongside the quay or to Hubberstone Pill, from
the third situation described; for the pilot £1.11s.6d.
If with a boat, an additional sum of £0.10s.6d.
For taking vessels of 14 draught of water and upwards,
from the quays of Hubberstone Pill to moorings in any of the
situations before mentioned, the like sums above specified.
Vessels under 14 feet draught of water, to or from the situation
before mentioned, three-fourths of the sums above specified.
For new mooring a vessel drawing 14 feet of water, in the
situation first described; for the pilot £0.10s.6d.
If with a boat, an additional sum of £0.10s.6d.
Each person employed, per tide's work £0.5s 0d.

Vessels not having British registers pay one-fourth in addition to the above rates.

Harbour Dues, by appointment of the Vice Admiral and Governor of Milford Harbour, Sir John Orren, Bart.

Payable by all vessels anchoring in the harbour of Milford, except such as belong to the harbour, and such as belong to the Cinque Ports, that produce their certificate of freedom:

Vessels	16 tons	£0.0s.4d.	Vessels	60 tons	£0.2s.1d.
"	20 tons	£0.0s.8d.	"	70 tons	£0.2s.4d.
"	25 tons	£0.1s.0d.	"	80 tons	£0.2s.7d.
"	30 tons	£0.1s.4d.	"	90 tons	£0.2s.10d.
"	40 tons	£0.1s.7d.	"	100tons	£0.3s.0d.
"	50 tons	£0.1s.10d.	"	And 3d for each 10 Tons above 100	

The above harbour dues are but partially paid, there being no Act of Parliament to enforce the payment, and most masters of vessels refuse doing so.

Quayage and Moorage, per Act 30, Geo. III., cap.55. – One half-penny per register ton. Vessels lying up alongside the quay for more than one month and not exceeding two months, 2d per register ton; and for every succeeding month, the additional sum of 10s. foreign vessels, 9d per ton. Coasters, 2d per ton, loading or discharging.

Anchorage in Hubberstone Pill, by prescription and Act 30 Geo. III. Cap.55. - 4d per vessel, laden or in ballast, charged on all vessels on a coasting or foreign voyage.

Vessels lying up may be removed for loading or discharging vessels.

Ballast.- Put on board 8d. per ton.

Depth of Water- Springs rise and fall about 30 feet; Neaps, about 20 feet. The depth of water in the middle of the harbour, from the entrance to Langum Poole, a distance of about 2 (sic) miles, is not less than 10 fathoms at low water Spring Tides.

HAVERFORDWEST, *a Creek in the Port of Milford.*

From the locality of this place, the narrowness of the river, and the shallowness of water, only small coasting vessels, to which the trade is confined, can come up to the town. The rates of pilotage are the same as at Milford. At high water, upon spring tides, there is not more than from 10 to 11 feet; when exceeding that, it extends over the marshes, and vessels cannot then be hauled up, which is always done by hands; at low neaps, the tide scarcely makes its appearance at the quay. There is no authorised rule established for men's pay; the haulers generally get 7s.6d. a-tide for towing a vessel up or down. Men employed working upon the quay are paid about the same amount per day.

   The only charge at this place is 1d. per register ton, on all vessels discharging or loading their cargoes, by order of the Mayor and Council, dated 30 May 1836. To take effect from 29 September 1836.

TENBY, *a Creek in the Port of Milford.*

Pilotage- As may be agreed on.
Harbour Dues- Vessels with cargoes, 3d; wind bound, 1¹/₂d. per ton. Per Act of Parliament, 9 May 1838.
Ballast- 1d. per ton, for wheeling; labourers, 1s 6d. to 2s per man.
Depth of Water- Springs, from 16 to 2 feet; Neaps, 10feet.

SAUNDERSFOOT, *a Creek in the Port of Milford.*

 Pilotage- As may be agreed upon; for vessels 100 tons register, about £1; and for vessels 300 tons, about £2 is usual. Pilots are only required by strangers. There is a day signal and pier light, free of charge.
 Harbour Dues- Every vessel which enters the harbour, the sum of 2d. per register ton; and if the same shall continue in the harbour beyond the space of twenty-one days, an additional sum of 1d. per ton register, for every week beyond the first twenty one days. Per Act of Parliament, 10 Geo.IV.c 118.
Ballast- Discharged by the men appointed by the Company, for 1d. per ton for wheeling; each man employed on board as may be agreed for.
Depth of Water- Springs, 19 feet; Neaps, 9 feet.

PEMBROKE DOCK, *a Creek in the Port of Milford.*

Quayage- Each vessel, 8d. There is no Act of Parliament for it, but it is a corporation charge. There are no harbour dues for vessels lying at Pembroke Dock or Pembroke. Harbour dues had been charged at this creek; but since Mr.L.Philipps' taking office here he has refused to collect them, there being no Act of Parliament to justify his doing so.
Pilotage, from Sea to Pembroke Dock.- Vessels under 14 feet, 2s 6d per foot; 14 feet and upwards, 3s 6d per foot.
Harbour Pilotage, from Milford to Pembroke Dock- Vessels under 14 feet, 2s per foot; 14 feet and upwards, 2s 6d per foot. Shifting vessels, or first mooring them, 10s 6d each.
Ballast- Put on board, 1s 2d per ton.
Depth of Water- Off the dockyard, with good anchorage, at high water, 9 fathoms; low water, 7 fathoms. Along the Hobbs Point Pier, at Springs, 26 feet; Neaps, 15 feet.

NOULTON, *a Creek in the Port of Milford.*

Pilotage- As may be agreed on. No other charges
Ballast- Free of charge.
Depth of Water- Springs, 10 to 12 feet; Neaps, 7 to 8 feet.

(I am grateful to Robin Craig for drawing my attention to this source)

APPENDIX M

Outputs from Cresswell Colliery/Quay 1770 to 1827

The Harcourt Powell papers at the Pembrokeshire Record Office, and the Owen and Colby papers at the National Library of Wales include a number of accounts in respect of some of the pits shipping coal and culm through Cresswell Quay. Simplified accounts for five selected years between 1770 and 1827 are shown here for comparison purposes, although the decline of the trade at Cresswell over this period is quite apparent.

Official government sources have provided some additional information about coal and culm shipments in the years after the Napoleonic Wars, and this material is also tabulated here.

CRESSWELL COLLIERY
OUTPUTS FOR INDIVIDUAL PITS IN COAL AND CULM FOR 1770

Working Pit	Worked By	Output		Proceeds
		Coal	Culm	£-s-d
Level	Alex Smith and Partners	98h 10c		593-0-0
			417h 7c	1013-4-5
				1606-4-5
Brince	John Griffith and Partners	28h		168-0-0
			56h 1c	144-2-10
			312-2-10	
Great Lake	William Smith and Partners	0h 8c		4-0-0
			45h 3c	110-17-3
				114-17-3
Underhill	Alex Smith and Partners	149h		894-0-0
			443h 4c	1051-8-11
				1945-8-11
Butchers Fortune	Henry Mends and Partners	-	5h 2c	11-16-11
Horse Park	Richard Phelps	-	1h 8c	4-1-8
Dirty Pools	John B. Allen	42h 8c		255-14-0
			92h 1c	214-4-3
			469-18-3	

Where h stands for Hundred and c stands for Carts.
Source: Pembs.R.O. D/POW/H/83
NOTE: For the sake of simplicity, the figures for coal sold for shipping, and coal sold from the coalfield have been put together, and similarly as regards culm sold for shipping, or sold from the coalfield, or from the pithead. In this group of pits in 1770 coal was priced at £6 per hundred at Lawrenny, or £5-16-0 per hundred at Cresswell.

CRESSWELL COLLERY
OUTPUTS FOR INDIVIDUAL PITS IN COAL AND CULM FOR 1787

Working Pits	Worked By	Output		Proceeds
		Coal	Culm	£-s-d
Smiths Hill	Partners		108h 9c	271-17-6
Level		12h 11c		77-10-0
	William Smith		269h 10c	672-12-8
				750-2-8
Mead		17h 6c		105-0-0
	Alex Smith		169h 4c	416-12-6
				521-12-6
Brince		3h 1c		18-10-0
	Richard Eynon		49h 11c	124-7-8
				142-17-8
Belth	William Belth,	5h 1c		30-10-0
	Stephen Gwyther and		77h 10c	202-11-2
	Alex Smith		233-1-2	
Quarry Backs	John James,	1h 2c		7-0-0
	Stephen Jones		50h 2c	125-8-4
	and William Belth		132-8-4	
Wedland	Thomas James and		23h 3c	58-2-6
	John Harris			
Islands	William Thomas and		35h 9c	89-7-6
	Thomas Rowe			
Bowling's Well	Alex Smith		7h 9c	19-7-6

Where h stands for Hundred and c stands for Carts.

SOURCE: N.L.W. Owen and Colby 1137

NOTE: In 1787 coal for shipping cost £6 per hundred, and culm for shipping cost £2-10s-0d per hundred. Culm sold at the pit cost £1-16-0d per hundred. A royalty of One Third was payable at each pit to the landowners jointly – Sir Hugh Owen, J. H. Powell and Mr Barlow – except at Smith's Hill and Brince, where the royalty was One Quarter.

NOTES TO TABLE OVER PAGE

NOTE 1: Bickening Moor also sent 29h of coal and 70h 11c of culm for shipment through Saundersfoot, and 1h 6c of coal and 16h 4c culm were sold at the pit. The total value of these sales was £533-16-11.

NOTE 2: As regards shipments at Lawrenny and Cresswell, in 1808 coal at Lawrenny cost £7-10-0 per hundred and at Cresswell £7-3-0. Culm cost £3-15-0 per hundred at Lawrenny, and £3-11-0 at Cresswell. The royalties payable at Brince, Brince Backs, Level, Langdon and Bickening Moor were a quarter. At all the other pits it was one sixth.

CRESSWELL QUAY and LAWRENNY
OUTPUTS FOR INDIVIDUAL PITS IN COAL AND CULM FOR 1808

Working Pits	Worked By	Output		Proceeds
		Coal	Culm	£-s-d
Brince	Richard Llewhellin	2h 2c (Lwy.)		16-5-0
			52h 9c (Lwy.)	197-16-3
			60h 8c (Cress.)	215-4-5
			Sold at Pit	30-10-0
				459-15-8
Brince Backs	ditto		10h 9c (Lwy.)	40-6-3
			22h 0c (Cress.)	78-2-0
				118-8-3
Level			6h 2c (Lwy.)	46-5-0
			11h 3c (Lwy.)	42-3-9
	Mrs Smith	1h 1c (Cress.)		7-15-5½
			22h 7c (Cress.)	80-3-5
			Sold at Pit	2-2-0
				178-9-7½
Rowes Meadow	J. H. Powell, J. H. Allen,		18h 7c (Lwy.)	69-13-9
	Thomas Philipps,	0h 4c (Cress.)		2-7-10
	Hugh Wilson		21h 7c (Cress.)	80-3-5
			Sold at Pit	2-2-0
				178-9-7
Furzey Park	ditto		12h 5c (Lwy.)	46-11-3
		0h 6c (Cress.)		3-11-9
			28h 6c	101-3-1
			Sold at Pit	5-13-0
				156-19-1
Fords Lane	ditto		0h 3c (Lwy.)	0-18-9
Bowling's Well	ditto		18h 3c (Lwy.)	68-8-9
			33h 4c (Cress.)	41-14-3
			Sold at Pit	1-16-0
				65-7-9
Rogers Park	ditto		5h 10c (Lwy.)	21-17-6
			11h 9c (Cress.)	41-14-3
			Sold at Pit	1-16-0
				65-7-9
Langdon		14h 8c (Lwy.)		110-0-0
			116h 0c (Lwy.)	435-0-0
	J. H. Powell	14h 4c (Cress.)		102-1-10
			289h 9c (Cress.)	1028-9-9
			Sold at Pit	162-2-4
				1837-13-11
Bickening Moor		4h 11c (Lwy.)		36-17-6
			11h 5c (Lwy)	42-16-3
	Thomas Williams	3h 9c (Cress.)		26-18-1
			35h 10c (Cress.)	127-11-2
				233-16-0

Where h stands for Hundreds and c for Carts; Lwy. for Lawrenny and Cress. for Cresswell.
SOURCE: Pembs.R.O. D/POW/H/83 NOTES TO THIS TABLE ON PREVIOUS PAGE

CRESSWELL QUAY
OUTPUTS FOR INDIVIDUAL PITS IN COAL AND CULM FOR 1814

Working Pits	Worked By	Output		Proceeds
		Coal	Culm	£-s-d
Bowling's Well	J. H. Powell, J. H. Allen, Mrs Philipps, Hugh Wilson		2h 6c (Lwy.)	10-0-0
			15h 9c (Cress.)	58-5-6
				68-5-6
Furzey Park	ditto		0h 4c (Lwy.)	1-6-8
			15h 4c (Cress.)	56-14-8
			Sold at Pit	7-11-6
				65-12-10
Quarry Backs	ditto	0h 5c (Lwy.)		3-7-8½
			2h 6c (Lwy.)	10-0-0
			17h 7c (Cress.)	65-1-2
			Sold at Pit	0-18-0
				79-6-10
Kilns	ditto		2h 7c (Lwy.)	9-13-4
			26h 7c (Cress.)	98-7-2
			Sold at Pit	3-10-0
				111-10-6
New Level	ditto	13h 5c (Lwy.)		109-0-2
			9h 4c (Lwy.)	37-6-8
		10h 9c (Cress.)		82-15-6
			251h 9c (Cress.)	931-9-6
			Sold at Pit	71-18-3
				1232-10-1
Belths Hill	ditto		4h 2c (Lwy.)	16-13-4
			31h 10c (Cress.)	117-15-8
			Sold at Pit	0-12-0
				135-1-0
Level	ditto		3h 6c (Lwy.)	14-0-0
			25h 11c (Cress.)	95-17-10
				109-17-10
Reynalton	J. H. Powell and Hugh Wilson	116h 4c (Lwy.)		945-4-2
			16h 2c (Lwy.)	64-13-4
		55h 1c (Cress.)		424-2-10
			232h 10c (Cress.)	861-9-8
			Sold at Pit	126-19-4
				2422-9-4

Where h stands for Hundred and c for Carts; Lwy. for Lawrenny and Cress. for Cresswell.
SOURCE: Pembs.R.O. D/POW/H/92
NOTE: In 1814 Cresswell Quay also shipped coal or culm from the pits of the other proprietors at Masterland, Waddock, Hill Wood, Morgans, Gold Inn, Broad lays, Binges. Coal at Lawrenny cost £8-2-6d, and at Cresswell Quay £7-14-0d. Culm at Lawrenny cost £4-0-0d, and at Cresswell £13-14-0d.
The Royalty, or Lord's Part, payable in each case was One Sixth, except in the case of the colliery at Reynalton, where it was One Fifth.

CRESSWELL QUAY
OUTPUTS FOR INDIVIDUAL PITS IN COAL AND CULM FOR 1827

Working Pits	Worked By	Output		Proceeds
		Coal	Culm	£-s-d
Brince Back	J. Harcourt Powell,		3h 2c	10-5-10
	J. H. Allen, Mrs Philipps		Sold at Pit	7-13-6
	and Hugh Wilson			17-19-4
Islands	ditto		2h 9c	8-18-9
			Sold at Pit	4-12-4
				13-11-1
Quarry Backs	ditto		23h 9c	77-3-9
			Sold at Pit	35-8-8
				112-12-5
New Level	ditto	3h 5c		25-12-6
			36h 0c	117-0-0
			Sold at Pit	21-18-0
				164-10-6

Where h stands for Hundred and c stands for Carts.
SOURCE: Pembs.R.O D/POW/H/98
NOTE: In 1827 Pembrokeshire coal sold at £7-10-0d per hundred and culm at £3-5-0d per hundred. In each case in 1827 the royalty payable was one sixth. However the total quantity of coal and culm dispatched for shipping was only 65h 8c.

A poor quality but rare photograph of coal loading at Hook Quay. The vessel is believed to be the SS. Foamville

M.R.C. Price Collection

APPENDIX N

Pembrokeshire total Output from 1876

Year	Output (Tons)	Year	Output (Tons)	Year	Output (Tons)
1876	79,721	1900	48,140	1924	51,640
1877	75,420	1901	42,190	1925	47,815
1878	36,421	1902	49,301	1926	28,093
1879	84,573	1903	60,790	1927	42,180
1880	79,386	1904	57,961	1928	50,670
1881	79,153	1905	52,358	1929	38,048
1882	71,615	1906	46,893	1930	28,427
1883	92,650	1907	49,694	1931	34,481
1884	94,687	1908	50,931	1932	39,013
1885	52,642	1909	49,938	1933	35,591
1886	96,177	1910	40,851	1934	49,925
1887	95,099	1911	46,209	1935	51,660
1888	74,453	1912	43,274	1936	39,874
1889	71,271	1913	55,045	1937	43,447
1890	71,908	1914	54,308	1938	70,879
1891	74,811	1915	56,483	1939	26,200
1892	80,942	1916	57,754	1940	23,739
1893	89,019	1917	46,600	1941	17,965
1894	82,460	1918	46,350	1942	30,383
1895	85,058	1919	63,376	1943	15,685
1896	80,858	1920	53,240	1944	20,213
1897	82,267	1921	38,853	1945	22,319
1898	82,384	1922	52,432	1946	23,124
1899	59,419	1923	49,081	1947	18,640
				1948	4,447

Source: G. Edwards, *A Study of the Daucleddau Coalfield (Pembrokeshire)* Appendix B, 111.

INDIVIDUAL COLLIERY OUTPUTS – 1912 TO 1948

Year	Borvilles Court		Hook		Reynalton		Wood Level		Broom		Loveston		Kilgetty	
	Tons	£	Tons	£	Tons	£	Tons	£	Tons	£	Tons	£	Tons	£
1912	34,486	30,032	8,419	3,570										
1913	42,544	36,162	12,361	5,356										
1914	42,162	25,297	10,646	4,524	1,500	1,000								
1915	37,639	26,347	10,469	4,187	8,375	7,075								
1916	37,044	29,635	10,062	5,577	10,648	12,000								
1917	35,172	36,931	10,528	7,844	900	1,000								
1918	38,063	49,006	5,797	4,057	2,490	3,408								
1919	39,884	55,685	12,277	9,207	11,215	11,413								
1920	36,390	54,130	7,326	7,362	9,524	17,154								
1921	29,189	57,527	7,809	4,685	1,355	3,000								
1922	37,573	70,293	12,286	10,796										
1923	37,867	63,585	11,174	8,380										
1924	39,949	58,925	11,553	8,665										
1925	39,177	61,051	8,614	6,460										
1926	17,369	26,198	10,724	8,043										
1927	28,345	54,210	13,581	10,186										
1928	31,599	45,555	19,071	14,303										
1929	30,814	40,829	7,148	5,361										
1930	8,583	11,551	19,394	14,545										
1931			34,481	20,860										
1932			38,853	30,760							160	160		
1933			34,835	29,609							756	756		
1934			42,235	37,276					4,270	3,736	3,420	3,002		
1935			32,112	29,548					19,248	18,045	300	300		
1936			7,795	8,902					30,007	27,756	2,072	2,072		
1937			12,078	14,999					28,243	26,831	1,765	1,765	1,361	1,293
1938			25,906	31,033					29,678	28,194			15,295	16,824
1939			25,265	30,427					635	603			300	330
1940			23,739	32,150										
1941			17,965	29,732										
1942			30,383	33,914										
1943			15,685	30,771										
1944			18,351	37,420			1,862	2,962						
1945			17,609	43,762			4,710	8,242						
1946			17,674	42,099			5,450	10,054						
1947			13,383	32,307			5,257	9,862						
1948							4,447	9,634						

Bibliography

A. Primary Sources
 (i) unprinted MSS collections
 (a) Carmarthenshire Record Office
    Derwydd MSS
    Dynevor MSS
    John Francis collection, Lewis of Henllan MSS
    Museum MSS
 (b) Cornwall County Record Office
    Harveys of Hayle MSS
 (c) East Kent Archives
    Cobb MSS
    E/KU 1453
 (d) Hereford and Worcester Record Office
    Pakington MS
    BA 2309/55
    BA 4416
 (e) National Library of Wales
    Coleman MSS
    Corston MSS
    Eaton, Evans and Williams MSS
    Great Sessions 4, Pembrokeshire Gaol Files
       775/6, 813/4 & 5, 814/3, 817/1 & 3, 823/6,
       824/1 & 825/5.
    Francis Green MSS
    Gogerddan Papers (uncatalogued)
    Hamilton-Greville MSS
    Haverfordwest (Williams and Williams) MSS
    Haverfordwest Deeds
    Jones MSS
    Lucas MSS
    Owen and Colby MSS
    Picton Castle MSS
    Slebech MSS
    Tithe Map of 1840
    25/8/14b
    MS1352B, fo. 231
 (f) Pembrokeshire County Library, Haverfordwest
    Francis Green MSS
 (g) Pembrokeshire Record Office
    Minute books of the Primitive Methodist
       Pembroke Dock Station
    Minutes of the Saundersfoot Railway &
       Harbour Co.

George Price and Dr. R. H. Blundell, *Report on
   the Pembrokeshire Coalfields*, (June 1955).
"The Hook Coalfield, Pembrokeshire", brief
   notes by T. W. Harcourt Roberts, c 1952.
Particulars of the estate of Harcourt Powell:
H/DX/238/1 and D/EE/7/338
D/EE/7/256 and 293
D/HIG/36, 50 and 51
D/HR/10
D/LLC/484, 546 and 547
D/LLW/298 and 300
D/MDC/5/5/11
D/POW/H/61, 66, 91, 96 and 163
D/RTB/Sir RBPP/6/79 and 81
D/RTM/HPO/209 and 290
D/RTM/HP4/292
D/RTM/JAV/74
D/RTM/13/46
H/DX/4/3
HDR/HT/2/10
HDX/476/4, 951 and 1190
Plans of Milford and St Brides Bay Light
   Railway
 (h) Public Record Office, Kew
    BT 31
    COA/38/817
    CUST 75/
    E 134
    E178/3493: Court of Exchequer – Special
       Commission of Inquiry
    HO 87/53
    J15
    POWE 7 (Annual Reports of Mines Inspectors)
    POWE 8 and 27
    RAIL 559, 640 and 1075
 (j) Privately Owned
    Cresselly Estate map of 1755
    Notebook and diary of M. Walters of Nolton
    Picton Castle – Accounts of William Evans to
       Lord Milford
    Vickerman papers
 (ii) Printed Primary Sources
 (a) Newspapers

The Cambrian (Swansea)
Carmarthen Journal
Haverfordwest and Milford Haven Telegraph
Herald of Wales
Llanelly & County Guardian
Narberth Weekly News
The Pembroke and County Guardian
Pembroke Dock and Pembroke Gazette
Pembrokeshire County Guardian
Pembrokeshire Herald
Pembrokeshire Telegraph
Tenby Observer
The Times
The West Wales Guardian
Western Telegraph

(b) Contemporary Magazines
Archaeological Journal No. 108 (1870).
Cambrian Register, 1796.
Mining Journal, July and August 1864.
Pembrokeshire Almanack, 1936.
The South Wales Coal Annual, 1903, 1908.
The Telegraph Almanack, 1929, 1937, 1951.
Transactions, Vol. V (South Wales Institute of Engineers).

(c) British Parliamentary Papers
16 and 17 Charles II, Cap 1
7 Geo I, Mich 17
33 Geo II, Cap 15
26 Geo III, Cap 60
37 Geo III, Cap 100
42 Geo III, Cap 29
42 Geo III, Cap 115
56 Geo III, Cap 127
59 Geo III, Cap 52
1 and 2 Geo IV, Cap 67
10 Geo IV, Cap 108
5 Vict, Cap 35
27 and 28 Vict, Cap 256
Calendar of Fine Rolls, 1347-56.
Report from the Select Committee Appointed to inquire into the State of the Coal Trade of this Kingdom, 1800.
*Report of the Committee on the Petition of the Owners of South Wales Collieries,*Volume 4, 1810.
House of Lords Select Committee on the Coal Trade*: Report of Committees,* Volume 8, 1830.
Report of the Select Committee on the Coal Trade, Volume 15, 1838.
Royal Commission of Enquiry into the Employment of Children and Young Persons in Mines, 1842 (Children's Employment

Commission): *Reports from Committees,* Volumes 15, 16 and 17, 1842.
Royal Commission of Enquiry for South Wales: Volume 16, 1844.
Royal Commission on the State of Education in Wales: *Reports from Committees,* Volume 27 parts 1 and 2, 1847.
Select Committee on Coal Mines: *Reports from Committees,* Volume 5, 1852.
Royal Commission on Coal Mining*: Reports from Commissioners,* Volume 18, 1871 (with supplementary volume containing maps).
Royal Commission on Mining Royalties: Volume 36, 1890.
Royal Commission on Land in Wales: Volume 36, 1894.
Royal Commission on Coal Supplies*:* Volume 16, 1905.

B. Secondary Sources
(i) Books
An Account of Tenby (London: 1820).
R. Page Arnot, *South Wales Miners (a history of the South Wales Miners Federation, 1898-1914)* (London: G. Allen and Unwin, 1967).
T. S. Ashton and J. Sykes, *The Coal Industry of the Eighteenth Century* (Manchester: Manchester University Press, 1929).
C. Baber and L. J. Williams (eds.), *Modern South Wales: Essays in Economic History* (Cardiff: University of Wales Press, 1986).
J. V. Beckett, *Coal and Tobacco: the Lowthers and the economic development of West Cumberland, 1600- 1760* (Cambridge: Cambridge University Press, 1981).
The Black Book of St. David's (Cardiff: University of Wales Press, 1902).
R. E. Bowen, *The Burry Port & Gwendraeth Valley, Vol.1, Canals & Tramroads* (Usk: Oakwood Press, 2001).
T. C. Cantrill and others, *Memoirs of the Geological Survey: The Geology of the South Wales Coalfield*, Part XII (London: HMSO, 1916).
B. G. Charles (ed.), *A Calendar of the Records of the Borough of Haverfordwest, 1539-1660* (Cardiff: University of Wales Press, 1967).
Roy Church, *The History of the British Coal Industry*, Vol. 3, 1830-1913 (Oxford: Clarendon Press, 1986).
Noel and Alan Cox, *Tokens, Checks, Metallic Tickets, Passes and Tallies of Wales, 1800-1993* (Cardiff: privately published, 1994).

L. M. Cullen, *Anglo-Irish Trade, 1660-1800* (New York: Augustus M. Kelly, 1968).

Sir F. Dashwood, *The story of Blackpool Mill* (Narbeth: privately published, 1975).

D. J. Davies, *The Economic History of South Wales prior to 1800* (Cardiff: University of Wales Press, 1933).

Margaret Davies, *The Story of Tenby* (Tenby: Tenby Museum, 1979).

Peter B. S. Davies, *Deadly Perils* (St. Davids: Merrivale Press, 1992).

P. B. S. Davies, *Pembrokeshire Limekilns* (St. Davids: Merrivale Press, 1997).

Robert L. Davies and Jane Nelson, *A River Never Sleeps* (Narberth: 1999).

R. R. Davies, *The Age of Conquest; Wales 1063-1415* (Oxford: Oxford University Press, 1987).

Walter Davies, *General View of the Agriculture and Domestic Economy of South Wales* (London: 1815).

Daniel Defoe, *A Tour through the Whole Island of Great Britain* (London, 1725 and 2nd ed. 1769).

E. W. Evans, *Mabon (William Abraham 1842-1922)* (Cardiff: University of Wales Press, 1959).

E. W. Evans, *The Miners of South Wales* (Cardiff: University of Wales Press, 1961).

R. Fenton, *An Historical Tour through Pembrokeshire, 1811* (London: Longman et. al., 1811).

R. S. Fenton, *Cambrian Coasters* (Kendal: World Ship Society, 1989).

Michael W. Flinn, *The History of the British Coal Industry*, Vol. 2, 1700-1830 (Oxford: Clarendon Press, 1984).

Hywel Francis and David Smith, *The Fed: A History of the South Wales Miners in the Twentieth Century* (London: Lawrence and Wishart, 1980).

Robert L. Galloway, *Annals of Coal Mining and the Coal Trade* (2 Volumes) (London: 1904; reprinted Newton Abbott: David & Charles, 1971).

Charles Hadfield, *Canals of South Wales and the Borders* (Newton Abbot: David & Charles, 1967).

S. C. Hall, *The Book of South Wales* (London: 1861).

Royston Harrison (ed.), *The Independent Collier* (Brighton: Harvester Press, 1978).

W. Harrison, *Some aspects of Tenby's History* (Tenby: 1979).

J. Harry, *The Pembrokeshire Coalfield* (Dyfed County Council, 1990)

J. Harry, *Living and Working in the Pembrokeshire Coalfield* (Dyfed County Council Education Dept., 1990).

Charles Hassall, *General View of the Agriculture of the County of Pembroke* (London: 1794).

John Hatcher, *The History of the British Coal Industry*, Vol.1, Prior to 1700 (Oxford: The Clarendon Press, 1993).

John de Havilland (ed.), *Industrial Locomotives of Dyfed and Powis* (London: Industrial Railway Society, 1994).

Arthur Horner, *Incorrigible Rebel, The life of Arthur Horner* (London: Macgibbon & Kee, 1960).

D. W. Howell, *Land and People in Nineteenth Century Wales* (London: Routledge, 1978).

David W. Howell, (ed.), *Pembrokeshire County History Vol.IV, Modern Pembrokeshire 1815-1974* (Haverfordwest: The Pembrokeshire Historical Society, 1993)

D. W. Howell, *The Rural Poor in Eighteenth Century Wales* (Cardiff: University of Wales Press, 2000).

B. E. Howells (ed.), *Pembrokeshire Life 1572-1843* (Pembrokeshire Record Series, I, Haverfordwest).

Brian Howells (ed.), *Elizabethan Pembrokeshire: the evidence of George Owen*, Pembrokeshire Record Series, 2 (Pembrokeshire Record Society, 1973).

Brian Howells (ed.), *Pembrokeshire County History Vol. III, Early Modern Pembrokeshire 1536-1815* (Haverfordwest: The Pembrokeshire Historical Society, 1987).

Roscoe Howells, *From Amroth to Utah* (Llandysul: Gomer Press, 2001).

R. Hunt, *Mineral Statistics of the United Kingdom, 1865* (London: 1866). *The Inland Trade* (1976).

J. Geraint Jenkins, *Maritime Heritage* (Llandysul: Gomer Press, 1982).

A. H. John, *The Industrial Development of South Wales 1750-1850* (Cardiff: University of Wales Press, 1950).

Angela V. John, *By the Sweat of Their Brow: Women Workers in Victorian Coal Mines* (London: Croom and Helm, 1980).

D. J. V. Jones, *Before Rebecca* (London: Allen Lane, 1973).

D. J. V. Jones, *Rebecca's Children* (Oxford: Clarendon Press, 1989).

F. Jones, *Historic Pembrokeshire Houses and their Families,* extended edition (Newport, Pembs: 2001).

P. N. Jones, *Mines, Migrants and Residence in the South Wales Steamcoal Valleys: the Ogmore and Garw Valleys in 1881* (Hull: Hull University Press, 1987).

R. Keen, *Coalface* (Cardiff: National Museum of Wales, 1982).

Eric Kerridge, *Trade and Banking in Early Modern England* (Manchester: Manchester University Press, 1988).

John Leland, *The Itinerary in Wales – John Leland, in or about 1536-1539*: extracted from his MS., arranged and edited by Lucy Toulmin-Smith (London: George Bell and Sons, 1906)

Brian Lewis, *Coal Mining in the Eighteenth and Nineteenth Centuries* (London: Longman, 1971).

D. J. Lewis, *Dai The Mill* (St. Davids: Merrivale Press, 1995).

E. A. Lewis (ed.), *The Welsh Port Books (1550-1603)* (London: Honourable Society of Cymmrodorion, 1927).

W. Linnard, *Welsh Woods and Forests* (Cardiff: National Museum of Wales, 1982).

H. A. Lloyd, *The Gentry of South West Wales, 1540-1640* (Cardiff: University of Wales Press, 1968).

A. K. Longfield, *Anglo-Irish Trade in the Sixteenth Century* (London: Routledge, 1929).

B. H. Malkin, *The Scenery, Antiquities and Biography of South Wales* (2nd edition, London: 1807).

K. D. McKay, *A Vision of Greatness: The History of Milford 1790-1990* (Haverfordwest: Brace Harvatt Associates, 1989).

Dillwyn Miles (ed.), *The Description of Pembrokeshire: George Owen of Henllys* (Llandysul: Gomer Press, 1994).

G. E. Mingay, *English Landed Society in the Eighteenth Century* (London: Routledge, 1963).

Mrs Mary Morgan, *A Tour to Milford Haven in the year 1791* (London: John Stickdale, 1795).

W. R. Morgan, *The Story of Begelly* (Llandysul: Gomer Press, 1980).

W. R. Morgan, *A Pembrokeshire Countryman looks back* (Tenby: Five Arches Press, 1988).

J. H. Morris and L. J. Williams, *The South Wales Coal Industry. 1841-1875* (Cardiff: University of Wales Press, 1958).

Lewis Morris, *Plans of Harbours, Bars, Bays and Roads in St. George's Channel* (London, 1748).

Sir R. Murchison, *Silurian System* (London: 1839).

J. U. Nef, *The Rise of the British Coal Industry* (2 volumes, 1st edition, London: Routledge, 1932, 2nd Edition, London: Routledge, 1966).

Paul O'Leary, *Immigration and Integration: The Irish in Wales, 1798-1922* (Cardiff: University of Wales Press, 2000).

G. Owen, *Description of Pembrokeshire*, Part 1, H. Owen (ed.) (London: 1892).

G. Dyfnallt Owen, *Elizabethan Wales* (Cardiff: University of Wales Press, 1962).

G. Dyfnallt Owen, *Wales in the Reign of James I* (Woodbridge, Suffolk: Boydell Press, 1988).

Michael Pollard, *The Hardest Work under Heaven: The Life and Death of the British Coal Miner* (London: Hutchinson, 1984).

J. A. Price (ed.), *Pembrokeshire County Plan* (1953).

M. R. C. Price, *Industrial Saundersfoot* (Llandysul: Gomer Press, 1982).

M. R. C. Price, *The Pembroke and Tenby Railway* (Oxford: Oakwood Press, 1986).

M. R. C. Price, *The Saundersfoot Railway,* 4th edition (Oxford: The Oakwood Press, 1989).

J. F. Rees, *The Story of Milford* (Cardiff: University of Wales Press, 1954).

W. Rees, *Industry before the Industrial Revolution* (Cardiff: University of Wales Press, 1968).

T. W. Harcourt Roberts, *Historical Survey of the Pembrokeshire Coalfield*, (1947).

William Shakespeare, *Cymbeline.*

Thomas G, Stickings, *The Story of Saundersfoot* (Tenby: 1970).

H. Stopes, *Malt and Malting* (London: 1885).

A. Strahan and others, *The Memoirs of the Geological Survey: The Geology of the South Wales Coalfield*, Part XI (London: HMSO, 1914).

M. V. Symons, *Coal Mining in the Llanelli Area, Vol.1 The Sixteenth Century to 1829* (Llanelli: Llanelli Borough Council, 1979).

W. G. Thomas, *Llangwm through the Ages, Part I, 1244-1800* (Haverfordwest: 1989).

H. M. Vaughan, *The Squires of South Wales* (London: Methuen, 1926).

Simon P. Ville, *English Shipowning during the Industrial revolution: Michael Henley and Son, London Shipowners, 1770-1830* (Manchester: Manchester University Press, 1987).

R. F. Walker, (ed.) *Pembrokeshire County History, Vol II, Medieval Pembrokeshire* (Haverfordwest: The Pembrokeshire Hisorical Society, 2002)

Where the River Bends - an illustrated History of Hook (Haverfordwest: 1996).

T. S. Willan, *The English Coasting Trade, 1600-1750* (Manchester: Manchester University Press, 1938).

T. S. Willan, *River Navigation in England, 1600-1750* (Manchester: Manchester University Press, 1964).

Chris Williams, *Democratic Rhondda: Politics and Society 1885-1951* (Cardiff: University of Wales Press, 1996).

D. Williams, *The Rebecca Riots* (Cardiff: University of Wales Press, 1955).

Stanley Williamson, *Gresford: The Anatomy of a Disaster* (Liverpool: Liverpool University Press, 1999).

H. R. Wyndham, *A Tour through Monmouthshire and South Wales, 1777* (Salisbury: 1781).

(ii) Articles

Colin Baber, "Canals and the Economic Development of South Wales", in C. Baber and L. J. Williams (eds.), *Modern South Wales: Essays in Economic History* (Cardiff: University of Wales Press, 1986).

T. Boyns, "Work and Death in the South Wales Coalfield 1874-1914", in *Welsh History Review*, Vol. 12, 1985, No.4

Richard Brinkley, "Religion, 1815-1974", in *Pembrokeshire County History*, Vol. IV, *Modern Pembrokeshire 1815-1974*, (Haverfordwest: The Pembrokeshire Historical Society, 1993).

Robin Craig, "Carmarthen vessels in deep sea trade 1785-1825", in *Carmarthenshire Antiquary*, XXXV1, (2000).

H. M. Davies, "Very Different Springs of Uneasiness: Emigration from Wales to the United States of America during the 1790s", in *The Welsh History Review*, Vol. 15, 3 (1991).

"The Diary of Charles Collins, 1806", in *Narberth Weekly News*, May 1934.

H. J. Dickman, "Wesleyan Methodism in Pembrokeshire", in *The Journal of the Pembrokeshire Historical Society*, No.3 (1989).

M. C. S. Evans, "The Pioneers of the Carmarthenshire Iron Industry", in *Carmarthenshire Historian, IV.* (1967).

Barbara J. George, "Pembrokeshire Sea Trading before 1800", in *Field Studies*, Vol. 2, No.1 (1964).

Margaret C. Gilpin, "Population Changes round the Shores of Milford Haven from 1800 to the Present Day", in *Field Studies* Vol.1, No.2 (1960).

F. Green, "Early Banks in West Wales", in *West Wales Historical Records*, Vol. VI (1916).

F. Green, "Dewisland Coasters in 1751", in *West Wales Historical Records*, Vol. VIII (1919-20).

Francis Green, "Pembrokeshire in Bye-gone Days", in *West Wales Historical Records* Vol. IX (1920-1930).

D. W. Howell, "Leisure and Recreation", in David W. Howell, (ed.), *Pembrokeshire County History Vol.IV, Modern Pembrokeshire 1815-1974* (Haverfordwest: The Pembrokeshire Historical Society, 1993)

Brian Howells, "Land and People, 1536-1642", in Brian Howells (ed.), *Pembrokeshire County History Vol. III, Early Modern Pembrokeshire 1536-1815* (Haverfordwest: The Pembrokeshire Historical Society, 1987).

John Howells, "The Countryside", in R. F. Walker, (ed.) *Pembrokeshire County History, Vol II, Medieval Pembrokeshire* (Haverfordwest: The Pembrokeshire Hisorical Society, 2002)

A. H. John, "Iron and Coal on a Glamorgan Estate 1700-1740", in *Economic History Review*, Vol. 13 (1943).

F. Jones, "White of Henllan", in *The Pembrokeshire Historian*, No.5 (Haverfordwest: 1974).

F. Jones, "Owen of Orielton", in *The Pembrokeshire Historian*, No.5 (Haverfordwest: 1974).

Francis Jones, "Agrarian Disorders at Pembroke", in *Treasury of Historic Pembrokeshire* (Newport, Pembs: 1998).

Gareth E. Jones, "Education 1815-1974", in D. W. Howell (ed.), *Pembrokeshire County History*, Vol.IV, *Modern Pembrokeshire 1815-1974* (Haverfordwest: The Pembrokeshire County Historical Society, 1993).

M. D. Matthews, "Mercantile shipbuilding Activity in South-West Wales, 1740-1829", in *Welsh History Review*, Vol. 19, No.3 (June 1999).

M. Nix, "North Devon Coal and Culm Trades, 1780-1830", in *The Devon Historian*, October 1999.

Henry Owen (ed.), *A Calendar of Public Records relating to Pembrokeshire*, Vol. 3, The Earldom of Pembroke and its members (London: Honourable Society of Cymmrodorion, 1918).

T. R. Perkins, "The Saundersfoot Railway", in *The Locomotive*, 15 September 1934.

R. Phelps, "We lived by the River", in *The Pembrokeshire Magazine*, No 22 (April/May, 1984).

M. R. C. Price, "Coal, Culm and Cresswell Quay", in *The Journal of the Pembrokeshire Historical Society* No.6 1995-95.

M. R. C. Price, "The New Reynalton Anthracite Colliery Company", in *Archive*, No.23 (September 1998) (Lydney, Glos: Lightmoor Press).

M. R. C. Price, "A glimpse of the Pembrokeshire Coal Trade in 1880", in *Archive*, No.27 (September 2000) (Lydney, Glos: Lightmoor Press).

M. R. C. Price, "The Saga of Vickerman's Siding", in *Archive* No.34 (June 2002) (Lydney, Glos: Lightmoor Press).

R. O. Roberts, "Bank of England Branch Discounting 1826-1859", in W. E. Minchinton (ed.), *Industrial South Wales 1750-1914* (London: Frank Cass & Co. Ltd., 1969).

R. O. Roberts, "Banks and the Economic Development of South Wales", in C. Baber and L. J. Williams (eds.) *Modern South Wales: Essays in Economic History* (Cardiff: Cardiff University Press, 1986).

R. F. Walker, "William de Valence and the Army in West Wales, 1282-83", in *Welsh History Review,* 18 (1997).

J. T. Ward, "Landowners and Mining", in J. T. Ward and R. G. Wilson (eds.) *Land and Industry* (Newton Abbot: David & Charles, 1971).

D. Williams "The Acreage Returns of 1801 for Wales", in *Bulletin of the Board for Celtic Studies*, Vol. XIV parts i-ii (1950 and 1951).

(iii) Unpublished Theses and Papers

P. F. Claughton, *Combe Martin: The History and Archaeology of SilverLead Mining* (unpublished paper, 1996).

Ian Cran, *Little Milford Colliery* (unpublished paper, 1989).

G. Edwards, unpublished M.A. thesis, *A Study of the Daucleddau Coalfield (Pembrokeshire)* (University of Birmingham, 1950).

Dorothy and Betty Phillips, *Local Study - Hook* (unpublished account, 1953).

T. W. Harcourt Roberts, "Brief Notes on The Hook Coalfield, Pembrokeshire", Pembrokeshire Record Office c1952.

R. P. Roberts, *The History of Coal Mining in Gower from 1700 to 1832* (Unpublished MA thesis: University of Wales, 1953).

(iv) Miscellaneous

Hugh Felton, "Liber Communis; a record of the accounts of St. David's Cathedrel for 1385", [Quoted by P. B. S. Davies].

Cresselly estate map of 1755 in possession of T. Lloyd, Esq., Cresselly.

Patent No.1596/1873.

Billy Howells' unpublished reminiscences, c 1891, "A Debtor to Grace".

"The Journal of Daniel Williams, 1848-1852", Ms 667, Folder 2, in the Special Collections and Mss. at the Brigham Young University Library, Salt Lake City, Utah, USA.

Index